Also by MAULANA KARENGA

The Book of Coming Forth By Day: The Ethics of the Declarations of Innocence (1990)

Reconstructing Kemetic Culture: Papers, Perspectives, Projects (ed.) (1990)

The African American Holiday of Kwanzaa: A Celebration of Family, Community and Culture (1988)

Kemet and the African Worldview: Research, Rescue and Restoration (ed.) (1986)

Selections From the Husia: Sacred Wisdom of Ancient Egypt (1984)

Introduction to Black Studies (1st Edition) (1982)

Kawaida Theory: An Introductory Outline (1980)

Essays on Struggle: Position and Analysis (1978)

Kwanzaa: Origins, Concepts, Practice (1977)

The Foundations of Kawaida Theory: An Essay in Communitarian African Philosophy (forthcoming)

Race, Ethnicity and Multiculturalism: Issues in Domination, Resistance and Diversity (forthcoming)

INTRODUCTION TO BLACK STUDIES

MAULANA KARENGA

SECOND EDITION

The University of Sankore Press
Los Angeles, California

1993

FRONT COVER:

First Panel	- Ancient Egyptians with hieroglyphic text
Second Panel	- Ancient Nubians with Meroitic text
Third Panel	- Queen and King of Benin with Vai text
Fourth Panel	- Kwanzaa set with outline of the history of Africans in America

COVER DESIGN: University of Sankore Press Collective

LIBRARY OF CONGRESS CATALOG NUMBER: LCN: 92-61391

ISBN 0-943412-16-1

TO

Fannie Lou Hamer *who taught us the morality of remembrance, saying there are two things we all should care about - never to forget where we came from and always praise the bridges that carried us over;*

Malcolm X *who taught us the instructiveness of history, saying "Of all our studies, history is best prepared to reward our research;"*

Mary McLeod Bethune *who taught us our mission in education, saying we must discover the dawn and share it with the masses and bring the benefits of science and knowledge to those who need it most;*

Paul Robeson *who taught us that "The battlefront is everywhere; there is no sheltered rear."*

Anna Julia Cooper *who taught us that what we do must be done together as male and female, saying "There is a female as well as male side to truth" and those who do not honor it do damage to both female and male;*

Amilcar Cabral *who taught us the challenge and protracted nature of struggle, saying "Mask no difficulties, tell no lies and claim no easy victories;"*

Lady Ta Aset of Kemet *who taught us the cardinal virtue of reciprocity, saying "Doing good is not difficult. In fact, just speaking good is a monument to one who does it. For those who do good for others are at the same time doing it for themselves,"*

and **Kheti of Kemet** *who taught us that "Every day is a donation to eternity and even one hour is a contribution to the future."*

Ase, Hotep, Heri

TABLE OF CONTENTS

Preface to the Second Edition

In the ten years since I wrote the first edition of this book, numerous developments have occurred in the discipline of Black Studies accompanied by a new body of literature. Among these developments are the consolidation and expansion of Black Studies professional organizations, the emergence of Afrocentricity as a major intellectual concept, the expansion and growth of Black women's studies, the focus on classical African Studies and the rise and challenge of multiculturalism. These occurrences and the new body of literature have required critical evaluation and inclusion, both to keep abreast with discourse and practice in the discipline and to make a substantive contribution to each. The present edition responds to these challenges.

I am grateful to my colleagues who have made suggestions for this edition and engaged in helpful exchanges with me in various subject areas, especially Molefi Asante, Felix Boateng, Sandra Collins, Roy Garrott, Charles Henry, William Nelson and James Stewart; to my skilled and valuable research assistants, Chimbuko Tembo and Limbiko Tembo, who have assisted me in more ways than I can acknowledge or repay; to Subira Kifano and Tulivu Jadi, who as Vice-Chairs of Us, relieved me of many responsibilities so I could finish this project; and to all the other advocates of my organization, Us, for constant support in these and other endeavors. I am also profoundly and permanently indebted to Tiamoyo, my friend, secretary, administrative assistant, colleague in this project, wife and constant companion in love, work and struggle, and in all things good and beautiful.

Maulana Karenga
Los Angeles
January 1993

Preface to the First Edition

This text is essentially a contribution to the efforts to develop a standard body of discipline-specific literature for Black Studies. Its basic aim is to offer a definitive introduction to the discipline. Moreover, as an introductory text, it seeks to provide the student with a concise but substantive intellectual base for a critical understanding and discussion of Black Studies. Although a survey approach is employed, stress is placed on inquiry and analysis as key to building the student's intellectual base in the discipline.

Toward achieving this basic aim, several objectives have guided the preparation of this text: (1) to introduce and define the origins, relevance and scope of Black Studies; (2) to introduce, define and discuss critically the seven core areas of Black Studies, i.e., Black History, Black Religion, Black Social Organization, Black Politics, Black Economics, Black Creative Production and Black Psychology; (3) to introduce and define key concepts in the discipline and each subject area; (4) to delineate fundamental issues and areas for critical discussion in the discipline and its subject areas; (5) to introduce and discuss critically major challenges facing Black Studies; (6) to introduce fundamental literature in the discipline of Black Studies and its core subject areas; and (7) to raise provocative questions about the Black experience which cultivate the use of and on appreciation for inquiry and analysis as indispensable tools to an effective grasp and critical discussion of Black Studies.

This text, then, is structured around these objectives. The first chapter introduces the discipline as a whole through discussion of its origins, relevance and scope. The main body of the text follows and is organized into seven chapters, each of which discusses critically one of the seven core subject areas of Black Studies and thus introduces the student to the basic internal dialogue of each subject area. The final chapter raises includes suggestions of how they might be met. At the end of each chapter are study questions and references aimed at encouraging and facilitating inquiry and analysis by the student.

This enterprise is self-consciously Afrocentric, critical and corrective in response to the internal demands of the discipline itself, whose subject matter and academic and social mission clearly demand this approach. An Afrocentric approach is essentially intellectual inquiry and production centered on and in the image and interest of African peoples. This responds to the early and continuing demands for academic and social relevance of the educational process and its contents. The critical thrust is the advancing of severe and ongoing criticism of the established order of things in order to negate myths, mystifications and insubstantialities of traditional white studies on Blacks, society and the world. And the corrective thrust is the correlative discovery and affirmation of the truth of the Black experience in its current and historical unfolding. It also means posing correctives to problems internal to the discipline of Black studies as well as to those which confront Black people, themselves.

Several other points should be made about the book. First, I have self-consciously used abundant references to introduce the student to the literature in the field and provide him/her with a bibliography which will facilitate research for term papers in Black Studies and its seven core subject areas. Secondly, in citations, I have not used the first names of the authors in hopes that this will encourage use of the bibliography. Thirdly, I have written an admittedly long chapter on Black History in order to give the student a general panoramic view and sense of the origins, challenges and achievements of Black people as a backdrop for the discussions in the particular areas which follow.

Moreover, I tried to deal substantively with vital issues and questions often raised by students but not normally dealt with at length or in a systematic Afrocentric manner by other texts, i.e., resistance in slavery, the DuBois-Garvey conflict, the fall of African societies, Black scientific achievements, and of course the dynamics and legacy of the Sixties. Fourthly, an

attempt has been made to avoid negative categories and introduce proactive and positive ones. Therefore, the word "negro"
except when it is part of a title is replaced with Black, African,
Afro-American, etc. in parenthesis and the text focus is on Black
struggle and achievement rather than on victimization.

By way of acknowledgements, I owe a great debt to
Tiamoyo, my wife, who lived up to her name "she who inspires."
For she inspired, typed, proofread, xeroxed, edited, researched,
raised questions, took notes and dictation, and understood and
appreciated the limitations on my time during the writing.

Special thanks go to Chimbuko Tembo and Limbiko
Tembo who did research, xeroxed, compiled bibliographies and
supported the effort in other ways. Thanks goes to Jitahadi
Imara, my administrative assistant, who conducted classes,
seminars and forums for me while I was writing and to the other
Executive Council members of Us, who shared other responsibilities to free me to finish this book. Thanks go to Ralph Tulivu
who helped edit and Chanzo Ndoto and Salimu Logan for the
long and many hours spent at the libraries on several campuses
collecting needed materials for me. Great thanks go to the
founders of the Kawaida Groundwork Committee (Us) who
supported my theoretical and practical efforts to preserve and
expand the legacy of the 60's out of which this gook grew, i.e.,
Tiamoyo Karenga, W. Sikivu Kabaila, Mark Tangulifu, Chimbuko
Tembo, Subira Kifano, Ujima Goode and Nzinga Ratibisha.

In addition to the founders, I am also grateful to other
advocates who critical questions in our regular discussions and at
seminars and institutes sponsored by the Institute of Pan-African
Studies helped lay the basis for this book. These are Chanzo
Ndoto, Brent Mshindaji, Jitahadi Imara, Robert Mpinduzi,
Limbiko Tembo, Imani Imara, Gerold Msadiki, Kweli Walker,
Robert Tambuzi, Salimu Logan, Haiba Collier, Nyenyekevu
Kumbufu, Arnold Kumbufu, Ralph Tulivu, Kamilisha Angalifu,
Andrew Angalifu, Jifunza Pinkston, Muhebi James and support-
ers, Walter Jitahidi and Joel Mjengaji.

I am indebted to the many students who took my classes
and listened to my lectures on the many campuses at which I

have taught and lectured and who also raised critical questions about Black life, history and struggle which this book seeks to answer. Special thanks to my friend and colleague, Professor Amen Rahh, who Afrocentric stress complements and reinforces mine; to Haki Madhubuti, Kalamu ya Salaam, Segun Shabaka, Mansong Kulubally and Kamau Tyehimba for intellectual exchange and support; to Eunice, my sister and Chestyn my brother, whose support has always been strong and timely; and to Clentine, my sister for whom the finishing of this book was a last aspiration.

I am indebted also to the Black scholars in these pages whose works provide the substance of Black Studies.

But the greatest debt is to Black people whose lives, achievements and aspirations fill this book and give it whatever message and meaning it has.

Maulana Karenga

Ingelwood, California
July, 1982

INTRODUCTION

1
INTRODUCTION

1.1   ORIGINS OF THE DISCIPLINE

Black Studies grew out of one of the most important, politically active and successful periods of Black history in the U.S. and cannot be separated from it without severe damage to analytical clarity. The discipline of Black Studies is rooted in the social visions and struggles of the 60's which aimed at Black power, liberation and a higher level of human life and thus from its inception, it has had both an academic and social thrust and mission. To clearly understand the relevance, objectives and developmental direction of Black Studies, then, a critical review of its history is imperative.

Fixing the starting point of the discipline firmly in the Sixties does not deny the pre-discipline intellectual history which laid fundamental ground for its emergence in the 60's. On the contrary, this pre-60's history represents both a rich resource of data on which to build and reflects a continuity and longevity of Black intellectual history central to both the discipline's self-conception and its mission (Crouchett, 1971; Turner and McGann, 1980; Stewart, 1984; Karenga, 1988; Woodyard, 1991). Thus Black Studies defines itself and its mission in the historically evolved intellectual-activist tradition which extends back to the freedom-directed and life-affirming work during the Holocaust of Enslavement and extends thru other periods of crisis, challenge, struggle and achievement, culminating in the liberational projects of the 60's.

3

Black Studies, then, evolving out of and building on a long intellectual-activist tradition, emerges as a self-defined academic discipline in the 1960's. It began as both a political and academic demand with grounding in both the general student movement and the social struggles of the 60's out of which the Student Movement evolved (Brisbane, 1974; Pinkney, 1976; Edwards, 1970; McEvoy and Miller, 1969). The 60's was a time of upheaval and confrontation and students, people of color and whites were at the center of the struggles which produced this process. Beginning first off campus in a struggle against the racist structure and functioning of society, students began to see the university as a key institution in the larger system of coercive institutions created by the established order to maintain and perpetuate its role. Pictured as a microcosm of society, the university was defined as racist, sick, unresponsive, rigid and supportive of war, exploitation, oppression and exclusion of Blacks, other peoples of color and the poor from the social knowledge, wealth and power of U.S. society. The decision was then made to take up the struggle against society at the point of its "brain," or put another way, at its "intellectual factory" which produced both its leaders and followers and cherished social myths (McEvoy and Miller, 1969).

The Civil Rights Movement

The Student Movement expressed itself in four different thrusts, the last thrust being the one which more directly demanded and achieved Black Studies. The first thrust of the Student Movement began in 1960 with Black Students who played a central and indispensable role in the Civil Rights Movement in the South (Forman, 1972; Carson, 1981; Morris, 1984; Williams, 1987; Branch, 1988; Chalmers, 1991). Essentially, the Movement sought to: 1) break down the barriers of legal segregation in public accommodations; 2) achieve equality and justice for Blacks; and 3) organize Blacks into a self-conscious social force capable of defining, defending and advancing their interests. The Student Non-Violent Coordinating Committee (SNCC) was obviously the vanguard group in the Civil Rights struggle and the Student Movement. As vanguard, SNCC not only mobilized, organized and politicized thousands of Black students, but also politicized many white students and their leaders thru recruiting and training them and bringing them to the South to work in the struggle. As Clay Carson (1981:129) notes, white summer volunteers in Mississippi "who returned home greatly influenced by their experiences...would bring a measure of SNCC radicalism into the student's rights and antiwar movements." This link would prove valuable for joint action later.

The Free Speech Movement

The second thrust of the Student Movement began with the Free Speech Movement at UC Berkeley in 1964. It was essentially white student protest against the rigid, arbitrary, restrictive and unresponsive character of the university, in a word, a demand for civil rights on campus (Draper, 1965; Lipset and Wolin, 1965; Rorabaugh, 1989). Mario Savio who had been one of the SNCC summer volunteers in Mississippi was the leader of this movement and expressed a link between the civil rights struggle on campus and in the larger society. He posed the Free Speech Movement on UC Berkeley's campus as "another phase of the same struggle," i.e., the civil rights struggle in the larger society, and expressed the similarity of suppression of powerless Blacks and students by the established order (Carson, 1981:129).

The Anti-War Movement

The third thrust of the Student Movement began in 1965 which was the general student protest against the Vietnam war and university complicity in it thru its cooperation with the government (McEvoy and Miller, 1969; DeBendetti and Chatfield, 1990). The anti-war movement was launched by New Leftists at the University of Michigan with a teach-in which was duplicated across the nation. On April 17, the largest New Left organization, the Students for a Democratic Society (SDS), held a massive anti-war demonstration at the Washington Monument in Washington, D.C. SNCC, which inspired leaders of SDS to organized activism, supported the demonstration and participated in it. New Leftists like Casey Hayden, Bob Zellner, Betty Garman, Maria Varela and Jim Monsonis had been SNCC workers. In 1962 SDS at its annual convention drafted the Port Huron Statement, which acknowledged their debt to the Black struggle in the South and SNCC in particular for their new consciousness and activism.

Tom Hayden, who had met with SNCC workers in McComb, Mississippi, in 1961 and helped write the Port Huron Statement, was also very impressed with the achievements of SNCC and the possibility of its model. Likewise, other white activists and scholars on the Left such as Staughton Lynd and Howard Zinn were impressed with and inspired by the SNCC model. Thus, the student protest against the Vietnam war and university complicity was lead by the white Left but informed and supported by SNCC and its theoretical and practical criticism of U.S. society (McAdam, 1988).

To SDS and others, "selective service regulation and revocation of student deferments for dissent, military recruiting and R.O.T.C., corporate recruiting by Dow Chemical Company and other military suppliers and traditional recruitment by the Pentagon" were all evidence of university collusion with the government's war effort (McEvoy and Miller, 1969:4). SNCC supported the anti-war movement, not only from a student position, but also from a Black and Third World position. Thus, SNCC's opposition was to: 1) the government's war against Third World liberation movements and peoples in general and Vietnam in particular; 2) the threat the draft posed to its male personnel not covered by student deferment and especially vulnerable in the South, and; 3) fighting an unjust war for a nation depriving

Blacks of basic civil and human rights. It was Bob Moses, one of SNCC's most distinguished leaders, who represented SNCC at both the Washington massive demonstration and a subsequent one at Berkeley, outlining this basic position making the link between the southern struggle, Third World Liberation and SNCC's opposition to the war (Carson, 1981:183-185). As Carson also reports, Jim Forman, another major SNCC leader, led SNCC's early opposition to the war criticizing "American involvement in Vietnam at a time when the federal government was unwilling to intervene on behalf of southern civil rights workers."

The importance of this third thrust of the Student Movement against the war and university complicity and unresponsiveness is that it included a general criticism of and struggle against the very structure and functioning of the university itself. This, in turn, had three basic results which were contributive to the Black Studies Movement: 1) it further exposed the university's political character and its reflection of social structure and power; 2) it revealed the university's vulnerability to student power; and; 3) it suggested the possibility of an expanded struggle to change the way the university related to Black students and the Black community as well as to other Third World students and communities. Thus, social change was linked to university change and the students again moved into the vanguard.

The Black Studies Movement

The final thrust of the Student Movement which led directly to the establishment of Black Studies began in 1966 at San Francisco State College (SFSC) and was again initiated and led by Blacks (Edwards, 1970). It came at the rising tide of the Black Power Movement and reflected its sense of social mission and urgency. By 1966, the Watts Revolt and the Black Power Movement had ushered in a more racially self-conscious and assertive activism and Black students at SFSC and on other campuses began to respond to this resurgence of nationalist activism. Thus, in 1966, the Negro Students Association changed their name to the Black Student Union (BSU) to indicate a new identity and direction. And in the fall of the same year, the BSU produced a document arguing for and demanding the first Department of Black Studies. Continuing their thrust, they established a Black arts and culture series in the Experimental College which was also created in 1966 and became involved in SFSC's tutorial program for the surrounding community. This and other community service activities signalled the social commitment and service Black Studies advocates would place at the center of the academic and social mission of Black Studies.

Since the Experimental College was set up with student money, there was no serious resistance to it, but the demand by the BSU for a legitimate Black Studies Department funded by the college and controlled by Black people brought stiff resistance. Moreover, the BSU demanded a special admissions program which would waive entrance requirements for a given number of Black students. This also was resisted, even though Black enrollment had been reduced drastically from over a thousand to a few hundred by the College's tracking system.

By 1968 the situation had escalated to the point where the BSU launched a strike on November 6th around a series of demands including a Black Studies Department, special admissions, financial aid and decisions on personnel. Influenced by Frantz Fanon's, SNCC's and the Black nationalist emphasis on Third World solidarity, other Third World groups joined with the BSU under the umbrella organization, the Third World Liberation Front. These other Third World groups included the Mexican American Student Confederation (MASC), the Asian-American Political Alliance (AAPA), the Intercollegiate Chinese for Social Action (ICSA), the Philippine American Collegiate Endeavor (PACE) and the Latin American Student Organization (LASO). Reflecting a common concern for Third World students and Third World Studies, they issued fifteen demands which served as a model for other Black Studies struggles. The

SDS, Peace and Freedom party and white students from the Experimental College formed a strike support committee and worked to join the struggle of Third World students with the struggle against the war, ROTC on campus and other issues which linked the university with the government. In this student thrust, however, it was Blacks (and other Third World students) who again led the way and the whites supported, as in the first thrust in the early 60's.

On February 9, 1968, Dr. Nathan Hare had been appointed as coordinator of Black Studies and been given the task of formulating an autonomous Black Studies Department. By April 16, he had completed his proposal which included, not only the structure for the department, but special admission for Black Students, and a B.A. degree in Black Studies. However, the board of trustees continually delayed implementation of the program and it is this which led to the November 6th strike. The school was closed; students clashed with police; presidents were changed with regularity; and the community became involved in the campus struggle in a way it had never done. Eventually, the students won at the end of 1968 and San Francisco State became the first institution to establish a Black Studies program and department.

As Robert Brisbane (1974:228) notes, Black students paid close attention to the struggle at State and were impressed with the capacity of students to win concessions from the administration. Thus, already "by fall of 1968, the experiences of San Francisco State were being duplicated on dozens of campuses throughout the country." On every occasion, these struggles were seen as linked to the overall struggle for Black liberation and was often led by Black nationalists or Black Power advocates. Among these were members of SNCC, Us Organization and other Kawaida formations on the West and East coasts, the Black Panther Party, Congress of Racial Equality and smaller local nationalist formations. As Alphonso Pinkney (1976:177) observed, the struggle for Black Studies was "seen as a necessary component of Black liberation" and white resistance seen "as an

attempt to preserve (Black) subordinate status in society. . . ." It
became important then to break the white monopoly on knowledge and its manipulation and create a new context for the
creation and dissemination of a new knowledge directed toward
service to the community rather than toward its suppression.

Thus, the struggle to win Black Studies coincided with the
general student revolt against the structure and functioning of the
university and at the beginning often was supported by other
Third World students and whites. Eventually, however, the Black
students, in a strong pursuit of self-determination, would reject
cooperation with whites. This left only the Black Panther Party,
which changed its nationalist philosophy to Marxism, to deal with
them. As a result of countless struggles and negotiations, most
of the major colleges and universities agreed to establish some
form of Black Studies by 1969.

The Black Studies struggle extended also to Black colleges
which had prided themselves on being pioneers in teaching the
Black Experience. What they actually taught was "negro history"
which both in content and consciousness was different from the
liberational thrust for which Black Studies advocates struggled.
Brisbane (1974:238-239) lists three reasons the Black colleges
resisted the challenge: 1) alleged financial problems; 2) assumption that only a militant faction advocated it; and; 3) the
"bourgeois mentality" of the staff which was "committed to
working within the system (and) completely rejected the notion
of Black liberation." However, after a series of struggles and
after "Harvard, Yale and Columbia universities provided
'legitimacy' by the adoption of such programs," leading Black
institutions like Atlanta, Fisk, Howard, Lincoln, Morgan and
Tuskegee initiated Black Studies Programs by fall of 1969.

1.2   RELEVANCE OF THE DISCIPLINE

One of the most important concepts in the general
Student Movement and especially in the Black Student Move-

ment which waged the struggle for Black Studies was the concept of relevance, a concept which had both academic and social dimensions. Relevance, as a fundamental category, was inevitably defined as emanating from education's contribution to liberation and a higher level of life for Blacks. Thus, Nathan Hare (1969:42), one of the guiding theorists and founders of the Movement, argued for an Afro-American education, which would contribute to solving "the problems of the race" by producing "persons capable of solving problems of a contagious American society." Moreover, he concluded, "a Black education which is not revolutionary in the current day is both irrelevant and useless." It is this stress on academic and social relevance of education that not only gave Black Studies its raison d'être, but also brought it its major opposition.

The push for relevant education in the university was thus joined with a thrust by Black Studies to establish and maintain its own relevance as both an academic and social project. Therefore, in developing a relevant Black Studies, Black Studies advocates expressed two sets of basic concerns, i.e., academic and social ones (Robinson, 1969; Blassingame, 1973).

Academic Concerns

On the academic level, they were concerned first with the quality and usefulness or relevance of traditional white studies. White studies was seen as incorrect, incomplete and exclusive of the majority of humankind, especially the fathers and mothers of humankind and human civilization, i.e., Blacks. Secondly, Black Studies advocates perceived white studies for the most part as so much propaganda for the established order which not only posed the white paradigm as the most definitive of human life and society, but also discouraged study and development of Third World models. Finally, the Black Studies advocates saw white studies as resistant or negative to social change inquiries and models. This they felt could only be countered by a self-conscious and viable discipline of Black Studies which would not only seek to study society and the world, but also to change them.

Social Concerns

The social concerns of Black Studies centered around the questions of exclusion, treatment on campus, academic conversions and production of a conscious, committed and capable intelligentsia and on what all this meant for the Black community. Black Studies advocates were first concerned with the low number of Blacks on campus which they saw as a racist exclusion to maintain the white monopoly on critical knowledge and to thwart the rise of a Black intelligentsia capable of effectively leading and serving Blacks. Thus, one of their first demands was special admission and recruitment efforts to correct this problem. Secondly, Black Studies advocates were concerned with treatment of Black students on campus. In fact, a key set of grievances and incidents on San Francisco State's campus centered around what was considered racist treatment of Black students in terms of news reports, counselling, instruction, representation on decision-making bodies, etc. The concern was to make Blacks respected and politically effective on campus and in campus politics in the broadest sense of the word (Hare, 1972:33).

Thirdly, Black Studies advocates were concerned about what they conceived as white academic conversion, i.e., transformation of Blacks into vulgar careerists with no sense of social commitment. Equally feared was that Black students would become what Frantz Fanon called "obscene caricatures" of Europe, pathetic imitators of their oppressors (Fanon, 1968:255). Finally, Black Studies advocates were concerned with the social problems of the Black community and how Black students and Black Studies could address them.

Basic Objectives

It is around these general concerns that Black Studies advocates across the country laid out some basic academic and social objectives which interlocked and mutually reinforced each other (Blassingame, 1973; Hare, 1969; Robinson, 1969). The first and seemingly most urgent objective was to teach what was called the Black experience in its historical and current unfolding. The category "experience" suggested all that Blacks had encountered, done and endured and sought to reflect the multidimensionality of the process. Moreover, this experience was to be greatly focused on the history and contributions of Blacks who were systematically denied history and contribution to society and humanity or relegated to minor historical significance. Finally, it was advocated that the data and instruction include both the Continental African and Diasporan African experience, the Diasporan focus treating first African Americans and then all other Africans spread across the world. Although this was the projected scope, in practice, data and instruction were essentially concentrated on the Continental and African American experience with some curricula offering a few courses on the Caribbean experience.

A second beginning objective of Black Studies was to assemble and create a body of knowledge which was contributive to intellectual and political emancipation. Intellectual freedom was posed as a prerequisite to political freedom. In a word, until the white monopoly on Black minds was broken, it was argued, liberation was not only impossible, but unthinkable. For there would be no categorical referent, no way to conceive it and thus, no way to carry it out. Political emancipation as a social goal, then, was dependent on intellectual emancipation as an academic goal. These contentions were reflective of Harold Cruse's (1967) and Franklin Frazier's (1973) positions on the crisis and responsibilities of the Black intellectual.

Logically linked to the above objective was a third objective of creating a body of Black intellectuals who were dedicated to community service and development rather than vulgar careerism. Restating W.E.B DuBois' (1961) argument against Booker T. Washington's overstress on vocation at the expense of education for social competence and contribution, Black Studies advocates stressed the need for Black intellectuals who were conscious, capable and committed to Black liberation and a higher level of human life. They argued like DuBois (1969) that the race would be elevated by its best minds, a "Talented Tenth" which did not sell itself for money and machines, but recognized and responded creatively to the fact of the indivisibility of Black freedom and their indispensable role in achieving it.

Fourthly, Black Studies advocates posed as an early objective the cultivation, maintenance and continuous expansion of a mutually beneficial relationship between the campus and the community. This relationship was best posed in Nathan Hare's statement which became a slogan and call to action of the Black Studies Movement, "We must bring the campus to the community and the community to the campus." The intent here was to serve and elevate the life-conditions and the consciousness of the community and reinforce the student's relationship with the community through service and interaction. Thus, the classic alienation between the intellectual and the community is thwarted in an ongoing mutually beneficial exchange, where knowledge is shared and applied in the service of liberation and development of the Black community (Hare, 1972:33).

Finally, an early (and continuing) objective of Black Studies advocates was to establish it as a legitimate, respected and permanent discipline. This was and remains both an academic and political problem. The political problem is to win the battle of acceptance with administrations and other departments who are threatened by Black Studies or incorrectly and reductively translate its relevance and viability. The academic problem is to answer the critics of Black Studies with counter arguments, critical research, solid intellectual production and effective teaching. Afterall, there are really only two basic arguments against Black Studies, i.e., a charge of academic insubstantiality and its having a political character.

These arguments, however, do not really hold weight given Black Studies' twenty-seven year history of teaching, research, intellectual production and service to students and the university. Moreover, to answer a tired contention, Swahili is no more frivolous or irrelevant to Blacks than Hebrew or Armenian is to Jews or Armenians who were not born in Israel or Armenia and will never go there. And if white studies or traditional college courses seek to produce socially competent and committed leaders for the white community, how does one justify calling such an academic and social mission political for Blacks and proper for whites? Afterall, the basic justification for all education is that it enhances our social competence and, therefore, our capacity to make a more significant contribution to society.

Grounds of Relevance

Through the twenty-seven year old practical and theoretical struggle to achieve and refine these early objectives, fundamental and undeniable grounds of relevance of Black Studies have been established which clearly define the academic and social contributions and purpose of Black Studies. The first ground of relevance of Black Studies is that it is a definitive contribution to humanity's understanding itself. As Samir Amin (1974:5) contends, there is only one possible science, the science of human society, of humans in the process of self, social and world construction. But humanity is an abstraction, a mere construction for the convenience of conversation unless it is seen in its diversity and particularity as well as its unity and universality. Black Studies, then, becomes important because it is a study of a particular people which aids in the study of humanity as a whole. In other words, Black Studies (and other ethnic studies) represents in its most definitive sense, a necessary and significant study of a particular form and part of humanity in certain socio-historical conditions. Moreover, Black Studies is an important contribution to humanity's self-understanding because Blacks, i.e., African people, are the fathers and mothers of both humanity and human civilization (Jackson, 1970; Diop, 1991). Thus, to omit a study of the parent people of humanity is to deprive oneself and humanity of a holistic and effective understanding of itself.

A second ground of relevance of Black studies is found in its contribution to U.S. society's understanding of itself. It is not an exaggeration to say that Black and other Ethnic Studies are the most trenchant criticism and most definitive mirror of American society. If it is true that one does not evaluate a society by its public pronouncements but by its social practice, then, the study of the Black experience in the U.S. would obviously give an incisive look at American life, from a race, class and gender perspective. U.S. society claims freedom, justice and equality for all, but Black Studies poses a more definitive view of inequalities of social wealth and power in the U.S. Moreover, as Rafael Cortada (1974:41) has argued, the curricular reform in American universities is as beneficial to whites as others "if the U.S. is to be socialized in a world where only 21.8 percent of the population is white" and where U.S. and European power is declining and Third world power is on the rise. It is thus to the credit of Black Studies and the social struggles which inform its focus, as I (Karenga, 1977:50) have argued elsewhere, that they "have provided the U.S. with an essential theoretical and practical self-criticism." Furthermore, Black Studies and struggle "have forced the U.S. into a necessary self-knowledge, unmasked its self-indulgent myths and confronted it with internal contradictions so elemental that only a broad and profound social change can resolve them."

Thirdly, and as a logical consequence of the first two contentions, Black Studies has established its relevance as a contribution to the university's realization of its claim and challenge to teach the whole truth, or something as close to it as humanly possible. No university can claim universality, comprehensiveness, objectivity or effectiveness in creating a context for the development of a socially competent and aware student, if it diminishes, denies or deforms the role of African peoples in history and society. Moreover, as has been so often noted:

> Until quite lately higher education in the
> United States of America has been almost completely
> under the sway of an illusion shared by nearly every-
> body of European descent since the Middle Ages -- the
> illusion that the history of the world is the history
> of Europe and its cultural offshoots; that Western
> interpretations of that experience are sufficient, if
> not exhaustive and that the resulting value systems
> embrace everything that matters (Wright, 1970:366).

However, a true appreciation of the multicultural character of humanity and human society shatters that illusion and compels a more realistic and thus a multicultural approach to truth and education. Indeed, an academic and cultural provincialism as expressed in a Eurocentric education can only discredit the university's claim of inclusiveness, objectivity and rigor for its curriculum. It also reflects an image of irreality in a world where Africans, Native Americans, Asians and Latin Americans have stepped back on the stage of human history in both dramatic and unavoidably significant ways and roles and must be on the educational agenda. In fact, quality education is impossible without a multicultural character (Karenga, 1992; Asante, 1992; President's Task Force, 1991).

Fourthly, Black Studies has demonstrated its relevance as a contribution to the rescue and reconstruction of Black history and humanity. As both an affirmative and negative academic and social project, Black Studies affirms the truth of our history and humanity and negates the racist myths assembled to deny and deform them. Refusing to answer frivolous racist contentions, it rises to challenge traditional white studies which have intellectualized their biases, omissions and distortions. It realizes the link between history and humanity and is conscious of the fact that Europe denied and deformed Black history in order to deny and diminish Black humanity. Black Studies, then, begins with rigorous research and critical intellectual production in the key social science, history, which lays the basis for and informs all others and which will affirm the truth of the Black experience and negate the racist myths which have surrounded it.

A fifth ground of relevance of Black Studies is that it is a critical contribution to a new social science and humanities which will not only benefit Blacks, but also the U.S. and the world. Joyce Ladner's (1973) announcement of the death of white sociology can only be answered with the creation of an alternative (affirmative and negative) sociology or more accurately, a new social science which sets a model for others by the standards it sets for itself and reflects. Likewise, Hazel Carby's (1987) critique of the race, class and gender limitations of the cultural production of the dominant society demands the creation of a new humanities not restrained and restricted in such ways. Black Studies, as a contribution to this academic project, has already developed along those lines in the light of Harold Cruse's (1967) and Franklin Frazier's (1973) criticism and the challenges posed by students, other departments and the demands of the discipline itself (Turner and Perkins, 1976; Karenga, 1988).

As a contribution to a new social science and humanities, Black Studies, which is interdisciplinary, becomes a paradigm for the multidimensional approach to social and historical reality. Secondly, it is a model of a holistic social science and an inclusive humanities, not simply focusing on Blacks, but critically including other Third World peoples and whites in appropriate socio-historical periods and places of interaction with Blacks and denying no people its relevance, unlike the case of traditional white studies. Thirdly, as a contribution to a new social science and humanities, Black Studies is critical and corrective of the inadequacies, omissions and distortions of traditional white studies. In fact, it is its severe and uncompromising critique that so disturbs its traditional critics who are secure in old assumptions from by-gone eras. Moreover, as a new discipline, Black Studies is not as restricted by old data and methods as white studies. It comes without the burden and baggage of sacred assumptions about society's righteousness and imperviousness to change and thus, it introduces generative ideas which are corrective to social science and stimulate innovation and deeper inquiry (Apter, 1977:36).

Moreover, Black Studies, as both an *investigative* and *applied* discipline poses the paradigm of theory and practice merging into active self-knowledge which leads to positive social change. In a word, it is a discipline dedicated not only to understanding self, society and the world but also to changing them in a positive developmental way in the interest of human history and advancement. In this quest, it challenges the false detachment of traditional white studies which contradicts reality and obscures clarity (Ladner, 1973; Hamilton, 1970).

A sixth ground of the relevance of Black Studies is its contribution to the development of a Black intelligentsia and professional stratum whose knowledge, social competence and commitment translate as a vital contribution to the liberation and development of the Black community and thus as a contribution to society as a whole. It is at this point that the academic and social missions of Black Studies merge most definitively and become an expression of knowledge self-consciously placed in the service of community, society and ultimately humankind. It is also an effective response to DuBois' (1969) call in his seminal essay, "The Talented Tenth," for the academic and social cultivation of a body of conscious, capable and committed men and women who would assume leadership of the Black community, set its ideals, direct its thoughts and aspirations and lead its social movements in the struggle for social change. It is also reflective of Mary M. Bethune's (1939:9) call for service oriented professionals and intellectuals who would "discover the dawn and to bring this material within the understanding of. . .the masses of our people." Thus, such stress reaffirms the historical, intellectual and activist thrust of Black education and reflects a vital continuity of thought and practice.

This goal of Black Studies, however, is also reflected on one level in the educational philosophy of American universities which have historically structured curricula and instruction to produce the social servants and leaders of society. Black Studies, then, as both an investigative and applied social science, follows a similar tradition. It simply focuses more intensely on a particular part of society, the Black community and self-consciously defines itself as an emancipatory project as distinct from the oppressive managerial project of the dominant society. And in this focus which seeks to cultivate persons capable of critical thought and problem-solving, Black Studies not only benefits the Black community, but society as well. For in essence, the problems of the Black community are the problems of the larger society, and their collective solution is clearly in the larger society's interest.

A seventh and final ground of relevance of Black Studies is that it is a vital contribution to the critique, resistance and reversal of the progressive Europeanization of human consciousness and culture which is one of the major problems of our times. By the Europeanization of human consciousness and culture is meant the systematic invasion and effective transformation of the cultural consciousness of the various peoples of the world by Europeans thru technology, education, and the media so that at least three things occur: 1) the progressive loss of historical memories of these people; 2) the progressive disappreciation of themselves and their culture as a result of a conscious and unconscious assessment of themselves using European standards, and; 3) the progressive adoption of a Eurocentric view not only of themselves, but also of each other and the world to the detriment of their own humanity and the increasing degeneration of the cultural diversity and exchange which give humanity its rich variousness and internal creative challenge.

The established tendency is to use the category "westernization" to express this process of the Europeanization of human consciousness and culture. But in fact, "westernization" is a cultural category that camouflages the fundamental racial reality of European dominance. Afterall, when one refers to western culture, it is not to indicate Hawaiian or Inuit cultures, the most western of peoples. Nor is it meant to suggest the various other cultures of peoples of color in the western hemisphere, i.e., Native Americans, Africans, Latinos or Asians. What one encounters then is a Eurocentric cultural hegemony camouflaged under a cultural category that hides more than it reveals.

Black Studies challenges both the cultural content of what is called western and the definition itself, arguing for a multicultural interpretation of the western hemisphere rather than a Eurocentric one. Moreover, Black Studies joins with other ethnic studies scholars in creating and posing paradigms for multicultural discourse and exchange and possibilities of a just and good society. This, of course, presupposes and necessitates respect for each people's right and responsibility not only to exist but also to speak their own special cultural truth and make their own unique contribution to the forward flow of societal and human history (Karenga, 1988:406ff).

1.3   SCOPE OF THE DISCIPLINE

The scope of Black Studies is expressed in its definition and by the parameters it has set for itself as an interdisciplinary or multi-field discipline. *Black Studies is the systematic and critical study of the multidimensional aspects of Black thought and practice in their current and historical unfolding.* It is systematic in that it is structured and coherent; critical in the sense of its focus on the search for meaning and concern with detail and bringing forth the hidden; and multidimensional in its thrust to examine the many-sidedness of each issue, process or phenomenon. This stress on the many-sidedness joined with concern for historical and current unfolding points toward emphasis on a holistic approach and contextualization in terms of both time and place. The thrust, then, is to view each thing in the context of the whole, to always ask historical as well as current questions about it and to identify, where possible, tendencies, directions, patterns and possibilities.

As a discipline dedicated to an inclusive and holistic study of Black life, Black Studies contains subject areas in social science and in humanities as well as any other subject areas within the Black experience. As Article II of the National Council for Black Studies (NCBS) Constitution states, the discipline "include(s) any subject area that has the Black Experience as the principle object and content of study." Thus, although the bulk of Black Studies focuses on social science and humanities subject areas, it includes other areas such as education, the care professions, athletics, the physical, natural, technological and applied sciences, and any other subject of concern and encounter in the Black experience.

In fact, an important exploration of the idea of including the so-called "hard" sciences has begun. Stewart (1992:5-4) argues that this inclusion of physical and natural sciences in the realm of Black Studies is vital to the ongoing development of the discipline. The inclusion of these fields, he maintains, does not require the development of a "Black Chemistry" or "Black Physics." Rather, he continues, it requires (1) "the exploration of the potential insights from the new field of 'science, technology and society' into a Black/Africana Studies framework," (2) exploration of the value and use of "new information technologies. . .to accelerate development of the field" as exemplified in Hendrix et al's (1984) discussion of Black Studies and computer use; and (3) the development by theoretical mathematicians and statisticians of "empirical techniques based on circular rather than linear models." Stewart is correct to reject a Black science which suggests a biological or racial base. But if he extends the prohibition to include cultural emphasis, which he does not seem to do, then, he undermines the very meaning of Black Studies, i.e., to speak African people's special cultural truth and make their own unique contribution to the forward flow of human history.

Thus, Black science like Black sociology will, of necessity, reflect a cultural context and conception. A primary task of the Black Studies scientist will be to ask is there a uniquely African as well as general human approach to science? And if so, is it of value today and again, if so, in what ways? In this regard, a key task of the Black Studies scientist will be to develop a philosophy of science rooted in and growing out of an African worldview. It will raise not simply epistemological questions but equally important, ethical ones about both the concept and use of science as an instrument of human good. This was the suggestion of Bethune's (1939) and DuBois' (1969) challenge to bring the fruits of science and other knowledge to the masses who most need it. Moreover, a history of African science -- Continental and Diasporan -- placed in the context of the development of science in the world is also important. The point here is that as a multi-field or many-subject-area discipline, Black Studies borrows from and builds on invaluable achievements of other disciplines which parallel various fields or subject areas in Black Studies. But Black Studies must and does bring its own critique, challenge and contribution or it is not a specific discipline only a variant discourse within other disciplines.

Black Studies, then, is both a particular and general social science and shares with the other social sciences similar foci of inquiry and analysis. It shares with political science the concern with the problems of gaining, maintaining and using power, especially as it relates to Blacks, and with economics, the concern of the relationship of race, class, and gender to economic opportunities and distributive inequalities. Likewise, Black Studies shares with psychology a critical concern with questions of identity, alienation, self-concept and mental health and development from a Black perspective, and with sociology, concern with social problems which range from crime, educational opportunities and race, class, and gender relations to interest group organization, family and male/female relations.

Also, Black Studies shares with history a profound concern for
critical interpretation of events, issues, important personages and
social units of the past which illuminate understanding of current
thought and practice and its concern for heritage and contribution to human advancement. As a humanities discipline, Black
Studies shares with other humanities disciplines a concern for
and commitment to creative production. It shares with literature,
art, music, and dance a definite concern with ongoing issues of
aesthetics, i.e., the nature of the artistic enterprise, art as social
and personal message and meaning, standards of creativity, issues
of artistic freedom and social responsibility, questions of critique,
of deconstruction, dislocation, cultural hegemony, representation,
transcendence, border crossing, text, subtext, marginality and
centrality, recovery and reconstruction. Likewise, it shares
concern about the race, class and gender articulation, language
use and misuse, and its ability to reveal the nature and structure
of social relations, and with signs, literature and other art forms
as contested terrains. But again, Black Studies brings its own
vision and voice to the discourse in humanities, contesting the
given, crossing boundaries and calling for a new way to understand and approach the human experience.

Black Studies in sharing similar concerns with other social
sciences and humanities disciplines draws from them and strives
at an ongoing synthesis and utilization of the most incisive and
productive theories, methods, techniques, models, strategies and
research designs. Since it has come into being as a critique of
and a corrective for traditional white studies, it is compelled to
produce generative ideas to encourage new ways of thinking
about and handling theoretical and practical problems. Thus, it
is committed to challenging the old and developing new analytical
frameworks for the study of the Black and human experience,
new techniques for the continuous acquisition of knowledge and
new criteria for the validation of claims both in and outside the
discipline.

Black Studies as an interdisciplinary discipline allows for
and encourages both a *specialized* and *integrative* approach to

subject areas within the discipline. Such approach not only satisfies Martin Kilson's (1973) concern that Black Studies students and teachers have a specialization in a traditional discipline, i.e., economics, political science, literature, art, but also Phillip Daniels' (1981) concern that Black Studies maintain its autonomy as a valid and valuable discipline. It is obvious that Black Studies cannot and should not be subsumed under a traditional discipline. Therefore, both Maurice Jackson's (1970) early suggestion to subordinate it to sociology and Martin Ijere's (1972) early suggestion to subsume it under economics are more discipline preferences than substantive recommendations for the development of the discipline. Likewise, if by "curricular control of an established discipline," Kilson means choosing one at the expense of Black Studies rather than as a subject area for specialization within the discipline of Black Studies, he too is incorrect and non-contributive to the developmental and autonomy demands of Black Studies.

Like all disciplines, Black Studies has subject areas of specialization which do not replace the discipline, but sharpen its focus in the given subject area. Thus, international relations, the study of parties or the politics of developing countries do not replace political science as a discipline, but rather sharpen its focus in given subject areas. Moreover, each discipline is integrative as well as specialized. This is necessary to check excessive specialization which can make sublevels of research alien, narrow and even counterproductive to the holistic thrust of a given discipline. Therefore, Black Studies, while allowing and encouraging specialization in one or more subject areas, demands as a coherent discipline the linking of these subject areas within it to the overall principles and fundamental thrusts of the discipline.

Black Studies, then, as an interdisciplinary discipline has seven basic subject areas. These intradisciplinary foci which at first seem to be disciplines themselves are, in fact, separate disciplines when they are outside the discipline of Black Studies, but inside, they become and are essentially subject areas which contribute to a holistic picture and approach to the Black experience. Moreover, the qualifier Black attached to each area in an explicit or implicit way suggests a more specialized and delimited focus which, of necessity, transforms a broad discipline into a particular subject area. The seven basic subject areas of Black Studies then are: Black History; Black Religion; Black Social Organization; Black Politics; Black Economics; Black Creative Production (Black Art, Music and Literature) and Black Psychology.

This volume is structured around these subject areas for they represent core courses in most Black Studies programs and departments and thus serve as excellent foci for a survey course in Black Studies, i.e., a broad but substantive introduction to the discipline of Black Studies. Furthermore, this conceptual framework is taken from *Kawaida* theory, a theory of cultural and social change, which has as one of its main propositions the contention that the solution to the problems of Black life demand critiques and correctives in the seven basic areas of culture (Karenga, 1980). These areas of culture are: religion, history, social organization, economic organization, political organization, creative production and ethos. The categories spirituality, creative motif and ethos were changed to coincide with course titles, but the definition and analysis of these subject areas in this volume are essentially the same.

It should also be noted that Kawaida theory "defines culture in the broadest sense to equate it with all the thought and activity of a given people or society" and focuses on the seven areas of culture as core areas of analysis and problem-solving, or in Kawaida terms, of critiques and correctives (Karenga, 1980:16-17). The Kawaida seven-area focus and definition of culture obviously coincides with the core focus of Black Studies on the totality of Black thought and practice. The similarity would not appear as amazing and coincidental, if we remember Cruse's (1969:6-7) contention that the historical "demand for Black Studies...falls under the heading of the movement, tendency (and) ideology of 'Black cultural nationalism.'" This theoretical and practical thrust of Black cultural nationalism emerged among "young Black intelligentsia, young Black students and young Black activists" and was, as Cruse states, "in response to the feeling that at (that time) there (was) no viable intellectual approach to the problems facing both Blacks and whites in American society." Black Studies was then posed as a critical alternative intellectual approach to the development of critiques and correctives necessary to understanding and changing the Black community and the larger society. As the guiding theory of Black cultural nationalism and the Black Cultural Revolution of the 60's, then, Kawaida theory played a key role in the definition and defense of the foci and academic and social mission of Black Studies (Pinkney, 1976: Chapter 7).

In summing up, the scope of Black Studies as a discipline is the systematic and critical study of the totality of historical and current Black thought and practice, but expresses itself most definitively in seven core subject areas: 1) Black History; 2) Black Religion; 3) Black Social Organization; 4) Black Politics; 5) Black Economics; 6) Black Creative Production (Black Art, Black Music and Black Literature); and 7) Black Psychology. As an interdisciplinary discipline concerned with the coherence and unity of its subject areas, Black Studies, of necessity, has core integrative principles and assumptions that serve as thematic glue which holds together these core subject areas. This volume, the survey approach it employs and the subject areas it includes are all given coherence and informed by four of these integrative principles and assumptions.

The first of these assumptions is that each subject area of Black Studies is a vital aspect and area of the Black experience and, therefore, contributive to the understanding and apprecia-tion of its wholeness. Secondly, the truth of the Black experience is whole and thus, any partial and compartmentalized approach to it can only yield a partial and incomplete image and under-standing of it. Thirdly, effectively integrated into the pattern of the discipline as a whole, each subject area becomes a microcosm of the macrocosm, the Black experience, which not only enriches our knowledge of the Black experience, but also enhances the analytical process and products of the discipline itself. Finally, all the subject areas mesh and intersect not only at the point of their primary focus, i.e., Black people in the process of shaping reality in their own image and interest, but also in their self-conscious commitment and contribution to the definition and solution of the social and discipline problems which serve as the core challenges to Black Studies.

1.4   SUBSEQUENT DEVELOPMENTS

If the 60's marked the definitive founding of the discipline of Black Studies, the 70's and 80's represent a multidimensional thrust toward consolidation and expansion (Young, 1984; Turner, 1984; Aldridge, 1988; Harris, Hine and McKay, 1990; Anderson, 1990). In this multifaceted process several new developments have occurred which have defined both the course and character of the discipline. Among these are the emergence of and focus on: 1) professional organizations of the discipline; 2) the concept of Afrocentricity; 3) Black Women's Studies; 4) Multicultural Studies; and 5) Classical African Studies.

Professional Organizations of the Discipline

African Heritage Studies Association (AHSA). The founding of the African Heritage Studies Association evolved in the context of the general thrust toward self-determination of the Freedom Movement in the 60's and the parallel efforts of Black Studies scholars within the Africana Studies movement to do likewise in the academy. The AHSA emerged from a year of discussions within the Black Caucus of the African Studies Association (ASA), the major professional organization of African Studies at that time, and simultaneous negotiations with the leadership of this organization. During the 11th Annual Convention of ASA held in Los Angeles in 1968, Black members met to discuss grievances against ASA and to list demands for it to change its Eurocentric treatment of both the subject matter of Africa and of them (Rowe, 1970:4). Moreover, they decided to form "a new organization to cater to Black scholars and to correct the teaching of Euro-Africa rather than Africa in U.S. colleges and universities."

In addition to the decision to form a new organization "to serve Black scholars and Black communities," several other decisions were made. Among them was the decision that the new organization act as a clearing house and liaison among Black scholars all around the world, "exchanging information, and establishing networks to correct the present monopoly of information about Black cultures and histories in white hands." Thirdly, it was decided that members of the new organization would "link with Africanists in Africa through embassies." Fourthly, the new organization was to "encourage active partici-pation of its members in all Black conferences at home or abroad." And finally, a decision was made to meet in December of that year in New York to consolidate agreements reached in Los Angeles.

After a follow-up meeting in December 1968, AHSA held its first convention in June 1969 at Federal City College in Washington, D.C. However, AHSA still maintained its links with ASA, defining its relationship with ASA as one "of a symbiotic nature." Thus, at ASA's conference in Montreal, October 1969, its Black Caucus inside petitioned ASA for equal representation in all decision-making committees, an equitable number of ASA fellowships, adequate representation at all national and interna-tional conferences relating to African or Black Studies, and encouragement of the involvement of Black scholars in various roles according to their expertise and interests. ASA, however, rejected these requests. John Henrik Clarke (1976:8), the first president of AHSA, read the rejection as resistance of the white majority to giving Blacks "the means of changing the ideological and structural bases of the African Studies Association." According to him and other AHSA members, ASA enjoyed its monopoly on the authoritative interpretation of all things African; "resented" the stress on the Pan-Africanist perspective and were threatened by the intellectual and practical challenge posed by African Americans claiming a special relationship with Africa and independent grounding in African Studies.

The Montreal conference was for Black Caucus members of the ASA a decisive point of rupture. They left the conference convinced that the leadership of ASA did not wish collaboration but monopoly and that only a totally independent African organization could do the practical and intellectual work neces- sary to serve the interests of Black scholars and Black people. Thus, they formed AHSA as an indispensable "association of scholars of African descent...committed to the preservation, interpretation and creative presentation of the historical and cultural heritage of African people, both on the ancestral soil of Africa and in the diaspora in the Americas and throughout the world" (Clarke, 1976:11).

Within this context, according to Clarke (1976:3ff), the Pan-Africanist scholars and activists set themselves several fundamental goals.   Among these were: 1) "to examine every aspect and approach to the history and culture of African people in this country and throughout the world;" 2) "to project (AHSA) influence into every organization that relates to Africans and the people of African descent;" 3) to challenge and question all who claim authority on African life and history; 4) "to use African history to effect a world union of African people;" 5) to establish "a new frame of reference in all matters relating to Africa," i.e., a critical pan-Africanist perspective which stresses especially the interrelatedness of African peoples and the linkage of the intellectual with the practical; and finally, 6) to define African heritage and "to put components of (this) heritage together to weld an instrument of liberation."

In the 23 years of its existence, AHSA has essentially served several functions. First, and foremost, it has served as a ground and context for scholarly encounter and exchange. Its annual conferences bring scholars from all over the world African community in fruitful exchanges and creative challenge. Secondly, AHSA has served through its individual members, an organizational role for other professional organizations. In her inaugural presidential address in 1989 titled "Agenda for AHSA: 21st Century," Charshee McIntyre (1989:3) listed several organizations in which AHSA members played a founding role, i.e., Trans-Africa, a lobby for African interests, the National Council for Black Studies, the National Association of Black Educators, the Association for the Study of Classical African Civilizations and the National Congress of Black Faculty. Thirdly, AHSA has been an advocacy organization for Black interests in education in general as well as on larger social issues organizing forums, engaging in demonstrations and participating in governmental and institutional policy discussions. It has been also a major participant in the overall thrust to link African peoples intellectually and practically in ongoing projects.

Finally, McIntyre (1989:5ff) has noted several other on going projects to which AHSA is committed. These include: 1) focus on transnational and international African world interests and cooperative relations among scholars throughout the African world as outlined in Locksley Edmondson's 1985 memo "Redefining the Role of AHSA;" 2) strengthening and expanding the AHSA student commission to mentor and support young scholars; 3) a publishing project to aid Africana Studies scholars in publishing their work and produce regular organization literature; 4) sustaining and expanding the AHSA newsletter; and 5) building a Pan-African research institute dedicated to the pursuit of truth and the reaffirmation of African heritage.

National Council for Black Studies (NCBS). The National Council for Black Studies (NCBS) was founded in 1976 and has since become the preeminent discipline organization. The process which led to its founding was initiated in 1975 by Bertha Maxwell, who was then the chair of the Department of Afro-American Studies at the University of North Carolina at Charlotte. Calling on Black scholars around the country to engage in dialog on critical issues of Black Studies, she created the interest and opportunity for the building of NCBS and played a central role in its formation and development. In 1976 at the founding conference, women and men of the discipline developed programs and strategies for organizational and discipline development and Maxwell became NCBS' first chairperson. She was followed by chairpersons William King, William "Nick" Nelson, Carlene Young, Delores Aldridge, Selasé W. Williams and now in 1992, Charles Henry. It is important to note here that since its inception NCBS has not only had an equal number of female and male chairpersons and leaders, but also a similar distribution of key players in its founding and development. This has helped produce, as argued below, a positive and productive male/female dialog and exchange and has thus expanded and enriched the organization and the discipline.

In a paper titled "A Synoptic History of NCBS and Its Future Direction" and presented at the NCBS Summer Faculty Institute in June 1991 at Ohio State University, then president Selasé Williams outlined the role of the organization in defining, defending and developing Black Studies. He (1991:1) noted the unique role of NCBS as a professional organization for a discipline which "always insisted on the inclusion of both the intellectual and political dimensions of the Black Experience in its curriculum, its research and other professional responsibilities." Thus, he (1991:2) calls attention to Article II of the NCBS Constitution which shows its commitment to both academic excellence and social responsibility, building on and drawing from not only educators but also students, interested citizens and other professionals. "The purpose of this Council," the Article reads, "is to promote and strengthen academic and community programs in the area of Black Studies. The Council believes that Black Studies academic programs should include any subject area that has the Black experience as the principle object and content of study."

Under successive administrations, NCBS emerged as the preeminent professional organization of the discipline. Having established its national office at Indiana University, Bloomington under the auspices of Herman Hudson, Dean of Afro-American Studies, it proceeded to produce its organizational voice, *Voices in Black Studies* and to expand its regional structures. Moreover, it began in the early 80's to produce a series of documents which defined its goals and informed its practice. Among these are: *The Black Studies Core Curriculum*, (The Hall Report) 1981; *The Black Studies 4-Year College and University Survey* (The Daniel and Zike Report) 1983; and *The Short-Range and Long-Range Goals Report* (The Williams Report) 1984. In addition, NCBS chairpersons Carlene Young and Delores Aldridge produced special Black Studies issues of journals on the state, future and direction of the discipline. Young (1984) edited a special issue of the *Journal of Negro Education* and Aldridge (1988) edited a special issue of *Phylon*, both of which deepened and expanded Black Studies discourse.

Important also to NCBS' development has been its establishment of an accreditation process for Black Studies programs, its creation of specialty caucuses, its workshops on multicultural education and Black women issues, its joint activities with AHSA, the Congressional Black Caucus and other academic, professional and community organizations; and its recent establishment of its discipline journal, *The Afrocentric Scholar*. Also, among its most significant programs has been the foundation sponsored projects such as the Summer Faculty Institute, the Administrative Training Workshop and Curriculum Development and Data Collection. Especially central are the Summer Faculty Institute which introduces new Black Studies faculty to the history, philosophy and varied discourses of the discipline, and provides them with a context of creative challenge and exchange with peers as well as major scholars in the discipline.

Finally, Williams (1991:4) lists as the future direction and goals of NCBS: 1) continued production of discipline literature and organizational documents; 2) ongoing and expanded grant and research proposals for development of the discipline, faculty, students and community -- NCBS projects; 3) continuing organizational professionalization and reorganization for improved performance and service; and 4) increasing and enriching contexts for discourse and exchange, i.e., conferences, symposia, workshops, etc. In addition to these goals, certainly the pursuit of curriculum development to meet new challenges and expand the discipline to include new discourse and issues, i.e., Black women studies, classical African studies, multicultural studies and international studies, also stand at the core of the NCBS mission (Aldridge, 1992).

The Concept of Afrocentricity

Clearly one of the most important recent developments in Black Studies is the emergence of Afrocentricity as a major conceptual framework within the discipline. As an intellectual category, Afrocentricity is relatively new, emerging in the late 70's and finding its most definitive treatment then in a work by Molefi Asante titled *Afrocentricity: The Theory of Social Change* and published in 1980. In this initial work Asante (1980:66) described Afrocentricity as the indispensable perspective of the Black Studies project and he has continuously maintained this position.

One could argue that the Afrocentric emphasis in Black studies is not new and that it reaches back to much earlier periods in Black intellectual history (Morgan, 1991). For example works on education by W.E.B. DuBois (1975), Anna Julia Cooper (1892) and especially, Carter G. Woodson's (1969) *Mis-education of the Negro* could certainly be called in part or whole Afrocentric works. But it is Asante (1980, 1987, 1990) who provided the category Afrocentricity and an accompanying literature which contributed definitively to establishing the concept as a central element in Black Studies discourse and practice. Since the introduction of the category, the discourse around both the category and its meaning to Black Studies has been extensive and varied. Thus, it is important to note that there is no single conception of Afrocentricity, only a general conceptual agreement that Afrocentric means essentially viewing social and human reality from an African perspective or stand-point.

Moreover, as Stewart (1992:3) points out, " a popular Afrocentricism" has emerged which "is being confused increasingly with systematic intellectual approaches in the field." He adds that "this confusion has contributed to a distorted view of the state of the field and is fueling uneasiness in some circles about the intellectual credibility of Black/Africana Studies." Here one can draw a distinction between Afrocentricity and Afrocentricism. Afrocentricism appears more often in ideological discourse between Afrocentric advocates and critics especially in popular pieces on the subject. *Afrocentricity* is, thus, used in my work rather than Afrocentricism for several reasons. First, it is to stress its intellectual value as distinct from its ideological use. For in the final analysis, it must prove its value as an intellectual category regardless of the ideological use advocates and critics make of it. Second, Afrocentricity is preferable to Afrocentricism to clearly distinguish it from Eurocentricism which is an ideology and practice of domination and exclusion based on the fundamental assumption that all relevance and value are centered in European culture and peoples and that all other cultures and peoples are at best marginal and at worse irrelevant. Afrocentricity is not built on or conceived as a denial of worth and values to others. On the contrary, it conceptually includes both a particular (African) and universal (human) dimension as indicated below.

Thirdly, Afrocentricity is preferred to establish it as a quality of thought and practice rather than thought and practice themselves. In a word, it is used to focus on the cultural and human quality of African thought and practice rather than on thought and practice as an ideological conception and conduct. Rejecting the "ism" becomes a way to avoid being labelled as simply another ideological posture. The category *African-centeredness* is also used to escape ideological associations (Keto,

1991). Having made such distinctions and conceding the variations in both definitions and approaches to it, nevertheless *Afrocentricity can be defined as a quality of thought and practice rooted in the cultural image and human interests of African people* (Karenga, 1988:403). To be rooted in the cultural image of African people is to be anchored in the views and values of African people as well as in the practice which emanates from and gives rise to these views and values. "To be rooted in the human interests of African people is to be informed and attentive to the just claims on life and society Africans share with other peoples, i.e., respect and concern for truth, justice, freedom, the dignity of the human person," nature, etc. (Karenga, 1992:10). Here, one notes that Afrocentricity, as an intellectual concept, contains both a *particular* and *universal* dimension. It self-consciously contributes a valuable particular cultural insight and discourse to the multicultural project and in the process, finds common ground with other cultures which can be cultivated and developed for mutual benefit.

The Afrocentric vision, critically defined and developed, then, demands that Black Studies root itself in the African experience and in the worldview which evolves from and informs that experience. However, having rooted itself in the African experience, which is the source and substance of its raison d'être, Black Studies as a mode of grasping reality, expands outward, to the acquisition of other relevant human knowledge and the knowledge of other humans as DuBois (1975:98) urges. For even as there are lessons for humanity in African particularity, there are lessons for Africans in human commonality. And African humanity is enriched and expanded by mutually beneficial exchanges with others. Moreover, in understanding human history as a whole, Africans can even more critically appreciate their fundamental role in the origins of humanity and human civilization and in the forward flow of human history.

Afrocentricity as an intellectual conception evolves out of and is based on several fundamental assumptions. First, it is based on the assumption that African culture is not only worthy of study, but critical to understanding society and the human experience given its key role in each (see the chapter on Black history below). Secondly, Afrocentricity or African-centeredness as a methodological orientation, contends that the most effective and fruitful way of studying and understanding African people is from their own perspective (Karenga, 1988:403-404). Thirdly, Afrocentric theory argues that Black Studies is not simply a body of data but also a way of approaching and interpreting data, i.e., from an African-centered perspective (Asante, 1990:7). Thus, Afrocentricity becomes an indispensable aspect of the Black Studies project and an important measure of the accuracy and value of a given work. And finally, Afrocentric theory is based on the assumption that if an African-centered approach is incorrect or of little value, then so is the discipline of Black Studies which is based on an equally important assumption that the African experience is both a valid and valuable subject of study.

Of course, Afrocentricity has its critics inside and outside the discipline. Often critiques outside the discipline appear more ideological than intellectual (Schlesinger, 1991; Ravitch, 1990) and have been noted and answered (Asante, 1992, 1991). Internal criticism, however, raises issues that have created an ongoing discourse which is valuable to the discipline's need to constantly question and refine its thought and practice (Hall, 1991; Oyebade, 1990). Among the essential challenges posed by critics and the discipline's own commitment to ongoing self-criticism and self-correction are the challenges to avoid the tendency: 1) to project Afrocentricity as a dogma of authenticity rather than an orientation and methodology; 2) to deny the reality and value of the diversity of perspectives and approaches within the discipline of Black Studies; 3) to promote a static, monolithic and unreal concept of African culture which denies or diminishes its dynamic and diverse character; 4) to overfocus on the Continental African past at the expense of recognizing the African American past and present as central to and constitutive of African culture and the Afrocentric enterprise; and 5) to be unable to prove its utility in intellectual production beyond declaration of its presence and aspirations.

Certainly, if Afrocentricity as an intellectual concept and a quality of thought and practice can avoid these tendencies and at the same time demonstrate constantly its capacity to define more accurately and explain the African experience, it will prove its worth. For it will then not only bring us a more accurate and informative view of the African experience, but also contribute to a more accurate and informative understanding of the human experience in all its rich and instructive diversity.

Black Women's Studies

Another major development in Black Studies is the emergence of Black women's studies as a fundamental, even indispensable, part of Black Studies. The lack of adequate scholarly treatment of Black women in Black Studies and in the academy as a whole posed both a serious problematic and challenge for Black Studies since its inception. But as Delores Aldridge (1992:171) notes, "Within the last several years, there has been increasing advocacy for recognition and correction of this failure to deal equitably with Africana women in scholarship and the academy." This development was not automatic nor easily achieved and is still marked by both continuing inattentiveness and outright resistance as well as support and achievement. Several factors have shaped and contributed to the emergence of Black women studies in the discipline of Black Studies.

The first and foremost of these factors is the intellectual and practical struggles waged by Black women in the discipline itself. These efforts have been directed towards creating and sustaining space for teaching and research in Black women studies in particular and gender studies in general. Challenging male-centered interpretations of African and human reality and the relationships which such interpretations cultivated and sustained, Black women scholars produced and insisted on alternative visions. Among some of the early works in the 70's which raised important Black women studies issues are Toni Cade's *The Black Woman* (1970), Joyce Ladner's *Tomorrow's Tomorrow* (1971), Inez Smith-Reid's *"Together" Black Women* (1972), Mary Helen Washington's *Black-Eyed Susans* (1975), Sharon Hurley's and Rosalyn Terborg-Penn's *The Afro-American Woman: Struggles and Images* (1978), and Roseann P. Bell's, Bettye J. Parker's and Beverly Guy-Sheftall's *Sturdy Black Bridges: Visions of Black Women in Literature* (1979). These works raised critical issues of race, gender and class and called for correctives.

In the 80's and 90's early Black women studies literature was built on and expanded in various fields, especially in literature. Among the most notable are La Frances Rodgers-Rose's *The Black Woman* (1980); Angela Davis' *Women, Race and Class* (1981); Gloria Hull's, Patricia Bell Scott's and Barbara Smith's *All the Women are White, All Blacks are Men, But Some of Us are Brave* (1982); Barbara Christian's *Black Feminist Criticism: Perspectives on Black Women Writers* (1980); Paula Giddings' *When and Where I Enter: The Impact of Black Women on Race and Sex in America* (1984); Gloria Wade-Gayle's *No Crystal Stair: Visions of Race and Sex in Woman's Fiction* (1984); bell hooks' many books including *Talking Back: Thinking Feminist, Thinking Black* (1989), *Yearning: race, gender and cultural politics* (1990), *Black Looks: race and representation* (1992); Vivian Gordon's *Black Women, Feminism and Black Liberation* (1987); Delores Aldridge's *Black Male-Female Relationships* (1989); Darlene Clark Hine's 10 volume *Black Women in American History* (1990); Margaret Simms' and Julianne Malveaux's *Slipping Through the Cracks: The Status of the Black Woman* (1986); Beverly Guy-Sheftall's *Daughters of Sorrow, Attitudes toward Black Women 1880-1920* (1990); Hazel Carby's *Reconstructing Womanhood: The Emergence of the Afro-American Woman Novelist* (1987); and Patricia Hill Collins' *Black Feminist Thought* (1991).

A second factor shaping Black women's struggle for space, recognition and egalitarian relationships was the key role

Black women played in building and developing the two major professional organizations of the discipline, the African Heritage Studies Association (AHSA) and the National Council for Black Studies (NCBS). In 1968 at the founding of AHSA, women were in the vanguard of the move for self-determination and self-definition in the discipline. They collaborated in both the intellectual and practical construction of the organization and have played a fundamental role in its maintenance, development and leadership. Some of the important pioneers in this process are: Shelby Lewis, Barbara Wheeler, Barbara Sizemore, Charshee McIntyre, Nancy Cortez, and Inez Smith-Reid.

Likewise, it was Bertha Maxwell whose conceptual and organizational initiative led to the founding of NCBS. Calling on Black scholars around the country in 1975 to come to the University of North Carolina to engage in dialog on critical issues in Black Studies, she created the interest and opportunity for building NCBS. Along with other women, she played a central role in its formulation and development and was its first chair in 1976; Maxwell led NCBS well through its beginning years of establishing a national office and regional structures producing its organizational voice, *Voices in Black Studies*, and initiating a conference process. Also, as in AHSA, women not only played leadership roles in the founding and development of NCBS but also in the definition and development of the discipline itself. Among the most noted, in addition to Maxwell, are Delores Aldridge and Carlene Young. These women of NCBS as well as those in AHSA have continuously advanced gender issues in both Black Studies discourse and organizational practice. And in this persistence, they have provided necessary creative tension for positive and productive discourse and change with their male colleagues, thus expanding and enriching the discipline.

A third factor which shaped the construction of Black women studies was the creative tension and discourse between Black feminists (womanists) and white feminists and between Black Studies and white women studies in the academy. Especially in the early period of Black women studies, work by

Black women tended to stress racial oppression more than gender oppression and to stress a common front of male and female for Black liberation (LaRue, 1970; Cade, 1970; Hare and Hare, 1970; Cooper, 1971; King, 1973). However, even later many Black women stressed the race, as well as gender character of their oppression and the need for white women to recognize the race and class nature of their own feminism, the differences as well as commonalities among women and the privileged position of white women in the racist white patriarchy which worked to Black women's and Black people's disadvantage (Rodgers-Rose, 1980; Gordon, 1987; hooks, 1990; Carby, 1987; Hill, 1991). This creative tension helped develop Black feminist thought and at the same time laid a basis for a current and historical criticism of sexism in the Black Movement and community.

Thus, a fourth factor which aided in shaping the development of Black women studies is the ongoing inquiry into and criticism of relations in the Black Freedom Movement (hooks, 1981; Hull, Scott and Smith, 1982; Giddings, 1984; Gordon, 1987). The women of SNCC under the leadership of Ruby Doris Robinson are credited with first raising in written form a serious critique of sexism in the movement. But this criticism became an enlarged discourse with a persistent demand for inclusion and the end of inequality in participation, power and representation (Clark, 1986; Giddings, 1984). In addition to criticism of current and historical practices of the movement by women and men, there are also genuine efforts of many men to be self-critical and self-corrective and a developing literature on the ethical basis for improving male/female relations (Aldridge, 1989; Rodgers-Rose, 1980; Rodgers-Rose and Rodgers, 1985).

As it continues to develop, Black women studies as a subject area of Black Studies faces several challenges. Aldridge (1992:179) outlines the challenges as follows: 1) continued and expanded scholarship by and about Black women "with increased focus in the social and behavioral sciences, the natural sciences, professions and policy studies;" 2) "increased contributions by women to conceptualization of the theoretical and empirical issues of the field in general;" 3) "continued involvement of Africana women with womanist perspectives in leadership positions in the professional bodies for Africana Studies so that programs and policies reflect their perspectives;" 4) "increased attention to developing new and restructuring old curricula to reflect a balance that is inclusive of Africana women;" 5) "increased balancing of speakers and cultural activities on campuses that draw upon both men and women not only from the literary tradition but other orientations;" and 6) "concentrated efforts to search out and quote works of both Africana women and men in the field...."

In addition to these, key to Black women's studies is the continued development of womanist theory so that it cannot only distinguish itself from white feminism but also move beyond its early concentration on oppression rather than agency (Carby, 1987; Gordon, 1987; hooks, 1990). As Carby (1987:16) notes, "Black feminist theory continues to be shaped by tensions apparent in feminist theory in general." These above all include concentration on what men have done rather than what women have done, and can and will do. It is as hooks notes, the struggle between concentrating on victimization or agency.

Moreover, as Gordon argues, much of the literature follows too closely white feminism without recognizing and taking into consideration vital differences.   In fact, even when Black women use the category womanist, there is little theoretical development of its distinctness as a defining characteristic of Black feminist thought. Certainly, Patricia Hill Collins (1991) has made a major contribution to this effort, but womanism still needs a more developed and distinctive theory.

Collins (1991:38-39) contends that "the primary guiding principle of Black feminism is a recurring humanist vision." She quotes Anna Julia Cooper's classic statement from *A Voice From the South* (1892) which states "We take our stand on the solidarity of humanity, oneness of life, and the unnaturalness and injustice of all favoritism whether of sex, race, country of condition...." She links this with Alice Walker's (1983:xi) concept of "womanist" and argues that Walker's concept of womanist, as one who is "committed to the survival and wholeness of an entire people, male and female," is an expression of the "notion of the solidarity of humanity." This is clearly part of it, but it also speaks of the unity of male and female without dominance, as does Cooper, of wholeness and of woman "audacious, coura-geous... responsible, in charge, serious" (Walker, 1983:xi). These are clearly concepts which offer excellent points of departure for not only a critical discourse on the reconstruction of womanhood, but also the reconstruction of male-female relations and society. And this challenge is, in the final analysis, the most daunting and promising one.

Finally, directly related to this theoretical challenge of distinctness is the challenge of developing more Black women studies literature in areas other than literary criticism. As noted above and in Chapter 7 on Black Creative Production, literature and related areas are well-represented. But as Aldridge (1992: 178ff) notes in her challenges, this is not so for other areas. The challenge thus is to develop both theory and major studies in these other areas which speak Black women's own special truth and serve as their unique contribution to both education and liberation (hooks, 1989).

Multicultural Studies

Another key development in Black Studies is its varied response to the emergence of multiculturalism as discourse and practice (Karenga, 1992; Asante, 1992; Marable, 1992; Carru-thers, 1990). Essentially there have been three responses inside the discipline to it. First, there is a tendency to see it as simply another attempt by the established order to dilute and divert the legitimate claims and demands of African people and maintain the power and worldview of the established order. Secondly, multiculturalism is seen as superficial cultural diversion from more serious issues of wealth and power. In a word, it becomes a preoccupation with cultural symbols rather than with the issue of wealth and power relations which either give or deny cultural substances and maintains white dominance.   And finally, multiculturalism is seen by others in the discipline as a continuation of the struggle for a quality education, and a just and good society under another category. It is in this later conception that multiculturalism becomes an important development and challenge to Black Studies (Karenga, 1992).

Seen as a new expression of a continuing struggle for quality education and a just and good society, multiculturalism becomes and is a part of a Black historical tradition in education and society. Marable (1992:15) makes the same determination, linking the political and ethical aspirations of the Black Freedom Movement to multicultural democracy. He states that "multicultural democracy must perceive of itself in this historic tradition, as a critical project which transforms the larger society...restoring humanity and humanistic values to a system which is materialistic, destructive to the environment, and abusive of fellow beings."

Moreover, the struggle for a multicultural education begins in full form in the 60's with the Black Student Movement demanding the end to exclusive white studies instruction. As noted in the Introduction above, the Black students' struggle for Black Studies and the end to the Eurocentric curriculum was joined and aided by Third World groups who formed with Blacks the Third World Liberation Front. Moreover, white progressives formed a support committee for the Front. Thus, this historic struggle for Black Studies was in fact a struggle for a multicultural education as opposed to a Eurocentric one. For it not only broke the Eurocentric monopoly on what was taught as relevant and truth, but it also opened to the door for an even wider challenge. Therefore, other ethnic studies, i.e., Native American, Latino and Asian Studies, and women studies built on this tradition and joined in demanding an education of quality and relevance. It is at this point that quality education unavoidably requires a multicultural content.

The challenge to Black Studies, then, is to recognize its vanguard role in initiating both the discourse and process of multiculturalism (Karenga, 1993; Carruthers, 1990:17). As Delores Aldridge (1991:24) states, "It was African American Studies scholars who dared initiate and embrace a new way of looking at and examining knowledge about the world with a focus upon the experiences of the people of African descent." She states, Black Studies scholars "should take the lead in defining the new multicultural curriculum and indeed the concept itself which is mired in confusion." In a word, she concludes, "Black Studies, then, must lead in resolving the issues and definitions of what is multicultural...."

The challenge to define multiculturalism and rescue it from the established order or the Eurocentric version is a key task. Jacob Carruthers (1990:3) has noted that "even the most carefully developed multicultural curriculum will be unavoidably centered in the culture of the community by or in which the program is developed and taught." He goes on to say that this "means that if nothing else is done in the United States, the curriculum will have a Eurocentric focus." Criticizing Diane Ravitch's (1990) view of multiculturalism, Carruthers (1990:5ff) notes that she refuses to recognize unequal power in society and its effect on the multicultural curriculum, and that it is not simply a question of teaching too little of cultures of the people of color, but also of what is taught, i.e., falsehoods. Moreover, she does not recognize the history of the struggle for a revised curriculum and wishes to pretend progress in this area simply happened. It is these problems and others that make Carruthers conclude, the established order cannot be left to define and impose its own version of multiculturalism.

Molefi Asante (1992) in his critique of Arthur Schlesinger's (1991) multiculturalism, also reveals problems of Eurocentric versions. First, he (1992:305) points out that Schlesinger's vision of multiculturalism evolves from a conception of "an American rooted in the past, where whites, actually Anglo-Saxon whites, defined the protocols of American society and white culture itself represented the example to which others were forced to aspire." It is thus a multiculturalism with a hegemonic role for European culture, a conceptual blindness to oppression and domination and a studied aversion to Afrocentric theory and practice which reveal flaws in the body politics and the hegemonic position of Euro-Americans in education and society. As a counter, Asante (1992:311) suggests that an Afrocentric conception of multiculturalism "becomes useful for the expansion of dialogue and the widening of discourse-the proper function of education." This, he concludes, would of necessity mean the development of "a curriculum of instruction that affirms all people in their cultural heritages" and the parallel end of "white self-esteem curriculum now present in most school systems."

As I (Karenga, 1992:1) have argued, "The current debate on the character and content of quality education in a multicultural context offers new possibilities not only for the reconception and reconstruction of public and higher education, but also for the reconception and reconstruction of society itself." This is because "the debate is in essence about power and place, standards of relevance and the quality of relations among various cultural groups which compose U.S. society and indeed the world." This multiculturalism is a critical thought and practice which cannot and should not be left to established order theorists. Conceived in an Afrocentric framework, multiculturalism can be defined as thought and practice rooted in and reflective of several basic commitments: 1) mutual respect for each people and culture; 2) common recognition that human diversity is human richness and that the challenge is not simply to tolerate it but to embrace and build on it; 3) mutual recognition that neither U.S. society nor the world is a finished white product, but rather an ongoing multicultural *project* and that each people has both the right and responsibility to speak its own special truth and make its own unique contribution to the forward flow of social and human history; and 4) mutual commitment to an ongoing search for common ground in the midst of diversity necessary to build a just and good society and a peaceful and freedom-respecting world.

Black Studies is also challenged to provide a rationale for multicultural education. This rationale will, of necessity, resemble and build on the rationale for Black Studies itself. For again, it is the struggle for Black Studies which layed the ground for multicultural discourse and practice. There are essentially three basic grounds for multicultural education -- moral, intellectual and social (President's Task Force Report, 1991:3ff; Karenga, 1992:2ff). The moral grounds of multicultural education rests in a real respect for the concrete human person in all her/his diversity. In such a conception, the student and teacher are not abstracted from concrete conditions for critical understanding but are engaged and challenged to generate reflective problematics from their own experience. In a word, they speak from their own experience and location in history and culture and thus enrich educational discourse.

The intellectual ground of multicultural education is established, as I (President's Task Force Report, 1991:3) have argued elsewhere, in its use and value as 1) "a necessary corrective for the conceptual and content inadequacy of the exclusive curriculum which omits and diminishes the rich (and instructive) variety of human cultures; 2) an equally important corrective for racist, sexist, classist and chauvinistic approaches to knowledge and education which deny, demean or diminish the meaning, experience and voice of the other; and 3) a creative challenge to the established order of things. For multicultural education, especially in its Afrocentric form, comes into being and establishes itself as an uncompromising and relentless critique of the established order. It then joins this critique with correctives pointed toward creating not only a richer and more varied educational experience but also a just and good society.

The social grounds of multicultural education are established in its function as: 1) a just response to the demand of marginalized and excluded peoples and groups for an education reflective of and relevant to their own life experience; 2) an indispensable preparation of students and teachers for the world in which they live, work, study and exchange; and 3) "part and parcel of the thrust to create a just and good society, to avoid civil strife, and to enhance the quality of social life through cultivation of democratic values.

A third challenge for Black Studies is to construct a model multicultural curriculum at various levels of education. If quality education is at the same time and of necessity multicultural education, then, the challenge here is not to provide an Afrocentric curriculum in schools and universities, but rather to propose an Afrocentric paradigm for a multicultural education. Thus, in a multicultural context, the curriculum cannot be totally Afrocentric or it will become hegemonic as is the current Eurocentric model. On the contrary, the curriculum will and should be multicultural with various cultural visions, including the Afrocentric vision, as fundamental constitutive parts of the educational process. This position in no way suggests that Africana Studies departments and programs should not be Afrocentric. On the contrary, they must be Afrocentric; otherwise the distinctiveness of their contribution to multicultural discourse is called into question and ultimately undermined. What is key here is to create and pose a paradigm which rises from particular African views and values but also reflects the human interests we share with others. And this, of course, is the true meaning of Afrocentric, i.e., a paradigm rooted in the cultural image and human interest of African people.

Finally, multiculturalism confronts Black Studies with the challenge to demonstrate the effective difference and value of Afrocentric or African-centered concepts and practices to the multicultural education and enterprise. At this point, it is important to state that use of the terms African-centeredness and Afrocentric does not intend to suggest any more for the conceptual category "African" than is indicated by the terms "European" (Western), "Asian" (Oriental) or "Latin American." The categories *African* philosophy, worldview, values, etc., simply suggest *shared orientations* born of similar cultural experiences. As

Kwame Gyekye (1987:x) notes, "(i)t is the underlying cultural unity or identity of the various individual thinkers that justifies references to varieties of thought as wholes, such as Western, European or Oriental philosophy." Therefore, to say African philosophy, worldview or values is to assume certain shared orientations based on similar cultural experiences. Among these shared orientations are: 1) the centrality of community; 2) respect for tradition; 3) a high level spirituality and ethical concern; 4) harmony with nature; 5) the sociality of selfhood; 6) veneration of ancestors; and 7) the unity of being. This is also not to say that there are not other African core values which one could focus on as central to the Afrocentric vision. However, these are a conceptual and indispensable minimum regardless of other additions.

Within the context of an Afrocentric cultural paradigm, then, several conceptual contributions can be offered as an enrichment of multicultural discourse and education. Among these are: 1) centeredness or groundedness and critical insight from one's own culture; (this is also called location or orientation); 2) the holistic approach to knowledge; 3) critique and corrective as a joint project in the educational enterprise; 4) the essentiality of an historical perspective (Sankofa); and 5) the centrality of the ethical dimension to the educational project both in terms of reaffirmation of the worth and dignity of the human person and knowledge in the service of humankind and the just and good society. All of these contributions are interrelated and mutually reinforcing and offer a paradigm of difference as possibility in a multicultural context. They also represent an excellent point of departure for further research and discourse.

Classical African Studies

Finally, one of the most important and challenging developments in Black Studies since the decade of the 60's is the emergence in the 80's of increased intellectual and academic stress on the study of classical African civilizations, especially

Egypt. Classes on Egypt in Black Studies departments and programs have increased and include history, culture, art, literature, language, religion and ethical philosophy. Moreover, major conferences and smaller symposia are held regularly. Also, works on ancient Egypt and using ancient Egyptian culture as a major research source have increased. Among the important works on ancient Egypt or with major reference to it which were published within the last decade are Jacob Carruthers' *Essays in Ancient Egyptian Studies* (1984); Molefi Asante's *Kemet, Afrocentricity and Knowledge*, (1990); Ivan Van Sertima's *Nile Valley Civilizations* (1985) and *Egypt Revisited* (1989); Rkhty Amen Jones' *Medu Neter: The Ancient Egyptian Hieroglyphs* (1990); Wade Nobles', Lawford Goodard's and William Cavil's *The Km Ebit Husia: Authoritative Utterances of Exceptional Insight for the Black Family* (1985); Maulana Karenga and Jacob Carruthers' *Kemet and the African Worldview* (1986); and Maulana Karenga's *Selections from the Husia: Sacred Wisdom of Ancient Egypt* (1984), *Reconstructing Kemetic Culture* (1990b), *The Book of Coming Forth By Day* (1990a), and his second dissertation, *The Moral Ideal in Ancient Egypt: A Study in Classical African Ethics* (1993).

The works of African Americans like David Walker, Hosea Easton, Martin Delaney and Henry Highland Garnet had exhibited an early interest in Egypt as a classical African civilization (Carruthers, 1992). And later the seminal work of George James, *Stolen Legacy* (1976) first and, then, the works of John Jackson (1972, 1980), Yosef ben-Jochannan (1970, 1971) and Chancellor Williams (1974) represent a continuing interest in Egypt and classical African civilization in general. In 1978 the Kemetic Institute in Chicago, dedicated to the recovery of ancient Egypt's legacy, was founded, and in 1979 the Institute of Pan-African Studies of Los Angeles also turned its attention to the critical study of Egypt and the rescue and reconstruction of its legacy. Moreover, Black Studies departments and programs have had courses on classical African civilization in general since their inception. However, full-fledged and widespread concern with Egypt as an intellectual development does not occur until the 80's. This period is marked by a flurry of intellectual and practical activity on a national level which lays the groundwork for this expanded and deepened focus.

An important factor in this flowering in the 80's is the planning and organizing by Us Organization of the First Annual Ancient Egyptian Studies Conference under the leadership of Maulana Karenga in February 1984 at Southwest College in Los Angeles which led to the founding of the Association for the Study of Classical African Civilizations (ASCAC). The Institute of Pan-African Studies, the research arm of Us, invited scholars and others working on ancient Egypt to come and present their work to the community and exchange among themselves on research in process. The Kemetic Institute under the leadership of Jacob Carruthers lent its name to the conference and joined in calling for a professional organization for those interested in ancient Egyptian studies. This marked the founding of ASCAC and Jacob Carruthers and Maulana Karenga became founding chair and vice-chair respectively. In its first three years ASCAC published important works, registered a membership of a thousand people which it took to Egypt in 1987, and reached deeply and widely into communities and campuses across the country to establish ancient Egyptian studies as a priority. However, afterwards, it seems to have lost its original focus on scholarship and education of the masses and, thus, lost its early driving force.

A second major factor shaping the development of classical studies was activities of the Nile Valley Civilization group headed by Ivan Van Sertima. It also held a major conference on Nile Valley Civilization in September 1984, seven months after the founding of ASCAC, calling together scholars and ancient Egyptian enthusiasts. But unlike the ASCAC group, they formed no professional organization. However, Ivan Van Sertima, who founded the *Journal of African Civilization*, built the journal into a major source for publication of critical research on Nile Valley and other classical African civilizations and African presence in civilizations around the world.

A third factor shaping the flourishing of ancient Egyptian studies was the increasing familiarity with and receptivity to the works of Cheikh Anta Diop (1974, 1978, 1981, 1987, 1991) and to a lesser degree, familiarity with works of his student and brilliant colleague, Theophile Obenga (1992, 1972). Because Diop wrote in French, English-speaking Africans, except for scholars, were for the most part not familiar with his work. But as Diop's works were translated, in part or in whole and discussed widely during this period, African American scholars and lay persons became very much influenced by his works.

It is Diop who, in fact, pioneered the African focus on Egypt as a classical African civilization. In his major works, *The African Origin of Civilization* and *Civilization or Barbarism*, he outlined both the basic arguments for the African character of Egypt and its importance to African and world history. Later Martin Bernal (1987), whose work would cause controversy in Eurocentric circles, would support many of Diop's contentions. However, he would not critically discuss Diop's work (Carruthers, 1992) nor reaffirm the African, i.e., Black, character of Egypt when challenged (*Arethusa*, 1989).

Diop presented several arguments for the African or Black character of Egypt. First, he (1989:9) presented the evidence of physical anthropology, i.e., iconography, melanin dosage tests, osteological (bone) measurements and blood group tests. And all of these, he argues, reveal a definite Africanness or Blackness to Egypt. Secondly, Diop (1989:20) argues from the self-definition of the Egyptians who called themselves *Kmtyw* or *Kemetiu* -- Black people -- stemming from *km* -- the ancient Egyptian word for Black. Eurocentric scholars, he notes, hardly ever mentioned this term and when they do translate it, it is as "the Egyptian" rather than the "Blacks" and they also prefer to use "*Rmt Kmt*" which means -- people of the country of Black people or people of the Black land, i.e., Black land (fertile) as opposed to Red Land (desert). Thirdly, Diop (1989:161ff) offered eyewitness "reports of Greek and Latin writers contemporary with the ancient Egyptians" who describe the Egyptians as having defiant hair, bold lips and thin legs, all characteristic of Africans. These witnesses include Herodotus, Aristotle, Lucian, Apollodorus, Strabo, Diodorus and others.

Fourthly, Diop (1989:22) offers the biblical evidence which states "the sons of Ham (were) Cush and Misraim (i.e., Egypt)." The Jews, he asserts, lived side by side with Egyptians and had no interest in misrepresenting their African ethnicity. Fifthly, Diop (1989:22; 1974) argues that cultural similarities prove the African character of Egypt. These include common elements with other African cultures such as circumcision, divine kingship, totemism, matrilineal focus, cosmogonies, architecture, musical instruments and religious practices. Related to cultural similarities, Diop (1989:23) points also to the linguistic affinity of ancient Egyptian with "Wolof, a Senegalese language spoken in the extreme west of Africa on the Atlantic Ocean" which he argues "is perhaps as close to ancient Egyptian as Coptic," the modern form of ancient Egyptian. The kinship with Wolof, he notes, cannot be ignored, especially since ancient Egyptian is not Semitic and displays a "genetic, that is non-accidental relationship" with other African languages.

Also, Diop offers artistic evidence presenting Egyptian sculpture and painting to show what is considered prototypical Africanoid features of the ancient Egyptians and their similarities to some Nubians. It is important to note here, however, that Diop is not obliged to prove that all Egyptians look like a Eurocentric conception of a prototypical West African. For Africa is the home of humanity as well as human civilization and thus would, of necessity, show varied physical features. Zulus, Ethiopians, Yoruba, Somali, Ashanti, Congolese and others resemble and differ at the same time. So it is, in a sense, playing Europe's racial game to concede that Egyptians are white or Asian if they don't look like a Eurocentric version of a West African. Ethiopians and Somalis, perhaps, resemble the ancient Egyptians and ancient Nubian more than any other peoples and they are, even by Eurocentric standards, African.

Finally, when all else is said, there is the evidence of geography. Egypt is in Africa and not in the political construction called the Middle East. And thus, it is an African culture. Ancient Egypt is, in fact, the only country in history that ever had to justify its geography--that is to say, explain why it's in Africa when it should not be there if racist scholarship is right. For racist scholarship since Hegel has claimed Africa had no history and thus could not be a suitable place for Egypt. Therefore, such scholars took Africans out of Egypt, Egypt out of Africa, and then Africa out of human history.

It is this removal process, which Diop calls the falsification of history, that leads him to place so much emphasis on the rescue and reconstruction of ancient Egyptian history and culture. Thus, he (1981:12) states that "For us, the return to Egypt in all fields, is the necessary condition" to achieve three basic goals: 1) "to reconcile African civilization with history, (i.e., end the great falsification of African and human history,);" 2) to enable Africans "to build a body of modern human sciences;" and 3) "to renew African culture."

He continues, saying "Far from being a diversion in the past, a look back toward ancient Egypt is the best way to conceive and build our cultural future." For, he concludes, having recovered Egypt, "Egypt will play in a reconceived and renewed African culture the same role that the Greco-Latin ancient past plays in western culture." It is this conception of the role of ancient Egypt in African history and culture that informed and guided the flowering of interest in and activity around the project of Egypt's recovery.

Critics have raised the question of the relevance of ancient history and especially ancient Egypt to the present and future. Not only has Diop answered this, but also it is obviously an ill-considered question, especially from people who read from ancient religious texts everyday and find meaning and from ancient secular texts and find cultural and intellectual grounding. Ancient Egyptian sacred and secular texts offer no less.

It is also said that ancient Egypt was a slave-holding society, and thus, is a flawed candidate for a paradigm of Black culture. There are several basic responses to this. First, if the whole of Egyptian culture is discredited and dismissed for slave-holding, so should be the societies of the ancient Hebrew, Greece, Rome and the U.S., since all were, at one time or the other, slave-holding also. Secondly, one should be clear about the difference between religious ideology and historical fact or between a narrative of faith (religion) and a narrative of fact (history). No scholar of any weight argues the biblical interpretation of Egypt as the epitome of oppression. In fact, the image of Egypt as having large-scale slavery or even slavery like Greece, is erroneous (Ruffle, 1977:36; James, 1972:37-38; Bierbrier, 1984:12-13). T.G.H. James (1972:37) asserts that "Herodotus may have been chiefly responsible for the belief that the pyramids were built by slave labor." But actually, the idea has been spread by Judeo-Christian literature which depends so much on the narrative of oppression, exodus and freedom. However, a more accurate assessment as Bierbrier (1984:12) notes, is that people were conscripted, hired and volunteered for public work projects, such as the pyramids, during the flood season when land was covered and agriculture impossible. Recent excavations have shown settlements around the pyramids and patterns of life and payment which do not indicate slavery. This is not to deny enslavement of foreign captives in Egypt. In fact, virtually all ancient societies, except communal ones, tended to enslave. And there is no reason for or morality in defending such practices. But claiming that Egypt used slavery to build the pyramids or held a whole nation in captivity does not correspond to historical evidence.

What is required morally, then, is to condemn anti-human practices in all societies. However, it is not required that we indict a whole society because of religious or racial bias and deny its contribution, not only to the world, but also to the very people who so severely and incorrectly indicted it. In fact, as Breasted (1934:xv) noted in his seminal work, *The Dawn of Conscience*,

Egypt was a center of moral development and teaching. He states, "It is now quite evident that the ripe social and moral development of mankind in the Nile Valley, which is three thousand years older than that of the Hebrews, contributed essentially to the formation of the Hebrew literature we call the Old Testament." He concludes saying, "Our moral heritage, therefore, derives from a wider *human* past enormously older than the Hebrews, and it has come to us rather *through* the Hebrews than *from* them." This historical fact in no way denies the Hebrews their originality and uniqueness in moral development and teaching. But it is worth noting that Egypt, the society which Judeo-Christian teaching so much associates with oppression, turns out to be a moral society which shared its moral concepts and philosophy with the Hebrews, Christians and the world (see also section on The Egyptian Legacy and Tradition in Chapter 3 and Karenga, 1989, 1984, 1990a).

The question is also raised of why Egypt and not other African civilizations for the classical paradigm. But it is not a question of one civilization to the exclusion of others. On the contrary, one is compelled to study the classical cultures of Yoruba, Akan, Ghana, Mali, Songhai, et al as well. Egypt is simply a priority focus for several basic reasons: 1) Egypt's antiquity, allowing for a long view of Africans in history; 2) the abundant availability of documents (books and writings in all forms and on all surfaces, art, architecture, cultural products, etc., thus, the capacity of Egypt to speak its own truth; 3) its level of achievements in so many of the basic disciplines of human knowledge; 4) its meaning to other African societies; and 5) its contribution to the world in the basic disciplines of human knowledge -- ethics, science, math, medicine, architecture, literature, astronomy, etc. It is this latter fact that makes it contested terrain but also makes it worthy of the contest and of its paradigm status. The challenge for Black Studies, then, is to rescue and reconstruct this rich ancient heritage and explore Diop's conception of the fertile field of possibilities ancient Egypt offers.

STUDY QUESTIONS

1. What is Black Studies?
2. What were the four thrusts of the Student Movement of the 60's and the focus of each?
3. How was the Black Studies Movement a basic component of the Black liberation struggle?
4. What were the early academic and political concerns of the advocates of Black Studies?
5. What were the early objectives of Black Studies?
6. What are the seven major contributions of Black Studies which establish its academic and social relevance?
7. What are some concerns Black Studies shares with other social sciences and humanities disciplines?
8. How does Black Studies handle the question of specialized and integrative approaches to subject areas?
9. What are the seven core subject areas of Black Studies?
10. What are four fundamental integrative principles and assumptions which serve as thematic glue to hold the subject areas together?
11. Discuss the history and goals of AHSA and NCBS.
12. What is Afrocentricity? Discuss its development and contentions.
13. Discuss the history and goals of Black women studies.
14. Discuss the relevance of classical African studies and the centrality of Egypt.
15. Discuss the definition and goals of multiculturalism.

REFERENCES

Aldridge, Delores (ed). (1989) *Black Male-Female Relationships: A Resource Book of Selected Materials*, Dubuque, IA: Kendall/Hunt Publishing Co.

Aldridge, Delores. (1991) "An Interview," *Word: A Black Cultural Journal*, 1, 1 (Spring) 19-28.

Aldridge, Delores. (1992) "Womanist Issues in Black Studies: Towards Integrating Africana Women into Africana Studies," *Journal of the National Council for Black Studies*, 1, 1 (May) 167-182.

Aldridge, Delores. (1988) *New Perspectives on Black Studies*, Special Issue, *Phylon*, 49, 1 (Spring).

Allen, Robert. (1974) "Politics of the Attack on Black Studies," *The Black Scholar*, 6, 1 (September) 1-7.

Amin, Samir. (1974) *Accumulation on a World Scale: Critique of the Theory of Underdevelopment*, Vol. 1, New York: Monthly Review Press.

Anderson, Talmadge. (1990) *Black Studies: Theory, Method and Cultural Perspective*, Pullman, WA: Washington State University Press.

Arethusa. (1989) Special Issue (Fall).

Asante, Molefi. (1980) *Afrocentricity: The Theory of Social Change*, Buffalo: Amulefi Publishing Co.

Asante, Molefi. (1987) *The Afrocentric Idea*, Philadelphia: Temple University Press.

Asante, Molefi. (1990) *Kemet, Afrocentricity and Knowledge*, Trenton, NJ: Africa World Press.

Asante, Molefi. (1991) "Multiculturalism: An Exchange," *The American Scholar* (Spring) 267-271.

Asante, Molefi. (1992) "The Painful Demise of Eurocentrism," *The World & I*, (April) 305-317.

Apter, David. (1977) *Introduction to Political Science*, Cambridge, MA: Winthrop Publishers.

Bailey, Ronald. (1970) "Why Black Studies?" *The Education Digest*, 35, 9 (May) 46-48.

ben-Jochannon, Yosef A.A. (1971) *Africa: Mother of "Western Civilization,"* New York: Alkebu-lan Books Associates.

ben-Jochannon, Yosef A.A. (1970) *African Origins of the Major "Western Religions,"* New York: Alkebu-lan Books Associates.

Bernal, Martin. (1987) *Black Athena: The Afro-Asiatic Roots of Classical Civilization, Vol. I*, London: Free Association Books.

Bethune, Mary McLeod. (1939) "The Adaptation of the History of the Negro to the Capacity of the Child," *Journal of Negro History*, 24, 9-13.

Bierbrier, Morris. (1984) *The Tomb-Builders of the Pharaohs*, New York: Charles Scribner's Sons.

Blassingame, John. (1973) *New Perspectives on Black Studies*, Chicago: University of Illinois Press.

Branch, Taylor. (1988) *Parting the Waters: America in the King Years, 1954-1963*, New York: Simon & Schuster.

Breasted, James. (1934) *The Dawn of Conscience*, New York: Charles Scribner's Sons.

Brisbane, Robert. (1974) *Black Activism*, Valley Forge, PA: Judson Press.

Cade, (Bambara) Toni. (ed.) (1970) *The Black Woman*, New York: New American Library.

Carby, Hazel. (1987) *Reconstructing Womanhood: The Emergence of the Afro-American Woman Novelist*, New York: Oxford University Press.

Carruthers, Jacob. (1992) "Bernal's Critique of Black Champions of Ancient Egypt," *Journal of Black Studies*, 22, 4 (June) 459-476.

Carruthers, Jacob H. (1990) "The Defenders of Western Civilization and the Battle Over the Multicultural Curriculum," unpublished manuscript.

Carruthers, Jacob H. (1984) *Essays in Ancient Egyptian Studies*, Los Angeles: University of Sankore Press.

Carson, Claybourne. (1981) *In Struggle: SNCC and the Black Awakening of the 60's*, Cambridge: Harvard University Press.

Chalmers, David. (1991) *And Crooked Places Made Straight*, Baltimore: Johns Hopkins University Press.

Clark, Septima. (1986) *Reading From Within: Septima Clark & the Civil Rights Movements*, New York: Wild Trees Press.

Clarke, John Henrik. (1976) "AHSA: A History," *Issue: A Quarterly Journal of Africanist Opinion*, 6, 1/3 (Summer/Fall).

Cooper, Anna Julia. (1892) *A Voice from the South: By a Black Woman of the South*, Xenia, OH: Aldine Printing House.

Cooper, Jean. (1971) "Women's Liberation and the Black Woman," *Journal of Home Economics*, 63, (October) 521-523.

Cortada, Rafael. (1974) *Black Studies in Urban and Comparative Curriculum*, Lexington, MA: Xerox College Publishing.

Crouchett, L. (1971) "Early Black Studies Movements," *Journal of Black Studies*, 2, 189-200.

Cruse, Harold. (1967) *Crisis of the Negro Intellectual*, New York: William Morrow Publishers.

Cruse, Harold. (1969) *Rebellion or Revolution?* New York: William Morrow Publishers.

Daniels, Phillip T.K. (1980) "Black Studies: Discipline or Field of Study?" *The Western Journal of Black Studies*, 4, 3 (Fall) 195-199.

Daniel, Philip T.K. (1981) "Theory Building in Black Studies," *The Black Scholar*, 12, 3 (May/June) 29-36.

DeBendetti, Charles and Charles Chatfield. (1990) *An American Ordeal: The Anti-War Movement of the Vietnam Era*, Syracuse: Syracuse University Press.

Diop, Cheikh Anta. (1974) *The African Origin of Civilization: Myth or Reality*, Westport, CT: Lawrence Hill & Co.

Diop, Cheikh Anta. (1991) *Civilization or Barbarism: An Authentic Anthropology*, New York: Lawrence Hill Books.

Diop, Cheikh Anta. (1981) *Civilization ou Barbarie*, Paris: Présence Africaine.

Diop, Cheikh Anta. (1989) "Origin of the Ancient Egyptians," *Journal of African Civilizations*, 10 (Summer) 9-37.

Draper, Hal. (1965) *Berkeley: The New Student Revolt*, New York: Grove Press.

DuBois, W.E.B. (1975) *The Education of Black People: Ten Critiques, 1906-1960*, New York: Monthly Review Press.

DuBois, W.E.B. (1961) *The Souls of Black Folk*, New York: Fawcett Publications, Inc.

DuBois, W.E.B. (1969) "The Talented Tenth" in Ulysses Lee (ed.) *The Negro Problem*, New York: Arno Press and the New York Times.

Edwards, Harry. (1970) *Black Students*, New York: Free Press.

Fanon, Frantz. (1968) *The Wretched of the Earth*, New York: Grove Press.

Ford, Nick Aaron. (1973) *Black Studies: Threat or Challenge*, New York: Kennikat Press.

Forman, James. (1972) *The Making of Black Revolutionaries*, New York: Macmillan.

Frazier, E. Franklin. (1973) "The Failure of the Negro Intellectual," in Joyce A. Ladner (ed.) *The Death of White Sociology*, New York: Vintage Books, pp. 52-66.

Frye, Charles A. (1978) *Towards a Philosophy of Black Studies*, San Francisco: R & E Research Associates.

Giddings, Paula. (1984) *When and Where I Enter: The Impact of Black Women on Race and Sex in America*, New York: William Morrow and Co.

Gordon, Vivian. (1987) *Black Women, Feminism and Black Liberation: Which Way?*, New York: William Morrow.

Gyekye, Kwame. (1987) *An Essay on African Philosophical Thought: The Akan Conceptual Scheme*, New York: Cambridge University Press.

Hall, Perry A. (1992) "Beyond Afrocentrism: Alternatives for Afro-American Studies," *Western Journal of Black Studies*, 15, 4 (Winter) 207-212.

Hamilton, Charles. (1970) "The Question of Black Studies," *Phi Delta*, 57, 7 (March) 362-364.

Hare, Nathan. (1969) "What Should be the Role of Afro-American Education in the Undergraduate Curriculum?" *Liberal Education*, 55, 1 (March) 42-50.

Hare, Nathan. (1972) "The Battle of Black Studies," *The Black Scholar*, 3, 9 (May) 32-37.

Hare, Nathan and Julia Hare. (1970) "Black Women 1970," *Transaction*, 8 (November-December) 68, 90.

Harris, Robert, Darlene Clark Hine and Nellie McKay. (1990) *Three Essays: Black Studies in the United States*, New York: Ford Foundation.

Hendrix, M. et al. (1984) "Computers and Black Studies: Toward the Cognitive Revolution," *Journal of Negro Education* 53, 341-350.

Hill-Collins, Patricia. (1991) *Black Feminist Thought*, New York: Routledge.

hooks, bell. (1981) *Ain't I A Woman: black women and feminism*, Boston: South End Press.

hooks, bell. (1989) *Talking Back: Thinking Feminist, Thinking Black*, Boston: South End Press.

hooks, bell. (1990) *Yearning: race, gender and cultural politics*, Boston, South End Press.

Hull, Gloria, Patricia Bell Scott and Barbara Smith, (eds.) (1982) *All the Women are White, All the Blacks are Men, but Some of Us are Brave*, Old Westbury, NY: Feminist Press.

Ijere, Martin. (1972) "Whether Economics in a Black Studies Program?" *Journal of Black Studies*, 3, 2 (December) 149-165.

Jackson, John. (1980) *Introduction to African Civilizations*, Secaucus, NJ: Citadel Press.

Jackson, John. (1972) *Man, God, and Civilization*, New Hyde Park, New York: University Books.

Jackson, Maurice. (1970) "Towards a Sociology of Black Studies," *Journal of Black Studies*, 1, 2 (December) 131-140.

James, George. (1976) *Stolen Legacy*, San Francisco: Julian Richardson Associates.

James, T.G.H. (1972) *The Archaeology of Ancient Egypt*, New York: Henry Z Walck.

Jones, Rkhty Amen. (1990) *Medu Neter: The Ancient Egyptian Hieroglyphs*, Orange, NJ: The Institute of Kemetic Philology.

Karenga, Maulana. (1992) "Afrocentricity and Multicultural Education: Concepts, Challenge and Contribution," unpublished manuscript.

Karenga, Maulana. (1988) "Black Studies and the Problematic of Paradigm: The Philosophical Dimension," *Journal of Black Studies* 18, 4 (June) 395-414.

Karenga, Maulana. (1990a) *The Book of Coming Forth By Day: The Ethics of the Declarations of Innocence*, Los Angeles: The University of Sankore Press.

Karenga, Maulana. (1977) "Corrective History: Reconstructing the Black Past," *First World*, 1, 3 (May/June) 50-54.

Karenga, Maulana. (1980) *Kawaida Theory: An Introductory Outline*, Inglewood, CA: Kawaida Publications.

Karenga, Maulana. (1990b) *Reconstructing Kemetic Culture*, Los Angeles: University of Sankore Press.

Karenga, Maulana. (1984) *Selections From the Husia: Sacred Wisdom of Ancient Egypt*, Los Angeles: University of Sankore Press.

Karenga, Maulana. (1989) "Towards a Sociology of Maatian Ethics: Literature and Context," in Ivan Van Sertima (ed.), *Egypt Revisited*, New Brunswick, NJ: Transaction Publications.

Keto, C. Tsehloane. (1991) *The Africa Centered Perspective of History: An Introduction*, Laurel Springs, NJ: K.A. Publishers.

Kilson, Martin. (1973) "Reflections on Structure and Content in Black Studies," *Journal of Black Studies*, 1, 3 (March) 197-314.

King, Mae C. (1973) "The Politics of Sexual Stereotypes," *The Black Scholar*, 4 (March/April) 12.

King, Richard D. (1990) *African Origin of Biological Psychiatry*, Germantown, TN: Seymour-Smith, Inc.

Ladner, Joyce A. (ed.) (1973) *The Death of White Sociology*, New York: Vintage Books.

LaRue, Linda J.M. (1970) "Black Liberation and Women's Lib," *Transaction*, 8 (November-December) 59-64.

Lipset, Seymour and S. Wolin (eds.) (1965) *The Berkeley Student Revolt*, New York: Doubleday Anchor.

Marable, Manning. (1992) *Black America: Multicultural Democracy in the Age of Clarence Thomas and David Duke*, (Open Magazine Pamphlet Series), Westfield, NJ: Open Media.

McAdam, Doug. (1988) *Freedom Summer*. New York: Oxford University Press.

McEvoy, James and Abraham Miller. (1969) *Black Power and Student Rebellion*, Belmont, CA: Wadsworth Publishing.

McIntyre, Charshee. (1989) "Agenda for AHSA: 21st Century." Unpublished manuscript, State University of New York at Old Westbury.

Morgan, Gordon J. (1991) "Afrocentricity in Social Science," *Western Journal of Black Studies*, 15, 4 (Winter) 197-206.

Morris, Aldon D. (1984) *The Origins of the Civil Rights Movement: Black Communities Organizing for Change*, New York: The Free Press.

Nobles, Wade W., Lawford Goddard and William Cavil. (1985) *The Km Ebit Husia: Authoritative Utterances of Exceptional Insight*, Oakland: The Institute for the Advanced Study of Black Family Life and Culture.

Obenga, Théophile. (1972) *L'Afrique dans L'Antiquité: Egypte pharaonique-Afrique Noire*, Paris: Présence Africaine.

Obenga, Théophile. (1992) *Ancient Egypt and Black Africa*, London: Karnak House.

Oyabede, Bayo (1990) "African Studies and The Afrocentric Paradigm: A Critique," *Journal of Black Studies*, 21, 2, 233-238.

Pinkney, Alphonso. (1976) *Red, Black and Green: Black Nationalism in the United States*, Cambridge: Cambridge University Press.

President's Task Force Report on Multicultural Education and Campus Diversity. (1991) *The Challenge of Diversity and Multicultural Education*, Long Beach: California State University, Long Beach.

Ravitch, Dianne. (1990) "Multiculturalism," *American Scholar* (Summer).

Robinson, Armstead, et al. (1969) *Black Studies in the University*, New York: Bantam Books.

Rodgers-Rose, La Frances (ed.) (1980) *The Black Woman*, Beverly Hills: Sage Publication.

Rodgers-Rose, La Frances and James T. Rodgers. (1985) *Strategies for Resolving Conflict in Black Male and Female Relationships*, Newark: Traces Institute Publications.

Rorabaugh, W.J. (1989) *Berkeley at War: The 1960's*, New York: Oxford University Press.

Rowe, Cyprian L. (1970) *Crisis in African Studies: The Birth of the African Heritage Studies Association*, Buffalo: Black Academy Press, Inc.

Ruffle, John. (1977) *The Egyptians: An Introduction to Egyptian Archaeology*, Ithaca, NY: Cornell University Press.

Säve-Söderbergh, Torgony (ed.) (1987) *Temples and Tombs of Ancient Nubia*, New York: Thames and Hudson Inc.

Schlesinger, Arthur. (1991) *The Disuniting of America: Reflections on a Multicultural Society*, Knoxville, TN: Whittle Direct Books.

Simms, Margaret C. and Julianne Malveaux (eds.) (1986) *Sliping Through the Cracks: The Status of Black Women*, New Brunswick, NJ: Transaction.

Stewart, James B. (1979) "Introducing Black Studies: A Critical Examination of Some Textual Materials," *Umoja*, 3, 1, (Spring) 5-17.

Stewart, James B. (1984) "The Legacy of W.E.B. DuBois for Contemporary Black Studies," *Journal of Negro Education*, 53, 296-311.

Stewart, James. (1992) "Reaching For Higher Ground: Toward an Understanding of Black/Africana Studies," *The Afrocentric Scholar*, 1, 1, (May) 1-63.

Turner, James. (1984) *The Next Decade: Theoretical and Research Issues in Africana Studies*, Ithaca: Africana Studies and Research Center, Cornell University.

Turner, J. and C. S. McGann. (1980) "Black Studies as an Integral Tradition in African American Intellectual History," *Journal of Negro Education*, 49, 52-59.

Turner, James and Eric W. Perkins. (1976) "Towards a Critique of Social Science," *The Black Scholar*, 7, 1 (April) 2-11.

Van Sertima, Ivan. (1985) *Nile Valley Civilizations*, Journal of African Civilizations.

Walker, Alice. (1983) *In Search of Our Mother's Garden*, New York: Harcourt, Brace and Jovanovich.

Woodson, Carter G. (1969) *The Miseducation of the Negro*, Washington, DC: Associated Publishers Inc.

Woodyard, Jeffrey L. (1991) "Evolution of a Discipline: Intellectual Antecedents of African American Studies," *Journal of Black Studies* 22, 2 (December) 239-251.

Wright, Stephen. (1970) "Black Studies and Sound Scholarship," *Phi Delta Kappan* (March) 356-368.

Williams, Bruce. (1989) "The Last Pharaohs of Nubia," *Journal of African Civilizations*, 10 (Summer) 90-104.

Williams, Juan. (1987) *Eyes on the Prize*, New York: Viking Penguin.

Young, Carlene. (1984) "An Assessment of Black Studies Programs in American Higher Education," *Journal of Negro Education*, 53.

BLACK HISTORY

2
BLACK HISTORY

2.1   INTRODUCTION

Black Studies begins with the study of Black history for two basic reasons. First, the core task of Black Studies, which is shared by all the core subject areas, is the rescue and reconstruction of Black history and humanity. This rescue, i.e., freeing both Black history and humanity from alien hands, and reconstruction is a theoretical and practical project. In fact, the work done to achieve this central goal in the academic world is an indispensable requirement for and contribution to its achievement in the social world. For to rescue Black history is not only to free it from denial, deformation and destruction academically, but also to free it socially from the same negatives by freeing the people who are both its producers and products. Likewise, the reconstruction of Black history demands intervention not only in the academic process to redefine and reestablish the truth of Black history, but also intervention in the social process to reshape reality in Black images and interests and thus, self-consciously make history.

Furthermore, the academic and social rescue and reconstruction of Black history is a contribution to and indispensable part of the rescue and reconstruction of Black humanity. For history is the substance and mirror of a people's humanity in other's eyes as well as in their own eyes. It is, then, not only what they have done, but also a reflection of who they are, what they can do, and equally important what they can become as a result of the past which reveals their possibilities.

Secondly, Black Studies also begins with Black history because it is relevant, even indispensable to the introduction and development of all the other subject areas. Black history places them in perspective, establishes their origins and development, and thus, aids in critical discussion and understanding of them. Moreover, each of the other subject areas of Black Studies teaches its own particular history which in turn is a part of general Black history. Black history, therefore, offers not only a broad framework for critically viewing and understanding Black people, but also a necessary background perspective for critical insights into other subjects.

2.2   DEFINITION

The understanding and appreciation of Black History begins with the definition of history itself and then uses that definition to define Black history and its relevance. *History is the struggle and record of humans in the process of humanizing the world, i.e., shaping it in their own image and interests.* To shape the world in a human image is to give it a human form and character and to shape it in human interests it to make it serve humans rather than threaten, deform or destroy them. In a word, shaping the world in a human image and in human interests is to make it a context which reflects and insures human defense, development and ultimate self-realization. African or Black history, then, is the struggle and record of Africans in the process of Africanizing the world, i.e., shaping it in their own image and interests. As a particular people, Africans shape the world in a particular way, i.e., they tend to Africanize it, or shape it in their own image and interests. This adds to the richness and beauty of human diversity and contributes to the overall effort of humans to transform the world from control by nature to control by humanity.

Put another way, history reveals itself as a human practice directed in its diversity toward self-construction, social construction and world construction. For as a people builds itself, it builds a society it lives and develops in and this effort becomes a contribution to and a vital part of the overall human construction of the world. Thus, as Africans developed agriculture, medicine, science, etc. to defend and develop themselves, they built societies and civilizations which contributed to the overall humanization of the world and to the forward flow of human history (Jackson, 1980; Diop, 1974; 1991).

But history does not just happen nor is it the work of unseen forces. On the contrary, it is a process which is defined by five basic characteristics. First, it is human in the fullest and most diverse sense of the word. Secondly, it is social, by and about people in definite social situations, in a definite society in relation to others, themselves and nature. Third, it is conflictual, that is to say, full of contradictions, i.e., conflicts and struggle to solve conflicts. In fact, the motive force of history is struggle against four major oppositions, nature, society, others and self which will be discussed below. Fourthly, history is fluid and changeable, i.e., in constant movement. Finally, history is manageable, i.e., subject to controlled and directed change. Humans make history but not always in their own image. Only thru self-conscious intervention in the social and historical process can history be managed or self-consciously made.

Self-conscious intervention in the social and historical process is intervention in the structure and tendencies of society and the world. The motive force and shaper of history is struggle. Thus to make history, humans must struggle against four major oppositions: (1) nature; (2) society; (3) other humans; and (4) their immediate selves. Even a cursory review of African history shows Africans in the process of solving these fundamental contradictions. The very battle to be human, to separate oneself from the animal kingdom is a struggle against nature. As the first humans, Africans began to humanize the world by controlling and breaking its hold on them (Clark, 1970). Thus,

they discover fire, make tools, clothes, shelter, and devise ways
to increase food. They collect seeds, learn the seasons, engage
in cultivation, harness the Nile and use it for irrigation and call
this science agriculture. They study disease and develop cures
and call it medicine; they dig in the earth and discover and
extract its resources and call it mining; they move beyond basic
structures and build large temples and pyramids and create
architecture; and they observe the stars, discover patterns and
movements, name them and call this astronomy. As they engage
in these activities, they reshape themselves, societies and the
world, distinguish and distance themselves from the animal world
and make true human history a reality.

The second major opposition humans face and must
overcome continuously in making history is society or more
precisely the limitations it imposes at various historical periods
on the defense and development of human life. It is a fundamental paradox that society which is designed and built as a
context for human freedom, defense and development often
becomes a context for suppression, exploitation and oppression.
In the long march toward human freedom, i.e., the absence of
restraint and the capacity for rational self-determination, society
has both impeded and aided progress toward this goal. In the
constant struggle to shape society in a more human, i.e., freer
and more positive image, humans have made bold strokes on the
canvas of history. The struggle to break the priests' monopoly on
knowledge and make it available to the masses, and the struggle
against dictatorship and to establish and maintain democracy, the
struggle to establish science over and against superstitions are
vivid and continuing examples. In African American history, the
struggle against society or more precisely society in its various
oppressive forms of enslavement, racism and capitalism has
clearly been its motive force. In fact, the periodization of Black
history reveals focal points of struggle against social exploitation
and oppression. The Holocaust of Enslavement, reversal of
Reconstruction and the rise of Jim Crow; lynchings and racism
in education, employment and other areas of social life; power-

lessness and police brutality are all categories not only of exploitation and oppressive social relations but foci of struggle against them.

But society is only context; other humans are actors who impose, exploit and oppress in that context. Thus at the heart of history is the struggle against others who threaten human life, freedom and development. Enslavement is imposed by the enslaver, racism by the racist, capitalism and colonialism by the capitalist and colonizer. The ruling ideas and dominant relations in any given society at any historical period are the ideas and relations of those who rule. This social grouping may be a ruling class or a ruling race or as in the USA and Azania (South Africa) a ruling race/class, i.e., a ruling class made up of and exclusive to the ruling race in a society where race is a category of human worth and social status. Moreover, "others" could be other smaller social units like ethnic groups, political parties or interest groups who challenge and check, or exploit and oppress them. And "others" could be other nations, whose nationalism deteriorates into pathological forms such as chauvinism, jingoism, apartheid, fascism, nazism, etc.

However, within this array of "others" who pose challenges contributive to making history, the struggle between classes and between nations or peoples are the most definitive struggles of history. Marxists argue that class struggle is the motive force of history (Bober, 1948). Black nationalists argue that it is the struggle of races and nations, two categories which are often used interchangeably (Williams, 1974). It is important to see however, that class struggle may or may not be the key struggle in every socio-historical setting and the same is true of racial or national struggles. Also, in the panoramic vastness of human history, it is, as argued at the outset, not just social struggle in and against society which makes history, but four basic struggles, the four major oppositions we are discussing. In a word, it is struggle in its full diversity which is the motive force of history, although a key struggle (race, class, etc.) tends to express itself in any given socio-historical setting (Rodney, 1974:89).

The final major opposition is the struggle of humans against themselves, against their conception of themselves and their conditions and the possibilities they see in them. That which *is* seems permanent and overwhelming. Thus the human personality is often prone toward submitting to or accepting the immediate. But history is made human when humans collectively and personally break beyond the current concept of self and distinguish between actuality, that which is; potentially, that which can be; and reality, that which ought to be and becomes when a person, people, society or thing realizes itself, i.e., fulfills its inherent potential. The Dogon astronomer who discovered Sirius B and C; the Ishongo mathematician who devised the abacus; the Egyptian physician Imhotep, who founded the science of medicine and the African American chemurgist, George Washington Carver, who created over 300 synthetic and organic products out of the peanut, all reached beyond the immediate, realized in part the unlimited potential of humankind, and thus, advanced human history. Fundamental to understanding this conception, then, is to see reality as not being, but as becoming and to see struggle as the motive force of both becoming and history. For human essence is human possibility and history is the process thru which that possibility is expressed and realized.

2.3   AFRICAN BACKGROUND

Introduction

The history of Black people, humans and human civilization began in Africa (Ki-Zerbo, 1990; Phillipson, 1985; Jackson, 1980; Williams, 1974; Clark, 1970; DuBois, 1965). Three major factors, however, have combined to obscure this fact and make the study and writing of African history problematic. The first factor is the vastness of the subject. African history is the history of a continent in flux and in contact and exchange with the world, and one can easily assume, especially given the

Eurocentric thrust and character of most histories of Africa, that others rather than Africans gave rise to Africa's many contributions to the forward flow of human history. As Williams (1974:33) remarked, "African history is complex and many-sided, and would be so (even) if we were discussing just one nation and not an entire continent." Thus, without the time or inclination to do the necessary research one ends up repeating what was written before in the image and interests of Europeans. An example of this is the tendency to pass along the French and English translations which call the founders of Ghana "white" (Gailey, 1970) although further investigation shows they were referred to as "red" or "reddish-brown" by the people of the region (Fage, 1969:8).

Secondly, the study of African history is complicated by the predominance of oral history in many places as the most definitive African perspective on the subject. That is not to say that Africans did not have several scripts. On the contrary, there were many scripts in Africa, including the three scripts of ancient Egypt -- hieroglyphic, hieratic and demotic; the Meroitic and Coptic scripts of Nubia; the Amharic, Sabean and G'eez scripts of Ethiopia; the Berber and Carthaginian scripts of North Africa; the Arabic script of North, Northeastern and Western Africa; the Swahili Perso-Arabic script of the East Coast of Africa; the Nsibidi script of Nigeria; the Mende script of Mali; the Toma and Vai scripts of Liberia; and the Mum script of Cameroun (Obenga, 1972: Chapter X). This long list clearly exceeds the two main scripts of Europe, Greek and Roman. However, these scripts do not always have abundant historical literatures of either a given people or larger areas of the continent. Documents, then, were not only few but often lost or destroyed, thus adding to the problem. Moreover, the European and Arab conquests led to much destruction also. However, although Europeans most likely duplicated destructions of documents in other parts of Africa, as in the burning of the library at Alexandria, Egypt by the Romans in 48 B.C.E. (Before the Common Era), in most parts of Africa, sources of history were essentially griots, a stratum or group of professional oral historians. It was their task to act as the collective memory of an ethnic group, nation or empire and pass on from generation to generation the history of its people. But whereas it is intellectually impressive to remember hundreds of years of key figures, phenomena and processes, it is also a vulnerable form of record keeping. For this "Heritage of the Ears," as the Hova of Madagascar call it, is subject not only to the problems of retention and repetition, but also to the unexpected deaths of the keepers (McCall, 1969:38-62).

Thirdly, and perhaps the most important of the problems of studying African history, is the European conquest of Africa and all that it meant to African history as both record and process. As suggested above, one cannot deny that Europeans destroyed many documents in Africa as well as other evidences of African presence and achievement (Williams, 1974; Diop, 1974, 1991). Moreover, European scholars often denied the value and authenticity of documents and/or their data, if it did not coincide with what they believed or wanted others and themselves to believe. The record of so-called Egyptologists in this matter has been documented by Cheikh Anta Diop. As Diop (1974:168) states, they operated on this principle, "Given what I've been taught about (Blacks), even if the evidence proves objectively that civilization was created by the said Blacks...it must be wrong."

Finally, with the conquest of Africa by Europe came the attempt also to Europeanize or "Caucasize" all important achievements and deny African presence and accomplishments (Drake, 1987). George James (1976) points this out in his book on the stolen legacy of Egyptian philosophy for which the Greeks are given credit. Diop (1974; 1991) shows how Egypt's entire civilization is claimed by whites thru falsification of history, discounting contrary evidence, and arguing racial and racist theories inapplicable to the ancient world. Also, Jackson (1980) and Van Sertima (1992) show how the Moors who aided in the "civilizing" of Europe are Caucasized and Arabized to deny their

Blackness. And then there are the useful mythical "Hamites" who are trotted out, whenever others are unavailable, to serve as founders of any civilization when it is important to deny its African origins (Fage, 1969:6-10). However, in spite of these obstacles, significant evidence of African genius and creativity still shine through and provide us with strong foundations for the rescue and reconstruction of Black history and humanity (Davidson, 1991; Bernal, 1987). Given the vastness of the subject, however, this text can in no way be exhaustive or comprehensive. What it will seek to do then is offer some of the many significant models of African political formations and achievements which tend to counter the racist lies and affirm the world historical achievements and significance of African civilization. More detailed and comprehensive treatment of African history can be found in the books cited as references. The student is thus encouraged to explore them, for the exploration will be most informative and engaging.

The Origins in East Africa

In spite of religious and secular myths about the origins of humans in Mesopotamia five or six thousand years ago, the reality is that humans originated in Africa (Ki-Zerbo, 1990; Phillipson, 1985). As J. Ki-Zerbo (1990:313) states, "all evidence suggests that the (African) continent was the first -- and indeed the principal -- center of human development." He notes that this was the case as far back as 14 million years ago when Kenyapithecus lived and "appears to have been the initial stock from which we came." *Australopithecus Africanus* was the first hominid, and "was followed by the Zinjanthrope -- from the word Zinj or East Africa -- which was the first direct ancestor of modern Man" and lived approximately 1.7 million years ago. Homo erectus came next, followed by the Homo sapien type whose features were Africanoid even in Europe. Thus, "All the links in the chain relating us to the earliest hominids and pre-hominians are to be found in Africa."

Phillipson (1985:60) notes that "(f)ully modern man H.s. sapiens (Homo sapiens sapiens) was present, at least in southern Africa, more than 100,000 years ago," but it was approximately 35,000 years ago, however, that modern humans began to lay the basis for true human civilization. It is at this point that humans began to diversify activities from the early total preoccupation with survival and engage in art and religious reflection. At about 10,000 years ago, humans began to establish cultivation as an alternative to hunting and gathering, thus allowing even more time to lay a basis for expanded cultural development (Curtin, et al, 1990:41). It is estimated that about this time, 8,000 B.C.E., Egypt rose from the waters of the Nile and its lakes and marshes; and thus the basis of habitation and cultivation in the Nile Valley was established.

The Nile Valley Civilizations

The flower of ancient African classical civilization originates and flourishes in the Nile Valley civilizations of Nubia, Egypt and Ethiopia. These civilizations represent a complex of cultures which interacted and mutually influenced each other and became a major source and resource of human culture and development.

Diop (1974; 1991), Jackson (1980) and Williams (1974) all argue that Egypt's origin is in Ethiopia, i.e., in the south. DuBois (1965:117ff) agrees stating that "In Ethiopia the sunrise of human culture took place, spreading down into the Nile Valley. Ethiopia, the land of the Blacks, was thus the cradle of Egyptian civilization." In the earliest times, DuBois continues, "the Ethiopians looked upon themselves as the source of Egypt and declared according to Diodorus Siculus that Egyptian laws and custom were of Ethiopian origin. The Egyptians themselves in later days affirmed that their civilization came out of the south." We know now that the term "Ethiopia," like "Nubia," was used for all of Africa and also meant the land to the south of

Egypt. Nubia was the first of those lands and had a long relationship with Egypt.

Nubia. It was once argued that Nubia had no civilization which Egypt, her northern neighbor, did not give her. But modern scholarship affirms an indigenous civilization in Nubia that was not only as old if not older than Egypt itself, but also was a rival, equal and ruler of Egypt at various times (Haynes, 1992; Olson and Wegner, 1992; Taylor, 1991; Williams, 1989; Säve-Söderbergh, 1987; Wenig, 1987; Adams, 1977).

The name Nubia seems to have originated from the ancient Egyptian word for gold, *Nub (nbw)* and is first used by the Greek, Strabo, in his Geography "to designate a land which the Greeks called Ethiopia" (Säve-Söderbergh, 1987:14). Nubia was indeed a land of gold, but the Egyptians themselves called it two basic names -- *Kash (K3s)* from which we later derive the terms Kush, and *Ta-Seti*, Land of the Bow, because of the skill and fame of Nubian archers who often served in and fought against the Egyptian army.

Nubia's history stretches back to approximately 3900 B.C.E. and continues in various forms to 1400 C.E. (the Common Era, i.e., this era) It evolves its own pharaonic or kingship system as early as 3800 B.C.E., approximately 800 years before Mena unites Egypt into a unified kingdom. New research and conclusions tend to suggest not only that Nubia developed a royal dynasty at the city of Qustul as early as Egypt, but perhaps even earlier (Williams, 1989). These Nubians, called A-Group by anthropologists, were both farmers and herdspeople who also traded with Egypt and acted as intermediaries for trade with other nations and societies further south. They produced highly refined pottery and jewelry and buried these things along with tools and weapons with the dead.

The A-Group Nubia (3900-2900 B.C.E.) was followed by a C-Group Nubian culture (2500-1500 B.C.E.). This culture interacts even more with the Egyptians and is controlled from about 2000-1800 B.C.E. Another Nubian culture which evolved simultaneously with the C-Group in Lower Nubia was the Kerma culture in Upper Nubia. This culture was politically complex and had powerful kings. It is this culture which the Egyptians called Kash or Kush. Nubia is effectively colonized by the Egyptians after almost a century of campaigns in 1500 B.C.E. and they continued to rule it until 1000 B.C.E. Here the Egyptians built temples and tombs, fortresses and trading posts, and exploited Nubia's human and material resources.

However, it is the Kingdom of Kush in its Napatan (900-295 B.C.E.) and Meroitic period (195 B.C.E. - 320 C.E.) that is most known in history. From the capital city of Napata, Kushite kings emerged as a powerful political force to unite Nubia and begin to extend their power north to Egypt. The first known leader is King Kashta, father of Piankhi, conqueror of Egypt and founder of the Twenty-Fifth Dynasty of Egypt. Piankhi, also known as Piye, at first simply ruled southern Egypt but upon request of Theban rulers went to Egypt ca. 734 B.C.E. to subdue a local ruler of the Delta, Tefnakht, who had ambitions of ruling all of Egypt. However, he retired to Nubia and left it to his successor to actually rule for approximately a century (756-656 B.C.E.)

He did, however, leave one of Egypt's and Nubia's most impressive pieces of literature, the *Victory Stela*, detailing his conquest of Egypt which "was discovered in 1862 in the ruins of the Temple of Amun at Napata, the Nubian capital at the foot of Gebel Barkal" (Lichtheim, 1980:66). Lichtheim also notes that the text reveals that Piankhi was a powerful, intelligent and generous king, "preferred treaties to warfare, and when he fought did not glory in the slaughter of his adversaries in the manner of an Assyrian king." A very religious man, Piankhi begins saying, "Hear what I did, exceeding the ancestors. I, the king, image of God, living likeness of Atum. Who left the womb marked as ruler. Feared by one greater than he! His father knew and his mother perceived that he would be a ruler from the egg. The good god, beloved of gods, the Son of Ra, who acts with his arms, Piye, beloved-of-Amun" (Lichtheim, 1980:68). Moreover, he tells his troops before battle to pray and give praise to Amen Ra. "For there is no strength for the mighty without Amen Ra. He makes the weak armed into the strong armed, so that the multitudes flee from the feeble and one alone takes a thousand captive." Therefore, he continues, "Anoint yourselves with the waters of his altars and bow down to the earth before Him and say make for us a way that we might fight in the shadow of your sword. For when young men who you have sent forth launch their attack, the multitudes flee from them."

Another important king of this period is Shabaka known for his copying and preserving "a work of the ancestors" called both "The Memphite Theology" and the "Shabaka Text." In any case, it is the earliest record of creation described as an act of creative thought and speech and prefigures the logos doctrine of Christianity (Breasted, 1934:37; Lichtheim, 1975;51ff; Karenga, 1989:375ff). Here the Creator conceives creation in his heart/mind (ib), as an expression of wisdom or exceptional insight (Sia) and through authoritative utterance (Hu), brings the world into being.

In Nubia, as in Egypt and other parts of Africa, there is sacred or divine kingship. Moreover, Nubian kings adopted the Egyptian custom of designating themselves as the Son of Ra and the queens followed this custom also. Two notable features of the Nubia Kingship and Queenship is the emergence of the office of High Priestess of Amun and the strengthening of the role of the Queen Mother. The High Priestess had three different titles -- the Wife of God, the Adorer of God and the Hand of God and was an office exercised by the King's daughter and passed on through adoption. This gave her equal economic and political power and influence in the government. Her representative was called Chief Steward as in the case of one Harwa, who was an important person in the administration of the country (Lichtheim, 1980:24ff). Harwa says of his patron, Amerindis, Adorer of God, "My Lady made me great when I was a small boy. She advanced my position when I was a child." He goes on to say he went on missions for the King and his Lady and that "Every mission on which their majesties sent me, I accomplished it correctly. I never told a lie about it." Moreover, he says, "I did not rob, I did no wrong. I maligned no one before them. I entered the Presence (i.e., before the king and/or queen) to resolve difficulties. To assist the unfortunate I have given goods to the have not(s). I endowed the orphan in my town. My reward is being remembered for my beneficence. My Ka enduring because of my kindness-Harwa."

The second female position of importance in government was that of queen mother. In Meroitic, the word is *Ktke* or *Kdke* or in English Candace or Kandake which became a well-known title in Greco-Roman times. The title transforms from queen mother with power to the office of queen in the second century B.C.E. under queen or Kandake Shanankdekhete (Hakem, 1990:175). Also, as Hakem points out, beginning with Queen Amanirenas in the first century B.C.E., another important development takes place. "This was the close association of the first wife of the king and perhaps their eldest son on so many of the important monuments." Such an association tends to suggest "some degree of coregency since the wife who survived her husband often became the reigning *Candace*."

The end of Kushite rule of Egypt which had lasted 100 years ended with the invasion of Assyrian armies and King Tantumani's retreat to the Nubian capital of Napata in approximately 656 B.C.E. This effectively ended the Twenty-Fifth Dynasty. However, the Kushite kings continued to use the titles of kingship from Egypt throughout the Meroitic period.

The Meroitic period (195 B.C.E. - 320 C.E.) begins with the shift of the capital to Meroe, a city located further south in Nubia. Meroe was a great city with exquisite palaces, an observatory, magnificent temples, pools and foundations, excellent arts and crafts, and large industrial complexes especially built around a large iron industry. They also engaged in trade and were like other Nubian kingdoms middle men in the trade between the south and the north. The relations with the Greeks, who had conquered Egypt in 332 B.C.E., tended to be mutually respectful, especially in the third century under King Ergamenes who was said to have had a Greek education. He also joined in temple-building projects with the Greek whom he allowed to build temples in the northern part of Lower Egypt and to live and work at his court (Säve-Söderbergh, 1987:39).

Meroe's relations with the Romans were less friendly and "following the Roman conquest of Egypt (30 B.C.E.), the Meroites attacked and sacked Philae and Aswan." And "in triumph, they carried home statues of the (Roman) Emperor Augustus erected at the Roman boundary" and buried at least one head under a palace (Säve-Söderbergh, 1987:39). In retaliation, the Romans sacked Napata in 25 B.C.E., but the Queen (Kandake) of Meroe, possibly Amenirenas, responded, driving the Romans back north and readjusting the borders between Roman-controlled Egypt and Nubia. She thus won back the whole of Nubia, a control which lasted until the conquest of Nubia by Axum in 325 C.E.

Even with the fall of Meroe to Axum, Nubia produced another kingdom called the Ballana culture (250-550 C.E.). By the 6th century C.E. three kingdoms had emerged in Nubia -- Nobadia, Makuria and Alwa. In this period the Nubians became Christians and maintained their kingdom until 1400 when the Muslims conquered them. Thus, Nubia has a history of 4200 years from 3800 B.C.E. to 1400 C.E. and a record of noteworthy achievements in the arts, industry and international relations.

Egypt. The civilization of Egypt represents the full flowering of African culture in antiquity. As Bruce Trigger (1983:1) states "Through pharaonic Egypt, Africa lays claim to being the cradle of one of the earliest and most spectacular civilizations of antiquity." In fact, one could say Egypt was the greatest civilization in antiquity, for neither Sumer, Babylonia nor any other earlier civilizations equalled her achievement (Trigger, 1983; Gardiner, 1961).

Egypt's chronology is divided into several periods: a prehistorical period, a predynastic period and a series of dynastic periods. It is the dynastic periods with which we will concern ourselves. The first period of Egyptian history is called the Early Dynastic period (c.3100-2686 B.C.E.). An important artistic and historical item in this period is the Narmer Palette which shows the King Narmer wearing both the White Crown of Upper Egypt (South) and the Red Crown of Lower Egypt (North), indicating he ruled the two kingdoms of Upper and Lower Egypt. The king came from the south and conquered the north, establishing a unified state approximately 3100 B.C.E., calling it the Two Lands, *Tawy*. Also Egypt was called *Kemet*, Land of the Blacks or the Black Land, and *Ta Meri*, the Beloved Land. In this same period, writing and irrigation are also established. Although the name Narmer is mentioned on this document, Menes or Mena is considered the traditional founder of the First Dynasty. However, it is not known whether Mena is King Narmer or King Aha or both. What is clear is that the state establishes a large bureaucracy and that "(I)n the course of the Early Dynastic Period, artisans and civil servants working for the central government were to fashion the highly sophisticated traditions of art and learning that thereafter were to constitute the basic pattern of Pharaonic civilization" (Trigger, 1983:50).

But it is in the Old Kingdom period (c. 2686-2182 B.C.E.) that Kemetic culture flowers. It is in this period that Imhotep, the master architect, under King Zoser or Djoser, builds the first pyramid, a step-pyramid at Saqqara. Imhotep is the world's first recorded multidimensional man, being, in addition to the royal architect, a philosopher, priest, astronomer, prime minister, engineer, teacher and chief physician to the king. In fact, it can be said he was the father of medicine and his "fame in later times was so great that he was ultimately venerated as a god and equated by the Greeks with Asklepios, their own god of healing" (James, 1979:44).

In the Fourth Dynasty, King Khufu builds the Great Pyramid at Giza which contained over 1,300,000 blocks of stone with an average weight of two and one-half tons a piece. King Khafra (Chephren) builds a smaller pyramid near Khufu's and a

Sphinx which is said to be in his image. The Fifth Dynasty sees the emergence of the oldest texts in history, the *Pyramid Texts*, found in the Pyramids of Unas, Teti and Pepi, the last king of the Fifth Dynasty, and the first two of the Sixth Dynasty respectively. Moreover, the *Declarations of Virtues*, statements of career and moral claims, evolve and give a moral portrait of Kemetic life. Already in the *Pyramid Texts*, Unas states that he wishes to be judged in the afterlife by what he has done on earth. And he affirms that "no one alive or dead accuses him and neither does beast or bird" (Lichtheim, 1975:35).

In his *Declarations of Virtue*, Harkuf, a noble, justifies himself before history and heaven saying, "I was one worthy. One beloved of his father, praised by his mother, and one whom all his sisters and brothers loved. I gave bread to the hungry, clothes to the naked and brought the boatless to (dry) land. I was one who spoke justly, who repeated that which was pleasing to hear. I never spoke evilly against any one to his or her superior. For I wished to stand well with God" (Karenga, 1984:94,95). Again, these *Declarations of Virtues* yield an important portrait of the Kemetic concept of morality.

Joined to this type of moral literature is the evolution of the *Sebait* or *Books of Wise Instruction* which also contained Egyptian moral philosophy. In the oldest complete *Sebait* the *Book of Ptah-hotep*, we are introduced to the concept of *Maat*, the central moral and spiritual concept in Kemetic society. *Maat* means many things, including truth, justice, propriety, harmony, balance, reciprocity and order -- in a word, rightness in the divine, natural and social realms. Ptah-hotep tells us "Maat is great, its value is lasting and it has remained unchanged since the time of the Creator. It lies as a (plain) path even before the ignorant and those who violate its laws are punished. Although wickedness may gain wealth, wrong-doing has never brought its wares to a (safe) port. In the end, it is Maat (the way of truth, justice and righteousness) which lasts and enables one to say it is the legacy of my father (and mother)" (Karenga, 1984:41).

It is this tradition of excellence and achievement which marks the Old Kingdom that continues throughout Egyptian history at varying levels through periods called the First Intermediate Period (c. 2181-2050 B.C.E.); the Middle Kingdom (c. 2050-1786 B.C.E.); the Second Intermediate Period (c. 1786-1567 B.C.E.); the New Kingdom (c. 1567-1085 B.C.E.); and the Late Period (c.1085-332 B.C.E.). The Intermediate periods were periods of decentralization and weak central government. And 332 B.C.E. marks the conquest of Egypt by Alexander, the Macedonian Greek. Within this 3000-year period of history, Egypt left an important and impressive legacy for both Africa and the world. And it is to this legacy to which we now turn.

The legacy of Egypt is awesome and occurs in several disciplines of human knowledge (Diop, 1987, 1991; Harris, 1971). One of the first major contributions ancient Egyptians made was in the field of agriculture. By 5000 B.C.E., they had transformed the Nile Valley from a food-gathering economy to a food-producing economy laying the basis for a settled life and thus a life of varied intellectual and cultural pursuits. In the field of agriculture, they developed the practice of irrigation and a nilometer to measure and control water levels. Moreover, animal domestication and husbandry were likewise a part of this body of knowledge.

Having gained the capacity for a settled life, the Kemites began to diversify thought and practice and produced various crafts and professions. These included cloth weaving, woodworking, shipbuilding, glass-making, leatherwork, pottery production, metallurgy and mining in gold, silver, and copper as well as its alloys, brass and bronze. Moreover, craftsmanship involved work in precious stones such as turquoise, carnelian, lapis lazuli, feldspar and amethyst. These activities in metal and mineral use required and produced techniques, i.e., forging, casting, riveting, soldering, stamping and hammering, and tools such as mallets, adzes, chisels, saws, drills, etc. These techniques, tools and the products were spread throughout the then known world.

Especially is Egypt known for its excellence in stone-masonry and architecture which included massive works in granite, diorite, limestone, basalt and gneiss. This work, of course, culminates in the masterful construction of the pyramids which are scientific, technical, aesthetic and religious masterpieces dedicated to God, Ra. As an allied field of architecture, the Kemites developed the discipline of engineering, laying out cities, building dams, dikes and canals, pools, ponds, gardens and courtyards, reservoirs, fortresses, and the instruments to measure, shape and complete these projects.

Egypt also contributed to science and math leaving "a valuable legacy in the fields of physics, chemistry, zoology, geology, medicine, pharmacology, geometry and applied mathematics" (El Nadoury, 1990:107). These include the science of mummification, surgery and medicine as outlined and explained in the *Edwin Smith Papyrus*, the *Ebers Papyrus* and the *Berlin Papyrus*. These documents reveal knowledge and treatment of major and minor diseases and disorders. In fact, as Rogers (1972:38-42) notes, the ancient Egyptians had diagnosed, treated and catalogued over 200 diseases and were conducting surgery and auscultation and were aware of blood circulation.

In mathematics, the *Moscow Papyrus* and the *Rhind Papyrus* reveal the Kemite knowledge of arithmetic, algebra and geometry. In fact, ancient Egyptians were credited by the Greeks (Herodotus and Strabo) as having invented geometry. They were knowledgeable of how to calculate a circle, triangle, the volume of a cylinder, a hemisphere and appear to be knowledgeable of pi. As shown in the *Carlsberg 1* and *Carlsberg 9 Papyri*, ancient Egyptians had an excellent knowledge of astronomy. They divided the year into 12 months, the day into 24 hours and gave us the 365-day calendar year on which the current calendar year is based.

In the discipline of art, the Kemites left countless examples of not only architecture of great aesthetic value, especially columns, temples, and palaces, but also fine paintings, reliefs and sculpture. In literature one has in ancient Egypt copies of the oldest books in the world. These include the *Pyramid Texts*, the oldest religious texts in the world; the oldest medical texts, as mentioned above; the oldest social justice text, the *Book of Khun-Anup* (The Eloquent Peasant); and the oldest ethical texts, the *Declarations of Virtues*. In addition, we find various forms of creative literature, poems, plays, narratives and histories. In the area of religion, as noted above, ancient Egypt has the oldest religious and ethical texts and apparently contributed to the formulation of both the Jewish-Christian-Islamic tradition as well as Greek philosophy (Diop, 1991; Bernal, 1991, 1987; James, 1976; Breasted, 1934).

Finally, ancient Egypt contributed both the technique of and the art of writing, using three systems, hieroglyphic, hieratic and demotic and also the paper on which to write. In fact the word paper has its origins in the word *papyrus*, the Greek word for the plant material on which the Egyptians wrote. The ancient Egyptians themselves called the plant by various names (*mnh*, *w3ḏ*, etc.); the blank papyrus roll -- (*shw*); and one with writing -- (*mḏ3t*, *t3w*, *sfdw*, etc.) Yet in considering all these achievements, it is important to remember DuBois' (1965:103) contention that the "first great experiment in human civilization" rose out of African problem-solving, out of the need to shape their world in their own image and interest. "The history of civilization which began in Egypt was not so much a matter of dynasties and dates," DuBois states. Rather, "It was an attempt to settle the problems of living together, of government, defense, religion, family, property, science and art." Therefore, to meet the challenges of nature and society, "African Egypt...made the beginning and set the pace...in these seven lines of human endeavor."

The legacy of ancient Kemet is an extensive and far-reaching one. It, thus, has become contested ground. For as Diop observes, its real history reveals a debt to Africa that Eurocentric and racist thinking can neither concede nor accept. And this has led to the falsification of both African and human history. Thus, new research and fresh and fruitful thinking are needed to reverse and end this state of things (Diop, 1991; Bernal, 1987).

Western Sudanic Civilization

The Sudanic civilizations of Ghana, Mali and Songhai are characterized by continuity and similarity (Osae, Mwabara and Odunsi, 1973: Part One; Davidson, 1977: Chapters 2-5, 7). They follow each other and build on each other's legacy. Moreover, they are heavily influenced by their interaction with the world Islamic community, especially Mali and Songhai. This interaction is expressed in the growth of commerce, scholarship and international relations. Also, they are societies defined by large and powerful armies, able rulers and industrious peoples.

Ghana. Ghana emerged as a state in approximately 300 C.E. It reached its height in the eleventh century and came to an effective political end in 1240. As early as 773-4 C.E., the Muslim author Al-Fazari wrote of Ghana, calling it the Land of Gold. Also, other Muslim authors wrote of Ghana and its wealth and importance to the trans-Saharan trade. Among these were al-Yaqubi in the ninth century, al-Mas'udin and Ibn Hawqal in the tenth century. But the most definitive report of the early Muslim writers was *The Description of North Africa* (1067) written by al-Bakri, a Moor who lived in the Moorish empire in Spain and who was also a geographer. However, two West African Muslims, Mahmud Kati who wrote Tarikh al Fattakh (*History of the Seeker After Knowledge*) and Abdal Rahaman who wrote Tarikh as-Sudan (*History of the Sudan*) also wrote on Ghana, as well as on the other Sudanic civilizations.

From al-Bakri's report and other sources, we know that Ghana's wealth was a result of the control of trade in two key items -- salt and gold. Strategically located along routes of the trans-Saharan trade, Ghana controlled the flow of trade and levied import and export taxes on the traders. Ghana controlled two main routes which stretched north to Morocco and Libya and West to the Bornu region near Lake Chad which tied in with the Nile Valley trade (Harris, 1972:51). Moreover, the report reveals that Ghana's capital city, Kumbi Saleh, had two sections - one for the King or Tunka and Ghanaian people and the other for the Muslim traders.

Tunka Menin, the king of the time, circa 1065, was an absolute monarch with an elaborate court of counselors, ministers, interpreters and a treasurer. Much revered, he held court with impressive splendor often ruling on great and small matters. Moreover, he maintained a large standing army of 200,000 and more than 40,000 were bowman. To gauge how impressive and politically powerful this was, one can remember that about this time, the Norman army which conquered England in 1066 was only 15,000 strong. Recognizing the rise of Islam and Muslim popularity in his empire, Tunka Menin showed political and economic wisdom by appointing several Muslims as ministers, treating all Muslims justly and allowing them to practice their religion freely. This not only contributed to peace in the empire, but received the economic benefit of good relations and increased trade with the Muslim North.

      The trans-Saharan trade was brisk and varied passing thru towns like Walata, Kumbi Saleh, Tichitl and Awdaghost. From the North, traders brought salt, daggers, silk, jewelry, time pieces and fine cloth. From other parts of the Sudan, they brought bars of iron, gold, leather, cotton, kola nuts, shea butter, millet and sorghum. At the peak of its empire, Ghana contained a population of several million and a territory of about 250,000 square miles. Its imperial might rested on the 200,000-man army, its control of trade and the revenues from it, as well as good political administration which was able to keep revolts at a minimum and put them down when and if they occurred. In 1076, religious reformers called Almoravids led a Berber army which captured Kumbi Saleh. By 1087, however, they had lost control of the empire and Ghana disintegrated into smaller states, laying the basis for the rise of Mali.

Mali. The empire of Mali has its roots in the state of Kangaba, a small state which was part of the Ghana Empire. The first Malian emperor was Sundiata, who defeated his rivals, established his rule approximately 1230 and reigned until his death in 1255. During this time, he took control of the trans-Saharan trade and set up Niani, his capital as a key trading and financial center. He also turned his attention to agriculture, transforming many of his soldiers, who now had no wars to fight, into farmers. This attention to agriculture paid off in a few years and Mali established itself as one of the richest farming areas in West Africa.

      Mali's most illustrious and well-known emperor was Mansa (emperor) Musa who came to the throne in 1312 and ruled until 1332. In his brief reign, he built Mali into one of the world's largest empires and his fame spread throughout the Muslim world and Europe. Conquering most of the major Berber cities of the western desert, Musa extended Mali into what is now Mauritania and southern Algeria in the north, and as far south as northern Nigeria to establish contact with the Hausa states. By the time of his death, he had made Mali twice the size of Ghana with a population of approximately ten million.

Mansa Musa is best known, however, for this famous hajj or pilgrimage to Mecca in 1324. With him he took 60,000 persons, many of them soldiers, baggage men, and royal secretaries to record this momentous trip. Also included were friends, doctors, teachers and local political leaders. To finance the trip, Musa took 80-100 camel loads of gold dust. Passing thru Cairo, he was honored and given royal assistance from the Sultan of

Cairo for the remainder of his trip. In Mecca and Medina, he gave gifts generously and on his return trip he passed thru Cairo again giving out so much gold, he depressed the price of gold in Egypt. One writer in the service of the Sultan stated that it took twelve years for the Egyptian economy to recover from Musa's generosity with gold.

Musa went through Cairo, Mecca, Medina and Tripoli and brought back many Muslim scholars, jurists, architects and other skilled men, among them African scholars from the University of Fez, Morocco. This had a tremendous impact on the development of African civilization. Among the many architects who returned with Musa was as-Saheli, a Moor from Granada who was also a poet. as-Saheli constructed many buildings in Mali, especially mosques and a palace for Musa. Most importantly, however, he built the University of Sankore at Timbuktu which became an intellectual center which attracted students and professors from all over the Muslim world. Also Musa encouraged learning, building many Quranic schools which taught reading and writing especially of the Quran. In addition, he sent ambassadors to Egypt and Morocco and representatives to many North African and Sudanic cities and the forest kingdoms near the Coast.

Mansa Musa laid the basis for European recognition and respect of Africa below the Sahara during that time. European scholars and traders were aware of his empire and in 1375 Charles V of France had an atlas drawn showing "Rex Melli" or "Musa Mali" in the area of West Africa wearing robes and a crown and holding a gold nugget in one hand and a scepter in the other. Mansa Musa left a strong impression on the African, Muslim and European world and a strong empire so that even when Mali was in decline in 1494, the Portuguese sought and established diplomatic relations and exchanged ambassadors with Mali. Mali began to decline in 1400 and in 1468, Songhai began its rise.

Songhai.   The largest and greatest of the Western Sudanic civilizations was Songhai. Songhai's foundation was laid by Sunni (Sonni) Ali Ber who came to the throne in 1464 and recaptured Timbuktu in 1468 from Mali, the year usually fixed as the beginning of the Songhai Empire. Sunni Ali was described by as-Sadi, author of *Tarikh as-Sudan*, *(History of the Sudan),* as a brutal and fierce tyrant. Sunni was the title of Ali's dynasty and Ber means "the Great," a name established thru fierce and uncompromising conquest by this warrior-king. During the

twenty-eight years of his reign, he was always at war and on the march, defeating all challengers and strengthening his army thru a systematic build-up of his cavalry. He even drafted soldiers from vassal states and built a navy of war canoes which sailed the Niger. By the time of his death, he had consolidated and greatly expanded his empire and laid the basis for the renowned glories of Songhai.

The most illustrious emperor of Songhai was Muhammad Toure, a distinguished general who served in Sunni Ali's army. Muhammad, who bore the title Askia (general), showed himself an able administrator as well as general. Ruling form 1493-1529, he built an effective army out of POW's and men formerly enslaved whom he freed and put into service to the empire. He based his administration on Islamic law, built a support system among the learned and the wealthy urbanites of Gao, Jenne and Timbuktu and surrounded himself with professionals in law and administration to insure uniform justice in the empire.

It is Askia Muhammad, also called Askia the Great, who built the largest empire in the history of West and Central Africa. DuBois (1975:47-48) states that Askia Muhammad "during his reign conquered and consolidated an empire two thousand miles long by one thousand miles wide at its greatest extent -- a territory as large as all Europe." He divided this great empire into a series of provinces and appointed professional administrators as governors. Emulating Mansa Musa of Mali, Askia Muhammad made a spectacular hajj to Mecca in 1495. With him he took 300,000 pieces of gold which he used for expenses, gifts and purchases. At Mecca, he was appointed as Caliph of the Western Sudan by the Sharif of Mecca, who was the spiritual ruler of all Islam. This had both political and religious ramifications, for it give him claim to allegiance of all Muslims westward to the Atlantic. It also put him in a united front of Muslims against the encroaching Christians and cemented his conquests and economic relations with the Muslim world.

Askia Muhammad is also responsible for a flowering of intellectual achievement. In Gao, Jenne and Timbuktu, many universities and schools were established. The universities taught philosophy, medicine, law, government, astronomy, math, literature, ethnography, hygiene, logic, rhetoric, grammar, geography, music and poetry writing. Scholars and students from other parts of Africa, Asia, the Muslim world and Europe visited the universities for study and exchange. One of the famous scholars at the University of Sankore at Timbuktu was professor Ahmad Baba, who was a faculty member, an author of forty books on such diverse fields as astronomy, ethnography, biography and theology, Islamic law, and owner of a library of 1600 volumes (Jackson, 1980:217). So enduring are his works that thirteen of them are still used in part of West Africa. This was also the time of the famous *Tarikhs* (Histories) of Western Sudanic civilization by Mahmud Kati and Abdul-Rahman as-Sadi.

In 1528, Askia the Great, who was now blind, was deposed by his son Musa, ending a brilliant and enlightened reign. The empire saw few dramatic developments after his reign and due to weak leadership, revolts sprang up and continuously increased. Finally, in 1591 a Moroccan army, led by a Spanish Christian who had converted to Islam and composed of captured Christians, Spanish Muslims and Moroccans, set out to attack and sack Songhai. The fire power of the army, which had lost many of its members crossing the Sahara, prevailed and the Songhai troops retreated down the Niger. Although the Moroccans held the main cities, they could not hold the empire, for Songhai troops continuously harassed them with guerilla warfare. Eventually, the empire disintegrated into city states and the Moroccans were assimilated into the indigenous populace. Songhai, the greatest and largest empire of the Western Sudanic civilization had thus come to an end.

The Moorish Empire in Spain

In his *Introduction to African Civilizations*, John Jackson (1980) devotes a chapter to "Africa and the Civilizing of Europe." In it he builds a strong case for Europe's debt to Africans, namely Moors, who pulled the Spaniards out of the Bleak Ages (500-1000 C.E.) which they call the "Dark Ages" and gave them a civilization no other country in Europe had at the time, but from which all Europe would eventually borrow. Recently, Ivan

Van Sertima (1992) has edited a text titled *Golden Age of the Moors* in which various scholars, including Jackson, offer critical perspectives on this extensive contribution, using the latest data in the field. James Ravell's (1991:407-454) bibliographic essay, titled "Annotated Bibliography of the Moors: 711-1492 A.C.," is extensive and extremely useful for further research and reference.

The Moorish conquest and civilizing of Spain began in 711. In that year, Tarik, a Moorish general, landed in Spain near a cliff later named Jebel Tarik, the Rock or Mountain of Tarik, i.e. Gibraltar, in his honor. After conquering some towns near Gibraltar, Tarik met and defeated Roderick, King of the Visigoths in Spain at the Battle of Xeres. This marked the beginning of Spain's golden age which she has never since duplicated (McCabe, 1935; Lane-Poole, 1886). The Moors brought Spain and thus Europe several gifts from African creativity and inventiveness, including agriculture, engineering, mining, industry, manufacturing, expanded commerce, beautiful skilled architecture and education and scholarship (Van Sertima, 1992).

In agriculture, the Moors brought new products, but also skill and literature in the field. They introduced rice, strawberries, cotton, sugar cane, ginger, lemons and dates. Ibn-al-Awam and Abu Zacaria produced scholarly works on agriculture and husbandry. As late as 1802, Ibn-al-Awam's treatise on agriculture was being translated and used in Spain. As first-rate engineers, the Moors built Spain its aqueduct system for irrigation, its reservoirs for water, underground silos for grain, tunnels thru mountains, raised sidewalks, lighted paved streets and dams. They also built a sewer system and artificial lakes to beautify cities. In the areas of mining and manufacturing they mined gold, silver, copper, tin, lead, iron and alum and made luxury and utilitarian items out of these and brass. In addition, the Moors were respected for their fine jewelry mosaics, pottery and glass work, tile and fine silk and cotton products. It is, in fact, the Moors who introduced cotton manufacture to Europe. Finally,

Jackson (1980:188) states that also "the Moors introduced the manufacture of gunpowder in Europe." Given this economic boom, the Moors also engaged in shipbuilding and expanded trade. This maritime commerce on the Mediterranean by the Moors and other Muslims was greater than that of the Christians and maintained its dominance up to the 12th century.

In terms of architecture, the Moors built structures not simply for use, but equally for aesthetic value. Their arches, courtyards and gardens are reflected in the architecture of California and the Southwest with its so-called Spanish motif. Actually, it is Moorish motif passed on thru the Spanish to the Mexicans from which the white Americans borrowed. In Cordova alone in the 10th century, there were 200,000 homes, 10,000 palaces of the wealthy and many royal palaces with exquisitely designed gardens. Also, there were 900 beautiful public baths and many private ones at a time when the rest of Europe considered bathing self-indulgent and a sin.

Finally, in terms of education and scholarship, the Moors were equally impressive in stature and contribution. At a time when even European kings could not read or write, and 99% of Christian Europe was illiterate, the Moors made education universal. And in the 10th and 11th centuries when Europe had no public libraries and only two significant universities, the Moors gave Spain more than 70 public libraries, built Spain seventeen famous universities and established an observatory at Seville. According to Rocker (1937:412) astronomy, physics, chemistry, geometry, philology, geography and math were taught at these universities. Also, artists and scholars formed professional associations and held regular conferences "where the latest achievements of research were announced and discussed which naturally contributed greatly to the spread of scientific thought." Carew (1991) also notes how Moorish scholarship was so respected that for centuries Arabic was seen as key to scholarship.

In addition to the subjects listed above, trigonometry, botany and history were taught in the university where students from Africa, the Middle East and Europe flocked. Lane-Poole (1886) reports that even women were encouraged to engage in serious study and that there were women doctors. Van Sertima (1991:11) notes what he calls "a benign influence" on the way Islam operated in Spain particularly in relationships to women. He also points out that the famous traveller Ibn Battuta had remarked on the freedom of Muslim women in Africa. Thus, in Moorish Spain, Van Sertima states that women "moved freely in public and engaged in various gatherings."

Jackson (1980:181) states that Moroccan science and scholarship were an integral part of the overall Muslim cultural achievement which produced advances in math, algebra, physics and astronomy. He points out that approximately 400 years before Magellan's trip in 1519 established for Europe that the world was round, Moors taught it in geography classes using a globe. In fact, El Idrisi, a Moor, wrote a book in the mid-twelfth century observing that according to astronomers and other learned men and philosophers, "the world is round as a sphere." He also suggested a concept of gravity, stating in his book that the earth draws "to itself all that is heavy in the same way as a magnet attracts iron."

By 1492, the Moorish empire in Spain came to an end with the fall of Granada. This was almost an 800-year Moorish reign of culture and science which developed as no other European country. For a brief while Spain tried to maintain her cultural standards and progress. Isabella and Ferdinand had used their wealth from Granada to finance Columbus' voyage to America when he found Blacks had already preceded him (Van Sertima, 1976:11). And then there was a push for trade and exploration in the New World which was no doubt aided by Moorish and other Muslim navigational experience and knowledge (Parry, 1966:Chapter 1). But as Lane-Poole (1886:vii-ix) observed, "this was but a last halo about the dying moments of a (once) mighty state." What followed with the vulgarity and unbridled violence of the Christian Inquisition, a condemnation of science, closing of universities and libraries with not one public library in Madrid in the 18th century, the decrease by four-fifths of the number of looms in Seville, destruction of the baths in the hysterical drive against imagined sin, deterioration of the irrigation and decline of agriculture production and decay in general. Jan Carew (1992) writing in *Golden Age of the Moors* confirms this disintegration not only of the economy, but also of the religious tolerance and multiculturalism which so defined the Moorish Empire. He (1992:249) notes that Isabella's reneging on her commitment to religious tolerance under the terms of Moorish surrender and subsequently expelling and launching attacks on the Moors and Jews established a "precedent...and tradition of treachery and racism that was adopted by all European colonizers...and it would endure throughout the Columbian era." Given Spain's deterioration, it is interesting to note that after all the commentaries on and claims about the tragedy that would descend on Africans if and when Europeans left Africa, it was a major European state, Spain, that deteriorated after Africans left. Such is the irony and severe instruction of history.

Other States and Empires

There are numerous other states, empire and ethnic-nations which need to be studies by serious students of African history. Among these are the ancient Ethiopian empire of Axum in the North East (El Madhi, 1965; Pankhurst, 1967; Shinnie, 1967). Secondly, there are the Hausa states and the Kanem-Bornu empire in the Western Sudan (Ajayi and Espie,1972); Trimmingham, 1962). Thirdly, there are the West African states and empires -- Ife, Oyo, Benin, Dahomey and the Akan states and empires of Ashanti and Fante (Murdock, 1959; Davidson, 1977). Fourthly, there are Central African states -- Kongo, Luba and Lunda (Collins, 1968; Vasina, 1968); and the lake states of Bunyoro and Buganda (Oliver, 1963; Beattie, 1960). Finally, there are the southeastern and southern states and empires, the Omani Sultanate, the civilization of Zimbabwe (The Mutapa

Empire) and the Zulu Empire (Davidson, 1959, 1967); Oliver
and Mathews, 1963; Vilakazi, 1962; Omer-Cooper, 1966). These,
however, are but selective examples of the rich variousness of
African history and the struggle for self, social and world
construction it represents.

The Decline of African Societies

Invariably students of Black Studies raise the question of
why did Africa with all its glory and achievement fall to the
European advance. There are several reasons, but before we
treat them, we should put the question in historical perspective
with three fundamental observations. First of all, one should
know that all civilizations, regardless of how great they are or
seem, eventually decline for various internal and external
reasons. Egypt, Ethiopia, Rome, Greece, Ghana, Mali, Songhai,
and of late the British, French and American empires all suffered
this tendency. So it should not be seen as a special weakness or
oddity that the civilizations of Africa eventually declined and fell
to the onslaught of Europe. Secondly, it should be noted that the
conquest and colonization of Africa took over 400 years, from
mid 1400's to the end of the 1800's which culminated in the
partition of Africa. Throughout this time, Africans continuously
resisted and won many battles and wars against the Europeans.
Queen Nzingha of Angola's long war with the Portuguese,
Samory Toure of the Western Sudan's ongoing war with the
French, the Zulu nation's defeat of the British at the Battle of
Isandlwana, 1896; Menelik's defeat of the Italians at the Battle
of Adua, 1898; the Asante's long wars with the British and the
Mahdi of Eastern Sudan's victories in the Sudan are but a few
examples of African resistance and victories (Ajayi and Espie,
1972; Rogers, 1972 Vol 1). In fact, as suggested above, Europe
first came to Africa as an equal and sometimes as an inferior on
the cultural and political power level. The exchange of
ambassadors between Portugal and Mali, the Moorish
domination of Spain and superiority in science and scholarship

to all Europe and the tribute and tax paid to kings and local rulers, all show an early deference and often higher level of culture of Africans at that time.

As July (1970:168) points out, the city-states of the Niger Delta offer another strong example of resistance to European penetration and of control of exchange by Africans. Although the Europeans built forts for stability, defense and as a launching base, "at first they gained not more than a minimum foothold for their garrisons remained by sufferance, unable to either exert political authority outside their walls or to enforce their *desired* trade monopoly." In fact, local leaders "characteristically extracted payment of tariffs, fines and rents while refusing traders access to the interior,...maintaining control over the inland trade." July argues that a typical situation was related by a European agent who reported the authority and power of the Fante who neither the English or Dutch "dare oppose...for fear of being ruined themselves." Finally, July states that perhaps "the degree of tenacity in opposition to European penetration was best exemplified by John Conny," a political leader of the then Gold Coast (Ghana) of the early 18th century. He fought off the Dutch for seven years when they attacked to take his fort and negotiated a settlement "only after seven years of combined diplomatic and military pressure."

Finally, to discuss critically the fall of Africa one must realize that Africa did not fall; separate empires, states, nations and ethnic groups were eventually conquered and colonized. To talk of Africa as if it were a self-conscious political unit rather than mostly a geographical fact with various cultural similarities is to obscure the reality and damage clarity. Africa did not fall with the defeat of the Asante and Zulu empires nor with the conquest of the Hausa states or the Sudan. There was no capital or central government for Africa. Africa was a continent in itself, but not self-consciously for itself. Only with the rise of Pan-Africanism did the peoples of Africa begin to see and define themselves as one. This was to Europe's advantage, but still the conquest and colonization of Africa proved to be a 400-year project which ended in great part in less than seventy-years as a result of the African independence struggles. Thus, it might be better to rephrase the question and ask, not why Africa fell, but rather what factors led to Europe's temporary conquest and colonization of African societies?

With these observations in mind, one can begin to answer the question by citing Europe's technological advantage. It is important to note here that Europe at first did not have serious technological advantage over Africa, especially during the Moorish occupation of Spain and up to the end of the 1400's. Also, Rodney (1974:10) states: "in the fifteenth century European technology was not totally superior to that of other parts of the world." In fact, Europeans imported African and Asian cloths and other consumer goods during this period. In terms of Europe's eventual technological advantage, it is also important to recognize that it was not simply the gun which gave Europe the advantage, for Africans and Asians often had guns. What is important to recognize is the complexity of factors of which the gun was only one, even though it was a central factor. In fact, there were three things which Europe possessed which would eventually give them a technological advantage over Africa: 1) guns; 2) long distance ships; and 3) capitalism as a system of production. Both Rodney (1974) and Parry (1966) agree with these, but Parry adds maps as a significant factor in the rise of European hegemony. Also, both give Africans and/or Muslims (Africans, Arabs, Persians, et al) credit for most of the basic knowledge which led to maritime science and capability.

The gun and the monopoly on it gave Europeans the capacity to impose; ships gave them the capacity to collect and synthesize technique and other knowledge from around the world, as well as control, block or bombard the African coast, and capitalism gave them the capacity to mass produce, monopolize and expand technology in great strides. Thus, by the colonial era in the 1800's Europe was able to: 1) conquer cities, states and empires thru force of arms; 2) dictate political developments in Africa; 3) force abandonment of productive processes like clothing manufacture and iron-smelting, and therefore encourage loss of technique and scientific inquiry necessary for technological advancement; and 4) refuse to share its borrowed and synthesized technology with Africans in spite of request. This process not only increased Europe's technological advantage, it also contributed to technological arrest in Africa.

A second factor which increased Europe's ability to conquer and impose its will on Africa was its economic advantage. In fact, the technological advantage and economic advantage are linked. Europe's ships which gave them capacity for long-distance travel and trade and valuable military capability, its guns which gave them the capacity to conquer and impose, and capitalism which gave them the capacity to mass produce and outproduce others clearly had both a technological and economic dimension. Therefore, with this combined power, they were able to: 1) graft African economies into the capitalist system; 2) disrupt African trade routes and relations as the Portuguese did in Upper Guinea with the cotton trade, in Angola with salt and in Kongo with cowries; 3) reduce African economies to a one-product or low number product economy, i.e., slaves, kola nuts, etc. to satisfy European demands; 4) force consumption of European goods; and 5) continue the European stranglehold on African consumer markets. Moreover, as Rodney (1974:106) points out, "the lines of economic activity attached to foreign trade were either destructive as slavery was, or at best extractive like ivory hunting and cutting comwood trees." This too produced developmental arrest and vulnerability.

Directly related to the economic and technological advantages was the holocaust of enslavement which deprived Africa of conditions for development and made security a priority over development. Furthermore, this trade deprived Africa of her youth, the major source of inventiveness and inquiry. Caught in a vicious cycle of needing to give Europeans what they demanded in order to get the guns Europeans had given their enemies, African rulers more and more got bogged down in the commerce in enslaved persons which not only cost

Africans many millions, but also created a context for insecurity, fear and lowered internal productivity. As July (1970:170) states, "no doubt an economy based on slaving was based insecurely, while nations devoted to slave mongering became brutalized and unproductive."

A fourth factor which led to the decline of African societies and their eventual conquest was internal and external problems of the various societies at given times of European penetration. Often they were too small for effective resistance to large well-armed European armies or contingents. Certainly, small ethnic groups were little match for states. And in fact the African states and empires put up a more effective resistance. Secondly, they might have been at war with various neighboring states or peoples, thus making them and their neighbors more vulnerable to European manipulation thru arms supplies. Thirdly, the class divisions and antagonisms in African societies were often played on where they existed and created where they did not. In this regard an example is the rise of mulatto strata or classes throughout Africa which acted as buffers, agents and middle men for Europeans. Also with the rise of the European imposition of the commerce in enslaved Africans, a new class of enslaved persons was developed by the late 18th century in parts of West Africa where once there were none. This further divided African societies in terms of class and color given Europe's fixation on race.

Finally, African societies found themselves culturally vulnerable to European penetration and conquest on several levels. First, except for Islamic societies, they lacked a unifying ideology which cut across the various socio-political formations to which they belonged. The Europeans had Christianity, capitalism and racism and though they often rivalled each other, these ideological focuses were also points of unity against the so-called Black heathen. Thus, "Pope Alexander VI issued a papal bull in 1493 giving, by the grace of an understanding god, the people of color of the world (all considered heathen) and especially their resources to Portugal and Spain" (Karenga,

1978:55). This had the effect of turning their immediate attention from killing each other to killing, enslaving and exploiting the so-called swarthy heathen.

Moreover, African vulnerability was increased by the communalistic character of African societies. This included a tendency toward xenophilia rather than xenophobia as with the European, the non-aggressive approach toward nature and thus, the likelihood of being technologically unable to meet the challenges of a society literally out to conquer and fully exploit nature. Such a people dedicated to the conquest of nature and others is more likely to be prepared for war than those deeply spiritual and deferential to nature and concerned with living in harmony with it rather than conquering it.

Even now such a cultural emphasis remains a problem for the development and defense of African and other Third World peoples. For the needed thrust to control and utilize nature often clashes with cultural values which are more spiritual than material. The question is raised here of how to synthesize the need and growth of science and technology with the need for human sensitivity and morality or how to humanize nature without denaturalizing and dehumanizing humans? Europe by its own admission had failed in this project. It now falls on Africans and other Third World people to demonstrate its possibility.

Conclusion

As stated in the Introduction, a comprehensive and detailed treatment of African history is not possible in this work. What was attempted were some definitive examples of African genius, creativity and historical struggles to shape the world in their own image and interests. Egypt and Nubia were chosen because together they represent the flowering of ancient African civilization in the Nile Valley and because Egypt is especially high achieving, important to the history of world civilization and contested terrain; the Western Sudanic civilization because of its high level of achievement and its being the source of many Africans brought to the New World; and the Moorish empire in Spain because it, like Egypt, shows Europe's immense debt to African and African peoples although they, through racial or racist immodesty, often mistakenly assume that African people owe them everything real and worth mentioning.

2.4   AFRICANS IN AMERICA

Introduction

It is important to restate here some of the basic concerns listed in the section on African Background. First, this section, as the one on Continental African history, will not seek to be an exhaustive treatment of African American history. The intention is rather to acquaint the student with major issues, processes, events and historical figures which have shaped the course and character of Black history. Secondly, in achieving this, focus will be placed more on modal experiences than on establishing neat chronological periods in which these experiences took place. By modal experience, I mean major experiences which defined Black life with Blacks in the roles of both producers and products of history, those who make and are made by these historical experiences.

Thirdly, stress will be placed on Blacks as historical actors rather than the object of historical action, struggling to define, defend and develop their interests rather than their being imposed on by others. The interest here is in the rich diversity of proactive responses Blacks had to life in a new and hostile land. It, thus, will not be a litany of lost battles, a dirge of endless defeats or a chronicle of simple survival. Rather this section will seek to show Blacks as they were and are, meeting major challenges with impressive adaptive vitality, durability and achievement. It will show them then, not simply surviving, but more importantly, self-consciously developing, a process which carries with it both the assumption and insurance of survival.

Finally this section will seek to present concise, critical summaries of major issues, events and processes so that the student can grasp the essence of each rather than get bogged down in insubstantial or less relevant data. The attempt here is to isolate and present the core and kernel of major phenomena and processes in Black History. The detailed presentations are in the general and specific works in the field. This, in a word, is a critical and concise introduction.

Egypt, Mali and the Olmecs

There is strong evidence that Africans did not come to America first on slave ships or as crew members and pilots on white ships, but on their own ships as early as 800-700 B.C.E. and afterwards in 1311 and 1312. This is obviously a contested contention but there is a strong body of evidence which invites consideration. However, if Europeans could reach America by accident, why couldn't Africans reach it by design and skill? Easily the seminal and most definitive work on African presence in ancient American is Ivan Van Sertima's (1976), *They Came Before Columbus*. In this major and controversial work, Van Sertima argues not only that Africans were here before Columbus but that they helped build the Olmec civilization, the parent civilization for all subsequent ones in Mesoamerica (Coe, 1962).

Since publication of his first work, Van Sertima (1992) has published new data to substantiate his claims. In this edited text, *African Presence in Early America*, other scholars join him in critical exploration of this contention. Among these is Alexander Von Wuthenau, author of *Unexpected Faces in America* who has done extensive work on the multicultural character of ancient America which supports Van Sertima's contentions of African presence in ancient America. In fact, Von Wuthenau provided

Van Sertima with new sculptures as evidence. Van Sertima (1992:5ff) gives an overview of what he feels has transpired in the 16 years since the publication of his work in 1976. He explains that more evidence has been unearthed to substantiate his contentions: more Olmec heads, especially one at Tres Zapotes showing Ethiopian type braids; more "clay sculptures of African types which evoke the coloration and texture of African hair;" reaffirmation of skeletal evidence; new evidence from ancient maps; new comparisons of African and South American

pyramids; and further discussion on dating of the voyages to America. In conclusion, he maintains, his earlier stance is fortified with new evidence.

The Olmec civilization, in which Van Sertima finds African presence, is the parent civilization of Meso-America informing the development of many subsequent ones. As Bernal

(1979:9) informs us, it "marks the dawn of civilization and the formation for the cultural areas of Mesoamerica." It is a civilization known for its magnificent temples and pyramids, ceremonial plazas, colonnaded courts for religious rituals, its reverence for the jaguar, its elegant and exquisitely carved figures in jade and other stones. It is also known for its hieroglyphic writing and calendar "which was used throughout early Mesoamerican history and represents an advanced knowledge of astronomy and mathematics, including knowledge of zero." But the most extraordinary and discussed monuments to and of Olmec artistic and technical skill are a series of eleven colossal heads in Southwest Mexico carved out of basalt, each standing nine feet tall and weighing about fifteen tons. Emmerich (1963:53) points out that these heads "portray men with characteristic Olmec features: thick, heavy lips, full cheeks, broad nostrils, almost swollen eyelids and a peculiar close-fitting headdress or helmet."

This helmet is not "peculiar" to Van Sertima. For he sees them as typical helmets used by Nubian soldiers of the 25th Dynasty of Egypt whom he argues came here and contributed to the building of the Olmec civilization. Moreover, nor are the bold features an unsolvable mystery, for they too show an unmistakable Africanoid character and origin.

Van Sertima (1976) offers and documents two main contentions to develop his thesis that Blacks did in fact come to ancient America. First, he argued that they came as Nubians from the 25th Dynasty of Egypt (751-656 B.C.E.) to the Olmec Heartland. This, he stated, would put them here in time to be at the founding of Olmec civilization. In his latest work, following the estimation of Rafique Jairazbhoy, Van Sertima (1992:14) says he is "persuaded by new evidence that the Egyptians came earlier in the Ramesside period between 1305-1080 B.C.E."

Secondly, he posits that Africans also came to America from the Mali empire. In 1310, Malian Emperor Abubakari II sent a fleet of 200 master ships and 200 supply ships into the

Atlantic Ocean toward America. Only one ship returned, but could not report the fate of the others which seemed to be swept away by ocean currents which drive anything in them inevitably to America. In 1311 Abubakari, undeterred from exploring the possibilities of a trans-Atlantic voyage, led a fleet of 2,000 ships to America, and never returned, leaving his brother Mansa Musa in authority.

Some of the major evidence supporting African presence, influence and achievement before the coming of Columbus, especially in Olmec civilization, which Van Sertima cites is as follows. First, he shows cultural and artistic influence, providing over thirty plates to show Africanoid heads, masks, symbols, shields and similarity in phallic cults in Egypt and Mexico. Secondly, Van Sertima demonstrates similarity in socio-religious beliefs and practices showing the Egyptian gods Sokar and Aken in Mexico, similar burial customs such as mummification, the Horus burial jar, golden mummy masks, and the bird-serpent motif in coats of arms and royal diadems. He (1992b:72) also argues that there was "a cluster of...royal traits shared by ruling circles in both civilizations, i.e., the double crown, the royal flail, the sacred bark, the use of purple, the artificial beard, etc." Thirdly, he (1976:155-156) contends that the step pyramid or ziggurat is a distinctive religious structure and that it is significant that "the very first American pyramid or stepped temple appears at La Venta, the site of the collosal (Africanoid) heads..." Moreover, he continues, not "only are the shape and religious function the same" for the Olmec pyramid and its presumed Egyptian prototype, "but also the astronomical and spatial relationships."

A fourth kind of proof Van Sertima offers is the similarities of plants in Africa and Mexico. Among those listed which appear to have been transplanted, he lists the banana, bottle gourd, cotton, Jack bean, yams and tobacco. Fifthly, linguistic evidence is offered in the form of similarities in Egyptian and Mexican words respectively like *Ra* for sun in both, and *kuphi* and *copal* for sacred incense. Moreover, Van Sertima also shows West African and Mexican word similarities. A sixth form of evidence offered for African presence and influence is observation and reports by European travellers as well as documents of East and West Africa reporting voyages to the West. In fact, he states (1992:29) in his address to the Smithsonian Institute that Columbus was the first person from Europe to suggest that there were Africans already in America. Afterwards, many other Europeans reported seeing them.

Also, Van Sertima presents a further proof, skeletal evidence, from studies by craniologist Andrzej Weircinski which reveal a clear presence of Africanoid skulls from Olmec B.C.E. sites. He also notes that 13.5% were evident in the pre-classic period and only 4.5% in the classic period indicating the fusion of Africans in the native population. Finally Van Sertima, argues the technological possibility in support of his thesis. He cites Thor Heyerdal's Atlantic crossing to prove the possibility of Egyptians' crossing the Atlantic, argues that both East and West Africans had the capacity for trans-Atlantic travel and makes the point that Africans navigated the Atlantic before the Christian era and conquered a part of Ireland in an early period. In further proof of the technical possibility, Van Sertima publishes an article by Joan Covey (1992:13ff) in which she argues that "the ancient Egyptian had the requisite mapping skills" to come to America.

Van Sertima has clearly shown the African presence and legacy in ancient America and thus, has given an alternative image and period of African arrival here. In a word, he has demonstrated that Africans came first to America, not as enslaved persons, but as explorers, traders, visitors and built with the Native Americans a great civilization that fortunately could not be erased by Europeans' wholesale book burning and vandalism in Mexico. In doing this, he has made a significant contribution to the rescue and reconstruction of Black history and humanity.

The Holocaust of Enslavement

It is clear from all historical evidence that the massive European enslavement and its accompanying violence, destruction and commercial aspect was one of the most catastrophic events in the history of humankind. If one objectively calculates the costs to Africa and Africans in terms of the 50 to 100 million lives lost thru mass murder, war, the forcible transfer of populations, and the brutal rigors of the Middle Passage and of enslavement as well as the attendant dehumanization and cultural destruction, one cannot help but conclude that of all the holocausts of history, none surpasses this one. By the use of the word holocaust in relation to the process of enslavement, I mean to introduce and stress the *moral* dimension of the tragedy as distinct from its *commercial* aspect. For the stress on the commercial aspect of enslavement often denies, ignores or diminishes the moral monstrousness that this massive destruction of human life, human culture and human possibility represents. As argued below, the severity of the violence undermines the use of the category trade as we usually think of it. What we will describe here is a holocaust. And a *holocaust is an act of genocide so morally monstrous it is not only a crime against a people themselves but also against humanity*.

The holocaust of African enslavement, then, was a holocaust in three basic ways: 1) the morally monstrous destruction of millions of human lives; 2) the savage destruction of cultures and civilizations, great works of art, literatures, buildings, cities, towns, villages, in a word, human culture and human heritage; and 3) the vicious destruction of human possibility through the destruction of the life-chances and cultural grounds for human aspirations, freedom, dignity and humanity itself. It is, in a word, the transformation of people into things and thus engineering their *social death* (Patterson, 1982).

What is intended here is to engage in a discussion using a language that constantly reminds us we are talking about real people, real lives destroyed and disrupted. Moreover, to use the category "slave" without a cultural, ethnic or national qualifier is to suggest the person has no identity outside of being enslaved, that s/he is a "slave" by nature not by social imposition. But to say "enslaved African" is to concede cultural identity and indicate the African was enslaved not simply a slave by birth or being. In a word, it is to begin to resurrect the enslaved Africans from the *social death* imposed on them. Finally, to say simply "slave" suggests a permanent and natural condition, but to say "enslaved" suggests an imposition and thus, the possibility of it being challenged and ended. To further discuss the basis for the contention we can begin by clearing up some of the basic misconceptions about African enslavement. Secondly, we will discuss its impact in more detail to demonstrate the toll it took in Africa and on African peoples.

Misconceptions.   First, as Rodney (1974:95) contends, the category "trade" does not reveal the reality of the process and practice. In fact, although there were transactions between Europeans and Africans which would be called commerce in enslaved persons, "on the whole the process by which captives were obtained on African soil was not trade at all." On the contrary, "it was through warfare, trickery, banditry and kidnapping." Thus, Rodney concludes, "when one tries to measure the effect of European slave trading on the African continent, it is essential to realize that one is measuring the effect of social violence rather than trade in the normal sense."

Secondly, Europeans do not escape moral indictment by blaming Arabs and Africans for participation in the trade. In terms of the Arabs, when the so-called Arab slave trade in East Africa was at its height in the 18th century and early 19th century, it was still tied to and controlled by Europeans (Rodney, 1974:97). For the destination of most of those captured by the Arabs "was the European-owned plantation economies of Mauritius, Reunion and Seychelles -- as well as the Americas, via Cape of Good Hope." Moreover, in the same centuries Africans who were enslaved in certain Arab countries "were all ultimately serving the European capitalist system which set up the demand for slave grown products such as the cloves grown in Zanzibar under the supervision of Arab Masters."

Furthermore, "as European political and economic influence in North Africa increased from the 1870's, the northern slave entrepots of the trans-Saharan and Nile valley were drawn into the European orbit..."(Harris, 1972:78). Thus, one discovers that what looked like an Arab-controlled trade was in fact a European dominated trade with Europeans using Arabs as middle men. None of this is to deny Arab involvement or even the involvement of some East Indians, but rather to focus the bulk of responsibility for the ultimate and greatest demand, and the wholesale destruction and depopulation of Africa where it belongs -- squarely on the shoulders of Europeans. Moreover, granted Arabs had slaves before Europeans demanded them for their labor systems, Arab slavery was domestic and escapable. In fact, there are many examples of servants or persons enslaved by Arabs who rose to power and social and political achievement in the world of Islam.

In terms of African involvement, it is true also that Africans enslaved others before the coming and demands of the European. But three other facts must be added to this statement to give a holistic picture. First, African enslavement was in no way like European enslavement. It was servitude which usually occurred "through conquest, capture in war or punishment for a crime" (Davidson, 1968:181). It could also resemble serfdom as in Medieval Europe where peasants were tied to the land and a lord for protection. They were thus obligated to provide certain goods and services. Moreover, they "were not outcasts in the body politics" as in European chattel slavery. They often lived as members of the family, married their masters' daughters and rose to political and economic prominence and did not face the brutalization and dehumanization which defined European chattel slavery.

Secondly, it is the European demand which forced Africans into a system whose implications few Africans realized at first. This forcing came from among other methods: 1) using their knowledge of local African politics to foment factionalism, launch war and thus get captives; 2) supplying arms to kings or local leaders to raid enemies' cities or villages in exchange for war prisoners; 3) demanding captives for guns from a king who needed them to counter an armed rival king; 4) hiring and launching raiding parties; 5) demanding captives in order to continue providing military supplies to given societies; 6) obtaining some African laborers under false pretenses and enslaving them afterwards; and 7) beginning in one kind of commerce and then demanding enslaved persons at a point when failure to comply would destroy a merchant's business.

Thirdly, it must be remembered that Africans also resisted this commerce in enslaved persons. In fact as Harris (1972:79) points out, "Resistance marked the whole endeavor from initial raid to sale abroad." Queen Nzingha of the Angolan state of Matamba fought fiercely for approximately thirty years against the Portuguese and their imposition of enslavement and its commerce until isolated and overwhelmed and forced back into the European economic orbit. The same is true of the political leader, Tomba, of the Baga people who lived in what is present-day Guinea. About 1720, he tried to build an alliance against the commerce in human persons, but was defeated by an alliance of Europeans, mulattos and Africans involved in the traffic in persons and forced also back into the system. King Nzenga Meremba (Alfonso) of the Congo also resisted Portuguese trafficking in persons vigorously, and is often cited as a strong example of African opposition to enslavement. Even King Agaja Trudo of Dahomey, a state known for enslavement later, sent armies to capture and destroy centers of commerce in enslaved persons on the coast in 1724, but was also forced into the system by superior arms and economic pressures. But as Harris notes, "Agaja, like Alfonso and other Kings in Futa Toro, Benin and elsewhere, all lacked local and international power to change the situation." Thus, they were forced into a system imposed from outside and the tragedy and loss were incalculable.

Impact of the Enslavement. The impact of the violence and destruction of European enslavement of Africans expressed itself in various tragic ways. First and most easily perceived is the depopulation through mass murder, societal disruption and destruction, and forced transfer of populations, especially in Angola and other parts of West Africa. Estimates run as high as 50 to 100 million persons lost to Africa. Secondly, the holocaust of enslavement caused the loss of youth and skilled personnel, thus affecting the scientific, technological and cultural progress of Africa. The youth were key, for it is among them that the thrust toward scientific inquiry and inventiveness is greatest. And loss of skilled people could only blunt and in some cases eliminate development and induce technical arrest.

Thirdly, the holocaust affected economic activity. It not only interrupted and destroyed markets and industries, but grafted African economies on and subordinated them to the commerce and violence of enslavement, leaving other branches of the economic activity underattended or unattended. This meant Africans entered into a vicious cycle of dependence and severely diminished ability to produce and provide for themselves and to continue the battle to control and utilize nature. Fourthly, as a source of constant war and violence, it created and sustained patterns of destruction of life and material achievements as well as conditions of uncertainty and insecurity which accompanied them. Finally, the European imposition of enslavement led directly to the underdevelopment of Africa and overdevelopment of Europe. In fact, Rodney (1974) points out, underdevelopment in Africa is dialectically linked to overdevelopment in the European society -- Continental and Diasporan. Eric Williams (1966) systematically shows how the holocaust of enslavement and its commerce in persons led to vast capital formation and expanded industries in shipbuilding, textiles, sugar refining, metal, insurance and banking in Europe.

This exploitation, oppression and appropriation of the vast human and material resources of Africa for their use in the European West unavoidably led to an interruption and deformation of Africa's development.

Moreover, it represented the combination of these two economic processes, underdevelopment and development, into a single system, capitalist imperialism. This system was/is characterized by the tendency to concentrate wealth at the European center and impose poverty in the so-called marginal areas, i.e., the Third World. It is further defined by an internal logic of competitiveness which pushes it to seek control of markets, raw materials and profitable fields of investment in less developed countries. Colonization grew to secure these necessary factors for capitalist growth and was possible because of the colonial power and wealth Europe had amassed at the expense of Africa and the rest of the Third World.

Thus, when one raises the question of why Africa is not where she was during the Egyptian or Mali Empire, in relation to Europe, one must focus on the period of the holocaust of enslavement by Europeans which interrupted African history and development, drained it of its human and material resources and thus, imposed the pattern of underdevelopment and poverty we witness in Africa today. Of course, the reasons Europe was able to do this which are explained in the above section entitled "The Fall of African Societies" can be argued. But it is impossible to deny that European exploitation and oppression of Africa, beginning in the 1400's, marks a clear turning point in African and world history at the expense of Africa and its peoples as well as other peoples of color.

Enslavement: Basis And System

The Basis of Enslavement.   The American system of enslavement had its basis in three major sets of factors: 1) its profitability; 2) its practicality; and 3) its justifiability in European racist thought. The profitability of enslavement and commerce in persons was alluded to above. Williams (1966), in his often quoted work, *Capitalism and Slavery*, has shown clearly the contribution of the system and the trade to capital accumulation and economic development by England. Some of these areas were: 1) shipbuilding, 2) rise of seaport towns and connected manufacturing centers, 3) banking and insurance houses like Barclay's and Lloyd's; 4) the textile industry; 5) sugar refineries; and 6) metal industries. This was true for other European countries as well.

The United States profited from the system of enslavement and its commerce in persons both as a colony and as a free interdependent part of the world capitalist system. In the USA, the enslaved African was profitable on three basic levels: 1) as a commodity to be sold; 2) as an object of labor to be rented; and 3) as a producer of cash products such as cotton, sugar, tobacco and rice. Around the economic process, commercial and industrial areas grew up, first in New England and New York and then the South. That growth led DuBois (1969) to conclude in his seminal work that this economic process, involving merchants and planters, became "the very life of the colonies." In fact, up to the mid-19th century, American economic development rested mainly on foreign commerce with enslavement and products grown by enslaved Africans at the center of the process.

Enslavement also had its basis in the practicality of the process. As Bennett (1975) states, forced labor was first tried on the Native American and then on indentured whites. But several factors made the enslavement of these groups unattractive and the enslavement of Africans more practical. The first factor was Africa's closeness to the Caribbean where plantations were set up early and where Africans were "seasoned," i.e., made manageable, and then re-exported. Secondly, Africans already had experience in large-scale agriculture with their own fields and European plantations in Africa, unlike the Native Americans who mainly hunted and gathered their food. Thirdly, Africans had relative immunity to European diseases due to long-term contact, whereas the Native Americans did not and were decimated at first by this.

Fourthly, the practicality of African enslavement rested in their low escape possibilities as opposed to Native Americans and whites due to unfamiliarity with the land, high social visibility and lack of a nearby home base. Fifthly, there were no major political repercussions for the enslavement of Africans, unlike the Native Americans who had people here to retaliate and the whites whose enslavement would challenge the tenets of Christianity and the age of enlightenment and reason on which Europe prided itself (Bennett, 1975:65).

Finally, the basis of the American system of enslavement was in its justifiability in European racist thought. Although the enslavement of Africans was based in economic reasons, it also rested in racism as an ideology (Davis, 1975). Racism as an ideology became a justification and encouragement for African enslavement. It expresses itself in religious absurdities, biological absurdities and cultural absurdities. Thus, religiously, it was argued God ordained whites to conquer, civilize and christianize the African "heathen" and of course, take his/her wealth in the process. Moreover, the biological absurdities included redefinition of Africans out of the human race, denying their history and humanity and giving them animal characteristics to suit their bestial treatment by whites. And finally, the cultural absurdities revolved around claims of white cultural superiority and social Darwinist claims of having both the natural right and responsibility to conquer and use the human and material resources of "lesser" peoples for the advancement of the more "noble and advanced" ones. Although Rodney (1974:88-89) at first argues that Africans were enslaved for economic rather than racists reasons, he later concedes the dialectical relation between the two. He correctly concludes that "oppression of African people on purely racial grounds accompanied, strengthened and became indistinguishable from oppression for economic reasons." Moreover, he maintained that "by the nineteenth century white racism had become so institutionalized in the capitalist world (and notably in the USA) that it sometimes ranked above the maximization of profit as a motive for oppressing Black people."

The System of Enslavement.   The American system of enslavement has been classified in several ways. Phillips (1963) a major apologist for enslavement, called it benign and civilizing. Stampp (1967) classifies it as peculiar, cruel and brutal. Genovese (1974) describes it as paternalistic. Elkins (1966) sees it as infantilizing. And cliometricians Fogel and Engerman (1974) think it was simply efficient. It is obvious that the first of the above descriptions are more apologetic than critical and that regardless of the various other descriptions, the system was brutal and defined by the domination, exploitation and oppression which permeate all systems of slavery (Campbell and Rice, 1991; Hurmence, 1990).

American slavery as a system, then, can be defined by: 1) the extent of its brutality; 2) its cultural genocide; and 3) its machinery of control. The brutality of slavery expresses itself on the physical, psychological and sexual level.   Physically, it included violence in various forms -- whippings, mutilations, torture, murder, overworking and deprivation of food, clothing and shelter. Psychological brutality included daily humiliation, denial and deformation of African history and humanity.

It was, in fact, an objectification of the enslaved African, reducing him/her to an object of labor, and using his "race" as proof and assignment of human worth and social status. Sexual brutality was imposed on enslaved African women, men and children. Each was subjected to the sexual lust and exploitation of the master and his family. "Breeding" and rape became the two principal forms of sexual abuse and brutality which they all suffered, but especially the women (White, 1991; Jacobs, 1987; White, 1987: Chapter 2).

It is here that we see the implications of Patterson's (1982:1-14) definition of slavery as "the permanent, violent domination of natally alienated and generally dishonored persons." He points out the need to concretely and symbolically dishonor the enslaved person and to humiliate and undermine the sense of self and connectedness with others and one's own community.

Harriet Jacobs (1987:77) one of the few enslaved African women to write a narrative of her life in enslavement noted that "slavery is terrible for men, but it is far more terrible for women." For "Superadded to the burden common to all, they have wrongs, and sufferings and mortifications peculiarly their own." And these peculiar forms of sufferings were sexual exploitation as well as racial and class oppression. They also included the burden of motherhood and being a wife in a system that devalued Black women, and allowed white men to rape, beat and sell mother, child and husband with impunity. As Deborah White (1991:102-103) points out, various aspects of the Black woman's life was seen in sexual terms and used against her; scarce clothing because of poverty, bending over to work, or lifting one's dress to keep it clean from dirt and water were seen by the slaveholder in sexual terms. In fact, she notes even "some whippings had sexual overtones." Enslaved Africans report beatings stripped naked and masters delighting in it in special ways. As Henry Bibb (1969:120) reports in his narrative as an enslaved African, his master stated that "he had rather paddle a female than eat when hungry." Jacqueline Jones (1985:37) concludes that generally speaking "the sexual violation of Black women by white men rivaled the separation of families as the foremost provocation injected into the Black family life by slaveholders...." And although they had few options in this situation and were brutally punished for resisting, still "Black women often struggled to resist and their fathers, sons and husbands often struggled to protect them" (see modes of resistance below).

The second major aspect of American slavery as a system was its cultural genocide against Africans. By cultural genocide is meant the wholesale intentional destruction of a people's culture and cultural identity and their capacity to produce, reproduce and expand themselves. It includes the destruction of: 1) political identities and ethnic units and identities; 2) families;

and 3) cultural leaders. These were all units of the preservation and transmission of African culture. But they were also units of real and potential resistance -- on the cultural and physical level and thus, the slaveholder sought to destroy them. As Patterson (1982) again notes, one aspect of social death is natal alienation from one's culture and community, one's ancestors and relatives. Thus Africans were systematically deculturalized and cultivated to be totally dependent and marginal.

Finally, American slavery can be defined and discussed in terms of its machinery of control. This machinery of control was one of the most brutal and extensive in the history of slavery. Basically, it involved five mechanisms of control: 1) laws; 2) coercive bodies; 3) the church; 4) politically divisive strategies; and 5) plantation punishments. The slave laws were directed toward defining Africans as property and depriving them of any legal or human right or personality (McIntyre, 1992: Chapter 4). Under these laws or Slave Codes, the enslaved African could not make a contract, could not testify against anyone except another African, could not strike a white man even in self-defense, could not leave a plantation without authorization; could not possess firearms; cold not visit whites, free Africans or entertain them in their quarters; could not assemble without whites; could not learn or be taught to read or write; and could not even beat drums or blow horns (Franklin, 1974:140-141).

The coercive bodies include first, local, county, state and federal armed bodies, soldiers and militias, patrols and vigilante committees dedicated to enforcing the laws even against whites who dared defy them, as in the case of teaching or allowing Africans to learn to read and write or fraternizing with them. Also the Church, as Bennett (1975:73) states was "an integral part of the governing mechanism" and thus, a part of the machinery of control. It was directly involved in upholding the law, buying and selling enslaved Africans and teaching doctrines supportive of the subordination and dehumanization of Africans.

A fourth aspect of the machinery of control was the use of politically divisive strategies to split consciousness and disrupt and deny unity among enslaved Africans. These included strategies to develop "class" or rather stratum divisions among enslaved Africans who worked in the house, yard and field and to develop a collaborator corps that spanned all strata and was used to stifle dissent, spread disinformation and mostly nip revolts in the bud.

Finally, the machinery of control included brutal plantation punishments. Stampp (1967:171-191) in his chapter "To Make Them Stand In Fear," lists some of the viciously ingenious ways whites punished Africans who would not accept or broke the laws and rules of the slave systems. Those included: demotions for the house Africans, foremen or drivers to field work; denials of food, clothing, shelter or recreation; splitting up families; imprisonment in private plantation jails; placing in stocks; brandings; whippings; torture; mutilation; and murder. Some of the most heinous and savage punishments were washing wounds in salt, purposely allowing dogs to maul rebels and forcing a person "to eat worms he failed to pick off the tobacco leaves."

None of this is said to shock or indulge in victimization history, but to clearly depict the system as it was. It is also presented to lay the basis for discussing slave resistance. For in depicting in stark detail the obstacles slavery posed to initiative and resistance, one can better appreciate the strength and depth of human will and spirit which led Africans to resist even in the most brutal and controlled situations.

Resistance to Enslavement

African resistance to enslavement began in Africa, as argued above, and continued in America throughout the period of slavery. In spite of works which question the equality or extent of African resistance to slavery, there is ample evidence to demonstrate real and unrelenting resistance to slavery by both enslaved and free African women and men (McIntyre, 1992; Yee, 1992). Given that enslavement threatened and affected even free

Africans and that they were thus constantly defending themselves as well as trying to liberate enslaved Africans, African resistance will be treated as a single process, even though more stress will be placed on the resistance activities of the enslaved. There are many works which discuss and analyze various forms for resistance, but no single volume deals thoroughly or extensively with all the ones listed below (Aptheker, 1968, 1943; Mullin, 1972; Price, 1973; Sorin, 1973; Quarles, 1969; Genovese, 1981). But the problem and truth are not that African Americans resisted less, but rather that interpretations of their resistance were less critical and often failed to take into consideration the different circumstances and variables involved. Thus, their comparative analyses were deficient and could not but make Black resistance in the U.S. look likewise.

Variables to take in account when comparing African resistance in the U.S. with African resistance in other societies in the Western hemisphere are: 1) the smaller population size; 2) the existence of less nearby unsettled regions for Maroon or independent societies of escaped Africans; 3) the isolated character of the U.S. plantations which hampered organized unified efforts; 4) the harsh winters which made survival maroon societies more difficult to maintain as opposed to tropical areas where food and shelter were less a problem; 5) the drastic decline of importation of large numbers of new Africans after 1807 with the federal prohibition of the slave trade, thus depriving enslaved Africans of a vital source of revitalization and rebellion; 6) the greater balance between the sexes and division into family units in the U.S. which often dampened male rebellion and flight in consideration for their family; and finally 7) the pervasive severity of the system which was not content to dominate physically but engaged in the most brutal and racist deculturalization process in the Western hemisphere. This process, as shown above, did not destroy all culture or cultural resistance, but joined to the fact of reduced and halted revitalization from newly imported Africans, the toll it took was significant.

Still, evidence reveals that resistance among African Americans was strong and continuous. But given the arguments surrounding resistance, it is necessary to define it as a preface to discussion of its forms. Resistance here then can be defined as any and all personal and collective acts designed to: 1) deny support to, challenge or overturn the established order; 2) deny, diminish or eliminate its hold; 3) force changes in its structure and functioning and/or; 4) escape its control and jurisdiction. From this definition and available evidence, free and enslaved Africans engaged in five basic forms of resistance to slavery: 1) cultural; 2) day-to-day; 3) abolitionism, 4) emigrationism, and 5) armed struggle.

Cultural Resistance.   Undoubtedly the most impressive and inclusive book on cultural resistance by enslaved Africans is Blassingame's *The Slave Community*. In this work Blassingame (1979:6) argues that the personality and initiative of the African in slavery was determined not simply by the impositions of the slave holder, "but rather the interaction between certain universal elements of West African culture, the institutionalized demands of plantation life, the process or enslavement and (the African's) creative response to enslavement."

Among the forms of cultural resistance, Blassingame lists the following: 1) cultural retention and synthesis; 2) cultural creation; 3) maintenance and development of a family against all odds. Blassingame observes that most distinctive survivals or retentions are dances, moral narratives, music, magic and language patterns and spiritual beliefs (Holloway, 1990; Webber, 1978). Synthesis took place in these same areas especially in religion and music where, as Blassingame (1979:20-21) notes, "in the process of acculturation, the slaves made European forms serve African functions."

Cultural creation was a form of cultural resistance in that the European sought not only to destroy the African's past but to limit and control his/her future. But the Africans carved out space for themselves wherever and whenever they could and proved that "however oppressive or dehumanizing the plantation was, the struggle for survival was not severed enough to crush the slave's creative instincts" (Blassingame, 1979:105).

A third form of cultural resistance was building and maintaining the African family against all odds (White, 1991; Jacobs, 1987; Jones, 1985; Gutman, 1976). The slaveholder's sexual abuse of African women, his division and selling of family members, his breeding practices, and the denial and restriction of the African man's ability to protect, provide for and exercise authority in his family, all militated against a viable and durable Black family. Yet not only did the Black family survive, but it developed and performed the basic functions of socialization and care all families provide. However, it was not only "an important buffer (and) refuge from the rigors of slavery," but also a space where values of resistance were taught, where the trust needed for successful resistance was found and where active support for resistance was often available (Blassingame 1979:191).

Day-to-Day Resistance. Most literature on resistance to slavery focuses on day-to-day resistance as the definitive form but as this section shows, there were equally important other forms which deserve critical study. Day-to-Day resistance was, however, very important to the resistance process (Bauer and Bauer, 1942). Its regularity and pervasiveness are suggested by the category used to define it, i.e., "day-to-day." This form of resistance reflects the daily refusal and challenge with which Africans confronted the enslavement system and include sabotage, i.e., breaking tools and destroying crops, shamming illness or ignorance, taking property, spontaneous and planned strikes, work slow-downs, self-mutilation, arson, attacks on whites and poisoning of slaveholders and their families. Also, this form included suicide and infanticide which was designed to prevent life in enslavement of both parents and children and then deny the slaveholder both the profit and the perverse pleasure of domination and commerce of enslaved persons. A final form of day-to-day resistance was flight. Although many writers list flight as distinct from day-to-day resistance, I included it because of its regularity and the daily preoccupation with it (Mullin, 1972). All these forms, however, not only prove the real and unrelenting daily presence of resistance, but also disproves the image of the docile slave that Phillips (1963) and Elkins (1966) contrived.

Abolitionism.   This form of resistance includes all efforts dedicated to abolishing slavery conducted by both free Africans and formerly enslaved Africans like Harriet Tubman, Frederick Douglass and Sojourner Truth, Maria Stewart, William Wells Brown, Ellen and William Craft and others (Yee, 1992; Quarles, 1969).   As early as 1797, African fugitives from enslavement petitioned Congress to consider "our relief as a people." And in 1800, a group of Philadelphian Africans petitioned Congress to revise federal laws concerning the enslavement of Africans and fugitive enslaved Africans and to adopt measures for eventual emancipation. By 1830 free Africans had organized fifty anti-enslavement societies dedicated to abolition of the system of enslavement and aid to enslaved Africans in escaping and to those who escaped or were freed by purchase or other means. They also were founding members of multi-racial anti-enslavement societies, such as the American Anti-Slavery Society and the New England Anti-Slavery Society and were 400 of the 450 original subscribers to William Garrison's famous anti-enslavement paper, the *Liberator* (Quarles, 1969).

The diversity and intensity of the activities of the Black abolitionist are extremely impressive. Among these activities were: 1) fundraising efforts for purchase, aid and legal defense of enslaved Africans and anti-enslavement literature; 2) provision of security forces for defense and anti-enslavement rallies and to prevent kidnappings of fugitive and free Africans by former holders and catchers of enslaved Africans; 3) a massive publication effort including at its height major narratives of enslaved Africans, anti-enslavement books and 17 newspapers, including the first Black paper in the U.S., *Freedom's Journal*, 1827; 4) establishment of a distinguished speakers bureau of both formerly enslaved and free Africans to disseminate information and call for support in the struggle in the U.S., Canada and throughout Europe; 5) boycott efforts against products which though largely unsuccessful were significant as an expression of exhausting all avenues; 6) establishment of legal committees to defend free and enslaved Africans against enslavement and return; 7) establishment of vigilance committees, self-help and mutual aid societies to aid formerly enslaved Africans in adjusting to freedom; and 8) the building and maintenance of the Underground Railroad, a system of freeing, transporting and placing formerly enslaved Africans in the North or Canada.

It is important to stress two of the activities above. First, the publication efforts also included such works as *David Walker's Appeal* (1820) which was a severe and famous criticism of the system of enslavement, a call for revolt by the enslaved Africans and for aid by the free; George Moses Horton's *Hope of Liberty* (1829), and Robert Young's *Ethiopian Manifesto* (1829); Mary Prince's *A West Indian Slave* (1831), Lucy Delaney's *From Darkness Cometh the Light or Struggles for Freedom* (n.d.), Henry Highland Garnet's Address (1843), Frederick Douglass' *Narrative of My Life* (1845); and Linda Brent's *Incidents in the Life of a Slave Girl* (1861) among others. Secondly, the Underground Railroad represented in "a most dramatic way the determination of the abolitionists to destroy slavery" (Franklin, 1974:198). For it was a direct act against the system of enslavement, depriving it of its key units, its objects of labor and inspiring in them thoughts of freedom and a sense of possibility. Both the fear and effectiveness of this underground effort to free enslaved Africans are expressed in a governor of Mississippi's claim that "between 1810 and 1850 the South lost 100,000 slaves valued at more than $30 million" (Franklin, 1974:203).

Although, it had many distinguished "conductors" or group leaders, none was as outstanding in legend and reality as Harriet Tubman (Conrad, 1943). Freeing herself, she also freed her children, her sister and mother and father as well as hundreds of others. With the largest bounty ever on the head of an enslaved African, she went South at least 19 times, defying death and capture, and refusing to let any enslaved African turn back under penalty of death. She was also an excellent lecturer and raised funds for the cause, setting an example of the determination of the enslaved to be free and their dedication to freeing others they had left behind. Moreover, as Franklin and Moss (1988:170) report, Tubman was so dedicated to the struggle for freedom that she "would take several months off whenever she was running low in funds and hire herself out as a domestic servant in order to raise money for conveying (enslaved Africans) to freedom."

　　　　Also, it is important to stress the role of the numerous Black women abolitionists who often were not given due recognition and credit for their work. Yee (1992) offers a valuable portrait of Black women who gave their lives to the cause of freedom. Confronting both the racism of the white women's movement and the sexism of the abolitionist movement they nevertheless worked for freedom with untiring energy (Foster, 1990; Bernard, 1990; Billington, 1981, Richardson, 1987). Explaining this focus on freedom and struggle, Frances Watkins Harper noted in 1852 that the work of abolitionism was an urgent and collective one. In a word, she said "the condition of our people, the wants of our children, and the welfare our own race demand the aid of every helping hand" (quoted in Sterling, 1984:159). Binding together in networks of friendship and sisterhood, they organized politically, lectured and taught and engaged in a myriad of activities that abolitionism required and encouraged. They also established models of sisterhood and struggle which informed and inspired subsequent women and men activists.

Emigrationism.   Another key form of African resistance to slavery was emigrationism, the push to emigrate back to Africa or go elsewhere where Africans could be free and self-determining. As early as 1773, a group of slaves in Massachusetts petitioned colonial officials for permission to work in order to

earn money for transportation to "some part of the coast of
Africa where we propose a settlement" (Aptheker, 1951:8). Also,
in 1787, "a group of eighty Boston Blacks "petitioned the state
legislature to assist them in getting to Africa, providing them
money to pay passage and buy land: (Quarles, 1976:96). These
Africans were members of the African Society which was
dedicated to encouraging emigration to establish a self-determining, self-reliant African nation on the West Coast of Africa. Paul
Cuffee, a Black Quaker, was also one of the early advocates of
emigrationism and used his own money to repatriate 38 Africans
to Sierra Leone in 1815. He also petitioned the U.S. President
and Congress for aid in this project in 1814 but to no avail. It is
in light of this that he used his own money and urged others to
help to repatriate as many Africans as he could before he died
in 1871.

In 1817 the Negro Convention Movement was organized
in Philadelphia and became in time a source for the ardent
advocacy of emigrationism. The Convention Movement was
abolitionist and emigrationist and though it focused on sending
Blacks to Canada, at an 1854 convention, it met to consider
emigration to other areas including Africa, the Caribbean and
Central America. Some of its best known members were Martin
Delaney, who argued for the indispensability of Black nation-
hood; James Holly, who stressed the need to go to Haiti and
develop it; and Daniel Payne and Alexander Crummell, giants of
the African Methodist Episcopal Church.

Although only some members of the Convention Movement advocated emigrationism, all of them opposed the colonization schemes of the American Colonization Society. This was
essentially a white initiated and dominated organization which
had supported the founding of Liberia and advocated that all
Blacks including free Blacks return to Africa. The free Africans
opposed this wholesale immigration for four basic reasons: 1)
they saw it as a way to get rid of free Blacks to better secure
slavery; 2) they considered it their duty to stay and fight for
emancipation; 3) they assumed it would give weight to the

arguments of Black inferiority and inability to cope with "civiliza-tion;" and 4) they reasoned that they were as much Americans as whites in terms of their contribution and birth. Given these strong positions and fear of emigrationist sentiments being manipulated by racists wanting to get rid of all Blacks, emigra-tionism lost much of its appeal and appeared strongest at times of extreme oppression and anti-Black agitation.

Armed Resistance.   Obviously, the ultimate criticism of and resistance to a society is armed action against it. And enslaved Africans engaged in this form of resistance not only in the U.S. but also on the disease-ridden death ships on which they were being transported here. Although much of the literature on armed resistance focuses on revolts, there were other forms (Aptheker, 1943; Carroll, 1938; Genovese, 1981). In addition to revolts, four other basic forms stand out: ship mutinies; guerilla warfare, Afro-Mexican alliance and struggle, and Afro-Native American alliance and struggle.

Over 250 revolts are recorded in the U.S., but only a few have been researched and written on at length. Among the most notable and most written on are: 1) the New York City Revolt in 1712; 2) the Stono, South Carolina revolt in 1739; 3) the southern Louisiana revolt in 1811; 4) the Nat Turner revolt in 1831. In addition, two planned revolts or conspiracies are also well-written about and well-discussed, i.e., the Gabriel Prosser conspiracy in 1800 and the Denmark Vesey conspiracy in 1822.

The importance of these and other revolts or attempted revolts lies not so much in their military effectiveness, for a revolt by definition is an unsuccessful revolution, i.e., an unsuc-cessful armed uprising which does not end in seizure of state power. Rather their significance lies in: 1) what is revealed about the rebels, especially their leaders; 2) the chilling effect they had on the slaveholders; and 3) the effect they had on the other enslaved Africans and eventually their descendants.

The major revolts reveal rebel leaders conscious of and prone toward use of religion as an instrument of unity and struggle. Both historical African religion and Africanized Christianity were used to call the rebels to arms, to justify the moral right to rebellion and freedom, and steel them against overwhelming odds. Moreover, the rebel leaders, especially Prosser, Vesey and Turner, were aware of and sought to use current political realities to their advantage. Prosser expected French help in his struggle; Vesey looked to Haiti for inspiration and support, and Turner saw in the internal debates on slavery a good omen reinforced by the religio-political visions he had of war and liberation. Each, having taught himself to read and write, kept up with the news and used the concepts and arguments for freedom and rights in the Declaration of Independence, the Constitution and the Rights of Man, demonstrating a grasp of the ideologies of the Age of Revolution. Finally, one is struck by the dedication, determination and audaciousness of these rebels, risking all to be free even though being as knowledgeable as they were, they knew the overwhelming odds. Given these odds, as Genovese (1981:50) notes, "only the most heroic souls, even as measured by the highest standards of revolutionary self sacrifice could contemplate such a course..."

The effect those rebels and revolts had on whites is clear from the record. The reactions of the slaveholders and other whites were invariably reflective of bloodthirsty hysteria. The bloodletting they engaged in and the stringent laws they passed after each revolt showed their fear and tended to erode their contrived image of invincibility. Often they imagined revolts and conspiracies where there were none, showing a respect for Blacks they would never admit and even many historians fail to observe. Thus, in spite of their writings about the docile, happy enslaved African, they could not easily deny their own deaths at the hands of African rebels. They could and did often hide these realities, but they knew them and were thus forced to face the constant fact and threat of revolt throughout slavery. What Franklin (1974:160) noted about the result of the Prosser conspiracy can be said of other conspiracies and revolts, "The large numbers (at least a thousand), together with the disregard the slaves seemed

to have for their own lives caused the whites to shudder."
Moreover, "the 'high ground' they took in maintaining silence
added to the *stark terror of the situation*" (emphasis mine).

The effect these rebels and revolts had on the other
enslaved Africans was strong and positive. Although some may
argue that their capture, death and lack of success discouraged
other enslaved Africans, this is only partly true. For as some
were discouraged, as in the case of revolts of the enslaved
throughout the world and throughout history, many were also
encouraged by the audaciousness and determination shown by
the rebels. One cannot but be impressed by the rebels'
willingness to risk their lives and those of their loved ones
against such overwhelming odds. One is also unavoidably
impressed by the political commitment and political awareness of
an enslaved African in 1800 slaveholding America, informing his
captors who asked what he had to say during the "trial" that:

> I have nothing more to offer than what General Washington
> would have had to offer, had he been taken by the British
> officers and put to trial by them. I have ventured my life in
> endeavoring to obtain the liberty of my countrymen, and am
> a willing sacrifice to their cause; and I ask a favour, that I may
> be immediately led to execution. I know that you have
> predetermined to shed my blood. Why then all this mockery
> of a trial?

The witnesses to this bold and well-presented statement and
stand were not only the captors but other enslaved Africans who
undoubtedly felt admiration and respect.

Nat Turner reports an exchange between himself and a
new comer to his group of rebels which indicates a similar
political commitment to the freedom struggle. He reports that
he:

> ...asked Will (the newcomer) how he came there? He
> answered (that) his life was worth no more than others, and
> his liberty as dear to him. I asked him if he meant to obtain
> it? He said he would or lose his life.

Again, this commitment was recognized and respected by other enslaved Africans. A strong evidence of this recognition and respect is found in the following popular song praising Nat Turner and noting the vulnerability of the slaveholder and slave system:

> You mought be rich as cream
> And drive you coach and four-horse team.
> But you can't keep de world from moverin' round
> Nor Nat Turner from gainin ground.
> And your name it mought be Caesar sure.
> And got you cannon can shoot a mile or more,
> But you can't keep de world from moverin' round
> Nor Nat Turner from gaining ground.
> (Quoted in Stuckey: 1973:141).

It is this legacy also which has: 1) inspired the descendants of the once enslaved Africans, 2) negated the lies their oppressors have told them about their foreparents' resistance, 3) taught possibilities of struggle and the strength to endure and prevail based on historical precedence and models; and 5) demonstrated to the enslavers, the enslaved Africans, their descendants, and the world, the impossibility of destroying the will and thrust of African peoples to resist and be free.

Ship mutinies constituted a second form of armed struggle to slavery. (Harding, 1981:Chapter 1). These struggles also stand out for overcoming the obstacles placed in their way to prevent them. Greene (1944:347) reports that "every possible precaution was taken to prevent the slaves from revolting." Not only were the crews well armed with canons, guns and knives, but guards stood on constant watch. Also the enslaved Africans -- men, women and children -- were chained in compartments only three feet three inches high and sometimes no more than 18 inches to prevent their sitting erect. Forced to lie spoon fashion to increase carrying capacity and prevent any defiance, the enslaved Africans often were rubbed raw by rolling ships, caught all kinds of diseases and died of suffocation.

But in spite of this oppressive and restrictive Middle Passage ride, the enslaved Africans, although weakened by confinement and ship-contracted disease, often rebelled and attempted to seize the ship and return to Africa. From evidence, ship mutinies seemed to have been more successful than revolts on land. Among the many successful mutinies were those on the Little George (1730), the Jolly Bachelor (1740) and the Amistad (1839). In the case of the Little George, the ship had sailed from the Guinea Coast in 1730 with ninety-six enslaved Africans. Freeing themselves from shackles, they put the crew to flight in the cabin below. They guided the ship into Sierra Leone River, removed all the women and children and left the ship. The Jolly Bachelor which was carrying captives down the Sierra Leone River in 1740 was attacked and captured by Africans who freed the enslaved Africans and stripped the ship of its sails and rigging and then left ship.

Perhaps the most famous ship mutiny in African American history, however, is the Amistad mutiny in 1839. In this mutiny, a group of Africans, led by Joseph Cinque, an African prince, seized the ship, killed their captors and attempted to return to Africa. Intercepted by a U.S. naval vessel, they were captured and brought to trial. Abolitionists hired John Quincy Adams to defend them and they were freed and allowed to return to Africa. Again, this form of armed resistance proves the will and spirit to be free among enslaved Africans and contributes definitively to an important legacy.

A third form of armed resistance to enslavement was guerrilla warfare conducted by members of Maroon or independent communities. Although attention and credit have been given to Maroon societies and struggles in other parts of the Western Hemisphere, comparatively little has been written on Maroon societies and warfare in the U.S. (Price, 1973; Aptheker, 1968; Mullin, 1972).

There is evidence of the establishment of at least fifty Maroon communities between 1672-1864 with varying life-spans. These communities existed in the forest, mountain and swampy

regions of several states, i.e., Virginia, North Carolina, South
Carolina, Georgia, Louisiana, Mississippi, Alabama and Florida.
However, the most notable and largest communities existed in
the Dismal Swamp, along the Virginia-North Carolina border
and in Florida in union with the Seminole Native Americans
which will be discussed under Afro-Native American alliance and
struggle. These Maroons sought in varying ways to duplicate the
African societies from which they came. They built communal
agricultural societies, raised crops and animals and fowl,
maintained families with African kinship patterns and even
engaged in trade with whites in certain areas.

The significance of the Maroon communities as a source
of resistance expressed itself on five basic levels. First, they
represented a reality and possibility of self-determination and
power to other enslaved Africans. Both their existence and their
victories against search-and-destroy expeditions and successful
attacks on plantations reaffirmed this reality and possibility.
Secondly, they were sources of asylum for fugitives daring enough
to escape and reach them. Thirdly, they were bases from which
to launch attacks on plantations for supplies or in retaliation and
thus, on the slave system itself, even if only in a minor and
isolated way. Fourthly, they often raided plantations to free
enslaved Africans. Fifthly, they often provided leadership and
inspiration for revolts among the enslaved. Thus, although
isolation, limited means of subsistence and regular search-destroy
measures reduced the Maroon communities' capacity to expand
and consolidate and wage a more effective guerilla warfare, the
contribution they did make to the overall process and legacy of
resistance stands out and must be recognized and respected.

Afro-Mexican alliance and struggle offers a fourth form
of armed resistance by Africans against enslavement. Enslaved
Africans began to come to Mexico early in the 1800's to seek
freedom. This was due to three basic reasons. First, Mexico was
close to the South, especially close to Texas, Louisiana and
Florida from which most came. Secondly, local Mexicans would
often protect them from pursuing Anglos whom they resented or

hated. Thirdly, the Mexican government was favorable toward
enslaved Africans, having abolished slavery in 1824 and put it in
the Constitution in 1857, the same year the U.S. Supreme Court
ruled in the *Dred Scott* decision that Blacks had no rights whites
were bound to respect (Schwartz, 1975).

      Mexico's antislavery position was both humanitarian and
political. In its war with Spain, it had raised the cry of freedom
for all and took it seriously. In terms of its political position, it
saw Africans as barriers against Anglo invasion and
encroachment on their lands. Thus, they offered Africans and
Native Americans land on the border in states such as
Tamaulipas and Coahuila where Blacks who have not totally
merged with the indigenous population still live today. In the
early 1850's hundreds of Seminoles (Afro-Native Americans)
migrated from Oklahoma to Coahuila forming military colonies
and buffers against Anglo soldiers and slave-raiders. Other
Blacks received land in the state of Vera Cruz for development
and were exempted from all taxes and from military service,
barring foreign invasions.

      A fifth and final form of armed resistance by enslaved
Africans to enslavement was Afro-Native American alliances and
struggle (Foster, 1935; Littlefield, 1977; Bennett, 1975). Africans
and Native Americans have a close history in community and
struggle which reaches back to the holocaust of enslavement and
the common ground they found first in struggle (hooks, 1992;
Katz, 1986; Forbes, 1980). One of the earliest known examples
of Africans and Native Americans allied in resistance and war
was in an uprising in Hartford, Connecticut in 1657 (Bennett,
1975:89). From 1657 on, Bennett reports a continuous series of
plots, insurrections and armed actions against Europeans by
Afro-Native American joint action. In fact, in the New York
City rebellion of 1712, Native Americans fought jointly with
Africans. These alliances and joint actions were rooted in their
association as fellow slaves, their common mistreatment by the
European, their intermixture and need to defend themselves
from the threat of conquest and enslavement.

Easily, the most clear and impressive example of Afro-Native American alliance is the Afro-Seminole Alliance in Florida. In no other Native American nation or ethnic group were Africans treated with such deference and did they rise to such leadership roles in politics and war. As early as 1738, enslaved Africans began to regularly escape from South Carolina taking refuge among the Creeks or Seminoles in Florida.

The Seminoles were a group of Creeks whose name in Creek means runaways and who in 1750 seceded from the Creek Nation and went to a territory in Florida. There they settled near African Maroons and began to build a strong bond. In fact, it can be argued that the Seminole Nation developed early into an Afro-Native American nation controlled and run by Africans. Even though Porter (1932:326) refers to enslavement among the Seminoles, he has to admit that "not only were the Seminole slaves not slaves in the usual sense of the word; they might even lay claim to being the *true rulers of the nation*" (emphasis mine). Porter attributes this rise to political leadership by Africans among the Seminole to four basic factors: 1) Africans' knowledge of the European and his culture and thus their value in war and peace exchanges; 2) their indispensability as negotiators, guides and interpreters, often speaking French, Spanish and English; 3) their agricultural skills and thus value in creating and sustaining agricultural economies; 4) their courage and skill in war. Therefore, he concludes, the Africans were valued as allies and associates and accepted as equals and later, leaders in war and politics.

Moreover, in the Seminole wars, Africans were both generals and often most of the soldiers. They fought fiercely, won many victories and would not often surrender because of the certainty of re-enslavement. They also used their key political and military positions in the Seminole Nation to refuse emigration to Oklahoma Territory suggested by the U.S. Government and prolonged the struggle to avoid re-enslavement and maintain self-determination. This is why Gen. Jessup, a U.S. commander in the war, argued that Seminole wars were "an (African) not a

(Native American) war which if not quickly put down would affect the enslaved African population."

Civil War and Reconstruction

The road to Civil War was most definitively laid in the stormy 1850's (Franklin, 1974:208ff). In this decade, a series of events made war almost inevitable. First, was the passage of the 1850 Fugitive Slave Law which made the fugitive guilty until proven innocent, denied his/her testimony and was retroactive. It gave the abolitionists another opportunity to expose the viciousness and recalcitrance of slaveholders and slavery advocates. Secondly, in 1854 Congress passed the Kansas-Nebraska Act which repealed the Missouri Compromise of 1850 which prohibited slavery in the Kansas-Nebraska Territory. This increased the bloody struggle in the territory and foreshadowed larger battles. Thirdly, the U.S. Supreme Court ruled in the Dred Scott case (1857) that neither free nor enslaved Africans were citizens and had no rights whites were bound to respect. Fourthly, John Brown, a white radical abolitionist attacked Harper's Ferry in 1859 to gain arms for at least 500 enslaved Africans and wage a war in the South. Although Black abolitionists like Frederick Douglass and Harriet Tubman thought correctly that this move was premature and unwise, he became a martyr of the abolitionist movement and foreshadowed the coming war. The final straw came with the election of Abraham Lincoln whom the South hated and whose election they saw as an abolitionist vote.

Civil War. The Civil War began with the Confederate attack on Fort Sumner, S.C. in April 1861. Although many factors can be cited as causes of the Civil War, the question of enslavement and by extension the question of the future of Africans in America stand at the core of its causes. The Civil War is important in African American history not only because it led to their emancipation, but even more important, because they fought heroically and in great numbers in the war and played other significant roles in it. As Quarles (1969:296) states, African Americans "took stock in the adage that they who would be free must themselves strike the blow." Thus, they took up arms and became self-conscious agents of their own liberation.

At first the whites resisted the idea of Blacks serving in the army, feeling that: 1) to call and depend on Blacks implied their inadequacies; 2) arming Blacks meant arming potential rebels; 3) serving in the armed forces would change the social attitude and status of Blacks and thus pose a problem for white rule and power. They also pretended to doubt the fighting qualities of Blacks, but this was irrational and based more on racist ego-needs than evidence as the war would prove. By the summer of 1862, after a series of military defeats by Union forces, Congress passed the Confiscation Act and Militia Act which opened the way for free and freed Africans to aid the war effort. Moreover, Lincoln, seeing the indispensability of African American participation in the war, if it were to be won, issued in the same year the Emancipation Proclamation.

The Proclamation was not a blanket declaration of freedom for all enslaved Africans, only for enslaved Africans in states and parts of states in rebellion against the U.S. government. Loyal slave states like Missouri, Kentucky, Maryland and Delaware were exempt. Moreover, it did not grant freedom; it only "declared" it--a declaration totally unenforceable. For the proclamation was declaring freedom for enslaved Africans in the Confederacy, a land which had already rejected U.S. jurisdiction and was at war with it to defend its decision. Its value was as a propaganda document to appease abolitionists and Radical Republicans, give the war the moral character it lacked and contribute further to the rebellion and flight among enslaved Africans which had already reached a high level (Quarles, 1953:117).

Africans, anxious to fight for freedom, respect and better status and role in society, enlisted in large numbers and served in various capacities. In addition to serving as regular soldiers and sailors, they served as guides, scouts, intelligence agents, engineers, nurses, surgeons, chaplains, construction workers, teamsters, cooks, carpenters, miners, farmers, commandos and recruiters. An estimated 186,000 Africans participated as soldiers and 29,000 as sailors accounting for 25% of U.S. sailors. The real number of participants is probably much higher but was disguised by many mulattos being registered as whites. Moreover, Blacks served in every theater of operations, fought in 449 engagements, thirty-nine of which were major battles and won seventeen Congressional Medals of Honor on land and four on sea. These achievements were made in spite of vicious racism exhibited in treatment, pay and time differentials, poor equipment, bad medical care, excess fatigue details, wreckless and hasty assignments and the no-quarter policy of the South against Black soldiers.

The Civil War ended April 9, 1865 with the surrender of Gen. Robert E. Lee to Gen. Ulysses S. Grant. The end of the war and the Union victory was important to both African Americans and the nation as a whole. For African Americans, it was an end to slavery which had lasted almost 250 years. Secondly, it represented a victory won only as a result of their entry and heroic participation in the struggle which was not only to free them but win respect and a new status in society. Thirdly, it meant the beginning of a new struggle to secure economic and political rights which did not automatically come with emancipation. For the nation, the victory meant the federal government had clearly established its sovereignty over the states, freed the South from a morally indefensible and politically and economically backward system and thus opened for the South and the nation a new era of economic growth and political change -- as well as the problems which accompanied this process.

Reconstruction. The period of Reconstruction (1865-1877) represented for African Americans "the best of times and the worst of times." It was a time of great leaps forward and hope and great disappointment and betrayal (Logan, 1954). For the

U.S., it represented a time of great possibility to realize its ideals of freedom, justice and equality for all. But after a strong start it betrayed its own ideals and failed in solving the problems the post-war period posed, i.e., the problems of Reconstruction. These problems were essentially: 1) rebuilding the South's economy on the basis of free labor and its industrialization and reintegration in the national economy; 2) politically subduing and transforming the South; and 3) integration of the freed Africans into the social fabric, especially in the South and protecting them from re-enslavement, exploitation and abuse. Out of these problems, only the reintegration of the South economically and politically were really achieved. This took place on the South's own terms and included the betrayal and sacrifice of the African American (Harding, 1981).

However, early events seemed to suggest an alternative outcome. The Freedman's Bureau was established by Congress in 1865 to guide and protect the freed Africans. It was to: 1) set up schools for them; 2) provide medical services, 3) write, supervise and enforce their contracts; 4) manage, lease and sell them confiscated and abandoned lands; 5) resettle them; and 6) provide them legal assistance and protection. Moreover, Congress passed three cornerstone Amendments directed toward integration of Blacks in the social fabric on the basis of equality, i.e., the Thirteenth, Fourteenth and Fifteenth Amendments. Essentially, the Thirteenth freed them; the Fourteenth made them citizens, and the Fifteenth gave them the right to vote. Also, Congress passed the 1866 Civil Rights Act (CRA) declaring Blacks citizens again; the 1870 Civil Rights Act to expand and strengthen the 1866 CRA; and the 1871 CRA which sought to establish equal rights in the public facilities and jury duties. Congress also passed the 1871 Enforcement Act which outlawed white terrorist societies like the Ku Klux Klan.

However, economically, Congress did not give Blacks the support they needed and they were essentially reintegrated back into the southern economy under semi-enslaved conditions as sharecroppers. Whites, never accepting the freedom and equality of African Americans, passed Black Codes, patterned after the antebellum Slave Codes which made "the control of Blacks by white employers...about as great as that which slaveholders exercised" (Franklin, 1974:241). In spite of the general assumption among Blacks that the federal government would give them lots of forty acres, and the tacit encouragement given this assumption by the creation of the Freedman's Bureau, the government never did, thus posing one of the main problems of Black economic adjustment. For with no land of their own, the majority of freed Africans slowly but inevitably returned to the plantation more or less at the mercy of their employers.

Moreover, those who did go to urban areas were met with crippling discrimination and severe exploitation. Black carpenters, bricklayers, painters, blacksmiths and other skilled workers were strongly opposed by white artisans in their employment efforts. Skilled and unskilled workers were denied union membership and white employers often used Blacks to break union strikes, thus, splitting the labor movement and casting Blacks as essentially strikebreakers and ones who would work for the lowest wages. In 1869 African Americans created two unions, the National Labor Convention of Colored Men and the National Negro Labor Union, and sought affiliation with white labor unions, but to no avail. By 1874, due to this exclusion and other factors, these Black labor union thrusts were effectively ended.

The Reconstruction period, however, did provide some political gains for African Americans although they were short-lived. During this period 22 African Americans served in Congress. Two served in the Senate, Hiram Revels and Blanche K. Bruce, both from Mississippi, and 20 served in the House. In spite of the racist claims that they were uneducated, ten had gone to college and five had degrees. Moreover, most had some political experience before going to Congress as delegates to constitutional conventions and as local and state officials and state senators and representatives. Although African American legislators were unable to pass much legislation in Congress, at the state levels they were able to achieve much more. They expanded suffrage, instituted free public education, improved the tax system, reorganized the judicial system and repealed imprisonment for debt laws as well as negative labor laws of 1865 and 1866 which were part of the Black Codes.

Eventually, however, the efforts to reconstruct the life of the African American and the South on the basis of freedom, justice and equality, failed for several reasons. (Harding, 1981:Chapter 16). These included: 1) the failure of the federal government to give Blacks land and equipment, thus forcing them into semi-enslaved status; 2) the return of Southerners to status of respect represented by the repeal of the loyalty oath requirement for re-entering national political life; 3) the rise of the white terrorist societies like the KKK and the Camelias in spite of the 1870 and 1871 laws against such societies; 4) the Supreme Court's eroding constitutional and legislative gains for Blacks through rulings favorable to the South; 5) the disintegration of the old coalition of abolitionists, Radical Republicans and northern industrialist through fatigue, retirement, disenchantment and the push for social peace in the South which would allow economic growth; and finally, 6) the Hayes-Tilden Compromise in 1877 which saw President Hayes grant the South federal troop withdrawal, assistance in internal improvements and better representation in Congress for its electoral votes. In 1878, federal troops were withdrawn leaving Blacks at the mercy of racist governments and terrorist societies. In 1894 federal marshals were withdrawn and in 1896 the Supreme Court issued its *Plessy v. Ferguson* decision, the "separate but equal" doctrine that lasted until 1954 with the *Brown v. the Board of Education* decision.

The Great Migrations and Urbanization

The end of the Civil War brought migrations in three basic directions, i.e., to the southern cities, southwestward to Arkansas, Oklahoma, Texas and Kansas and to the northern cities. The Kansas migration in 1879 was the largest southwest movement and included over 7,000 Blacks going to Kansas with lesser numbers to Missouri, Iowa and Nebraska. But the greatest migrations were to the northern and southern cities -- and between 1890 -- 1910, the urbanization of Blacks moved from 20 to 27 percent. At first the southern cities received the majority of Black migrants, but by the 1900's the tide was turning in favor of the northern cities. Thus, by 1903 DuBois noted that "the most significant economic change among (Blacks) in the last ten or twenty years had been their influx into northern cities."

The Great Migration of the World War I era was due to several factors. First, it was due to the dissatisfaction with and determination to escape the oppressive and exploitative race relations in the South. Secondly, it was prompted by the depressed economic situation in the South which included crop failures, the ravage of the boll weevil and natural disasters like the 1915 floods in Alabama and Mississippi which had disastrous results on the agricultural economies. A third factor was the growth of industry in the North, especially with increased semi-skilled and unskilled labor demands due to World War I. Fourthly, the world war had cut off immigration from Europe and with it its pool of unskilled laborers and domestic servants. And finally, there were intense efforts by manufacturing companies who sent recruiting agents in the South to solicit Black labor as well as by Black newspapers who induced Blacks to come North for greater opportunities (Quarles, 1969:193-194).

But the North was not the heaven promised. On the contrary, racial violence, discrimination and abuse continued in the North. As Drake and Cayton (1962, Vol. 1:174) noted, the migration led to the rise of the ghetto or "Black Belt," a segregated residential area "whose inhabitants can neither scatter as individuals nor expand as a group..." Moreover, it was defined by its dilapidated houses, overcrowdedness, poor health, high mortality rate, police brutality and other social ills. Secondly, Blacks encountered continued white terrorism and violence evidenced in lynchings and racial riots by whites. In the summer

of 1919, often called the "Red Summer," there were twenty
incidents of white mob violence of riots, against Blacks in the
North and South. Ida B. Wells, a journalist, author and anti-
lynching activist, played an important role in exposing this white
terrorism and unmasking the self-serving sexual ideologies of
white racists (Carby, 1987:110ff; Duster, 1970).   In her
autobiography, *Crusade for Justice* she recounts in detail the
vicious practices of lynching and her tireless crusade against it
under daily threat to her life. Her pamphlets against lynching,
Southern Horror (1892), *Red Record* (1895) and *Mob Rule in New
Orleans* (1900) were important in providing both statistical and
literary witness to the terror and a critical analysis of race and
gender relations in the U.S. at this time. In the first year of the
century, there were a hundred lynchings and by 1914, there were
more than 1,100. Although most occurred in the South, as with
the riots, the North had its share. Finally, the Black migrant met
worsening conditions of the labor market.   After the war,
employment declined rapidly due to the decrease in government
contracts with industry, the return of 4,500,000 soldiers and
traditional discrimination which made Blacks the "last hired and
first fired."

Organization Against Injustice

To aid in readjustment and fight discrimination, the
Niagara Movement, the NAACP, the Urban League and the
Black Woman's Club Movement and other organizations were
formed. The Niagara Movement was formed in 1905 by W.E.B.
DuBois and others to fight against injustice. It demanded the
right to justice, the vote, education, the abolition of Jim Crow,
equal treatment in the armed forces and enforcement of the
13th, 14th and 15th amendments. This militant organization gave
way to the National Association for the Advancement of Colored
People which was formed by 1909 by African Americans and
white liberals.   The NAACP, which absorbed many of the
Niagara Movement's members including W.E.B. DuBois, adopted

much of the Movement's philosophy but was not as militant, due to the whites that controlled its executive board. In fact, DuBois was the only African American among its original executive officers. However, the NAACP went on to launch and win effective campaigns against lynching and Jim Crowism, and to secure the vote. Also, the Urban League was founded in 1911 and dedicated itself to social welfare programs. Like the NAACP, white liberals controlled it and devoted itself to social service programs for jobs, housing, recreation facilities and health clinics, etc., shunning politics and the social struggles of African Americans.

Although Black women served in each of the above organizations, they saw a need to also build a Black Woman's Club Movement to add extra strength to the struggle for justice. Between 1892-1894, Black women began to organize clubs throughout the country to deal with the various problems confronting them and all Black people (Neverdon-Morton, 1989; Carby, 1987; Giddings, 1984). In 1895, the First National Conference of the Colored Women of America convened and established the National Association of Colored Women (NACW) with Mary Church Terrell as its first president. The concerns of the NACW can be summed up in its model "Lifting as we climb" and included issues of: 1) sexual abuse and attacks on the moral character of the Black woman; 2) lynching of Black men, women and children; 3) education; 4) inadequate health care; 5) lack of child care services; and 6) poverty.

Within twenty years of its founding, NACW represented over 1,000 clubs and 50,000 Black women. Some of the major figures in this movement were Mary Church Terrell, Ida B. Wells-Barnett, Anna Julia Cooper, Charlotte Brown, Fannie Barrier Williams, Margaret Murray Washington and Mary McLeod Bethune. As the NACW was losing some of its momentum, its then president, Mary McLeod Bethune, had a vision of a larger and more powerful organization, The National Council of Negro Women (NCNW), which she organized and founded in 1935. "We need an organization to open new doors for our young women (which) when (it) speaks its power will be felt" she proposed (quoted in Giddings, 1984:212). Expressing her commitment to vision and the development of women, she stated "I am interested in women and I believe in their possibilities. We need vision for larger things, for the unfolding and reviewing of worthwhile things" (Giddings, 1984:214). But Bethune was also for the welfare of the masses of Black people and she directed the development of the NCNW toward service to Black people. And she worked tirelessly in the areas of race, women, education and youth (Giddings, 1984:215).

Accommodationism, Confrontation and Black Nationalism

In the wake of the failure of Reconstruction, African Americans were confronted more and more with discrimination and mob violence. By the end of the century, Jim Crowism, the racist system based on the separate-but-equal doctrine and the political, economic and social subordination of Blacks, was firmly in place. Most of the Southern states had passed such discriminatory laws and in 1896 in the *Plessy v. Ferguson* case, the Supreme Court had upheld and enshrined such practices, a ruling that would last until the 1954 Brown Decision. In the areas of politics, economics and justice, African Americans were excluded from voting, jobs and unions, and jury duty. And white terrorist societies rose to ensure such exclusion and subordination.

Moreover, Southern patterns of race relations and racist ideology were shaping public opinion in the North and West. The doctrine of African inferiority was supported by most white anthropologists, historians and political scientists reinterpreted Reconstruction in the interest of the whites. Social Darwinism, which advocated the right and responsibility of the assumed strong to conquer and use the assumed weak for their own more noble ends, not only served as a justification for Blacks subjugation in the U.S., but also for American imperialism against other Third World peoples. In this precarious context, two major leaders rose and were later followed by a third.

Separately and through their ideological struggles with each other they established political tendencies which even today serve as models and points of debate concerning the future and struggle of Blacks in the U.S. These leaders were Booker T. Washington, W.E.B. DuBois and The Hon. Marcus Garvey.

Booker T. Washington.   The career of Booker T. Washington was indisputably an impressive one. Having been born in slavery in Virginia, he rose to national and international fame and was accepted in the North and South as the major Black leader of his time. In 1903, even DuBois (1969:79), his major opposition, was compelled to state that "Easily the most striking thing in the history of the American (Black) since 1876 is the ascendancy of Mr. Booker T. Washington." Washington's base was at Tuskegee where he arrived in 1881 to found a school which would serve as a model of the vocational education he saw as the way for Blacks to raise themselves and gain the respect and tolerance of whites.

Washington's thought and practice were molded and informed by four major factors: 1) his experience in slavery; 2) his education at Hampton Institute; 3) the tasks before him at Tuskegee; and 4) his reading of the socio-historical setting in which he operated. The system of enslavement taught him the viciousness, violence and power of whites; Hampton taught him the need to conciliate whites in order to get necessary resources and stay operating; and his reading of the times brutally suggested that protest in the South was counterproductive and extremely dangerous (Washington, 1968).

The core contentions of Washington's philosophy were advanced in his famous Atlanta Exposition Speech in 1895 (Washington, 1968:218-224). In it he advanced propositions which he would repeat and expand on throughout his life. First, he argued that vocational education was the key to Black economic success and urged Blacks to get into practical occupations such as agriculture, mechanics, commerce, domestic service and the professions. Secondly, he advanced the concept of social separation with economic integration in his famous statement "In all things that are purely social we can be as separate as the fingers, yet one as the hand in all things essential to mutual progress."

Thirdly, Washington suggested Black accommodation to social inequality and disenfranchisement, arguing that "agitation of questions of social equality is the extremist folly" and that not "artificial forcing" but productive labor and business would end discrimination. "No race that has anything to contribute to the markets of the world, " he stated, "is long in any degree ostracized." Fourthly, he asserted the essentiality of Black-white cooperation in social progress with whites as superior benefactors and Blacks as a subordinate pliant work force and the "most patient, faithful, law-abiding and unresentful people."

In later interviews, speeches and writings, Washington expanded on these themes (Thornbrough, 1969). He also argued that economic progress was both a way to and substitute for equality and political rights. Moreover, he stated that economic progress could not only raise Blacks but make "the white man partly dependent on (Blacks) instead of all the dependence being on the other side." Stressing economic self-help and racial solidarity, he urged Blacks to pull themselves up by their own bootstraps and not let grievances blind them to opportunities. Finally, he emphasized the need for moral regeneration of Blacks, i.e., the cultivation of virtues and values which would destroy the slave legacy of laziness, immorality and wastefulness and other vices.

However, Washington's policy of accommodation was contradicted by his private efforts against racism (Meier, 1957). He was deeply involved in the struggle against disenfranchisement and other forms of discrimination. He not only lobbied in the background against disenfranchisement and other forms of discrimination, he also raised money to pay lobbyists and fight court cases against racism. Moreover, he was for Black economic power and built the National Negro Business League to advance Black economic interests. Furthermore, he was an expert politician himself, and in spite of his talk against political participation, ran the Black Republican campaign for Roosevelt and was instrumental in both the appointment and rejection of Blacks in high office and employment throughout the country.

Although Black leaders like DuBois and Monroe Trotter strenuously opposed Washington for his open accommodationism, he nevertheless maintained his power until his death in 1915. Washington's success was obviously rooted in his mastery and manipulation of three major socio-political and economic tendencies, i.e., capitalism, racism and Christianity. His stress on vocational education, pliant industrial and agricultural workers and social peace provided capitalism with its supply of cheap, non-striking and apolitical workers. His stress on separateness, his disinterest in political and civil rights and his promise to be loyal to whites, not compete with them, and start at the bottom, satisfied the demands of racism.

Finally, his emphasis on the need for the Black moral regeneration and putting behind the assumed moral negatives developed in slavery appealed to the Christian mentality. Thus, he spoke to the spirit and motion of the times, much of which was accepted by Blacks as well as whites. For many middle class Blacks had recognized the problems of political participation, accepted literary and property qualifications if equally applied to both races, saw the economic realm as the key area of advancement and advocated self-help, racial solidarity and the cultivation of middle class virtues.

W.E.B. DuBois.   Washington's foremost critic was W.E.B. DuBois, an impressive leader in his own right whose rise to national and international fame was based not on white patronage, but on his own intellectual genius and role as an activist-scholar. DuBois studied at Fisk University and the University of Berlin, received three degrees from Harvard and became in 1895 the first African American to receive a Ph.D. An historian and sociologist, DuBois' doctoral dissertation, *The Suppression of the African Slave Trade*, was the first published work in the Harvard Historical Studies and his *Black Reconstruc-*

tion, a monumental and voluminous work, as well as his *Philadelphia Negro* became classic studies of Blacks.

Washington had been understandably impressed with DuBois' scholarly achievement and at first tried to enlist him as an aid, but intellectual achievement, self-conception as a leader and his opposite political approach to social struggle all militated against such a relationship. In 1903 in his classic work, *Souls of Black Folk*, DuBois (1969) wrote an essay "Of Mr. Booker T. Washington and Others" in which he offered the core points of his opposition to Washington. Through his ideological struggle with Washington, he repeated and expanded on these with the severe and incisive criticism which so characterized his writings.

DuBois said that Washington's leadership was not so original as it was reflective of the times. He called Washington's Atlanta Exposition speech the "Atlanta Compromise," criticized him for silencing his critics in unprincipled ways and trying to maintain a monopoly on Black leadership. He defined three basic kinds of historical Black leadership and response to oppression -- revolt, accommodation, and self-realization and self-development. Nat Turner and David Walker represent the first kind; Washington represented the second; and Frederick Douglass whom he called "the greatest of American (Black) leaders" represented the third.

Washington, DuBois argued, had not only assumed and advocated "the old attitude of adjustment and submission," but in catering to the times, had introduced "a gospel of Work and Money to such an extent as apparently almost complete to overshadow the higher aims of life." Moreover, he criticized Washington for not only catering to triumphant capitalism, but also to Southern racism which demand Black subordination. He cited three basic paradoxes of Washington's program: 1) advocacy of Black business and ownership of property and denunciation of struggles for political rights to defend them: 2) insistence on thrift and self-respect yet counseling "a silent submission to civil inferiority...bound to sap the manhood of any race...;" and 3) advocacy of common schools and industrial

training and disappreciation of institutions of higher learning
from which teachers for his industrial and common schools came.

DuBois rejected Washington's demand that Blacks give
up "political power, insistence on civil rights and higher education." He noted he did not oppose industrial training, only the
exclusive emphasis on it; he did not oppose reconciliation in the
South, only "the industrial slavery and civil death" of Blacks
which it demanded.   And he complimented Washington's
practical achievement in open and behind-the-scenes efforts
against racism and oppression, but he opposed his apologies for
injustice, support of the caste system and opposition to higher
education.

DuBois, however, did not simply oppose Washington, he
offered his own form of confrontation and agitational leadership
(Broderick, 1969; Moon, 1972; Weinberg, 1970). First he argued
for a "Talented Tenth," an intellectual and political vanguard
which would lead Black people to freedom and a higher level of
human life. Secondly, he advocated a multidimensional education which would enable Blacks to grasp, confront and be
effective in society and the world. He abhorred the vulgar
careerism which reduced education to money-making at the
expense of an effective social competence and social commitment. Thirdly, he advocated a cultural nationalism and plural-
ism, which stressed pride in Black heritage and unity yet a full
and effective membership in American society.

Fourthly, DuBois insisted on confrontational activities in
the struggle for social, political and economic rights and gains.
He also saw political rights as the basis for economic opportunities and defense of economic gains. Moreover, he too argued for
self-help and racial solidarity. Fifthly, DuBois advocated Pan-
Africanism and called and presided over four of the five pre-
independence Congresses from 1919 to 1945. He recognized and
advocated the unity and common interests and struggle of all
Africans and the world historical importance of Africa. In his
later years, he went to live in Africa and died in 1963 at the age
of 95 in Ghana working on the *Encyclopedia Africana*. Finally,

DuBois proposed cooperative economics for the community at first and later advocated socialism for the country. In this, he saw socialism as an alternative to capitalism's unequal distribution of wealth, enslavement of labor and reduction of human aspiration to material pursuits.

Marcus Garvey. Born in Jamaica, Marcus Garvey arrived in Harlem in 1916, an ardent Pan-Africanist dedicated to the liberation of Africa and building a nation-state in Africa that would demand the rights and respect of Africans everywhere. He had admired and written to Booker T. Washington and expected to see him when he arrived in the U.S., but Washington died a year earlier. It might seem strange to some that Garvey, the father of modern Black Nationalism, would admire Washington, the assumed paradigm of Tomism. But, as argued earlier, a one-dimensional portrait of Washington is not an accurate one. Garvey admired Washington's stress on social separateness, racial solidarity, economic self-help and self-sufficiency and institution building.

Moreover, Garvey, while condemning whites' denial of Black rights, did not see Blacks' political salvation in the U.S., but in Africa and thus, like Washington, put no real emphasis on political struggles in the U.S. However, he did not reject politics as Washington and he argued that "If Washington had lived he would have had to change his program." For the problem of Black power "must be solved not by the industrial leader only, but by the political and military leaders as well." In a word, the new leader must recognize that the New African "does not seek industrial opportunity alone, but a political voice" (Garvey, 1977, Vol. 1:56).

Garvey and DuBois clashed openly in their struggle for leadership preeminence. Garvey criticized DuBois for a year in his paper *The Negro World* before DuBois responded. He accused DuBois of being equivocal and unvigorous in his criticism of imperialism. Agreeing with A. Phillip Randolph, he argued that DuBois was controlled by the white capitalists on the

NAACP's board. Also, he criticized DuBois' elitism, his theorizing while Garvey was acting, and his focus on integration.

DuBois' first public response to Garvey was in the *Crisis*, his NAACP organ, in December 1920. He called Garvey an "extraordinary leader of men" and acknowledged that Garvey was "essentially an honest and sincere man with a tremendous vision, great dynamic force, stubborn determination and unselfish desire to serve." But he also thought him a "dictatorial, domineering man" and without any real business sense. He also criticized him for introducing the Jamaican Black-mulatto division, alienating the British whom he needed for his international trade, alienating Liberia where he hoped to establish his base and unnecessarily antagonizing and attacking other Black leaders. Eventually, they both began to argue ad hominem, questioning each other's sanity and sincerity.

The source of their conflict was both their different philosophies and their struggle for leadership preeminence. Garvey was a global Pan-Africanist engaged in the practical redemption of Africans everywhere, posing a liberated Africa as a base. DuBois focused on continental Pan-Africanism and stressed continental self-determination. Garvey was an effective mass leader, organizing over six million Blacks (working class and petty bourgeoisie) in the Universal Negro Improvement Association (UNIA), whereas DuBois was elitist and by his own analysis unable to reach the masses. His concept of the Talented Tenth was both positive and problematic. Garvey was a man of action, an institution builder; DuBois was more the theoretician and scholar. Garvey argued for race purity and race first; DuBois was for integration. Finally, Garvey advocated statehood and state power for Blacks while DuBois stressed political participation within the U.S. system.

Garvey, however, advanced a larger strategy for liberation and a higher level of life for Blacks. As the father of modern Black Nationalism, he wrote and spoke extensively on all four emphases of nationalism -- economics, politics, religion and culture -- and thus laid the theoretical bases for all subsequent nationalist assertions.   Likewise, his practice -- politics, organization and institution building -- has served as models for all subsequent practical nationalist thrusts (Garvey, 1977, Vols. I & II).

Economically, he advocated economic autonomy, arguing that "A race that is solely dependent upon others for its economic existence sooner or later dies."   Thus, there is a need for factories, businesses and commerce based on self-help and self-reliance.   Moreover, he saw class struggles and revolution as a fundamental feature in the rise and fall of nations, and argued for checks on corporate ownership to prevent monopoly and the rule of the few at the expense of the masses.

Politically, Garvey posited "Race First" as a principle of theory and practice, i.e., an Afrocentric approach to the definition, defense and development of Black interests. He used nation and race interchangeably and thus argued for a global Pan-Africanism which sought to free "Africa for the Africans at home and abroad."   His Pan-Africanism stressed anti-imperialism, global unity of Blacks and continental liberation and reconstruction. He sought to establish a national power base to defend African interests all over the world, to raise the level of the African masses and return an effective number of Diasporan African pioneers to start and sustain the project. Garvey also advocated armed struggle in the liberation of Africa stating that "any sane man, race or nation that desires freedom must first of all think in terms of blood, " i.e., costly struggle.

On the question of religion, Garvey advocated a race-specific God. It is only human, he stated, to see God through one's own eyes, thus Black people must see God in their own image and interests. He criticized the bankruptcy and hypocrisy of white Christianity, attacking white Christian control of Africa through mass murder and brutality and Christians preaching brotherhood while everywhere killing Third World people. A forerunner of Black liberational theology, he posited the need for religion to be socially rooted and socially relevant. Thus, he posed Jesus as a social reformer, organized and used ceremonies to reinforce nation-building, painted Jesus and Mary Black and posed God as a warrior God whose assertive defense of his rights humans should emulate. Moreover, he gave humans the central role after creation in building the world. "Man is supreme lord of creation," he contended, and in him "lies the power of mastery of all creation."

Finally, Garvey advocated cultural nationalism, a bold redefinition of reality in Black images and interests. This thrust, he contended, should begin with a rescue and reconstruction of Black history, for little can be expected from whites who "have tried to rob the Black man of his proud past." Blacks, he said, "have a beautiful history of their own and none of any other race can truly write it but themselves." Moreover, he urged encouragement of Black authors "who are loyal to the race" and exhibit race pride and severe criticism for those who prostitute their skills for white patrons and allies. Also, he urged an education that was socially relevant, i.e., applicable and inspirational in the struggle of Blacks to free themselves and rebuild the world in their own image and interests. To do this, Garvey called for a Black Vanguard, "men and women who are able to create, originate and improve, and thus make an independent racial contribution to the world and civilization."

Black Science and Inventions

One of the most important factors contributing to the rapid industrialization of the U.S. was the increase in inventions. Between the period of 1860 and 1890 which transformed the U.S. from an agricultural to an industrial nation, hundreds of thousands of patents were registered. Some of the most important inventions contributing to this industrialization process were by African Americans (Diggs, 1975; Adams, 1979; Carwell, 1977; Hayden, 1972; Haber, 1970; Klein, 1971). By 1913, Blacks had patented an estimated one thousand inventions, especially in the fields of electricity, transportation and industrial machinery, and the records showed that more than twenty of the approximately 190 Black inventors were Black women.

Before the Civil War, Black inventions were hardly recognized or known due to the fact that enslaved Africans could not patent their inventions. In fact in 1858, the U.S. Attorney General ruled that since a slave was not a citizen and a patent was a contract between the government and a citizen inventor, a slave could not make a contract with the government or assign the invention to his slaveholder. Nevertheless, reports are numerous of enslaved Africans inventing useful devices. At first the inventions centered on household and agricultural devices, but eventually the field of Black inventions widened to include achievements in nearly all branches of industrial inventions.

The first African American to receive a U.S. patent was Henry Blair who in 1834 registered a seed planter and in 1836 registered a corn harvester. In 1846, one of the most important inventions by an African American was patented. In that year, Norbert Rillieux patented the revolutionary multiple-effect vacuum evaporation process for refining sugar. Today, his basic technique is not only used in manufacturing sugar, but also condensed milk, gelatin, glue, soap, etc.

After the Civil War, the most significant inventors near the turn of the century were Lewis Latimer, Jan Matzeliger, Elijah McCoy, Garret Morgan and Granville T. Woods. Lewis Latimer invented the first electric lamp with a carbon filament, an inexpensive production technique for making carbon filaments for lamps, and the cotton thread filament which made electric light bulbs practical and inexpensive. Thus, although Edison is credited with inventing the bulb, it is important to note that this bulb continuously burnt out quickly, and it was Latimer's inventions which made it last and become a useable item. Latimer also drew designs for Alexander Bell's telephone patent, worked for Thomas Edison, General Electric and Westinghouse and in 1890 wrote the first book of the electrical lighting system.

Jan Matzeliger revolutionized the shoe industry with his invention of the shoe lasting machine in 1891. Within the first twenty years of Matzeliger's invention, the shoe industry doubled its production in dollars from $220,000,000 to $442,631,000 and shoes became 50% cheaper and of much better quality. Elijah McCoy's most important invention was the automatic lubricator for use on locomotive engines in 1872. This drip cup eliminated the need to stop and restart engines in order to lubricate them. His product was so respected, the phrase "the Real McCoy" was used to question or confirm the genuineness of his and other products.

Garret Morgan invented a belt fastener for sewing machines in 1921, the smoke inhalator in 1914 and the automatic traffic light in 1923. His smoke inhalator was a life-saver used by fire departments and was transformed into a gas mask in World War I to protect soldiers. His automatic traffic light was sold to General Electric for $40,000. The most productive inventor was Granville T. Woods who patented over one hundred inventions. His first patent was in 1884 for an improved steam boiler furnace. In 1887, he patented his most important invention, the Induction Telegraphy System which permitted communications between moving trains and between them and the stations, and thus made rail travel safer. Thomas Edison attempted twice to claim priority in this invention but Woods won both cases and was certified by the U.S. patent office as the real inventor. His other inventions include a telephone transmitter (1884); an apparatus for transmission of telephone and electric messages (1885) which was bought by the American Bell Telephone; an electro-mechanical brake and apparatus (1904-1905) both of which were sold to Westinghouse Electric Company, and an electric railway (1901) which was sold to the General Electric Company of Thomas Edison. Edison tried to hire him, but he remained independent forming his own company, Woods Electric Company.

There were, of course, other significant inventors and inventions during this period among which were John Parker, a screw for tobacco presses, 1884; William Purvis, over a dozen inventions in machinery for making paperbags; J.A. Burr, a lawn

mower, 1899; G. Grant, the golf tee, 1899; J. Winters, a fire
escape ladder, 1878; J. Standard, a refrigerator, 1891; and A.
Miles, an elevator, 1887. The importance of these inventions lies
not only in their value to industrial growth, but also in their
being a model of achievement under the most severe discrimination and oppression.

Finally, it is important to mention the significant contribution of Afro-America's most distinguished scientist, George
Washington Carver, even though most of his work was done after
the major period of industrialization. Carver was a chemurgist,
i.e., a chemist pioneer in the field before it become a recognized
science. Determined to free the South from overdependence on
cotton, he encouraged farmers to grow peanuts, sweet potatoes
and soybeans and developed hundreds of products from them.
In his small ill-equipped laboratory at Tuskegee, he made over
300 synthetic products from the peanut, over 100 from the sweet
potato and over 75 from the pecan. Some of his synthetic
products were adhesives, axle grease, bleach, facial cream, dyes,
fuel briquettes, ink, insulating board, linoleum, metal polish
mucilage paper, rubbing oils, soil conditioner, shampoo, shoe
polish, shaving cream, synthetic rubber, woodstain, wood filler,
buttermilk, cheese, flour, instant coffee, mayonnaise, meal, meat
tenderizer, milk flakes, sugar and worcester sauce.

He also developed dehydrated foods and the U.S. army
used his sweet potato flour during WWI. Although Thomas
Edison and Henry Ford offered him large sums to come to their
laboratories, he stayed at Tuskegee. He never patented any of
his discoveries, refused to profit from them and instead donated
them all to humanity.

Crisis and the New Deal

The decade of the great depression was especially difficult
for African Americans. The New Deal, under President Franklin
Roosevelt, held out hope and relief for Blacks through its focus
on social welfare and public work programs. Blacks recognizing

the importance of this new focus shifted dramatically from their traditional Republican voting to support Roosevelt and the Democratic party by 1936. Also, the New Deal marked a significant turning point in Black-white relations for the better. This was due to the continuous struggle of Blacks for equality and the end of discrimination as well as to the humanitarian focus of the administration.

Through the initiative of the NAACP and the Urban League, several social activist organizations established the Joint Committee on National Recovery (JCNR) to oversee federal government policy and oppose discriminatory aspects of it. The JCNR exposed unequal wage rates, lobbied for race relation advisors in major federal departments and generally fought for federal respect and defense of Black rights. Blacks were also successful in getting the Public Works Administration to stipulate numerical goals for Blacks in slum clearance projects. The Civilian Conservation Corps and the Works Progress Administration (WPA) were valuable to the employment of Blacks during this period. The Federal Arts Project which was a branch of the WPA employed many Black actors and writers. In addition, the National Youth Administration had a Black division headed by Mary McLeod Bethune.

The New Deal passed two major Acts which were of great importance to Blacks. The first was the Social Security Act of 1935 which not only guaranteed old-age and unemployment insurance for workers, but also provided federal monies for social welfare. Secondly, the Wagner Labor Relations Act of 1935 guaranteed the right of collective bargaining and outlawed company unions. In the same year, the Congress of Industrial Organizations (CIO) was formed, began to organize workers and opened up to Blacks. At first distrustful, based on past discrimination, Blacks urged by the Urban League and other Black organizations joined and were very instrumental in organizing the steel workers in the Steel Workers Organizing Committee. Moreover, they joined and helped build the Ladies' Garment Workers Union and the Amalgamated Clothing

Workers Union, the International Longshoreman's Union and the United Auto Workers. Through these struggles and gains, Black workers penetrated organized labor and thus gained a strong base from which to wage even larger struggles.

Finally, Blacks achieved an increased respectability in the Roosevelt Administration as specialist and advisors in various governmental departments. This marked a change in the Washington model of unofficial advisor whose relationship with the president, more than his skill, fitted him/her for the job. These were highly respected specialist and advisors who were civil servants. They were called the "Black Cabinet" and the "Black Brain Trust" due to their academic and professional achievements.

Among the most notable of this brain trust were Robert Weaver, an economist who served in the Department of Interior and several federal agencies; Mary McLeod Bethune, founder-president of Bethune-Cookman College, National Youth Administration; Eugene Jones, Executive Secretary of the Urban Leagues, Department of Commerce; Ralph Bunche, Department of State; Rayford Logan, Coordinator of Inter-American Affairs, and Abram Harris, economist, National Recovery Administration. Although these positions were not cabinet level, they were a breakthrough in appointment by merit and paved the way for advances in the 60's and 70's.

Civil Rights and Revolts

This slightly revised summary of the 60's appeared first in the Black Collegian, February/March 1980, under the title "From Civil Rights to Human Rights: Social Struggles in the 60's."

In spite of reductive translations by liberals, Marxists and established historians, the Sixties marks one of the most definitive and significant decades in the history of Black people in the U.S. It is in this decade that major civil rights and nationalist organizations and personalities reached their height. This is also the decade in which Blacks made the most severe and successful theoretical and practical criticism of the structure and content of U.S. society. And it has become through its achievements and often exaggerated "failures" the unavoidable historical referent-both for analysis of the 70's and 80's and the projections for the 90's (Carson, 1987; Williams, 1987; Harding, 1987; McAdam, 1983).

To discuss the Sixties as a unified process is not to deny that there were varying tendencies and interpretations of what was to be done. There were, in fact, two main tendencies, the integrationist and the nationalist. Chronologically speaking the integrationist tendency reached its height first and through its failures laid the historical groundwork for the resurgence of nationalism. The logic of the process seems to suggest that only after the integrationist thrust had proved itself unworkable and historically exhausted, was the nationalist alternative able to challenge it successfully and eventually overshadow it (Brisbane, 1974). Thus, in 1963 and most definitively in the period of 1965-1968 the strategy of non-violence was challenged by the urban revolts and in 1966 SNCC led the move from integrated groups and aspirations to Black groups and Black power. It was also in the mid-Sixties that the "Back to Black" thrust expanded to reach beyond the U.S. to Africa for models and inspiration. Thus, though we speak of the 60's as a unified process on one hand, it is instructive on the other hand to recognize the two basic tendencies which shaped and informed this critical decade (Robinson and Sullivan, 1991).

The Civil Rights Movement

The Civil Rights Movement, which was essentially integrationist, gave Black people in the U.S. their first major accomplishments of the decade. The integrationist thrust, in its political sense, was an effort to break down barriers to full participation in U.S. society and remove the penalties and other negative consequences of racial distinctions. Thus, a major accomplishment of this period and tendency was not only major civil right executive orders and legislation to overcome these negatives, but also the building of a mass movement which mobilized and politically educated millions of Black people. It is a significant number of these mobilized and politically educated people who would go beyond the vision and aspirations of civil rights to demand human rights and Black power. Therefore, it can be said that the Civil Rights Movement produced activists and organizations which would prove effective in transforming it into its Black nationalist alternative (Carson, 1981).

The Civil rights struggle was led by major groups such as SNCC, CORE and SCLC, although countless smaller groups played fundamental and indeed indispensable roles in the civil rights struggle. Likewise, major personalities like Fannie Lou Hamer, Bob Moses, Ella Baker and Martin Luther King, Jr. were key to the civil rights struggle, but there were countless "unknown soldiers" without whom the struggle could not have begun or been sustained (Lomax, 1962; Clark, 1963; Youth of the Rural Organizing and Cultural Center, 1991; Robinson, 1987; Morris, 1984).

The turning point in the Black civil rights struggle is usually considered to be the winning of the NAACP of the 1954 Supreme Court Decision *Brown v. The Board of Education* (Tushnet, 1987; Kluger, 1976). The decision put a legal end to the "separate but equal" doctrine established in the 1896 Supreme Court decision of *Plessy v. Ferguson.* Even though the decision was hampered in implementation, it gave a necessary psychological boost to the Black struggle and gave legal support to the struggle against segregation.

The beginning of the Montgomery Bus Boycott in 1956 marked another key event in the civil rights struggle (Robinson, 1987). On December 1, 1955, Rosa Parks, having decided that she was not going to give up her bus seat in servile deference to whites, became the catalyst to a struggle which not only catapulted Martin Luther King to national fame, but also built a model that Blacks in other Southern cities were soon to emulate. The economic boycott was thus established as an effective instrument of breaking down segregation barriers (King, 1958).

On February 1, 1960, four students from North Carolina Agricultural and Technical College in Greensboro, N.C., decided they would no longer accept segregation of public facilities and moved to protest and challenge the state of things by sitting down at lunch counters in a variety store and ordering coffee (Wolff, 1972; Proudfoot, 1962). This marked the beginning of the sit-in movement and a sustained period of Black activism and societal confrontation that would last a decade, only declining with police suppression in the late Sixties and defection in the early Seventies.

In May, 1961, the Congress of Racial Equality developed another strategy to force the civil rights issue -- the Freedom Rides (Farmer, 1985; Farmer, 1965; Peck, 1962). CORE, an essentially integrationist group, developed the Freedom Rides to challenge segregationist laws and practices in interstate transportation which forced seating by race. However, the strategy had the spinoff effect of forcing the federal government to take a more vigorous stand on protection of the civil rights guaranteed by the Constitution. The Kennedys (John and Robert, who were in power at the time as President and U.S. Attorney General respectively) were disturbed by the assertiveness of these activists and asked for a cooling-off period. But the activists continued their thrust and forced the Attorney General to dispatch a force of 600 marshals and other federal officers to intervene in a Freedom Ride confrontation in Montgomery.

In 1963, the centennial year of the Emancipation Proclamation, Black people launched a series of massive demonstrations to expose the contradictions in U.S. society and demanded serious social change. One of the most notable of these was the Birmingham Demonstration of April 3 under the leadership of Martin Luther King and the Southern Christian Leadership Conference (King, 1962; Branch, 1988, Fairclough,

1987; Garrow, 1986). Again, racist violence flared, but the marchers were adamant in their push for fair employment, desegregation of public facilities and dropping of politically motivated charges against the thousands of demonstrators arrested. Easily the largest and most dramatic was "The March on Washington for Jobs and Freedom," August 28, 1963, which involved over 200,000 participants.

It is important to note here that throughout this period, the Student Non-Violence Coordinating Committee (SNCC) from its inception had been the most effective and largest contributor of freedom fighters to the struggle (Carson, 1981; Forman, 1972; Stoper, 1989; Zinn, 1964). It had participated in great numbers in the major strategies of the Civil Rights Movement -- including boycotts, sit-ins, voter registration campaigns, cooperative projects and even political party building. It was SNCC who, along with Fannie Lou Hamer and Bob Moses, built the Mississippi Freedom Democratic Party and the Lowndes County Freedom Organization which was popularly called the Black Panther Party. Later, Huey Newton and Bobby Seale of Oakland would use both the symbol and inspiration of the Black Panther Party of Lowndes County to launch their group. It was also SNCC, as mentioned above, who would lead the movement discussion and organizational move away from one of integration to one of Black power (Carmichael and Hamilton, 1967).

A critical analysis of the civil rights struggle, then would reveal a series of major accomplishments. As mentioned above, its first and perhaps most important achievement was the increased liberalization of the U.S. system. Through legal, economic and political challenges, Blacks were able to achieve among other things: 1) the 1954 Brown Decision; 2) the Civil Rights Act of 1957; 3) the 1960 Civil Rights Bill; 4) the Interstate Commerce Commission ruling September, 1961, against racial segregation on interstate carriers and terminals; 5) the Civil Rights Act of 1964 which was the most far-reaching and comprehensive civil rights law passed by Congress; 6) mass voter

registration; 7) the 1965 Voting Act; and 8) widespread desegregation of public facilities.

Secondly, as mentioned above, the Civil Rights Movement
severely exposed the contradictions of the American dream in
both the eyes of U.S. society and the world. This uncompromising and fierce exposure contributed to the internationalization
of the Black struggle which was another gain for the Movement.
It brought world attention to the struggle and won it moral and
political allies around the world. The U.S. was thus forced to
operate under the attentive world eye and, therefore, sought to
check its excesses against Blacks in a way it was not compelled
to do before. Thirdly, the Movement mobilized and politically
educated people who before were, in fact, outside the political
process. It is significant to note here that King, believing in and
teaching the social function of religion, turned religion into a
political force for massive social change. King, stressing the
social aspect of religion, taught civil disobedience against unjust
practices as a moral imperative, gave Blacks boldness by stressing
that they were God's soldiers in an unjust world and thus enabled
an otherwise reluctant people to dare take control of their
destiny and daily life.

Fourthly, the Civil Rights Movement laid the organizational and political-educational basis for continued struggle in
other areas. The mobilized and organized masses did not simply
disband at the end of the Civil Rights Movement, but went on to
win elections, build co-ops and unions and in general build
institutions that housed, defended and expanded their interest.
Finally, the Civil Rights Movement, by its uncompleted tasks, the
non-attainment of its core and social objectives, the timidity of
its methods and its eventual historical exhaustion, laid the
historical basis for the rise of its nationalist alternative.

The Civil Rights Movement was thus limited in its goals
and methods for their achievements. Moreover, its Black
leadership was unnecessarily concerned with and deferential to
the wishes and support of white allies. Whites, through financial
contributions and organizational positions, limited the Move-

ment's possibilities and ultimately had to be confronted and rejected for leadership positions. And it is in the process of reassessment of the goals, methods and leadership of the Black Civil Rights Movement that the nationalist alternative appeared, grew and eventually checked and surpassed the thrust toward integration.

It is important at this point, however, to stress that all the gains made during the 60's, both of the Civil Rights and Nationalist Movements, were not the gifts of presidents, Congress or liberal allies, but the result of a people's self-conscious struggle to free and realize themselves. As evident in the case of the liberal Kennedys, Black needs and the political concerns of liberals easily clash. But through the self-conscious collective struggle of Blacks to control their destiny and daily lives, presidents, Congress and shaky allies were time and time again forced to act even against their will.

The painful process of reassessment which occurred in the middle 60's produced, perhaps, the most definitive aspect and achievement of the Sixties -- the self-conscious decision of Africans in the U.S. to initiate a theoretical and practical thrust to redefine and restructure society in Black images and interests. Even the integrationist wanted Black interests to be recognized and respected. Even they fought for a society which did not penalize Blacks for their color and which would concede to affirmative action to end and compensate for such behavior. But it was the nationalist tendency which redefined both society and the world in Black images and interests.

The Black Power Movement. The thrust for self-determination, self-respect and self-defense, as the Black Power Movement was defined by Us Organization, gave the Black Power Movement a new vitality and dynamics. It was this thrust which began to solve the Crusian-posed crisis of the Black intellectual, raised the political and cultural consciousness of the Black masses, linked our struggle with African and other Third World peoples and introduced the concept and practice of armed

struggle in urban centers among other things. The nationalist
struggle can be, for analytical purposes, divided into three basic
tendencies or thrusts: 1) the religious thrusts; 2) the cultural
thrust; and 3) the political thrust.

The Religious Thrust.   The religious thrust was both Islamic
and Christian. The Islamic section was personified by the Nation
of Islam (NOI) under the leadership of the Honorable Elijah
Muhammad (Muhammad, 1965; 1973). Muhammad posed Islam
as a necessary alternative to Christianity, which he saw as the
oppressor's religion. Secondly, he argued that Blacks were the
chosen people of God, and that God was Black and the devil was
white. This reversal of the world order was a bold redefinition
of reality and was instrumental in reinforcing the concept of the
beauty and creative genius of Blacks. Thirdly, Muhammad
contended that separation of Blacks was a divine imperative.
This was central in order to escape the degenerative effect of
white society and the wrath of Allah who would destroy the U.S.,
a modern-day Babylon. Muhammad also argued for economic
self-help and national racial solidarity in a Black United Front.
Finally, he stressed the need for racial and Islamic solidarity
throughout the world.

        Although the Nation had its beginning in   1930, it
reached its height in the early Sixties. Muhammad's achievements, as leader of the NOI, lie in both the area of theory and
practice. He broke the monopoly whites had on good and God
by revealing an alternative truth and reconstructing reality in
Black images and interests. Moreover, he likewise broke the
traditional monopoly Arabs and other Asian Muslims had on the
doctrinal interpretation of Islam in the U.S. Thirdly, in doing
this, he established a socio-historically specific form of Islam for
Blacks. And fourthly, through this theological achievement and
the building of its practical, organizational and institutional
complement, the NOI, he placed himself in the ranks of the most
significant Black men in the history of the African American
people.

The Christian nationalist focus was best personified by Albert Cleage, the minister of the Shrine of the Black Madonna (Cleage, 1968; 1972). Cleage began this thrust by arguing that the Judeo-Christian heritage was, in fact, Black and needed to be redefined and reappropriated. He portrayed Jesus as a Black revolutionary who led a national liberation struggle against a white power, Rome. Moreover, he argued God is Black and partisan and demands social struggle, not submission. Power, he contended, is a basic aspect of group existence and Blacks can only demand and establish respect and end oppression through unity and power. Cleage finally argues that the church must assume its historical revolutionary role and lead "God's Chosen People," Blacks, to liberation and social reconstruction.

The Cultural Thrust. The cultural thrust during the 60's was most definitively represented by Us organization under the leadership of this author (Karenga, 1980; 1978). Us, established in 1965, was organized around the ideology and practice of *Kawaida*. The basic concepts of Kawaida centered around the contention that the key crisis in Black life is the cultural crisis, i.e., a crisis in views and especially, values. The need, thus, is for a cultural revolution which would break the monopoly the oppressor has on Black minds and begin to rescue and reconstruct Black history and humanity in their own image and interests.

The ideology of Kawaida, which is essentially a theory of cultural and social change and which seeks to draw from and synthesize the best in nationalist, Pan-Africanist and socialist thought, became the most structured and widespread body of Black nationalist thought in the country. It is Kawaida out of which this author developed *Kwanzaa* and the *Nguzo Saba*. The Nguzo Saba (Seven Principles) were advocated as a communitarian African value system necessary to build community and serve as social glue and moral orientation for cultural practice. These principles in Swahili and English are: *Umoja* (Unity), *Kujichagulia* (Self-Determination), *Ujima*

(Collective Work and Responsibility), *Ujamaa* (Cooperative Economics), *Nia* (Purpose), *Kuumba* (Creativity), and *Imani* (Faith). Since their introduction in 1965, the Nguzo Saba has become the basis for the philosophical orientation of many independent schools, rites of passage, community and professional organization's programs and is best known as the values of *Kwanzaa*, an African American holiday celebrated throughout the world African community. It is a holiday which celebrates African family, community and culture and serves as a fundamental way of reinforcing the bonds between African people (Karenga, 1989).

Also, Kawaida, as a system of thought, affected in varying degrees the early political development of people like Angela Davis, Amiri Baraka, Haki Madhubuti, Kalamu ya Salaam, and Jitu Weusi. Also Kawaida laid the ideological and organizational basis out of which grew Black United Fronts like the Black Congress in Los Angeles, the Black Federation in San Diego, Committee for A Unified Newark, the Congress of African Peoples and the National Black Assembly, and provided the theoretical framework which shaped the three national Black Power Conferences in the 60's.

Another definitive cultural achievement of the Sixties was the widespread positive turn toward Africa for revitalization and roots which was fostered by all Black nationalist groups. It was a logical outgrowth of the rejection of white values. It represented a defiant acceptance of Blackness and search for an Afrocentric perspective and national program. This turn toward Africa was not simply symbolic in terms of dress and hairstyle, but was both cultural and political. It expressed a Pan-Africanism which culminated in the African Liberation Support Committee, the Congress of African Peoples, the Sixth Pan-African Congress and FESTAC in the Seventies.

Finally, the cultural thrust was defined by its stress on a new education for Blacks. From this came the Black Students' and Black Studies Movements. SNCC had been at the center and head of the student movement during the Civil Rights Movement and during the Nationalist Movement, it remained vital. It was joined by Us, the Panthers, CORE and small groups in building both Black Student Unions and a climate and structure for the demand and achievement of Black Studies.

It was, thus, during the Sixties that the Black Student Movement came into being, won Black Studies programs and challenged the traditional wisdom and structure of white academia (Robinson, et al, 1969; Edwards, 1970; Hare, 1972). The Black Student Movement stressed the need to bring the campus to the community and the community to the campus. Thus, inherent in its assumptions and aspirations was the thrust toward a new educational process which would be focused not only in established academia, but also in alternative institutions in the community. Some definitive examples were the School of African American Culture of Us, the Ahidiana Work/Study Center, Uhuru Sasa of the East, and the Institute of Positive Education. (Kawaida served as the ideological base for these new institutions.) These structures sought to define, introduce and reinforce new Afrocentric values and visions of self, society and the world and their impact on the Movement was central and continuing.

The Political Thrust. The political thrust of the Nationalist Movement was best exemplified by Malcolm X who served as a model, ideologically and personally, for countless nationalist groups and leaders (Malcolm X, 1965; 1966; 1970, 1992). Malcolm X was schooled and reached his height in the Nation of Islam. There, he laid the organizational basis for its national expansion and introduced it to the country and world. Malcolm, however, came into conflict with a changed direction and character of the NOI. He was first suspended in 1963, and then, left to set up his own organizations, Muslim Mosque, Inc. and the Organization of African American Unity, in 1964.

Malcolm advocated several concepts which informed and inspired the Movement (Karenga, 1979). Thus, although he was a Muslim, he reached beyond the religious and had a profound effect on the entire Movement. Malcolm, like his former teacher Muhammad, argued that Blacks needed a moral and spiritual regeneration and that it was best achieved through Islam. He stressed also the need for a Black United Front and built the Organization of African American Unity modeled after the Organization of African Unity on the continent. Moreover, Malcolm taught the need for Pan-Africanism and Third World solidarity. He emphasized the values of breaking the "minority mentality" by seeing ourselves as part of the majority in the U.S. He, therefore urged a linking of struggles and a worldview of our problems using the spirit and movement of the Bandung conference as a model (Malcolm X, 1965:ff).

Closely linked with this concept was Malcolm's contention that Blacks needed to redefine the Black struggle from one of civil rights to human rights. This, he argued, would break the UN and international prohibition against interference in domestic affairs. He reasoned that the domestic character of issues prohibit world intervention, but issues of human concern demanded humanity's intervention both morally and politically in terms of the UN charter.

Finally, Malcolm stressed the right and responsibility of self-defense. Joined to this was the logical extension of the right and responsibility to struggle for freedom by any means necessary. He argued that it was criminal to teach Blacks not to defend themselves and to leave them defenseless in the face of violence. Moreover, he contended, that it was equally criminal and dispiriting to teach Blacks that they do not have the right to win their freedom by struggle -- armed and otherwise -- like all other peoples in the world. To the end of his life, Malcolm served as a model of audaciousness, defying threats from the system, and travelling to world capitals to gain support for the Black liberation struggle.

That the Sixties witnessed Black people becoming less convinced about the viability of non-violence and daring to explore armed struggle and self-defense against racist violence was not due entirely to Malcolm. Robert Williams, who had been the president of the NAACP in Monroe, North Carolina, had argued in the late Fifties that self-defense against racist violence was a natural and constitutional right (Williams, 1973). Moreover, he contended that the capacity for self-defense often limited the need to use it. For the attackers would be less likely to attack if they knew swift and effective penalties would follow. To illustrate this in practice, Williams organized a defense group which successfully protected the Black community against Klan attacks and intimidation and in doing so, he gave Black people a new method and model of struggle. His model produced the Deacons for Defense in Louisiana, which protected civil rights workers in the South and served as inspiration to urban nationalist groups in the North.

Moreover, Williams deserves much credit for helping to internationalize the Black struggle. Fleeing a trumped-up charge (which was later dropped) and death threats, he travelled to Canada, Cuba, China and Tanzania, where he wrote extensively on the African American struggle. In China, he succeeded in getting the country's leader, Mao Tse-tung, to issue a statement in support of the African American liberation struggle in 1963 and was asked for comments on a subsequent support statement in 1968.

The Sixties also saw the rise and transformation of the Black Panther Party from a nationalist community defense structure to a Marxist-integrationist structure (Marine, 1969; Seale, 1970; Newton, 1972). Its early history is marked with bold, physical challenges to police structures in the name of self-defense and the Black community. In 1968 with Huey Newton in jail, Eldridge Cleaver made alliances with white radicals and denounced nationalism and other Panther leaders followed suit. What followed was a transformation of the Panther Party into a "revolutionary" surrogate for the left. This forced them into "custer stands" with the police which they were ill-prepared to deal with, put them at odds with nationalist groups, helped contribute to their violent internecine struggle with Us Organization and their effective reduction to essentially a legal

defense committee. In fact, their legal cases consumed the bulk
of their efforts. Their contribution to the Movement was
essentially in their early period and must be seen, then, as a
contribution of the Williams-Malcolm legacy.

Finally, the Sixties saw the rise of and focus on the land
question. Although the Nation of Islam had stressed the
question during the Malcolm period, after '64 it was stressed less.
Stokely Carmichael (Kwame Toure) also raised it in the end of
the 60's and stressed it in the 70's. However, it was the Republic
of New Africa (RNA) under the leadership of Imari Obadele,
which pressed it in a political and practical way (Obadele, 1975).
Borrowing from Malcolm and Muhammad, Obadele argued that
Blacks were not citizens of the U.S. and were due a referendum
to choose among three options: 1) U.S. citizenship; 2)
nationalism in Africa or a country of choice; 3) building of a
nation on this soil. Obadele and the RNA chose this land,
declared independence from the U.S. in 1968 and demanded five
southern sates (South Carolina, Georgia, Alabama, Louisiana
and Mississippi) to construct a Republic of New Africa.
Moreover, the RNA demanded reparations from the U.S. to
build the nation and solicited world support. The question is still
a burning one and is not solved by non-believers dismissing it as
utopian.

The nationalist thrust, thus, contributed greatly to the
character, course and achievement of the 60's. It included: 1) the
building of economic institutions mainly though the NOI; 2)
alternative educational institutional constructions; 3) the building
of Black Student Unions and a Black Student Movement; 4) the
construction of Black Studies Programs; 5) the necessary
relinking with the African people on the continent and in the
Diaspora; 6) the exploration of armed struggle and self-defense
as a right and responsibility; 7) the redefinition of the world in
Black images and interests; and 8) laying of the foundations for
any and all benefits enjoyed in the 70's.

In conclusion, it is important to note that the Sixties left
a fundamental lesson both in the process of its development, as

well as in its comparison with the 70's. It is a lesson written in life struggles all over the world, i.e., the liberation of a people depends primarily on its own strength and struggle -- regardless of the sincerity or support of its allies. In the final analysis, the Sixties taught Black people that a people that cannot save itself is lost forever. It was in opposition to their erstwhile allies that Blacks charted a new course and made the new gains listed above. And if one reviews the 70's and 80's, the lull and the losses they reflect, one cannot help but see the dismantling and weakening of Black structures as a significant factor in that development.

The *Bakke* and *Weber* cases, the rise of the vulgar right and the cutback in social welfare gains in the 70's and 80's all point to the structural incapacity of African Americans to check these assaults on previous gains. It was Black structural capacity and struggle which brought Black gains and it was the absence of these which emboldened their adversaries. To paraphrase Frederick Douglass, if you want to know how much a tyrant will impose on a people, find out how much they will take. The misinterpretation of Black history and gains in the Sixties led to faculty reassessments and wholesale defections from the Afrocentric ideological and practical thrust. This resulted in the structural incapacity to respond to assaults on previous gains and reduced petty bourgeois leadership to making moral denunciations rather than taking concrete political steps to challenge and check such assaults.

Finally, it might be of use to note that if a people are assaulted in their identity, they have no alternative but to organize in defense and development of it. This, perhaps, was the most significant and provable legacy and lesson of the Sixties.

Post-Sixties

The Seventies. The decade began with recovery from the massive suppression and havoc wreaked on the Black Movement by the Cointelpro or counterintelligence program launched by the FBI in 1968. Hoover in a November 1968 memo asked 41 field officers for hard-hitting ideas to disrupt, discredit and destroy all real and potentially threatening Black leadership. This included groups such as the Black Panthers, Us, CORE, SNCC, the Nation of Islam and leaders as moderate as Martin Luther King. From this, violent internecine struggles were provoked and sustained as between the Panthers and Us, activists shot and murdered, put in captivity on trumped-up charges or driven into exile, and families as well as organizations disrupted and destroyed (O'Reilly, 1989).

Hoover feared the unity of the Movement and rise of a Messiah who could unify it and create the basis for a real Black revolution. Cautioning the media never to advertise Black activists, especially nationalists, except to discredit them, he created and fed disinformation to them. Using agent-provocateurs, he penetrated organizations, provoked them into internal struggles and violence and adventuristic acts which led to their arrest and deaths. This and other information was obtained through the Senate Select Committee Hearings on Intelligence and the Freedom of Information Act which allowed citizens to get copies of files kept on them by intelligence agencies.

The violence and shock of the suppression destroyed morale, provoked both critical and uncritical reassessment and made many wonder whether organized activism was any longer a valid strategy for social change. Much which passed as critical assessment of the Sixties was in fact Black self-condemnation and reflected both a loss of heart and vision of what the 60's were all about and certainly what was achieved. As I have argued, the 60's was the most important decade in Black history and its achievement was substantial. And even though Blacks lost ground during the Seventies, they also made gains.

Easily the greatest gains of African Americans during the Seventies were their penetration and victories in electoral politics. Taking advantage of the Voting Rights Act of 1965, Blacks went to the polls in great numbers, especially in the

South. Whereas in 1966, there were only six Blacks in Congress, ninety-seven in state legislatures and no mayors, by 1976, Blacks had elected eighteen Blacks to Congress, several hundred to state legislatures, two lieutenant-governors in California and Colorado and several mayors of major cities, including Los Angeles, Atlanta, Washington, D.C., Newark and Cleveland. Moreover, thousands had been elected to other state and local offices (Conyers and Wallace, 1976).

Also, Blacks sought to build national independent power structures throughout the decade, beginning with the first National Black Political Convention in Gary, Indiana, March 1972. Here over 3,000 delegates and approximately 5,000 alternates and observers passed resolutions, produced an historic document titled The Black Political Agenda and created a structure, the Black Assembly, that was posed as both a national body for collective planning and an organizing structure for independent electoral participation. The Black Political Agenda called for a new vision and bold and independent politics to meet the challenge of a clear social crisis in the U.S. (Gilliam, 1975: Chapter 6). Although the Agenda criticized the Democratic and Republican parties, it did not call for an independent Black one. Not until August 1980 at the Fourth National Black Assembly Convention in New Orleans was the decision made to form an independent Black party. In November, over 1,300 delegates from various organizations and political tendencies met to form the National Black Independent Political Party (NBIPP) "to advance a new Black politics of social transformation and self-determination" including, organizing, party-building, mobilization and "lobbying around private and public policy" and effectively and independently participating in electoral politics.

The Seventies also brought a resurgence of Pan-African-ism and the formation of two key organizations to advance its principles and practice. The first was the African Liberation Support Committee, a united front of Nationalist, Pan-Africanist and Marxist tendencies, dedicated to supporting liberation struggles on the continent of Africa through yearly massive

African Liberation Day rallies in May, political education, and raising material and financial resources for the struggles. ALSC was eventually split by the Nationalist/Marxist ideological struggle for hegemony within it and lost the massive support it once had (Salaam, 1974). Still, however, various Pan-Africanist and nationalist groups continue to support the Continental liberation struggle and celebration of African Liberation Day, May 25. The second major organization founded was TransAfrica, an African American lobby for Africa and the Caribbean. It has grown through the years and still monitors legislation and policy concerning Africa and the Caribbean and conducts political education through lectures, conferences and its bulletins. Also, it has developed a journal on U.S. policy toward Africa and the Caribbean.

Affirmative Action was another major issue and struggle in the Seventies. Growing out of Title VII of the 1964 Civil Rights Act, it was extended and reinforced by Executive Orders and the Equal Employment Opportunities Act of 1972. Although there were other cases such as the *DeFundis* and *Weber* court cases which challenged affirmative action terming it "reverse discrimination," none was so argued and followed as the *Bakke* case. The Bakke case which originated in California over the special admissions policy of U.C. Davis's medical school, brought to a head the struggle over the questions of numerical goals vs. quotas, preferential treatment vs. corrective measures for historical injustices and racially weighted criteria vs. race-conscious criteria for school admission as well as employment.

Blacks parted company with many of their traditional allies among Jews, liberals and labor who felt threatened by the implications of affirmative action. Although moral and philosophical arguments were understandably raised, the basic problem centered around the fact that Black entrance into law, medical and other professional schools and areas of employment meant increased competition and struggle for critical social space with those who traditionally held a monopoly on them. The Supreme Court seemed to straddle and ruled in 1978 that reservation of places for people of color and uncompetitive evaluation was prohibited, but that consideration of race and ethnic origin as one criteria for selection as well as consciously seeking diversity were permissible (Sindler, 1978: Chapter 4).

Key also to the Seventies was the emergence of an open and ongoing discussion among Black men and women on the quality, forms and future of their relationships and the transformation this produced. Major Black journals and magazines like *Black Scholar* and *Black Books Bulletin, Essence* and *Ebony* regularly carried articles and sometimes dedicated whole issues to the question of Black Male/Female relationships. Books, poems and plays self-consciously concerned themselves with this pressing issue, and debates and discussions on campuses, in the community and on TV and radio were regular occurrences. Moreover, psychologists Nathan and Julia Hare started a new journal, *Black Male/Female Relationships*, dedicated entirely to critically discussing, understanding and improving them. The impetus for this reassessment was rooted in three basic factors: 1) the general reassessment of the thought and practices of the Sixties; 2) collective agreement on its urgency; and 3) the influence of the general struggle of women for social equality. Although Black women did not join the Women's Liberation Movement in great numbers, they raised many of its questions, influenced and were influenced by much of its literature and were thus part of the overall struggle to end sexism in social and personal relations.

Finally, Vincent Harding (1980, Chapter 30) lists in addition to the above key issues and events of the Seventies, the prison revolts as at Soledad and Attica, the transformation of the Nation of Islam, and the awesome tragedy of Jonestown. The prison revolts reflected a continuing relationship with the struggles of the Sixties and the transformation of the NOI represented the loss of an important Black "religiously based challenge to the structures of White American life" and a symbol of defiant Blackness. And Jonestown represented the great dangers of unguided and uncritical searches for spiritual community in the context of cynicism, hedonism, materialism, individualism and alienation which marked the Seventies. It also underlined the absence of a Black mass movement which historically served as a base of meaningful relationships, community and hope. As Blacks moved into the 80's, they were keenly aware of the value and urgency of the need to rebuild a self-conscious united and active community which characterized the 60's.

The Eighties. The decade began with three major challenges to African Americans: 1) the continuing crisis of U.S. society; 2) the rise of the vulgar and "respectable" right; and 3) the continuing struggle to rebuild a Black mass movement and appropriate alliances and coalitions in order to defend Black gains, win new ones and minimize losses. The continuing crisis in U.S. society is marked most definitively by severe economic problems including high level inflation and employment, especially among Blacks, a perennially unbalanced budget, an aging productive structure, resource shortages, large military spending and massive cutbacks and cutoffs of government spending in other areas, especially in social welfare. And it is clearly complicated by self-confessed confusion at the highest levels of government as to how exactly to address these problems (Greider, 1981).

The rise of the right, which continues from the Seventies, expresses itself in the return of violent racist groups like the Klan and other neo-nazi formations, the rise of Christian fundamentalists and perhaps most importantly, Reagan's presidential victory and the various successes of right-wing candidates in state and local elections (Dalleck, 1984). With this turn of events came several related occurrences: 1) the tendency to declare social entitlement programs morally wrong and financially too costly; 2) strong and continuing demands for tax cuts, reduced social services and especially, reduced and more stringently restricted social welfare; 3) the progressive diminishing of the government's role in achieving social justice and equality for Third World peoples and the poor; and 4) the steady reversal of gains of the 60's and 70's.

In addition to the rise of the white right in and out of government, there is a parallel rise of a Black right (Daniels, 1980). These Black conservatives who are also in and out of government serve the Reagan/Bush Administrations and right-wing thrust by supporting policies and developing arguments against the minimum wage, government intervention to correct injustices for ethnics and the poor, affirmative action, equal opportunity programs and most other programs and proposals won in the general thrust for civil rights in the 60's and early 70's. This rise of Black conservatism and the challenge it poses for the liberal civil rights approach clearly has its historical parallel in the Washington-DuBois conflict concerning approaches to Black social advancement. Like Washington, the Black conservatives reject Black protest and emphasize vocational education and self-help. On the other hand, the liberals, like DuBois, stress protest, multidimensional education and the obligation of U.S. society to live up to its claims and of government to facilitate and insure this.

In this context, the liberal and radical Black leadership and the mass movement requires national organizations with adequate vision, structure and resources to meet the challenge of leadership and cooperation necessary to form a national Black united front which will stand at the center of the mass move-ment. Both radical and liberal organizations have attempted to build such a united front formation. The liberal forces have created the Black Leadership Forum which is made up of approximately sixteen national organizations. However, it is not well-known and is not visibly engaged in collective planning, organizing the national Black community or confronting the system. Secondly, the liberal forces often use the yearly Congres-sional Black Caucus Legislative Weekend structure as a means to gather, get briefings on the latest governmental policies, decisions and proposals, and to discuss possible defensive and development strategies. But the CBC is not really suited for activist leadership and the Weekends are more for briefings and informal exchanges than for the development of concrete action plans.

The radicals also have produced two national structures which they see as possibly providing an ideological and structural center for the mass movement necessary to define, defend and develop Black interests. Those are the National Black United Front and the National Black Independent Political Party, both of which were formed in 1980, the former in June and the latter in November. NBIPP, as mentioned above, seeks to be a genuine party which gives Blacks a clear alternative to the two traditional parties. Following in the tradition of other Black political parties, it seeks to point out the inability of the traditional parties to meet Black needs and build a powerful alternative structure to accomplish this (Daniels, 1980; Flewellen, 1981). The Party, however, remains in the formative stages and is having the traditional problems of third parties, i.e., resources, strategy, membership, community legitimacy and electoral success. (Walton, 1972).

NBUF is the largest of the two organizations, more active and more solidly based in the national community with chapters throughout the country (Daughtery, 1981). Although it is essentially a nationalist formation, NBUF's constitution sets for itself the task of "delicately" formulating "the conservative, moderate, reform, radical and nationalist concerns, problems and goals of the carried constituencies in the Black community into a dynamic black agenda, which speaks to our collective interests as a people." This is obviously its chief task and will decide whether it succeeds and grows or flounders.

The problem of alliance and coalition was also a challenge for Blacks in the 80's. For they are a necessary complement to the building of a self-conscious and effective mass movement. Although strains developed in the traditional Black-labor-liberal coalition in the late 60's and 70's, the Black liberal forces continued to see it as vital to defense of gains and the struggle for broad social change and thus, strove to rebuild it.

And the radicals, who see alliances with Third World people and labor as necessary political projects, likewise attempted to rebuild and build those and make them active and effective.

The 80's also witnessed a heightened level of electoral political activity among African Americans. In Chicago, Harold Washington waged a brilliant campaign to become mayor. He put together a coalition of Blacks, Latinos, workers, professionals, nationalists, white liberals and leftists to achieve his victory. Key groups in this process were the African Community of Chicago, PUSH (People United to Save Humanity), the Black United Front, and People's College. Also Jesse Jackson ran in 1984 and 1988 for president, mobilizing and registering millions of voters which were instrumental in getting other Blacks and progressives elected. His campaign in '88 garnered seven million votes and brought into the political process many formerly marginalized groups. Moreover, he raised issues of substance in a context of mediocre political discourse and challenged the country to live up to its highest ideals. Although he did not win office, his campaign was seen as an important tool for mobilizing, organizing and politically educating Blacks and progressives and building the Rainbow Coalition for the inauguration of a new progressive politics.

In 1989, Douglas Wilder was elected governor of the State of Virginia, a former bastion of the Confederacy. This was occasioned by several factors: 1) African Americans who gave him 96 percent of their vote; 2) women who favored him by 53%; and 3) his moving between moderate and conservative politics. It was a pattern called cross-over politics which bode ill for Black politics in some analysts' opinions. For it seemed at times to sacrifice Black interests on the altar of compromise. Also, David Dinkins was elected in 1989 mayor of New York. He too was the recipient of the support of an active African American community, the Latino community, liberals, Jews and labor. A progressive politician, his greatest challenge was to build a truly interactive and mutually respecting multicultural city. But as the 90's would prove, it remains a desirable but difficult goal in the context of the racist legacy of this country's history.

The Nineties. The 90's opened with celebrations of the above-mentioned elections of Wilder and Dinkins and appreciation for Jackson's political mobilization. But there were carryover problems from the 80's that required sober assessment. Among these problems were: 1) the increasing negative attitude of the Supreme Court to racial justice and affirmative action; 2) continuation of hate crimes against African Americans, which tripled in the last seven years (1983-1990); 3) the veto and later passage of the 1991 Civil Rights Act; and 4) the increase in poverty among Blacks and in the country as a whole.

Easily the most dramatic events in the early 90's were the Clarence Thomas-Anita Hill confrontation in October 1991 and the Los Angeles Rebellion in April 1992 (Chrisman and Allen, 1992; Morrison, 1992; Madhubuti, 1993). The Thomas-Hill confrontation revolved around the confirmation hearing of Clarence Thomas for a seat on the Supreme Court. Hill charged him with sexual harassment as her former supervisor and argued with allies that he was unfit to serve. He countered saying the charge was a lie and the interrogation which began to resemble a trial was a high-tech lynching. The Black community split around the issues of race and gender and the controversy revealed an ongoing problematic of race and gender relations and the need to constantly confront them (see below in Black Sociology).

The Los Angeles Revolt or Rebellion of April 1992 grew out of smoldering resentment of oppression in the Black and Latino communities. But it was triggered by the acquittal of four white Los Angeles policemen who beat a Black man, Rodney King, mercilessly while he was on the ground and incapacitated. The anger overflowed not only in response to the beating but also because the beating had been caught on video and the jury seemed to be racist to concede that it ever happened. Moreover, the verdict appeared to declare that Black men as Black men were a real and continuing menace, that they were less deserving of rights and that thus anything done to restrain and deter them is both understandable and justified. The Rebellion was the most destructive in recent U.S. history, leading to the loss of 58 lives and millions of dollars in property (Madhubuti, 1993). Rodney King became a symbol of police brutality and the Rebellion became a reminder of the injustice Black people face. It also had a Latino dimension and reflected similar injustices that are suffered by them and that they too will dare to struggle to correct them.

Finally, the 90's brought many African Americans a measure of political optimism with the election of Bill Clinton to the presidency and the presence of thirty-nine Black members of Congress and one Black Senator, Carol Mosely Braun. However, others remained cautious because in spite of Clinton's more liberal attitude and cabinet appointments of Blacks, these gestures do not translate into a substantive programs for the masses of Black people or deal with the challenges of urban life and politics (Browning et al, 1990). Likewise, the election of new faces to Congress and one person to the Senate is important, but they do not equal a critical mass necessary to determine policy. Thus, the caution is to realize that the struggle for a just and good society is a long and difficult one and, therefore, as Amilcar Cabral says concerning this, one should "mask no difficulties, tell no lies and claim no easy victories" (1969:89).

In conclusion, the 90's promise to be a decisive decade whose conflicts and struggles will be over the shape and future of the country. Thus, the decade poses not only a challenge to Blacks, but also to other peoples of color, progressives and liberals to be actively concerned about what kind of country this should be. Clearly, however, it is in the interest and historical tradition of African Americans to serve again as catalyst and vanguard of the struggle which resists reversals of fundamental humanistic gains and begins to build a society which successfully defends and expands the national ideals of freedom, equality of access and opportunity and social justice. Symbolic placements in government and a liberal president are not enough. Structures and strategy must be built and put in place. As Harding (1980:231) contends, it is African Americans who must, at "so elemental a time of turning" and coming from such a rich history of social change and leadership, pose the question to themselves and others of "how do we move forward, beyond our best leaders of the past, beyond our best declarations, beyond our best actions, beyond our best dreams, to participate fully in the creation of a fundamentally new reality, in ourselves, in our people, in this nation, and in this world?"

STUDY QUESTIONS

1.   What is history and what is its relevance?
2.   Cite some of Egypt's major contributions to the advancement of humankind.
3.   List and discuss the major empires of the Western Sudanic civilization.
4.   What were some of the major contributions of the Moorish empire to Europe through Spain?
5.   What are the basic factors leading to the fall of African societies?
6.   What arguments does Van Sertima make to prove African presence in Olmec civilization?
7.   What are some basic misconceptions about the "slave trade"? Discuss its impact.
8.   What was the basis for enslavement and some of its basic aspects?
9.   List and discuss the major forms of resistance to enslavement.
10. Discuss Black participation in the Civil War.
11. What were some of the basic reasons for the failure of Reconstruction?
12. What were the reasons for the Great Migration?

13. What were some of the major organizations founded to struggle against injustice? Especially discuss the Black Women's Club Movement.
14. What were some of the major Black inventors and inventions during the period of industrialization?
15. What are some of the major philosophical contentions of Washington, DuBois and Garvey?
16. Discuss the New Deal period.
17. What were the two main tendencies of the 60's and what were their organizations and achievements?
18. What are some major challenges and achievements of the 70's and 80's?

REFERENCES

Introduction/African Background

Adams, William Y. (1977) *Nubia: Corridor to Africa*, Princeton: Princeton University Press.

Ajayi, J.F.A. and Ian Espie (eds.) (1972) *A Thousand Years of West African History*, New York: Humanities Press.

Beattie, John. (1960) *Bunyoro, An African Kingdom*, New York: Holt, Reinhart, Winston.

ben-Jochannon, Yosef A.A. (1971) *Africa: Mother of "Western Civilization,"* New York: Alkebu-Ian Books Associates.

ben-Jochannon, Yosef A.A. (1970) *African Origins of the Major "Western Religions,"* New York: Alkebu-Ian Books Associates.

Bernal, Martin. (1991) *Black Athena: The AfroAsiatic Roots of Classical Civilization, Vol. II*, New Brunswick, NJ: Rutgers University Press.

Bernal, Martin. (1987) *Black Athena: The AfroAsiatic Roots of Classical Civilization, Vol. I*, New Brunswick, NJ: Rutgers University Press.

Billington, Ray A. (ed.) (1981) *The Journal of Charlotte Forten: A Free Negro in the Slave Era*, New York: W. W. Norton.

Bober, M.M. (1948) *Karl Marx' Interpretation of History*, New York: W.W. Norton & Co.

Bracey, John H. et. al. (1970) *Black Nationalism in America*, New York: Bobbs-Merrill Co.

Breasted, James. (1934) *The Dawn of Conscience*, New York: University Books.

Budge, E.A. Wallis (transl.). (1960) *The Book of the Dead*, New York: University Books.

Carew, Jan. (1991) "Moorish Culture-Bringers: Bearers of Enlightenment," *Journal of African Civilizations*, II (Fall) 248-277.

Clark, J. Desmond. (1970) *The Prehistory of Africa, New York*: Praeger Publishers.

Collins, Robert O. (1968) *Problems in African History*, Englewood Cliffs: Prentice Hall, Inc.

Conrad, Earl. (1943) *Harriet Tubman*, Washington, D.C.: Associated Publishers, Inc.

Curtin, Philip et al. (1990) *African History*, London: Longman.

Davidson, Basil. (1991) *African Civilizations Revisited*, Trenton, NJ: Africa World Press.

Davidson, Basil. (1967) *East and Central Africa to the Late Nineteenth Century*, Nairobi: Longman, Green & Co.

Davidson, Basil. (1966) *A History of East Africa to the Nineteenth Century*, Garden City, N.Y.: Doubleday & Co.

Davidson, Basil. (1977) *A History of West Africa, 1000-1800*, London: Longman.

Davidson, Basil. (1959) *The Lost Cities of Africa*, Boston: Little, Brown & Co.

DeGraft-Johnson, John C. (1966) *African Glory*, New York: Walker & Co.

Diop, Cheikh Anta. (1974) *The African Origin of Civilization: Myth or Reality*, Westport, CT: Lawrence Hill & Co.

Diop, Cheikh Anta. (1991) *Civilization or Barbarism: An Authentic Anthropology*, New York: Lawrence Hill Books.

Diop, Cheikh Anta. (1981) *Civilization ou Barbarie*, Paris: Présence Africaine.

Diop, Cheikh Anta. (1978) *The Cultural Unity of Black Africa*, Chicago: Third World Press.

Diop, Cheikh Anta. (1987) *Pre-Colonial Black Africa*, Westport, CT: Lawrence Hill & Company.

Drake, St. Clair. (1987) *Black Folk Here and There: An Essay in History and Anthropology*, Los Angeles, Center for Afro-American Studies, University of California.

DuBois, W.E.B. (1975) *Black Folk: Then and Now*, New York: Kraus-Thomson.

DuBois, W.E.B. (1965) *The World and Africa*, New York: International Publishers.

El Mahdi, Mandour. (1965) *A Short History of the Sudan*, London: Oxford University Press.

El Nadoury, R. (1990) "The Legacy of Pharaonic Egypt," in G. Mokhtar (ed.) *General History of Africa, Vol. II, Ancient Civilizations of Africa* , Berkeley: University of California Press.

Fage, J.D. (1969) *A History of West Africa*, London: Cambridge University Press.

Forbes, Jack. (1980) *Black Africans and Native Americans*, Cambridge, MA: Blackwell.

Gailey, Harry A. (1970) *History of Africa From Earliest Times to 1800*, New York: Holt, Rinehart and Winston.

Gardiner, A.H. (1961) *Egypt of the Pharaohs: An Introduction*, New York: Oxford University Press.

Garvey, Amy Jacques (ed.) (1977) *Philosophy & Opinions of Marcus Garvey, I & II*, New York: Atheneum.

Hakem, A.A. (1990) "The Civilization of Napata and Meroe," in G. Mokhtar (ed.) *General History of Africa, Vol II, Ancient Civilizations of Africa*, Berkeley: University of California Press, pp, 172-202.

Harris, J.R. (ed.). (1971) *The Legacy of Egypt*, Oxford: Oxford University Press.

Harris, Joseph. (1972) *Africans and Their History*, New York: New American Library.

Haynes, Joyce L. (1992) *Nubia: Ancient Kingdoms of Africa*, Boston: Museum of Fine Arts.

Jackson, John G. (1980) *Introduction to African Civilizations*, Secaucus, N.J.: Citadel Press.

James, George. (1976) *Stolen Legacy*, San Francisco: Julian Richardson Associates.

James, T.G.H. (1979) *An Introduction to Ancient Egypt*, New York: Harper & Row.

July, Robert W. (1970) *A History of the African People*, New York: Charles Scribner's Sons.

Karenga, Maulana. (1977) "Corrective History," *First World*, 1,3 (May/June) 50-54.

Karenga, Maulana. (1978) *Essays on Struggle: Position and Analysis*, San Diego: Kawaida Publications.

Karenga, Maulana. (1980) *Kawaida Theory: An Introductory Outline*, Inglewood, CA: Kawaida Publications.

Karenga, Maulana. (1984) *Selections From the Husia: Sacred Wisdom of Ancient Egypt*, Los Angeles: University of Sankore Press.

Ki-Zerbo, J. (ed.) (1990) *General History of Africa, I: Methodology and African Prehistory*, CA: UNESCO.

Kling, Susan. (1979) *Fannie Lou Hamer*, Chicago: Women For Racial and Economic Equality.

Lane-Poole, Stanley. (1886) *The Story of the Moors in Spain*, New York: G.P. Putnam's Sons.

Lichtheim, Miriam. (1975) (1976) (1980) *Ancient Egyptian Literature: A Book of Readings, Vol. I, Vol. II, Vol. III*, Los Angeles: University of California Press.

Massie, Dorothy C. (1974) *The Legacy of Mary McLeod Bethune*, Washington, D.C.: National Education Association.

McCabe, Joseph. (1935) *The Splendour of Moorish Spain*, London: Watts and Co.

McCall, Daniel F. (1969) *Africa in Time-Perspective*, New York: Oxford University Press.

Murdock, G.P. (1959) *Africa: Its People and Their Culture History*, New York: McGraw Hill.

Murphy, E. Jefferson. (1972) *History of African Civilization*, New York: Dell Publishing Company.

National Education Association. (1974) *Mary McLeod Bethune*, New York: National Educational Association.

Obenga, Théophile. (1992) *Ancient Egypt and Black Africa*, London: Karnak House.

Obenga, Theophile. (1972) *L'Afrique Dans L'Antiquité: Egypte Pharonique-Afrique Noire*, Paris: Presénce Africaine.

Oliver, Roland and G. Matthews. (1963) *History of East Africa*, *I*, Oxford: Clarendon Press.

Olson, Stacie and Josef Wegner. (1992) *Ancient Nubia: Egypt's Rival in Africa*, Philadelphia: University Museum of Archeology and Anthropology, University of Pennsylvania.

Omer-Cooper, John D. (1966) *The Zulu Aftermath*, London: Longmans.

Osae, T.A. and S.N. Nwabara, et al. (1973) *A Short History of West Africa*. New York: Hill and Wang.

Pankhurst, Richard Keir. (1967) *The Ethiopian Royal Chronicles*, Addis Ababa: Oxford University Press.

Parry, J. H. (1966) *The Establishment of the European Hegemony*, New York: Harper & Row.

Petry, Ann. (1955) *Harriet Tubman*, New York: Robert Books.

Phillipson, David W. (1985) *African Archaeology*, Cambridge: Cambridge University Press.

Ravell, James. (1992) "An Annotated Bibliography of the Moors: 711-1492 A.C.," in Ivan Van Sertima (ed.) *Golden Age of the Moors, Journal of African Civilizations*, II (Fall) 407-454.

Rocker, Rudolph. (1937) *Nationalism and Culture*, New York: Couici-Friede.

Rodney, Walter. (1974) *How Europe Underdeveloped Africa*, Washington, D.C.: Howard University Press.

Rogers, J.A. (1972) *World's Great Men of Color, Vol. I*, New York: Macmillan Publishing Co.

Säve-Söderbergh, Torgny (ed.) (1987) *Temples and Tombs of Ancient Nubia*, New York: Thames and Hudson Inc.

Shinnie, Peter L. (1967) *Meroe: A Civilization of the Sudan*, New York: Frederick A. Praeger, Inc.

Taylor, John H. (1991) *Egypt and Nubia*, Cambridge: Harvard University Press.

Thorpe, Earl. (1971) *Black Historians*, New York: William Morrow.

Trigger, B.G. et al. (1983) *Ancient Egypt: A Social History*, New York: Cambridge University Press.

Trimingham, John S. (1962) *A History of Islam in West Africa*, London: Oxford University Press.

Van Sertima, Ivan. (1992) *Golden Age of the Moors*, New Brunswick: Transaction Publishers.

Van Sertima, Ivan. (1976) *They Came Before Columbus*, New York: Random House.

Vasina, Jan. (1968) *Kingdoms of the Savanna*, Madison: University of Wisconsin Press.

Vilakazi, Absolam. (1962) *Zulu Transformations, Natal*, S.A.: University of Witwatersrand Press.

Wenig, S. (1978) *Africa in Antiquity, Vol. II, Arts of Ancient Nubia and Sudan*, New York: The Brooklyn Museum.

Williams, Bruce. (1989) "The Last Pharaohs of Nubia," *Journal of African Civilizations*, 10 (Summer) 90-104.

Williams, Chancellor. (1974) *The Destruction of Black Civilization*, Chicago: Third World Press.

Africans in America

Adams, Russell L. (1969) *Great Negroes Past and Presents*, Chicago: Afro-Am Publishing Co.

Aptheker, Herbert. (1951) *A Documentary History of the Negro People in the United States*, New York: Citadel Press.

Aptheker, Herbert. (1943) *American Negro Slave Revolts*, New York:International Publishers.

Aptheker, Herbert. (1968) *To Be Free*, New York: International Publishers.

Bauer, Raymond and Alice Bauer. (1942) "Day-to-Day Resistance to Slavery," *Journal of Negro History*, 27 (October) 388-419.

Bennett, Lerone. (1975) *The Shaping of Black America*, Chicago: Johnson Publishing Company.

Bernal, Ignacio. (1979) *Great Sculpture of Ancient Mexico*, New York: William Morrow & Company.

Bernard, Jacqueline. (1990) *Journey Toward Freedom: The Story of Sojourner Truth*, New York: The Feminist Press at the City University of New York.

Berry, Mary Frances and John W. Blassingame. (1982) *Long Memory: The Black Experience in America*, New York: Oxford University Press..

Bibb, Henry. (1969) *Narratives of the Life and Adventures of Henry Bibb, An American Slave, in Puttin' on Ole Massa*, New York.

Billington, Ray A. (1981) *The Journal of Charlotte Forte, A Free Negro in the Slave Era*, New York: W. W. Norton & Co.

Blackett, R.J.M. (1983) *Building an Anti-Slavery Wall: Black Americans in the Atlantic Abolitionist Movement*, Baton Rouge: Southern University Press.

Blassingame, John. (1979) *The Slave Community*, New York: Oxford University Press.

Bracey, John et al. (eds.) (1971) *Blacks in the Abolitionist Movement*, Belmont, CA: Wadsworth Publishing Co.

Branch, Taylor. (1988) *Parting the Waters: America in the King Years, 1954-63*, New York: Simon & Schuster.

Brent, Linda. (1973) [1861] *Incidents in the Life of a Slave Girl.* Edited by Lydia Maria Child, New York: Harcourt Brace Jovanovich. (see Harriet Jacobs)

Brisbane, Robert H. (1974) *Black Activism*, Valley Force, PA: Judson Press.

Broderick, Francis. (1969) *W.E.B. DuBois: Negro Leader in Time of Crisis*, Stanford: Stanford University Press.

Browning, Rufus, et al. (1990) *Racial Politics in American Cities*, NY: Longman's.

Cabral, Amilcar. (1969) *Revolution in Guinea*, New York: Monthly Review Press.

Campbell, Edward D.C. Jr. and Kym S. Rice. (1991) *Before Freedom Came: African-American Life in the Antebellum South*, Charlottesville: University Press of Virginia.

Carmichael, Stokely and Charles Hamilton. (1967) *Black Power*, New York: Vintage Books.

Carroll, Joseph. (1938) *Slave Insurrections in the U.S.*, Boston: Little, Brown & Co.

Carby, Hazel. (1987) *Reconstructing Womanhood: The Emergence of the Afro-American Woman Novelist*, New York: Oxford University Press.

Carson, Claybourne. (1987) *Eyes on the Prize: America's Civil Rights Years - A Reader and Guide*, New York: Penguin Books.

Carson, Claybourne. (1981) *In Struggle*, Cambridge, MA: Harvard University Press.

Carwell, Hattie. (1977) *Blacks in Science*, Hicksville, NY: Exposition Park.

Chrisman, Robert and Robert L. Allen. (eds.) (1992) *Court of Appeal: The Black Community Speaks Out on the Racial and Sexual Politics of Clarence Thomas vs. Anita Hill*, New York: Ballantine Books.

Clark, Kenneth (ed). (1963) *The Negro Protest*, Boston: Harper Press.

Cleage, Albert. (1972) *Black Christian Nationalism*, New York: William Morrow & Co.

Cleage, Albert. (1968) *The Black Messiah*, New York: Sheed & Ward.

Coe, Michael. (1962) *Mexico*, New York: Praeger Publishers.

Conrad, Earl. (1943) *Harriet Tubman*, New York: Paul S. Erikson.

Conyers, James E. and Walter L. Wallace. (1976) *Black Elected Officials*, New York: Russell Sage Foundation.

Covey, Joan. (1992) "African Sea Kings in America: Evidence from Early Maps," in Ivan Van Sertima (ed.) *African Presence in Early America*, New Brunswick: Transaction Publishers.

Cruse, Harold. (1967) *Crisis of the Negro Intellectual*, New York: William Morrow & Co.

Dalleck, Robert. (1984) *Ronald Reagan: The Politics of Symbolism*, Cambridge, MA: Harvard University Press.

Daniels, Ron. (1980) "The National Black Assembly: Building Independent Black Politics in the 1980's," *Black Scholar*, 11, 4 (March/April).

Daughtery, Herbert. (1981) "An Interview," *The Black Nation*, (Fall) 8-11.

Davidson, Basil. (1977) *Africa in History*, London: Macmillan Company.

Davis, David Brian. (1975) *The Problem of Slavery in the Age of Revolution, 1770-1823*, Ithaca, NY: Cornell University.

De Roo, Peter. (1990) *History of America Before Columbus*, Philadelphia: J.B. Lippincott.

Diggs, Irene. (1975) *Black Innovators*, Chicago: Third World Press.

Drake, St. Clair and Horace Cayton. (1962) *Black Metropolis*, New York: Harper & Row.

DuBois, W.E.B. (1969) *Souls of Black Folk*, New York: New American Library.

Duster, Alfred A. (ed.). (1970) *Crusade for Justice: The Autobiography of Ida B. Wells*, Chicago: University of Chicago Press.

Edwards, Harry. (1970) *Black Students*, New York: Free Press.

Elkins, Stanley. (1966) *Slavery*, Chicago: University of Chicago Press.

Emmerich, Andre. (1963) *Art Before Columbus*, New York: Simon and Schuster.

Fairclough, Adam. (1987) *To Redeem the Soul of America: The Southern Christian Leadership Conference and Martin Luther King*, Athens: University of Georgia Press.

Farmer, James. (1965) *Freedom Win*, New York: Random House.

Farmer, James. (1985) *Lay Bare the Heart: An Autobiography of the Civil Rights Movement*, New York: Arbor House.

Fauset, Arthur H. (1938) *Sojourner Truth, God's Faithful Pilgrim*, Chapel Hill: University of North Carolina.

Flewellen, Kathryn. (1981) "The National Black Independent Political Party: Will History Repeat?" *Freedomways*, 21, 2, pp. 93-105.

Forbes, Jack. (1980) *Black Africans and Native Americans*, Cambridge, MA: Blackwell.

Forman, James. (1972) *The Making of Black Revolutionaries*, New York: Macmillan Co.

Fogel, Robert and Barry Engerman. (1974) *Time on the Cross*, Boston: Little, Brown & Co.

Foster, Frances S. (1990) *A Brighter Coming Day: A Frances Ellen Watkins Harper Reader*, New York: The Feminist Press and the City University of New York.

Foster, Laurence. (1935) *Negro-Indian Relationships in the Southwest*, Philadelphia: AMS Press.

Franklin, John H. and Alfred Moss, Jr. (1988) *From Slavery to Freedom: A History of Negro Americans*, New York: Alfred A. Knopf.

Franklin, John H. (1974) *From Slavery to Freedom*, New York: Alfred A. Knopf.

Garrow, David. (1986) *Bearing the Cross: Martin Luther King Jr. and the Southern Christian Leadership Conference, 1955-1968*, New York: Morrow.

Garvey, Amy Jacques (ed.). (1977) *Philosophy & Opinions of Marcus Garvey, I & II*. New York: Atheneum.

Genovese, Eugene. (1981) *From Rebellion to Revolution*, New York: Vintage Books.

Genovese, Eugene. (1974) *Roll, Jordan, Roll,* New York: Pantheon Books.

Giddings, Paula. (1984) *When and Where I Enter: The Impact of Race and Sex in America,* New York: William Morrow & Company.

Gilliam, Reginald E. (1975) *Black Political Development,* Port Washington, NY: Kennikat Press.

Greene, Lorenzo. (1944) "Mutiny on the Slave Ships," *Phylon,* 5 (4th qtr.)

Greider, William. (1981) "The Education of David Stockman," *The Atlantic Monthly,* (December) 27-54.

Gutman, Herbert G. (1976) *The Black Family in Slavery and Freedom, 1750-1925,* New York: Pantheon.

Haber, Louis. (1970). *Black Pioneers of Science and Invention,* New York: Harcourt, Brace and World, Inc.

Hakem, A.A. (1991) "The Civilization of Napata and Meroe," in G. Mokhtar (ed.) *General History of Africa II, Ancient Civilizations of Africa,* London: UNESCO, pp. 172-184,

Harding, Vincent. (1987) *Hope and History: Why We Must Share the Story of the Movement,* Maryknoll, NY: Orbis.

Harding, Vincent. (1980) *The Other American Revolution,* Los Angeles/Atlanta: Center for Afro-American Studies/ Institute of the Black World.

Harding, Vincent. (1981) *There is a River,* New York: Harcourt, Brace Jovanovich.

Hare, Nathan. (1972) "The Battle for Black Studies," *The Black Scholar,* 3, 9 (May) 32-47.

Harris, J.R. (ed.). (1971) *The Legacy of Egypt,* Oxford: Oxford University Press.

Harris, Joseph E. (1972) *Africans and Their History,* New York: New American Library.

Hayden, Robert C. (1972) *Eight Black American Inventors,* Reading, MA: Addison-Wesley Co.

Haynes, Joyce L. (1992) *Nubia: Ancient Kingdoms of Africa,* Boston: Museum of Fine Arts.

Holloway, Joseph E. (ed.). (1990) *Africanisms in American Culture*, Bloomington: Indiana University Press.

hooks, bell. (1992) *Black Looks, Race and Representation*, Boston: South End Press.

Hurmence, Belinda (ed.). (1990) *Before Freedom: 48 Oral Histories of Former North and South Carolina Slaves*, New York: A Mentor Book.

Jackson, John G. (1980) *Pagan Origins of the Christ Myth*, San Diego: The Truth Seeker Company.

Jacobs, Harriet A. (1987) *Incidents in the Life of Slave Girl Written by Herself*, Cambridge, MA: Harvard University Press. (See also Linda Brent)

Jairazbhoy, R.A. (1974) *Ancient Egyptians and Chinese in America*, Totowa, NJ: Rowan and Littlefield.

Jones, Jacquelin. (1985) *Labor of Love, Labor of Sorrow: Black Women, Work, and the Family from Slavery to the Present*, New York: Basic Books.

Karenga, Maulana. (1989) *The African American Holiday of Kwanzaa: A Celebration of Family, Community and Culture*, Los Angeles: University of Sankore Press.

Karenga, Maulana. (1977) "Corrective History," *First World*, 1, 3 (May/June) 50-54.

Karenga, Maulana. (1978) *Essays on Struggle: Position and Analysis*, San Diego: Kawaida Publications.

Karenga, Maulana. (1980) *Kawaida Theory: An Introductory Outline*, Inglewood, CA.: Kawaida Publications.

Karenga, Maulana. (1979) "The Socio-Political Philosophy of Malcolm X," *Journal of Black Studies*, 3, 4 (Winter) 251-262.

Katz, William. (1986) *Black Indians*, New York: Macmillan Children's Book Group.

King, Martin Luther, Jr. (1958) *Stride Toward Freedom*, New York: Harper & Row Publishers.

King, Martin Luther, Jr. (1962) *Why We Can't Wait*, New York: Harper & Row Publishers.

Klein, Aaron E. (1971) *The Hidden Contributions: Black Scientists and Inventors in America*, New York: Doubleday and Co.

Kluger, Richard. (1976) *Simple Justice: The History of Brown v. Board of Education, Black America's Struggle for Equality*, New York: Alfred A. Knopf.

Lawrence, Harol. (1962) "African Explorers in the New World," *The Crisis*, (June-July) 321-332.

Littlefield, Daniel Jr. (1977) *Africans and Seminoles*, Westport: Greenwood Press.

Logan, Rayford. (1954) *The Negro in American Life and Thought: The Nadir, 1877-1901*, New York: Van Nostrand Reinhold Co.

Lomax, Louis E. (1962) *The Negro Revolt*, New York: Signet Books.

McAdam, Doug. (1983) *Political Process and the Development of Black Insurgency 1930-1970*, Chicago: University of Chicago Press.

McIntyre, Charshee C. (1992) *Criminalizing a Race: Free Blacks During Slavery*, Queens, NY: Kayode Publications.

Madhubuti, Haki R. (ed.). (1993) *Why L.A. Happened: Implications of the '92 Los Angeles Rebellion*, Chicago: Third World Press.

Malcolm X. (1965) *Autobiography of Malcolm X*, New York: Grove Press.

Malcolm X. (1970) *By Any Means Necessary*, New York: Grove Press.

Malcolm X. (1992) *February 1965: The Final Speeches*, New York: Pathfinder Press.

Malcolm X. (1966) *Malcolm X Speaks*, New York: Grove Press.

Marable, Manning. (1985) *Black American Politics: From Washington Marches to Jesse Jackson*, London: Verso.

Marine, Gene. (1969) *The Black Panthers*, New York: New American Library.

Martin, Tony. (1976) *Race First*, Westport: Greenwood Press.

Meier, August. (1975) "Toward A Reinterpretation of Booker T. Washington," *Journal of Southern History*, 23, pp. 220-227.

Moon, Henry. (1972) *The Emerging Thought of W.E.B. DuBois*, New York: Simon & Schuster.

Morris, Aldon. D. (1984) *The Origins of the Civil Rights Movement*, New York: The Free Press.

Morrison, Toni. (1992) *Race-Ing Justice, En-Gendering Power: Essays on Anita Hill, Clarence Thomas, and the Construction of Social Reality*, New York: Pantheon Books.

Muhammad, Elijah. (1973) *The Fall of Africa*, Chicago: Muhammad's Temple of Islam, No. 2.

Muhammad, Elijah. (1965) *Message to the Black Man in America*, Chicago: Muhammad's Temple of Islam, No. 2.

Mullin, Gerald W. (1972) *Flight and Rebellion*, New York: Oxford University Press.

Neverdon-Morton, Cynthia. (1989) *Afro-American Women of the South and the Advancement of the Race, 1895-1925*, Knoxville: University of Tennessee Press.

Newton, Huey. (1972) *To Die For the People*, New York: Random House.

Obadele, Imari. (1975) *Foundations of the Black Nation*, Detroit: Songhay Press.

O'Reilly, Kenneth. (1989) "Racial Matters": The FBI's Secret File on Black America, 1960-1972, New York: The Free Press.

Patterson, Orlando. (1982) *Slavery and Social Death*, Cambridge, MA: Harvard University Press.

Peck, James. (1962) *Freedom Ride*, New York: Simon & Schuster.

Phillips, Ulrich B. (1963) "Life and Labor in the Old South," Boston: Little, Brown & Co.

Porter, Kenneth. (1932) "Relations Between Negroes and Indians with the Present Limits of the United States," *Journal of Negro History*, 17 (July) 287-367.

Price, Richard. (1973) *Maroon Societies*, Garden City, NY: Anchor Books.

Proudfoot, Merrill. (1962) *Diary of a Sit-In*, Chapel Hill, NC: University of North Carolina Press.

Quarles, Benjamin. (1969) *Black Abolitionists*, New York: Oxford University Press.

Quarles, Benjamin. (1988) "Harriet Tubman's Unlikely Leadership," *Black Leaders of the Nineteenth Century*, Urbana: University of Illinois Press.

Quarles, Benjamin. (1953) *The Negro in the Civil War*, Boston: Little, Brown & Co.

Quarles, Benjamin. (1976) *The Negro in the Making of America*, New York: Collier Books.

Richardson, Marilyn. (ed.). (1987) *Maria W. Stewart: America's First Black Woman Political Writer*, Bloomington, IN: University Press.

Robinson, Jo Ann Gibson. (1987) *The Montgomery Bus Boycott and the Women Who Started It: The Memoir of Jo Ann Gibson Robinson*, Knoxville: University of Tennessee Press.

Robinson, Armstead et al (eds). (1969) *Black Studies in the University*, New York: Bantam Books.

Robinson, Armstead and Patricia Sullivan. (eds.) (1991) *New Directions in Civil Rights Studies*, Charlottesville: University Press of Virginia.

Rodney, Walter. (1974) *How Europe Underdeveloped Africa*, Washington, D.C.: Howard University Press.

Rogers, J.A. (1961) *Africa's Gift to America*, New York: Helga M. Rogers.

Salaam, Kalamu ya. (1974) "Tell No Lies Claim No Easy Victories," *Black World*, 23, 12 (October) 18-34.

Schwartz, Rosalie. (1975) *Across the Rio to Freedom*, El Paso: Texas Western Press.

Seale, Bobby. (1970) *Seize the Time*, New York: Random House.

Sindler, Allan P. (1978) *Bakke, DeFunis and Minority Admissions*, New York: Longman.

Sorin, Gerald. (1973) *Abolitionism*, New York: Praeger Publishers.

Stampp, Kenneth. (1967) *Peculiar Institution*, New York: Alfred Knopf, Inc.

Sterling, Dorothy. (1984) *We Are Sisters: Black Women in the Nineteenth Century*, New York: W. W. Norton & Co.

Stirling, Matthew, W. (1939) "Discovering the New World's Oldest Dated Work of Man," *National Geographic Magazine*, 76 (August) 183-218.

Stoper, Emily. (1989) *The Student Nonviolent Coordinating Committee: The Growth of Radicalism in a Civil Rights Organization*, Brooklyn: Carlson Publications.

Stuckey, Sterling. (1973) "Through the Prism of Folklore: the Black Ethos in Slavery," in *American Negro Slavery*, (eds.) Allen Weinstein and Frank Gatell, New York: Oxford University Press, 134-152.

Thornbrough, E.L. (ed.) (1969) *Booker T. Washington*, Englewood Cliffs: Prentice-Hall, Inc.

Tushnet, Mark V. (1987) *The NAACP's Legal Strategy Against Segregated Education, 1925-1950*, Chapel Hill: University of North Carolina Press.

Van Sertima, Ivan. (1992) *African Presence in Early America*, New Brunswick: Transaction Publishers.

Van Sertima, Ivan. (1976) *They Came Before Columbus*, New York: Random House.

Von Wuthenau, Alexander. (1969) *The Art of Terracotta Pottery in Pre-Columbian South and Central America*, New York: Free Press.

Walton, Hanes Jr. (1972) *Black Political Parties*, New York: Free Press.

Washington, Booker T. (1968) *Up From Slavery*, New York: Magnum Books.

Webber, Thomas L. (1978) *Deep Like the Rivers: Education in the Slave Quarter Community, 1831-1865*, New York. W. W. Norton & Co.

Weinberg, Meyer. (1970) *W.E.B. DuBois: A Reader*, New York: Harper & Row Publishers.

Weiner, Leo. (1972) *Africa and the Discovery of America*, Philadelphia: Innes and Sons.

White, Deborah Gray. (1987) *Ar'n't I A Woman? Female Slaves in the Plantation South*, New York: W. W. Norton & Co.

White, Deborah Gray. (1991) "Female Slaves in the Plantation South," in Edward D.C. Campbell, Jr., (ed.) *Before Freedom Came*, Richmond: The Museum of the Confederacy.

Williams, Eric. (1966) *Capitalism & Slavery*, New York: Capricorn Books.

Williams, Juan. (1987) *Eyes on the Prize*, New York: Viking.

Williams, Robert. (1973) *Negroes With Guns*, Chicago: Third World Press.

Wolff, Miles. (1972) *Lunch at the Five and Ten*, New York: Stein & Day Publishers.

Woodson, Carter G. and Charles H. Wesley. (1972) *The Negro in Our History*, Washington, D.C.: Associated Publishers.

Yee, Shirley J. (1992) *Black Women Abolitionists: A Study in Activism, 1828-1860*, Knoxville: University of Tennessee Press.

Youth of the Rural Organizing and Cultural Center. (1991) *Minds Stayed on Freedom: The Civil Rights Struggle in the Rural South, and Oral History*, Boulder: Westview Press.

Zinn, Howard. (1964) *SNCC: The New Abolitionist*, Boston: Beacon Press.

BLACK RELIGION

3
BLACK RELIGION

3.1   INTRODUCTION

Religion has always been a vital part of Black life in both Africa and the U.S. In Africa, religion was so pervasive that distinctions between it and other areas of life were almost imperceptible (Mbiti, 1970). In the U.S., the extent of Black religiousness is clear and has been well-documented (Lincoln, 1974a). Although there are numerous definitions for religion, for the purpose of this chapter, *religion can be defined as thought, belief and practice concerned with the transcendent and the ultimate questions of life* (Karenga, 1980:23). Among such questions are those concerning human death, relevance, origin, destiny, suffering and obligations to other humans and in most cases, to a Supreme or Ultimate Being. Within the context of the concern with the ultimate is also the clear division between the sacred, i.e., the set apart and exalted, and the profane, i.e., the common and non-exalted (Yinger, 1970).

The religion of Black people in the U.S. is predominantly Judeo-Christian, but Islam, both Black and orthodox, and ancient African religious and ethical traditions, are growing among African Americans (Wilmore, 1989). Among these other varied traditions are the Black Hebrew tradition (Ben Yehuda, 1975), the Rastafarian tradition (Barrett, 1988; Morrison, 1992) and the Yoruba tradition which is an international tradition including a Continental Yoruba practice (Lucas, 1948; Abimbola, 1976; Awolalu, 1979; Thompson, 1983; Drewal, 1992), a Santería Yoruba practice (Murphy, 1988; Gonzalez-Wippler, 1982;

Gleason, 1975) and a Candomblé Yoruba practice (Bastide, 1978; Richards, 1976). Also in recent years, the Maatian tradition from ancient Egypt has emerged and is discussed below (Karenga, 1984, 1988).

Given the fact that Black religion is so predominantly Judeo-Christian, the tendency is to see it as "white religion in Black face." However, as Lincoln (1974a) and Wilmore (1973) contend, such an interpretation is grossly incorrect. For regardless of what external details of white Christianity are similar to Black Christianity, the essence of Black Christianity is different. The essence of a people's religion is rooted in its own social and historical experiences and in the truth and meaning they extract from these and translate into an authentic spiritual expression which speaks specifically to them. Thus, Black religion represents in its essence then, not imitation but "the desire of Blacks to be self-conscious about the meaning of their Blackness and to search for spiritual fulfillment in terms of their understanding of themselves and their experience of history" (Lincoln, 1974a:3).

3.2   ANCIENT AFRICAN TRADITIONS

General Themes

Black religion like Black people began in Africa and thus, it is important to discuss its historical forms before turning to its current expressions. The study of traditional African religions is made difficult by Europeans' interpretations which exhibit a need to make Christianity seem superior and African religions primitive (Evans-Pritchard, 1965) and by African Christian interpretations which strive to make African religions more "normal" by making them look more Christian or Western (Idowu, 1975; Mbiti, 1970). To appreciate African religions, one must admit similarities and differences without seeing the similarities as "less developed" and the differences as evidence of psychological or cultural defectiveness.

Thus, if African stories of creation and divinities are myths, so are Christian, Jewish and Islamic ones. However, a better category for both African and other creation stories would be "narratives." Moreover, Jehovah, Yahweh and Allah are no more arguable than Nkulunkulu, Oludumare and Amma. And the abasom of the Ashanti and the orisha of the Yoruba are no less effective as divine intermediaries than Catholic saints like Jude and Christopher. All non-scientific approaches to the origin of the world and the forces operative in it are vulnerable to challenge. And the choice of one over the other is more a matter of tradition and preference than proof of any particular one's validity. Therefore, my use of Western religious examples will not be to force comparisons or contrasts, but to demonstrate parallels where appropriate which would help to lessen a person's tendency to reductively translate African religions in a mistaken assumption of superiority for his/her own.

Although African religious traditions are complex and diverse, there are some general themes which tend to appear in all of them (Mbiti, 1970, 1991; Ray, 1976; Zahan, 1979; Wright, 1984; Gyekye, 1987). First, there is the belief in one Supreme God: Oludumare among the Yoruba, Nkulunkulu among the Zulu and Amma among the Dogon, etc. This God is the Father in most societies, but also appears as Mother in matriarchal societies like the Ovambo in Namibia and the Nuba in Kenya. Moreover, in Dogon religion, Amma has both male and female characteristics, reflecting the Dogon concept of binary opposition as the motive force and structure of the universe (Ray, 1976:28-29; Griaule, 1978).

Secondly, in ancient African religious traditions, God is both immanent and transcendent, near and far. In this framework, then, Africans engage in daily interaction with divinities, who are seen as God's intermediaries and assistants (Mbiti, 1970, 1991). These divinities are both similar to and different from Jesus, angels and Catholic saints as intermediaries and assistants to the Supreme Being. It is this deference and exchange with the divinities which made the less critical assume Africans were polytheistic rather than monotheistic. However, evidence clearly argues against this assumption.

Thirdly, African religions stress ancestor veneration. The ancestors are venerated for several reasons which reinforce the concepts of linkage, heritage and spiritual relevance (Richards, 1989:7,8). They "are venerated because they are: 1) a source and symbol of lineage; 2) models of ethical life, service and social achievement to the community; and 3) because they are spiritual intercessors between humans and the Creator" (Karenga, 1988: 20, see also Mbiti, 1970:108, 1991). The Ashanti have a special Day of Remembrance of the Ancestors called *Akwasidae* in which ceremonies focus on linkage between those who have passed, the living and the yet unborn. As Mends (1976:8) notes, by participating in the ceremony to honor ancestors one is stressing "the common bonds of kinship and association which make for solidarity among the people." And it is also a way to reinforce the value and honor due those whose ethical life and service make them worthy members of the community.

Fourthly, ancient African religions stresses the necessary balance between one's collective identity and responsibility as a member of society and one's personal identity and responsibility. Like religion itself, a person is defined as an integral part of a definite community, to which she/he belongs and in which she/he finds identity and relevance. Summing up this conception, Mbiti (1970:141) states that "I am because we are, and since we are, therefore I am." The Dinka have captured this stress on the moral ideal of harmonious integration of self with the community in their word *cieng* which means both morality and living together. In this conception, the highest moral ideal is to live in harmony, know oneself and one's duties through others and reach one's fullness in cooperation with and through support from one's significant others (Deng, 1973).

Another key theme in African religions is the profound respect for nature. Because humans live in a religious universe, everything that is has religious relevance (Richards, 1989:6-7). The whole world as God's creation is alive with His/Her symbols and gifts to humans, and bear witness to His/Her power, beauty and beneficence. Thus, there are sacred trees, rivers, mountains and animals (as in Western religions). Nature is not only respected because of its association with God, but also because of its relevance to humankind. This respect is grounded in the belief that there is an unbreakable bond between the divine, the human and the natural and that therefore damage to one is damage to the other and likewise respect and care for one is respect and care for the other. The stress, then, is to show nature due respect, not abuse it in any way and to live in harmony with it and the universe. Dona Marimba Richards (1989:10) notes that African culture is a "culture that perceives the interrelationships and interdependence of all beings within the universe." Thus, she says the African approach is that "if we take or destroy, we must give or rebuild; for there is one spiritual unity that joins us all...."

Finally, the conception of death and immortality is an important theme in African religions. Death in African religions is seen in several ways. First, it is seen as another stage in human development. Humans are born, live, die and become the ancestors. Death is thus not the end, but a beginning of another form of existence, i.e., as ancestor and spirit. Therefore, it is seen as a transition in life rather than an end to it. After a period of mourning there is celebration for the human conquest of death. For after the funeral, the dead are "revived" in the spirit world and, as ancestors, are close and relevant. Secondly, death is seen as reflective of cosmic patterns, i.e., the rising and setting of the sun, and often graves are dug east and west to imitate this pattern.

Thirdly, death is seen as a transition in life to personal and collective immortality. Personally, one lives after death through four media: 1) children; 2) other relatives; 3) rituals of remembrance; and 4) great works or significant deeds. The living remember and speak one's name and deeds, and one's works speak of one's significance throughout time. Thus, without relatives to keep one's memory alive or significant achievements and deeds, one is what Africans call "utterly dead." Collective immortality is achieved through the life of one's people and through what one means to them. For as long as they live, the person lives and shares in their life and destiny.

The Dogon Tradition

One of the most complex and impressive African religious systems is that of the Dogon. The Dogon, who live in Mali, have astounded the world by their astronomical knowledge and impressed it with the logic and intricacy of their thought. So impressive is their knowledge, especially of the Sirius star-system, that some Europeans have argued that the Dogon's knowledge was given to them by space beings (Temple, 1976) or by mysterious Europeans (Sagan, 1979). However, Europeans did not know themselves until the 1800's what the Dogon knew about the Sirius star-system 700 years ago (Adams, 1979).

The socio-religious thought of the Dogon evolves from an elaborate cosmogony and an extremely complex cosmology (Griaule, 1978; Griaule and Dieterlen, 1965). It is these constructions around which the Dogon understand and organize their world and seek to carry out their social and spiritual tasks. For the sake of brevity and clarity, I have tried to reduce the story of creation to its most basic elements while at the same time, trying to remain faithful to its logic and content.

In the beginning everything that would be already potentially was. The substances and structure of the universe was in Amma, the Supreme God, who was in the image of an egg and divided into four quarters containing the four basic elements of air, earth, fire and water, and the four cardinal directions-north, south, east and west. Thus, Amma was the egg of the universe, and the universe and Amma were one. As egg, Amma symbolized and was fertility and unlimited creative possibility. Through creative thought, Amma traced within himself the design and developmental course of the universe using 266 cosmic signs which contained the essence, structure and life-principle of all things. Placing the four basic elements and sacred signs and seeds on a flat disk, Amma set the disk revolving between the two cosmic axes. But the spinning disk threw off the water drying up the seeds. The first creation was thus aborted and Amma began again, deciding that this time he would make humans the preservers of order and life in the world.

Placing a seed at the center of himself, the cosmic egg, he spoke seven creative words. From this, the seed (matter) vibrated seven times unfolding along a spiral path, conserving itself on one hand and transforming itself on the other through alternations between opposites. Thus, the principal of twinness or binary opposition directed its movement and its form and established a pattern for the structure and functioning of the universe, i.e., up/down, man/woman, action/inaction, hot/cold, etc. From the infinitely small (seed, atom), the infinitely large (universe) evolved. The seed, vibrating seven times and turning in a spiral fashion, extended itself in seven directions in the womb of the world, pre-figuring the shape of a human being, i.e., two directions for the head, two for the arms, two for the legs and one for the genital. The world was thus created in the image of humans and would later be organized around them.

Transforming the egg into a double placenta, Amma placed two sets of twins, male and female in each, again underscoring the principle of opposites which informs the structure and functioning of the universe. In the twins, He placed the sacred signs, words and seeds of creation. Before gestation was completed, however, one of the male twins, Yurugu (Ogo), feeling lonely and incomplete, bursts through the womb to seize his female twin. Unable to acquire his twin, he rebelled against the established order of things. Imposing disorder on a orderly process, Yurugu descended into the void in an attempt to create a world himself. But his knowledge was incomplete and he could not speak the creative words. Then Amma, using the piece of placenta which Yurugu took as he broke from the celestial egg-womb, created the earth. This creation of earth restored the human shape of the world. The celestial egg became the head of man; the lower incomplete placenta, now earth and forming an incomplete circle, became the hips and legs; and the space and lines which divide and connect heaven and earth became the trunk and arms. Binary opposition is thus, again established in that heaven is the head (mind, spirit) and earth, the lower region of the body (the physical). Joined together, they form the structure and essence of humans.

To restore order in the world, Amma scattered Yurugu's male twin, Nommo, i.e., creative word, over the expanse of the universe. Also, He created four other Nommo spirits from Nommo and their offspring became the eight ancestors of the Dogon. Amma then sent Nommo and the eight ancestors down to Earth, with all species of animals and plants, and all the elements of human culture, thus laying the basis for human development and a prosperous earth. Descending, Nommo shouted out the creative words, therefore transmitting the power of creative speech and thought to Earth, making it available to humankind. Through this power, they would be able to push back the boundaries of ignorance and disorder and impose creative order on the world. To punish Yurugu for his disorder and revolt, Amma transformed him into a Pale Fox. Deprived of his female half, the Pale Fox is an incomplete and lonely being wandering though the world in a vain quest for wholeness. But as he wanders, he leaves tracks through the mysteries of life, revealing the dangers humans must avoid. Finally, sending rain to Earth, Amma made the Earth flourish and humans began to cultivate the land and cover it with ever-increasing numbers. Possessing creative intelligence through Nommo, humans walk the way of Yurugu as well, alternating between disorder and order, destruction and creation, rationality and irrationality, conformity and revolt.

There are several aspects of this cosmogonical construction which reveal the profundity of Dogon thought and its susceptibility to interesting and expansive interpretations. First, it stresses the binary oppositional character and functioning of the universe, i.e., creation/destruction, order/disorder, male/ female, perfection/imperfection, self-conscious action/unconscious action, etc. This is essentially an African dialectic, posing opposites necessary to the explanation and functioning of the world. In fact, each opposite explains and necessitates the other. Thus, Yurugu rebels because he feels deprived of his female half which he needs for his wholeness. He fails because he represents action without critical consciousness, and Nommo, who reflects the creative thought and action of Amma, succeeds in establishing order and promoting development. Secondly, the concept of God as the cosmic womb, already containing in the beginning everything that would come into being in Him, suggests a concept of God as the universe and of its already having at the beginning all the building material (matter) for everything in it. This reflects the scientific principle that matter was always and already here, and only its forms changed and change.

Thirdly, the concept of God as egg is reflective of His fertility, productiveness and infinite creative possibilities, as well as the idea of them. As infinite creative possibility in the universe and of the universe, God is infinite in a logical and meaningful way. Fourthly, the Dogon pose God as making a mistake in the first creation and thus, maintain logical consistency even in discussing God. For God is both perfect and imperfect, male and female, thought and action and therefore reflects and reinforces the principle of binary opposition.

Also, there is a clear contention that the world is not perfect either and is in the process of perpetual becoming. This process again is marked by binary opposition in structure and functioning and strives toward the creative and ongoing harmonizing of the two opposites. Especially profound and far-reaching is the concept that becoming of necessity requires rebellion or oppositional thought and action against the established order. Yurugu comes into being by breaking through the cosmic egg and thus, sets up conditions for a new world. Breaking from Amma, God, he becomes truly man rather than a cosmic baby. In this action, he reminds one of the young adult leaving his/her parents' house in order to build a world for him/herself. In a word, independence and development requires a break from the established state of things. And even though Yurugu fails to make the world, he contributed to its origin and still leaves tracks through the mysteries of life which humankind can read and from which they can learn vital lessons.

Finally, Dogon thought is clearly impressive in its stress on humans as the indispensable element in the world's becoming and functioning. As noted above, the universe was created in the image of the human personality; he/she is the world in micro-cosm, containing its basic elements, the four cardinal directions, and the sacred cosmic seeds, signs and words. Moreover, Amma/ God could not make the world without humans, for not only did the world need man/woman to flourish, but so did God. For if God is idea and creative possibility, only man/woman can know and appreciate it. Only humans are capable of creative thought; trees will not pray or praise, and dogs do not discuss spiritual or social duties. But if God needs man/woman, the binary oppositional logic of Dogon thought requires that man/woman also needs God. For if idea and creative possibility (God) cannot exist without man/woman, man/woman cannot exist without idea and creative possibility (God).

The Egyptian Tradition And Legacy

Egypt's contribution to Western religions and indeed to Western civilization in general is a well-argued and well-docu-mented contention (Harris, 1971). In fact, given the deeply religious character of Egyptian society, all activities whether science, government or art were informed and inspired by its religion (Morenz, 1984:6ff). Within the context of Continental African and African American intellectual history, works by Cheikh Anta Diop (1991, 1974), John Jackson (1972), George G. James (1976), Jacob Carruthers (1984), and Maulana Karenga (1984, 1986, 1988) as well as others (Karenga and Carruthers 1986) cogently and consistently represent this position. More-

over, some European scholars such as E. Wallis Budge (1961),
James Breasted (1933), Gerald Massey (1970), Henri Frankfort
(1948), Flinders Petrie (1914), and most recently Martin Bernal
(1987, 1991) have assumed a similar position in varying degrees.
In fact, it is Breasted (1933:xv), the U.S.' pre-eminent orientalist,
who conceded as early as 1933 that "It is now quite evident that
the ripe social and moral development of mankind in the Nile
Valley, which is three thousand years older than that of the
Hebrews, contributed essentially to the formation of the Hebrew
literature which we call the Old Testament. Our moral heritage
therefore derives from a wider *human* past enormously older
than the Hebrews, and it has come to us rather *through* the
Hebrews than *from* them."

John Jackson (1972) cites several legacies of Egypt to
Christianity. First, he argues that the concept of the Virgin and
Child in Christianity is clearly based on the Virgin Isis and Child
Horus of Egypt. Jackson (1972:123) states that "Gods, heroes,
born of virgins, were quite common in olden times and the
sources of most, if not all of these divinities seem to have been
Egypt." He then quotes Jocelyn Rhys' *Shaken Creeds*, which
notes that "In the catacombs of Rome, black statues of this
Egyptian divine Mother and Infant still survive from the early
Christian worship of the Virgin and Child to which they were
converted."

Secondly, Jackson contends that Horus, the Egyptian
Savior and light of the world, is the model for Jesus who has
similar qualities. He points out that, as Charles Vail contends in
his *The World's Saviors*, there were fifteen saviours of miraculous
birth which preceded Jesus among which were Krishna and
Gautama (Buddha) of India, Tammuz of Babylonia, Zoroaster of
Persia, Quetzalcoatl of Mexico, and Horus of Egypt. But of all
the virgin-birth saviors, Horus appears to be the model of Jesus.
In fact, on the inner walls of the Holy of Holies in the Temple
of Luxor inscribed about two thousand years B.C.E., he (1972:-
124) states, "the birth of Horus is depicted in four scenes which
suggests how much Jesus' story is modelled after Horus." These

four scenes are: 1) the Annunciation, in which the God, Thoth, announces to the Virgin Isis, she will bear a son; 2) the Immaculate Conception in which the God Kneph (the Holy Spirit) and the Goddess Hathor mystically impregnate Isis by holding the ankh to her head and nostrils; 3) the Birth of the Son of God, Horus; 4) the Adoration with men and gods paying homage to the child, including three kings or magi who are giving him gifts.

Also, Jackson notes how an ancient Egyptian passion play enacts the arrest, trial, death, burial and resurrection of Osiris, often used interchangeably with Horus, as Savior, providing more evidence of Christianity's borrowing of models from Egypt. Finally, Jackson points out that even the celebration of Christmas on December 25th has its roots in Egypt. For "In Egypt, three thousand years ago, the birth day of the sun God (Ra) was celebrated on the 25th of December, since it was the first day to noticeably lengthen after December 21st (the day of the winter solstice)" (Jackson, 1972:134).

No one to date has done as much work toward the rescue and reconstruction of the rich cultural legacy of ancient Egypt to the world as Cheikh Anta Diop. A truly Imhotepian man, he was an historian, linguist, anthropologist and archeologist, and he used each of these fields to rescue and reconstruct this legacy and make it a vital part in the vindication, revitalization and continued development of African culture. For him, as with those who build on his work, Egypt is Africa's paradigmatic classical culture in the same way Greece is for Europe. His *The African Origin of Civilization* (1974) and his last major work, *Civilization or Barbarism* (1991), were especially dedicated to establishing and explicating the richness, relevance and African rootedness of this world historical legacy.

Diop (1981) argues cogently Egypt's contribution to science, math, philosophy, and religion, more precisely to the "revealed religions," i.e., Judaism, Christianity and Islam. For Diop (1981:388ff), Greek and Judeo-Christian thought borrows from and builds on an Egyptian cosmogony expressed in the so-called Pyramid Texts, which were written around 2600 B.C.E. "in an epoch in which the Greeks themselves did not exist and the notion of a Chinese or Hindu philosophy was nonsense" (Diop, 1981:388; 1991:310). From this cosmogony, Diop contends, one finds several key philosophical concepts which informed Greek philosophy and Judeo-Christian thought: 1) a universe of uncreated eternal matter (Anaximander's and Hesiod's aperion); 2) archetypes of essence of all future things which would be called into existence (Plato's archetypical ideals); 3) the law of transformation and the principle of evolution through time expressed in the concept of Kheper (actualization of archetypes in Plato); 4) the emergence of Ra (God) (Plato's demiurge); 5) Ra's creation through the word; i.e., logos, in Greek and later Judaism, Christianity and Islam.

Speaking of Christianity in particular, Diop (1991:312) states that the very term "Christ" "is not from an Indo-European root but comes from a pharaonic Egyptian expression, *kher sesheta*, 'one who is in charge of the mysteries' and which was applied to Jesus in the fourth century through reli-gious...(diffusion)." Moreover, Diop points out that Osiris is the religious paradigm for the Redeemer "who three thousand years before Jesus, dies and rises from the dead to save humans." He is thus the "redeeming God of humanity: he rises in the sky on the right hand of his father, the Great God, Ra. He is the son of God." Also, he notes that Egyptian religious philosophy provides a source of the concept of trinity. In fact, "the notion of trinity appears throughout Egyptian thought and is found in the many divine triads such as Osiris-Isis-Horus or Ra in the morning, at noon and in the evening," i.e., Kheper in the morn-ing, Ra at noon and Atum in the evening.

Finally, Diop posits that the goddess Hathor's receiving a ray of light from heaven which engenders the god Apis is clearly "a prefiguration of the immaculate conception of the Holy Virgin." He refers to J. Pirenne's *History of the Civilization of Ancient Egypt* for further explication. In one sense, Diop's work is a scholarly and well-documented expansion of George James' work, *Stolen Legacy* which was seminal in its conception and presentation at an early stage in the African project of rescuing and reconstructing the Egyptian legacy. James' work was essentially philosophical but Diop brought to bear a multidimensional knowledge base, as well as did scientific field and lab work, to prove his contentions and explicate the African/Egyptian legacy.

George James (1976) argues in his major work, *Stolen Legacy*, that it is out of Egyptian socio-religious philosophy that so-called Greek philosophy came. In fact, he (1976:1) contends at the outset that "The term Greek philosophy, to begin with is a misnomer," since it is essentially a derivative from the Egyptian socio-religious educational philosophical system called "the Egyptian Mysteries System." Realizing the awesome burden of proof such a contention incurs, James develops historical, textual and conceptual evidence to support it.

In terms of historical evidence, James cites the following information. First, the teaching of the Egyptian Mysteries System was the source of higher education in the ancient world with students from Europe, Asia and other parts of Africa studying there. Not only did the Greeks study there, but also Jesus and Moses. As a result, they returned to their various countries to set up EMS schools or variations of them. Secondly, Pythagoras, from whom all Greek philosophers borrowed, studied in Egypt as did Thales, Democratus, Plato, Diogenes, Timaeus and Herodotus and all confirm this in their writing. Thirdly, other Greek philosophers -- Anaximander, Anximenes, Parmenides, Zeno and Melisus studied in Ionia in Asia Minor, a stronghold of EMS schools.

Fourthly, immigration of Greeks to Egypt for education began as early as 525 B.C.E. after the Persian invasion of Egypt. Fifthly, the conquest of Egypt by Alexander (332 B.C.E.) prepared the way for greater absorption of Egyptian knowledge from its schools and libraries. In fact, the schools of Aristotle moved from Athens to Egypt, converted the Egyptian Royal Library to a research center and university and compiled a vast body of scientific and other knowledge from documents and oral instruction from Egyptian priests, and called it the history of Greek philosophy. Sixthly, there is an historical and logical problem of establishing that Aristotle wrote 400 to 1,000 books and learned from Plato who learned from Socrates a math, science, politics and economics Socrates did not know. Historical evidence says Alexander gave Aristotle money to buy books on science, but in order to obtain them they had to be in existence, and if they were in existence, he cannot be credited with having written them. In fact, he got them from the libraries of Egypt. Finally, the persecution of Greek philosophers for teaching *foreign* doctrines and the edicts of Roman emperors Theodius (4th century) and Justinian (6th century) which abolished EMS in Greece as well as Egypt, point strongly to the historical link between the two.

The textual and conceptual evidence shows also the historical link and borrowing. First, the Memphite Theology (c. 4,000 B.C.E.) with its three-part text on Gods of Chaos, Gods of Creation and Primate of the Gods, contains within it concepts that the Greeks appear to have borrowed. In sum, these borrowings are: 1) the concept of summon bonum--highest good and discipline and cardinal virtues which make humans god (Aristotle, Socrates, Plato); 2) the EMS curriculum, i.e., the Seven Liberal Arts, the Sciences of the 42 books of Hermes; the Sciences of the Monument (Architecture, Masonry, etc.), the Secret Societies (numerical geometric and religious symbolism), the Social Order and its Protection (social sciences); 3) proof of God, used by Aristotle, i.e., purpose in the universe and God as the Unmoved Mover; 4) concept of the Soul, immortality and salvation; 5) concept of the key elements--air, earth, fire, water; 6) the principle of opposites in the structure and functioning of the universe (dialectics); 7) the concept of creation as a product of Nous (mind, intelligence) and logos (creative utterance); 8) the concept of the atom as the basic building block of the universe (from the God, Atum, whose name and attributes are the same as those ascribed to the atom). "This is the legacy of the African continent to the nations of the world," James (1976:

151) concludes. And since it is she who "has laid the foundations of modern progress...she and her people deserve the honor and praise which for centuries have been falsely given to the Greeks."

J.A. Rogers (1972) credits Pharaoh Akhenaton (c.1350 B.C.E.) with making significant contributions to world religious development. He (1972:57-66) states that 1,300 years before Jesus, Akhenaton taught and lived "a gospel of perfect love, brotherhood and truth. Two thousand years before Muhammad, he taught the doctrine of one God." And "three thousand years before Darwin, he sensed the unity that runs through all living things." Breaking from the Egyptian stress on one God with many manifestations, Akhenaton stressed the worship of one God. Moreover, Akhenaton's God "unlike that of Moses was not a jealous God, but a God of perfect love, a God compassionate even toward the chicken that 'crieth in the egg shell.' Others have suggested that his psalms were the model for David's psalms which were written 500 years later and Rogers points out the similarity. Rogers also notes that Akhenaton advanced the concept that "the Kingdom of God is within you," centuries before Jesus did.

Finally, in the *Husia*, which is a collection of selected writings from the sacred texts of ancient Egypt, Maulana Karenga (1984) presents textual evidence of parallels and/or sources for many concepts in the Judeo-Christian tradition which emerge from Egypt which the above scholars have argued. In *The Book of Knowing The Creations* several fundamental concepts appear (Karenga, 1984: 6ff). Here one finds the concept of logos, as Diop has observed, which in Medu Neter or the ancient Egyptian language would be Hu Sia, i.e., authoritative utterance of exceptional insight. Ra, in his name of Ptah, conceives in his heart and mind and commands it to be. Thus, "by means of the Word, all (things) are fashioned and created" (Karenga, 1984:-6ff). Also, one encounters the concept of free will and human equality in Ra's statement of his Four Good Deeds. Ra says "I made every person like his or her fellow" and made wind, water and religious consciousness "so that the humble might benefit from it like the great." And he allowed free will in that he "did not command them to do evil." On the contrary, "it was their own hearts and minds which caused them to disobey that which I commanded" (Karenga,1984:7-8).

In the *Book of Prayers and Sacred Praises* (Karenga, 1984:13-25) one finds psalms or sacred praise songs and poetry which predate and prefigure David's in conception and imagery as Rogers noted. Ra is the Good Shepherd (more precisely Good Herdsman) who leads his flock to green pastures. He rescues the humble and the needy and hears and answers the prayers of the prisoner and the oppressed. He is the prime minister of the poor, judge that takes no bribes. "He makes the weak-armed into the strong-armed so that the multitudes flee from the feeble and one alone takes a thousand captive" (Karenga,1984:13ff). Also, noteworthy is Akhenaton's hymn to Aton, which Breasted (1933:202ff) and others have compared to Psalms 104.

In the *Book of Khun-Anup*, (Karenga, 1984:31-35; Lichtheim, 1975:169ff) one has the oldest text on social justice. The command is to "Speak justice and do justice. For justice is mighty. It is great; it endures. Its worth is real and it leads one to blessedness. Wrongdoing does not achieve its goal, but one who is just reaches dry land." Especially should this justice be directed toward the most vulnerable of society. For if there is no justice, the vulnerable cannot survive. Therefore, the righteous and just are commanded to be "the father of the orphan, the husband of the widow, a protective garment for the motherless" and to "come at the voice of the caller" (Karenga, 1984:29ff).

The Book of Declaration of Virtues (Karenga, 1984:91-98) reveals a similar stress on social justice and preference for the poor and vulnerable. One is instructed by example to give "bread to the hungry, water to the thirsty, clothes to the naked and a boat to cross over for those who have none." Moreover, there is a call to "rescue the weak from the strong," honor one's mother and father, speak truth, do justice, support the aged, satisfy the needs of the have-nots so that one "may come before God blameless and without blemish" (Karenga,1984:91ff).

In the *Books of Wise Instruction*, (Karenga, 1984:39ff) one finds several seminal theological and ethical concepts as well as the source of direct Hebrew borrowing. The *Book of Ptah-hotep* teaches the intrinsic worth and inevitable triumph of *Maat* (the way of Truth, Justice and Righteousness), the central ethical and religious concept in Egyptian spirituality (Karenga,1984:41ff; Lichtheim,1975:61ff). "Maat is great, its value is lasting," he says. Although wickedness may gain wealth, wrongdoing has never brought its wares safe to port. In the end it is Maat that endures..." (Karenga,1984:41). He also teaches due process, honor for father and mother, reciprocity and the concept of the chosen of God based on righteousness, not race or ethnicity. *The Book of Kheti* teaches the *imago dei* concept along with the concept of human stewardship on earth saying: God "made the sky and earth for their sake. They are in his image and came from his body" (Karenga, 1984:52; Lichtheim, 1975:106).

From the *Book of Amenomope* (c. 1405-1370 B.C.E.), Solomon (c. 976-939 B.C.E.) borrows heavily for his *Book of Proverbs*. As Breasted (1933:371ff) has maintained, "All Old Testament scholars of any weight or standing now recognize the fact that...a whole section...of the Book of Proverbs is largely drawn verbatim from the Wisdom of Amenomope; that is the Hebrew version is practically a literal translation from the Egyptian." For example, he cites Amenomope first and then Solomon as follows: 1) "Incline thine ears to hear my sayings (words). And apply thine heart to their comprehension."/ "Incline thine ear and hear the words of the wise and apply thine heart to my knowledge"; 2) "(riches) have made themselves wings like geese and they have flown to heaven."/ "riches certainly make themselves like an eagle that flies toward heaven"; 3) "Better is poverty in the hand of God than riches in the storehouse."/ "Better is little with the fear of Yahweh, than great treasure..." There are, of course, many more examples of this borrowing by the Hebrews as both Breasted (1933) and Griffith (1926) contend. Griffith cites at least twenty other borrowings including the "planted by the rivers of water" analogy, found in Psalms 1:3 and Jeremiah 17:18. He concludes that this borrowing was not abnormal, for "when the Hebrews were becoming civilized under Solomon and his successors, they looked especially to Egypt and Babylonia for instruction in the arts of life."

In the *Book of Neferti* (Karenga,1984:85ff; Lichtheim, 1975:139ff) one finds the concept of the messianic king which preceded David of the Hebrews. The messianic righteous king is "One Ameni, the son of man, born of a woman of Nubia" who shall return *Maat* (righteousness and order) to its place and drive away *isfet* (evil and chaos) (Karenga,1984:87; Lichtheim,1975:143-144). And finally, in the *Books of Rising Like Ra*, or the Pyramid Texts and the Coffin Texts (Karenga, 1984:101ff; Faulkner, 1969, 1973) one finds the Hall of Judgment, appearance before the Risen Savior, resurrection, the immortality of the soul through righteousness, the celestial paradise of heaven, and a source or parallel of the Ten Commandments. In the *Book of Coming Forth By Day* (Karenga, 1990), often called the Book of the Dead, one finds the forty-two Declarations of Innocence which contain clearly eight of the Ten Commandments thousands of years before Moses of the Hebrews.

These were Declarations of Innocence one made to justify or vindicate her/himself before God and thus indicates an ethical code key to eternal life through righteousness. These eight among the 42 are: 1) I have not blasphemed against God; 2) I have not told lies in the seat of Truth; 3) I have not mistreated my family and associates; 4) I have not committed murder, ordered murder or turned over anyone to a murderer; 5) I have not stolen; 6) I have not committed adultery; 7) I have not violated sacred times; and 8) I have not coveted other's property. The two missing from the Declarations are the prohibition against graven images which runs counter to African religious art and symbolism and the prohibition against gods *before* God which obviously was not a major issue with Egyptians. For Egyptians recognized one great God with many manifestations. Thus, the *Book of Prayers and Sacred Praises* says of Amen Ra, "You are the only God and there is none like you." And other prayers talk of Ra in his many forms, i.e., Kheper, Atum, etc. Thus, in so many areas, Egypt's legacy proves itself both profound and far-reaching. It is for this reason and the racism which denies African contribution to the forward flow of human history, that Europe has taught that Egypt was European or Asian rather than African in both color and culture. And it is the task of critical scholarship in Black Studies to correct this error and distortion, so that truth can be served and Africa can receive its due credit and place in human history.

As part of both an intellectual and cultural project, the Us organization, under the leadership of Maulana Karenga, and other organizations like the Kemetic Institute of Chicago have begun the recovery and reinstitution of the ancient Egyptian religious and ethical tradition. Concentrating more on the ethical tradition of ancient Egypt, Us has initiated what it calls the Maatian ethical tradition (Karenga, 1986; 1989; 1990). Rooted in the concept of *Maat* which in ancient Egyptian means among other things, truth, justice and righteousness, the organization has introduced *The Husia*, quoted above, as its sacred text and the Seven Cardinal Virtues of Maat as the core of its ethical value system (Karenga, 1984, 1989).

These virtues can be and are translations of the word *Maat* itself. They are Truth, Justice, Propriety, Harmony, Balance, Reciprocity, and Order. A discussion of these virtues and Maatian ethics can be found also in Karenga's article "Toward A Sociology of Maatian Ethics" (1989) and in his dissertation for his second doctorate "The Moral Ideal in Ancient Egypt: A Study in Classical African Ethics" (1993).

3.3   THE CHRISTIAN TRADITION

Reasons For Conversion

It is common knowledge that African Americans were converted to Christianity during enslavement. But what is less known and less discussed are the reasons for the conversion both from the point of view of the slaveholders and the enslaved Africans. The slaveholders reasons for Christianizing the enslaved Africans began with their perception of Christianity as a way to reinforce and maintain dominance. Thus, in 1743, a white minister prepared a book of dialogue for slaveholders to teach enslaved Africans which stressed contentment and thanks for being enslaved and ended saying "I can't help knowing my duty. I am to serve God in that state in which he has placed me. I am to do what my master orders me" (Frazier, 1974:19). As the indoctrination progressed, then, slaveholders soon discovered that many of the most amenable and submissive enslaved Africans were those who were Christians.

Secondly, the slaveholders were equally and at times more interested in uprooting Africans from their own religious heritage, in order to deprive them of cultural distinction and motivation for revolt. As Frazier (1974:17) points out, "whites were always on guard against African religious practices which could provide an opportunity for slave revolts, and they outlawed such practices." Finally, slaveholders converted Africans because they and other whites believed it was their duty to bring light to "benighted and lost heathens." It was, in a word, based on a culturally chauvinist assumption that their religion was the only real and correct one and that all others were pagan and an abomination to their intolerant and jealous God.

Although many Africans accepted Christianity, many others resisted it for a long time, maintaining their commitment to ancient African religions or Islam. Moreover, most of those who accepted Christianity transformed it in their own image and interest (Blassingame, 1979; Wilmore, 1973). Given the importance of religion to Blacks and the reverence they had for their God, one must raise the question, what compelled them to exchange their God for that of the slaveholder? The first reason for African American conversion to Christianity was obviously the conquest and coercion by the slaveholder. Alex Haley's (1976) description of the brutally coerced transformation of Kunta Kinte into Christianized Toby in his popular family saga, *Roots*, is representative of the process. Moreover, at one point as Frazier (1974:15) notes, the slaveholder and the "Missionaries recognized its difficulty of converting adult Africans and concentrated their efforts on children."

Secondly, Africans began to accept Christianity more as they gradually began to accept the slaveholders' religious and cultural contentions which posed Christianity and the Christian God as more powerful. This gradual acceptance was encouraged by the fact of their enslavement, the religious doubt and self-doubt it raised, the gradual loss of historical memory and the end of revivifying contacts from Africa through the end of the enslavement period. Thirdly, Christianity came to be seen as a coping strategy on the social and psychological level. Social acceptance meant avoidance of humiliation, punishment and beatings reserved for recalcitrant "heathens." Psychologically, it meant a transferred hope for deliverance, which the old religions seemed unable to fulfill.

Fourthly, Christianity and the religious meetings it allowed became, even more under severe restriction, a means of establishing and maintaining a sense of community. This was a time for the enslaved Africans to meet, to reinforce bonds between them, discuss hopes, problems and also, as in the Turner, Vesey and Prosser revolts, a time to plan liberation strategies. Finally, after years of forced conversion and tentative and partial acceptance Christianity became a heritage, and subsequent generations born in a Christian context simply accepted it. However, it is important to stress that in spite of this conversion to Christianity, Africans did not accept it totally in its racist African enslavement-supporting form. In fact, "a distinctive African American form of Christianity -- actually a new religion of an oppressed people -- slowly took root in the Black community" (Wilmore, 1973:36). This new "Black folk religion carried within its perspectives a definitive moral judgment against African enslavement and a clear legitimation of the enslaved Africans' and later the freedman's struggle against the forces of injustice and inequality."

The Historical Role Of The Church

The role of the Black church in African American life has been substantial and enduring since its inception (Woodson, 1945; Lincoln and Mamiya, 1990; Wilmore, 1989). Although Frazier (1974) divides the church into the "invisible church" in African enslavement and the institutional church which began with the founding of the African Methodist Episcopal Church in 1787 and the first African Baptist Church in 1788, for the purpose of this section and to stress historical continuity, the division will not be made. Moreover, although the Black church has rightly been and continues to be accused of support for the established order at various times (Washington, 1964), it does have a history of social activism and social service of which it can be proud (Lincoln, 1974a; Wilmore, 1983; Paris, 1985). And it is this history which will be stressed.

The Black church obviously began as a spiritual sanctuary and community against the violent and destructive character of the Holocaust of Enslavement. And even after enslavement, it remained a wall of defense and comfort against racism and its accompanying attacks on Black dignity, relevance and social worth. Secondly, the Black church served as an agency of social reorientation and reconstruction, providing reinforcement for the old values of marriage, family, morality and spirituality in the face of the corrosive effects of enslavement (Blassingame, 1979; Lincoln and Mamiya, 1990).

Thirdly, the church became a center for economic cooperation, pooling resources to buy churches, building mutual aid societies which provided social services for free Blacks purchasing and helping resettle enslaved Africans, and setting up businesses for economic development. Fourthly, the church engaged in both public and internal educational projects, setting up schools and training ministers and teachers and raising funds to carry out these projects. Finally, the Black church, from its earliest days as an invisible spiritual community, supported social change and struggle, providing leaders and leadership at various points in the struggle for Black liberation and a truly higher level of human life.

The Social Ethics of Martin Luther King

The death of Bishop Henry M. Turner left the Black community with "no clergyman of his stature who could, by temperament or ideology, assume the leadership role he played in a persistent but unsuccessful attempt to radicalize the Black church" (Wilmore,1973:187). Turner had been an advocate of the social role and responsibility of the church and religion, had engaged in a merciless criticism of U.S. society, and advocated the Blackness of God, draft resistance, armed self-defense and emigrationism (Angell,1992). Not until King did another Black Christian leader rise to his level of relevance and social effectiveness. "It was Martin Luther King," Lincoln (1974:114) observes, "who made the contemporary church aware of its power to effect change." Moreover, he also revived its tradition of self-conscious social activism and thus broke it from the moderate accommodating tendency which was also a part of its history and which it had exhibited since the death of Turner.

King developed a theory and practice which combined the best of Black religion with socially-focused concepts borrowed from Ghandi, Thoreau, Hegel, Rauschenbush, Tillich and others (King, 1958, 1963, 1964, 1967; Washington, 1986; Branch, 1988). Within his socio-political philosophy, five key concepts stand at its core. First, King posed Blacks as a people whose suffering and social situation has prepared them for and, in fact, gives them a divine historical mission of not only liberating themselves, but also of restructuring and spiritualizing U.S. society.

Secondly, King argued that Blacks had both the moral right and responsibility to disobey unjust laws in their resistance to social evil. This stress, as Walton (1976:44) notes, combines Henry David Thoreau's concept of "the rightfulness of civil disobedience," Jesus' stress on humanity, forgiveness and love, and Ghandi's stress on loving non-violence as a method of social transformation. "Your highest loyalty is to God" King (1963:128) stated, "and not to the mores, or folkways, the state or the nation or any man-made institution." Thus, when any of those "conflict with God's will, it is your Christian duty to oppose it."

Closely related to the above concept is King's contention that it is immoral and cowardly to collaborate in one's own oppression. "To accept passively an unjust system is to cooperate with that system," he (1958:188) maintained. And in doing this, "the oppressed becomes as evil as the oppressor." Moreover, such non-action says "to the oppressor that his actions are morally right." Thus, he (1958:189) concludes, acquiescence to oppression is not only morally wrong and corruptive, "it is (also) the way of a coward."

Fourthly, King posed the necessity of religion having a social as well as spiritual function. Having read Walter Rauschenbush's *Christianity and the Social Crisis*, he (1958:72) developed "a theological basis for the social concern" which he felt religion should have "as a result of his experiences." Therefore, he stressed that true religion was obligated to deal "with the whole man, not only his soul, but his body, not only his spiritual well-being but his social well-being." A final core concept in King's socio-political philosophy was his contention that human nature is perfectible through struggle. He (1958:82) asserted that Hegel's "analysis of the dialectical process...helped me to see that growth comes through struggle." Central to this concept is the emphasis on "creative tension," non-violent struggle which not only changes the oppressor, but also the oppressed in the process.

King's socio-political philosophy was important to Black religion and the Civil Rights Movement in several ways. First, it gave religious sanction to social resistance, although of the non-violent type, and thus spiritually inspired an oppressed people who would not have been moved as deeply by other doctrines in their quest for freedom. Secondly, it made social passivity immoral, an act in contradiction with the will of God and His desire for truth, freedom and justice in the world, and therefore, reinforced the need to resist social evil. Thirdly, it placed on preachers a continuing responsibility and pressure to take an active stand in the Freedom Movement and make religion more socially relevant. And finally, King's socio-political philosophy served as a transition in Black religion which encouraged self-criticism and pointed toward a Black liberation theology.

Black Liberation Theology

Historical Background. In July 1966 and in the midst of the period of Black urban revolts, a group of Black clergy met in Harlem to develop a position on the struggle for Black power in the U.S. There, they assumed a position which made a definitive contribution to the emergence of Black liberation theology. Breaking from King's negative position on Black power as "nihilistic," they affirmed the right and need of Black power, criticized the Black church for too often steering "its members away from the reign of God in this world to a distorted and complacent view of an otherworldly conception of God's power" and committed themselves to "use more of the resources of our churches in working for human justice in places of social change and upheaval" where God is truly already at work. This statement and other highly significant Black liberation theology documents appear in Wilmore and Cone's (1979) excellent documentary history of Black Theology from 1966 to 1979. Finally, the body of clergy who began in 1966 as the National Committee of Negro Churchmen changed their name to the National Committee of Black Churchmen (NCBC), and became the practical expression and representative of the new Black liberation theology.

Black liberation theology, however, did not come into being by itself. It evolved from several fundamental sources. First, it was developed in response to the dynamics of the decade of the 60's with its stress on Blackness and social activism and struggle. The 60's demanded a redefinition of the world in Black images and interests and Black religion was no exception. Also, the 60's demanded active engagement in the Black struggle for liberation and a higher level of human life and challenged the church to participate or disband. Secondly, Black liberation theology was inspired by both emulation and criticism of King. King's stress on the social relevance and role of religion and on active engagement in the struggle against social evil were accepted and applied, but his stress on non-violence was challenged or played down, his denunciation of Black power rejected, and his emphasis on redemptive suffering translated as redemption through liberating struggle.

Thirdly, Black liberation theology evolved from an ongoing internal criticism and push for a more relevant religion in light of the activist tradition of the Black church as well as the temper of the time. This process was given support and intensified by the dynamics of the 60's and forced Black churchmen and women and theologians to redefine the meaning and role of God in history and His relationship to Black oppression and struggle for liberation. Finally, Black liberation theology helped inspire and was in turn inspired by Third World Theology (Wilmore, 1979). Especially key here is Latin American Liberation Theology represented by Gustavo Gutierrez (1974, 1973) and Sergio Torres (1981, 1976) who translate religion in the most socially relevant and demanding ways.

One could argue there is a distinction between Black Theology and Black liberation theology, the former being all forms of Black systematic religious thought and the latter being one particular form of it. However, this distinction will not be made; for the quest for a Black Theology is firmly and clearly rooted in the search for religious answers to the questions of Black liberation. Some of the major writers who have sought to pose and answer such questions are Gayraud Wilmore (1983), Major Jones (1971, 1974), William Jones (1973), J. DeOtis Roberts (1974, 1971), Joseph Washington (1967), Joseph Johnson (1978, 1971) and Cornel West (1982, 1988).

In addition to the above writers, two others stand out as definitive of the two trends in Black liberation theology, i.e., Black nationalist Christianity and Black Christian Nationalism. These are James Cone (1969, 1970, 1975, 1983, 1984) and Albert Cleage, Jr. (1968, 1972). Moreover, both Cone and Cleage were key to the development of Black liberation theology. James Cone, a professor of systematic theology at Union Theological Seminary, "more than anyone else...set the tone and described the context of Black Theology with the publication of his book *Black Theology and Black Power* in 1969" and helped shape the movement as a practical project (Wilmore and Cone, 1979:77). Albert Cleage, the dean of Black Nationalist Christians and founder and head of the Shrine of the Black Madonna as early as 1963 "was also an active member of the NCBC almost from its inception and took part in the first theological discussions of the new movement of militant Black clergy in 1967" (Wilmore and Cone, 1979:67). Given their relevance to and work in this theoretical and practical thrust, their contentions can serve as a framework for discussion of Black liberation theology in general.

James Cone. Establishing the basis for a Black liberation theology, James Cone maintains that it must above all speak to the condition and struggle of Black people. "Black Theology has as its starting point the Black condition," he (1969:18) asserts. "It is a theology which confronts white society as racist Antichrist, communicating to the oppressor that nothing will be spared in the fight for freedom" (1969:135).

Secondly, Cone (1970:120) insists on the Blackness of God and Jesus. "The Blackness of God and everything implied by it in a racist society is the heart of Black Theology's doctrine of God." For "there is no place for a colorless God in a society (where) people suffer precisely because of their color." Thirdly, Cone (1970:116) argues that the God of Black liberation theology is and must be "the God of and for the oppressed of the land who makes himself known through their liberation." For Cone (1969:47) then, Black power and Black liberation are "doing God's work in history by righting the wrongs done against his people..." Thus, Blacks become God's covenant community. His later books, *God of the Oppressed* (1975), *For My People* (1983) and *My Soul Looks Back* (1984), reaffirm this stress on God's role in Black life and history as dictated by biblical assertions.

A fourth contention of Cone is the need for vindication of the Black church and the call upon it to recapture its radical tradition in the struggle for freedom, justice and equality. Citing Henry Garnet and Nat Turner as models, he (1969:94) argues that "the Black church was born in protest" and "in this sense, it is the precursor of Black Power." The need, then, is to revive this "heritage of radical involvement in the world." For "this past is a symbol of what is actively needed in the present" (1969:112-113). Fifthly, rejecting non-violence as "a technique of the rich to keep the poor poor," Cone declares that "if the system is evil, then revolutionary violence is both justified and necessary to end it." In fact, "sacrificing love" must be revolutionary love which "may mean joining a violent rebellion" (1969:113).

Sixthly, Cone in his later works has been very insistent on the need to address and end sexism in the Black church. In both *My Soul Looks Back* (1983) and *For My People* (1984), Cone devotes a chapter to critically delineating the problematic of sexism in Black theology and the Black church and the urgency of ending it in order to build an egalitarian religious community. Also in his co-edited work with Gayraud Wilmore, *Black Theology* (1979), he has written a chapter which challenged the church to divest itself of sexist ideas and practices negative to the liberation project. Finally, Cone, beginning especially in his *God of the Oppressed* (1975), has consistently stressed the need for a class analysis and class approach to liberation. For him, as his title suggests, God is the God of the oppressed and requires a preferential practice toward the poor and vulnerable. Thus liberation is a freedom won in struggle not only against racism and sexism but also against classism.

Albert Cleage (Archbishop Jaramogi Abebe Agyeman). The theology of Albert Cleage (1968:38) maintains at the outset that the Judeo-Christian heritage is a stolen heritage that must be recaptured. For "the white man captured the religion of a Black Nation (Israel), the revelations of a Black God, the teachings of a Black Messiah (Jesus) and he used them to keep Black men enslaved." This contention already leads Cleage to his second contention that God is and must be Black, as of course, is Jesus. Thirdly, Cleage (1972:3-4) argues for a rejection of the "Pauline perversion" of God's words in the New Testament with its emphasis on loving submission and concentration on the Old Testament's emphasis on struggle and liberation. The need is to make a distinction between salvation (spiritual) and liberation (social), and to struggle to eliminate "oppression, powerlessness and the white man's declaration of Black inferiority through Black unity" within the framework of Black Christian Nationalism.

Fourthly, like Cone, Cleage identifies the church as a key instrument in the liberation of Blacks. Thus, he (1972:xxxiv) calls for Blacks to "rediscover the historic roots of Christianity, strip from them the mystical distortions...bring the Black Christian church into the liberation struggle and make it relevant to the lives of Blacks."

Finally, Cleage (1972:403) argues that there is a dual aspect to the liberation struggle, an internal as well as external dimension. Given Blacks' history of oppression, they "have two beasts to fight: the beast within and the beast without." Externally, their enemy is whites, in fact, white Christians (Cleage, 1968:55). For "...within the system in which we live, we are not only separate, we are in conflict. We seek our freedom in a power struggle against them and in the context of this struggle, they are the enemy." Internally, the struggle is against what white society has made African people, i.e., individualistic, addicted to mysticism about God and using religion as psychic relief rather than inspiration to actively seek liberation.

Summary. In sum then, Black liberation theology is centered around several core contentions which appear in varying and similar forms in most writings on it. Among these are 1) the need for a God in Black people's own image and interest, i.e., Black and of and for the oppressed; 2) the imperative that religion must reflect the interests of Blacks and concretely and actively benefit them; 3) the contention that Blacks are a "chosen people" or "covenant community," i.e., have a special relationship with God; 4) the recognition of the Black church's radical history and a call for its resuming this role in the liberation struggle of Black people; and 5) the indispensability of social struggle to liberate Blacks -- socially and spiritually -- and realize God's will to bring truth, freedom and justice to society and the world.

Black Womanist Theology and Ethics

Clearly, one of the most important developments in Black religion in general and in Black Christianity in particular is the emergence of a distinctly Black womanist or feminist discourse. An excellent early corpus of such literature can be found in Wilmore and Cone's *Black Theology* in which several Black women theologians and writers delineate the history and challenge of Black women in the church (Grant, 1979; Hoover, 1979; Murray, 1979). Moreover, much work has been done on these issues by Black women scholars in the context of writing M.A. theses and doctoral dissertations. These include Jualynne Dodson (1983), LaTaunya Marie Bynum (1980), Delores Williams (1975) and Katie G. Cannon (1983), whose dissertation has since been published as a book titled *Black Womanist Ethics*, (1988), and is discussed below.

Jacquelyn Grant. Certainly, one of the most important theologians of this emerging discourse is Jacquelyn Grant (1979, 1989). Her major work, *White Women's Christ and Black Women's Jesus*, offers an important discussion of womanist issues in theology. Grant is concerned first of all with self naming, that is to say, giving specific name and voice to Black women in the historical and current church. She seeks to recover the hidden and denied role and relevance of Black women and speak their special truth. To do this she both criticizes and borrows from white feminist theology. It is her contention that white feminist theology cannot and does not adequately address the Black womanist tradition in the faith, for it is both white and racist (Grant, 1989:195ff). Moreover, she criticizes Black male religionists for their having both denied and diminished the vital role and relevance of Black women in the construction and maintenance of the Black religious tradition. However, she also cites both James Cone (1979,1983,1984) and James Evans (1981) for their critique of sexism in theology and the church and their call for corrective measures.

What is needed, she (1989:205) contends, is a Black womanist theology which "begins with the experiences of Black women as its point of departure." This theology will and does respect the tridimensional character of Black women's life, i.e., its vulnerability to racism, classism, and sexism (1989:209). It thus locates itself in the struggle against these forms of oppression and in the struggle to create free space to speak and act in Black women's own terms. Moreover, Black womanist theology challenges Eurocentric and androcentric interpretations of both text and context, scripture and history, building on Black women's experience as both oppositional and contributive.

Secondly, Grant argues for a gender-free Jesus, given the problematic of maleness as a metaphor for oppression and superiority. Thus, she (1989:212) envisions Jesus as "the divine co-sufferer, who empowers them (Black people) in situations of oppression." Here Jesus is both inclusive God and essential human, containing both male and female and also transcendent.

Thirdly, Grant argues for a concrete intimacy with Jesus in the womanist tradition. This of course allows her to draw the distinction made in the title and theme of her book between white women's Christ and Black women's Jesus. Again she contends Jesus in the womanist tradition is more intimate and concrete and less transcendental. Thus, he is "my sweet Jesus," friend, healer, hope-giver, co-sufferer and Black women's central religious frame of reference.

Fourthly, Grant (1989:211ff) argues for building on the emancipatory biblical tradition as central to the Black womanist project. She maintains that womanist theology must and does engage in an internal critique of biblical patriarchal views while at the same time brings its narratives to life, extracting their emancipatory possibilities. This means meeting the challenge to "investigate the relationship between the oppression of women and theological symbolism" and then moving to correct and transcend oppressive theological tendencies in the thrust to build an egalitarian theology of human wholeness (Grant, 1989:219ff).

Finally, Grant argues for a constructive Christology and theology that reject racist, sexist and classist interpretations and practices. This theology of necessity, Grant maintains, will be rooted in and rise out of the life, teachings and narratives of the bold, assertive and creative Black women whose lessons of resistance, love, construction and commitment inspire and inform the best of Christian and Black tradition, i.e., Sojourner Truth, Fannie Lou Hamer, Ida B. Wells, Jarna Lee, Mary McLeod Bethune, et al. However, it will not deny the contribution or humanity of Black males, for a theology or Christology which negates Black male humanity is still destructive to the Black community (Grant, 1989:221). What is needed then, she concludes, is a constructive rather than destructive practice, which rejects the unusable past and builds in reconciliation a future which grounds and reflects maximum human flourishing.

Katie Cannon. Katie Cannon's project of developing a Black womanist ethics begins with the privileging of ordinary experience. She (1988:5) wishes to use Black women's literary tradition "to interpret and explain the community's socio-cultural patterns from which ethical values can be gleaned." It will be the development of an ethics by which persons "learn to glean directives for living in the here and now" (Cannon, 1988:126). This will in turn "help Black women and others who care to understand and to appreciate the richness of their own moral struggle through the life of the common people and oral tradition" (Cannon, 1988:5). It is thus in Zora Neale Hurston's writings and life that she believes she has discovered a rich source of ethical values and insights.

Secondly, Cannon (1988:6ff) seeks to contextualize her ethics by focusing on "the interrelationship of white supremacy and male superiority which has characterized the Black woman's moral situation." She focuses on the historical context which "generates the conditions for the patterns of ethical behavior and moral wisdom which emerged in the Black female community." This "untangling of the Black woman's history sheds light on the values and virtues" that will undergird and inform a Black womanist ethics. And it also helps "to further understanding of some of the differences between ethics of life under oppression and established moral approaches which take for granted freedom and a wide range of choices" (Cannon, 1988:5-6).

Thirdly, Cannon (1988:104) argues that a womanist ethics is a virtue ethics and she defines virtue in a Hurstonian way as a "feistiness about life that nobody can wipe out no matter how hard they try." This, in a word, is an adaptive vitality and durability under pressure and oppression. For she asserts the moral quality of life of Black women has been defined by "the balancing of complexities in such a way that suffering did not overwhelm and endurance with dignity was possible." This, of course, is a vital element in the definition of "womanist."

Fourthly, Cannon posits the concept of "invisible dignity" or "unshouted courage" as a key virtue in womanist ethics. For her, Hurston and other strong Black women exhibited this quality, demonstrating "a moral wisdom wherein grace and truth constitute each other" (Cannon, 1988:128). Grace for her is grounding in a situation of struggle, a struggle to survive and develop in two contradictory worlds "one white, privileged and oppressive, the other Black, exploited and oppressed."

Finally, Cannon (1988:159ff) borrows from and builds on three fundamental themes from the works of Howard Thurman and Martin L. King to round out her womanist ethics. This is an important act because it expresses and reaffirms her commitment to the community as a whole--male and female--and to the richness of its various ethical teachings. The first of these themes is the *imago dei* anthropological concept. This concept of being in the image of God undergirds and propels the quest for wholeness and the urgency of freedom. It compels one to reject the oppressor's devaluation of one's humanity and to struggle for the inalienable rights of freedom and justice, etc. Here again, Cannon poses Hurston and other strong Black women as models of this quest for wholeness and struggle for "'living space' carved out of the intricate web of racism, sexism and poverty."

A second theme useful to womanist ethics is the interrelationship of love and justice. A love ethics for both Thurman and King is the basis of community and human relatedness. But whereas Thurman stresses reconciliation, King stresses struggle for justice and the achievement of justice as grounding for reconciliation and community. Thirdly, Cannon poses the centrality of community based on love and justice in both womanist ethics as expressed by Hurston, and in the ethics of Thurman and King. She concludes reaffirming the rich moral resource of the Black religious tradition and the need for it to be transformed to include space and opportunity for Black women's deserved recognition and continued contribution in a context of love, equality and common struggle for the paradigmatic "beloved community."

3.4   THE ISLAMIC TRADITION

Islam is clearly the largest and most effective religious challenge to Christianity among Blacks. In fact, as Lincoln (1974b:154) contends, "It has an inevitable appeal to Blacks who have difficulty with American Christianity because of its racism, and with the Black Christian church because of it posture of accommodation." Beginning in 1913 with Noble Drew Ali's establishment of the Moorish Science Temple and growing to its highest point in the early 60's in the context of the Nation of Islam, headed by the Hon. Elijah Muhammad, Islam has become a major religion among African Americans. Moreover, it has served as a creative challenge to Black Christianity in its internal criticism and struggle to create a more socially relevant religion, as expressed in Black liberation theology.

The Moorish Science Temple

In 1913, Noble Drew Ali established the Moorish Science Temple in Newark, New Jersey and began to teach a synthesized version of orthodox Islam, Garveyism, Christianity and various extractions from oriental philosophy (Bontemps and Conroy, 1945:175; Moorish Science Temple, 1991). From Newark, Ali's teaching spread to the northern cities of Detroit, Harlem, Chicago, Pittsburgh, Philadelphia and various cities in the South, eventually embracing an estimated membership of 20-30,000 (Lincoln, 1961).

The main contentions of Noble Drew Ali's religious nationalism were that: 1) the key to the salvation and liberation of African people in the U.S. lay in the discovery and acceptance of their national origin as Moors; 2) Islam was "the only instrument for (Black) unity and advancement;" 3) whites were the opposite of and negative to Blacks and were soon to be destroyed; 4) the need to obey the law and refrain from radicalism; and finally, 5) the essentiality of love, harmony and peace in the world and especially among Blacks. Urging his followers to struggle to be righteous and build a better world, he sums up his teachings saying:

> "In conclusion, I urge you to remember there is work enough for all to do in helping to build a better world. The problems of life are largely social and economic. In a profound sense, they are moral and spiritual. Have lofty conceptions of your duties to your country and fellowmen in general and especially those with whom you deal. This includes such honesty and righteousness as will cause you to put yourself in the other fellow's place. Look for the best in others and give them the best that is in you. Have a deeper appreciation for womanhood. Brighten the hopes of our youth in order that their courage be increased to dare and do wondrous things. Adhere at all times to the principles of love, truth, peace, freedom and justice (Moorish Science Temple, 1991:52).

As Essien-Udom (1964:76) maintained, Ali's basic contentions and principles laid a basis for the Nation of Islam which came into being afterwards. His stress on name, land and nationality, his division of the world into dark and white peoples, his political conservatism and his conception of divine retribution of Allah on whites all find subsequent expression in the ideology and practice of the Nation of Islam. However, although the Black Islamic tradition owes its origins to Nobel Drew Ali, it realized its most definitive development and recognition under the Hon. Elijah Muhammad and the Nation of Islam.

The Nation Of Islam

The Nation of Islam began in 1930 with the splitting into two factions of the Moorish Science Temple, one following a newcomer, W.D. Fard, to Detroit, and the other faction remaining faithful to Noble Drew Ali. Those following Fard eventually deified him when he disappeared in 1933 and became the founding members of the Nation of Islam under the leadership of Messenger Elijah Muhammad (Lincoln, 1961:181,182). Within the context of building the Nation of Islam, Muhammad developed an oppositional theology which is presented in his three basic works (1965, 1973, 1992).

The first and most fundamental aspect of the socio-religious thought of Muhammad is the posing of Islam as the true religion of Black people and Christianity as the religion of their opposite and enemy, white people. Islam is a Black religion because it means submission to the will of Allah and Black people are submissive to God by nature. Secondly, it is the "religion of freedom, justice and equality" and thus, serves Black people's interest better than Christianity which "is a white man's religion and...contains no salvation for the Black man" (Muhammad, 1973:8,4).

The second aspect of Muhammad's socio-religious philosophy is his contention that Allah (God) is in reality a Black man and the Black man is God (Muhammad, 1992:92ff). As Lincoln (1961:73) observed, "all Black men represent Allah or at least participate in Him for all Black men are divine." Thirdly, Muhammad argues that Black people are a chosen people who are "righteous by creation" and "righteous by nature."

Reversing the religious and world order ideologically in a way no one else had done, Muhammad defines the white man as the devil. By this he meant two things: 1) that logically if God is Black, the devil of dialectical necessity must be white; and 2) that if the devil means the embodiment of evil, the historical record of the white man both exposes and confirms his true identity. Thus, he (1965:134) states, that the white man's claim to be God or the chosen of God is in fact a lie. It is this part of Muhammad's doctrine of deliverance, the God-devil thesis, which has proved the most controversial and at the same time and most effective organizing principle (Muhammad, 1992:191ff).

Fifthly, Muhammad argues that separation on the social and political level from whites was a divine imperative. This he (1965:273-275) contended is necessary in order for Blacks to avoid the corruptive influence of white civilization which is "floating in corruption," to avoid the divine destruction Allah has for America, and to establish a nation in their own image and interests. Also, Muhammad stresses the need for economic self-help and racial solidarity. To accomplish this, Muhammad calls for "a united front of Black men of America" who will join hands in a program of economic, political and spiritual upliftment of Black people. Lastly, Muhammad stressed the need for racial and Islamic solidarity throughout the world. He argued that all Third World people were original people and that they were destined to unite in spite of the evil influence of the West which divided them.

The Socio-Ethical Teachings of Malcolm X

Muhammad's message was raised and taught at a national and international level by the NOI's most eminent and competent spokesman, Malcolm X (Al Hajj Malik Shabazz). Malcolm (1965a, 1965b, 1968, 1970, 1989, 1992) not only translated Muhammad's message into its most trenchant and compelling form, but he also went beyond it to produce and articulate one of the most effective and cogent critiques of domination in U.S. history. It is this severe incisiveness of his analysis, along with his bold stands and organizational ability that made him the most definitive symbol of the Black liberation movement in the 1960's (Clarke, 1969; Karenga, 1979, 1982; Cone, 1991).

Malcolm's critique of domination focused on the religious, racial and class restraints on Black and human freedom. He chastised white Christianity for its role in African enslavement, racism and oppression and its hypocrisy in dividing the secular from the sacred. He (1965a:244) states that "the Holy Bible in the white man's hands and his interpretations of it have been the greatest single ideological weapon for enslaving millions of human beings of color." In fact, Malcolm continues, "every country the white man conquered with guns, he has always paved the way and salvaged his conscience by carrying the bible" and using it to justify his dominance and destruction. Having rejected Christianity, he urged moral and spiritual regeneration in the colorblind religious community of Islam. As he states, "The teaching of Islam seeks to clear up our morals and (thus) qualify us to enter into this new righteous nation of God" (Lomax, 1963:151). And therefore, one becomes a worthy member of the righteous community, able to stand upright without either vice or shame before both history and heaven.

Secondly, he taught the social rootedness and responsibility of religion, its need to be an instrument and support of social change. His strategy for regeneration and liberation through struggle for the masses was to "wake them up, clean them up and then stand them up." Malcolm argued for an engaged community that was not simply a witness of history, but rather a midwife of history. Religion for him was a historical practice. Thus he (1970:140) states, "I believe in a religion that believes in freedom." And to any religion that does not respond accordingly to the struggle for freedom, "I say to hell with that religion."

Thirdly, Malcolm taught preference for the human interests of the masses against the narrow class interests of the middle class. For him, the masses were the core and conscience of the movement while the middle class was dedicated to integrationism, tokenism, compromise and self-mutilation. Here, he makes his classic distinction between the slavish behavior of the "house Black" and the resistance behavior of the "field Black." In modern terms, he (1983:95) cites the integrationist Black who "waits to beg white people to accept him or to force himself into white society" and "the new type of Black man who wants to think for himself, stand on his own feet, and walk for himself."

Fourthly, Malcolm argued for an ethics of self-defense. In fact, his famous slogan "freedom by any means necessary" is rooted in his ethics of self-defense. Freedom is constitutive of what it means to be human. As he says, "freedom is essential to life" (Lomax, 1963:150). Thus to deny one freedom is to deny one's life as human. Given this, Malcolm concludes one is justified in using any methods necessary to gain freedom and therefore secure one's humanity. Moreover, direct defense to save one's life is also justified. "We are not for violence in any shape or form" he (1992:46) states, "but believe that the people who have violence committed against them should be able to defend themselves." This, Malcolm (1992:47) clarifies, does not mean that one should "initiate acts of aggression...but where the government fails to protect... (one) is entitled to do it himself." Malcolm bases these contentions on Quranic teachings, constitutional guarantees in the Second Amendment and the Natural law assumption that self-preservation is the first law of nature. The Quran (2:190-191) teaches that one is permitted to "fight in the way of Allah against those who fight against you but be not aggressive (for) Allah loves not the aggressor." Also one should fight because "oppression is worse than death." Finally, the Quran (42:41) teaches that "whoever defends himself from oppression, these it is against whom there is no blame." Thus, Malcolm (1968:175) concludes "I'm for peace, yet I believe any man facing death should be able to go to any length to assure that whoever is trying to kill him has no chance."

Finally, Malcolm saw history as a field for both human and divine action and a need for African and other oppressed people to self-consciously struggle to regain their history and humanity and build a new world. Thus, he (1965:233) notes that the African American struggle is "part of a global rebellion of the oppressed against the oppressor, the exploited against the exploiter." And this was for him God's hand in history on the side of the righteous and truly human.

Schism, Transformation and Rebuilding

The Schism.   In 1963 the Nation of Islam (NOI) began to show signs of unravelling as evidenced by the underlying reasons for the suspension and eventual ouster/resignation of Malcolm X. His ouster/resignation had a tremendous impact on the NOI and the Black Movement and indicated a series of problems that would eventually lead to factionalization and transformation of the NOI. Although the NOI gave the reason for Malcolm's suspension as his disobeying an order not to comment on the Kennedy assassination, the underlying political basis for it was the conflict between two major tendencies in the NOI, the radicals represented by Malcolm and the conservatives represented by the ruling stratum in charge of daily administration. Each vied for and was dependent on Muhammad's decision and support for victory in the daily battle and the ultimate struggle itself (Carson, 1991; Evanzz, 1992).

As I (1982:5) have argued in a paper on the conflict, four major factors appear to have shaped and fed it. First, the transformation of the NOI from a small marginal group to a multi-million dollar budget and huge bureaucracy changed both its political character and its conception of what was politically acceptable. As Lincoln (1961) predicted and Lomax (1963) reported, the ruling stratum became increasingly conservative in its desire to protect its gains and Malcolm could not adjust to the new conservatism.

Secondly, then, the conflict was shaped by the ruling stratum's fierce opposition to Malcolm. Although they recognized his worth and significance to the NOI, they resented and opposed him because of: 1) his moral posture against the corruptive materialism which permeated the ruling stratum; 2) his unwillingness to moderate his radicalism in the face of changed circumstances; and 3) the likelihood of his succeeding Muhammad and establishing a radical position. Thirdly, the conflict was shaped by the ruling stratum's ability to eventually alienate Muhammad and Malcolm in spite of their prior closeness. This was achieved essentially by their being in the pivotal position of daily administration and thus of briefing the Messenger everyday and arguing Malcolm's refusal to moderate his disruptive radicalism and to accept Muhammad's divine authority (Evanzz, 1992).

Having been convinced of these charges, Muhammad suspended Malcolm at first and later denounced him. Malcolm in turn denounced the NOI and Muhammad and the ensuing conditions set the stage for his assassination. Finally, evidence suggest that the FBI had a significant role in provoking and sustaining the leadership struggle within the NOI. For as early as 1959, it had placed people in the leadership stratum. Moreover, documents from the FBI's Counter Intelligence Program (Cointelpro) obtained through the Freedom of Information Act reveal the FBI's decision to divide the NOI and either transform it or destroy it (Evanzz, 1992; Carson, 1991).

Transformation.   After Muhammad's death in 1975, the NOI underwent a drastic transformation and fragmentation involving severe criticism of Muhammad, rejection of the early Muslim belief on whites, and the introduction of a strong Americanism and orthodox Islam (Muhammad, 1980). This process "has its roots in the unsolved political and economic problems which shaped and fed the conflict between Malcolm and the ruling stratum" (Karenga, 1982:339). In other words, "the non-engagement, isolation and general conservatism which Malcolm fought in the 60's expresses itself in similar forms in the 70's...with the added dimensions of Americanism and orthodox Islam advocated by Muhammad's son, Wallace." In addition to the above factor, four others contributed to the transformation (Karenga, 1981: 339ff). A second factor contributive to the transformation then was the ideology and structure of the Nation itself. The theocratic leadership structure based on divine wisdom and authority allowed for corrupt officials to act without check, denied mass participation in decision-making and debates, and prevented criticism necessary to check the transformation carried to its ultimate by Wallace and the ruling stratum. Also, the ideological tendency toward non-engagement in social struggle, obeying laws and the stress on material acquisition cultivated an appreciation for political conservatism and vulgar materialism of the ruling stratum (Lincoln, 1961; Essien-Udom, 1964).

A third contributing factor was the leadership style and problems of succession of Imam Wallace Muhammad who succeeded his father. Wallace's leadership style leaned toward decentralization and orthodox Islam even before his father's death. Once at the helm, he reshaped the Nation. Also, his problems of succession were ones of establishing his authority; creating a new image of the NOI; and winning new converts and allies. Thus, he disavowed his father's divine authority and his God, disbanded the paramilitary arm, the Fruit of Islam, eliminating a possible challenge and changing the military or coercive image of the NOI. Moreover, he changed the doctrine of the NOI from religious Black nationalism to Americanism and orthodox Islam, winning new converts and allies who once opposed the race-and-earth focused religious doctrine of his father. Finally, as argued above, there is evidence of the U.S. government's intervention and role in the process of transformation and fragmentation. From positions at the top, it appears they not only provoked conflict and helped eliminate the radicals, but encouraged the transformation which insured an accommodationist religious structure.

The Rebuilding.　　　Although Minister Louis Farrakhan, the national spokesman after Malcolm, had at first gone along with the transformation, he eventually objected. In 1978, he announced publicly that he could no longer accept in silence the transformation of the Nation and its members. He listed among other things the following which he found intolerable: the ingratitude and disrespect for Messenger Muhammad which the transformed NOI was exhibiting; its open admission of whites; the deterioration of discipline and the emphasis on orthodox Islam as opposed to a people-specific Islam for Blacks which Muhammad had developed (Overbea, 1978:9).

To offset the disintegration he perceived in the NOI which was then called the World Community of Islam in the

West, Farrakhan moved to rebuild the NOI in its original Black image. He formed discussion groups around the country, lectured, published and republished the Messenger's works, reproduced tape recordings of the Messenger and himself, started a newspaper, *The Final Call*, and began to rebuild the Mosque structures and leadership cadres across the country. At the heart of his efforts to rebuild the NOI is the struggle to rescue and reconstruct the image of Messenger Muhammad. To accomplish this, Farrakhan argues: The truth and currency of Muhammad's message; his moral and material achievement and the praiseworthiness of his character as a leader (Karenga, 1981:379; Eure and Jerome, 1989). The success of Farrakhan in rebuilding the NOI will depend on several factors: 1) his own leadership capacity; 2) the extent of opposition from other Islamic groups claiming the Messenger's mantle; 3) his success in building a capable and committed cadre; and finally, 4) his ability to relate positively and effectively to the larger Black community.

STUDY QUESTIONS
1.   Define religion and list some of the major African American religious traditions.
2.   What are some general characteristics and general themes in African religions?
3.   Discuss the ideas suggested by Dogon cosmogony.
4.   What is the Egyptian legacy and some of the basic ethical teachings of the Maatian tradition?
5.   Why did enslaved Africans convert to Christianity?
6.   What has been the historical role of the Black church?
7.   Cite some basic tenets of Dr. Martin Luther King's socio-political philosophy and his ideological impact on Black religion and the Civil Rights Movement.
8.   What are some of the basic contentions of Malcolm X's social-ethical philosophy and his ideological impact on Black religion and the liberation movements of the 1960's?

9.   Who are two major Black liberation theologians and what
        are some of their basic theories?
10.   What are the challenges posed by Black womanist
        theology as argued by Jacqueline Grant? How does she
        address them?
11.   Discuss Katie Cannon's womanist ethics and her use of
        Black women's literature to develop them.
12.   Discuss the contentions and religious legacy of the
        Moorish Science Temple in relationship to the Nation of
        Islam.
13.   Discuss the philosophy of Messenger Muhammad.
14.   What factors contributed to the conflict between Malcolm
        X and the Nation of Islam?
15.   What are some of the factors which contributed to the
        transformation of the NOI after the death of Messenger
        Muhammad?
16.   What are the challenges posed for Minister Louis Farra-
        khan in rebuilding the NOI?

REFERENCES

Abimbola, Wande. (1976) *Ifa: An Exposition of Ifa Literary
        Corpus*, Ibadan: Oxford University Press.
Adams, Hunter III. (1979) "African Observers of the Universe:
        The Sirius Question," *Journal of African Civilization*, 1, 2
        (November) 1-20.
Ammi, Ben. (1990) *God, the Black Man and Truth*, Washington
        D.C.: Communicators Press.
Angell, Stephen W. (1992) *Bishop Henry McNeal Turner and
        African American Religion in the South*, Knoxville: The
        University of Tennessee Press.
Awolalu, J.O. (1979) *Yoruba Beliefs and Sacrificial Rites*, Lon-
        don: Longmans.
Barrett, Leonard E. (1988) *The Rastafarians*, Boston: Beacon
        Press.

Bastide, Roger. (1978) *The African Religions of Brazil: Towards A Sociology of the Interpretations of Civilizations*, Baltimore: John Hopkins University, Book Associates.

Ben Yehuda, Shaleak. (1975) *Black Hebrew Israelites: From America to the Promised Land*, New York: Vantage Press.

Bernal, Martin. (1991) *Black Athena: The AfroAsiatic Roots of Classical Civilization, Vol. II*, New Brunswick, NJ: Rutgers University Press.

Bernal, Martin. (1987) *Black Athena: The Afroasiatic Roots of Classical, Civilization Vol. I*, London: Free Association Books.

Blassingame, John W. (1979) *The Slave Community*, New York: Oxford University Press.

Bontemps, Arna and Jack Conroy. (1945) *They Seek A City*, Garden City, NY: Doubleday, Daran and Company, Inc.

Branch, Taylor. (1988) *Parting The Waters: America in the King Years, 1954-1963*, New York: Simon and Schuster.

Breasted, James. (1933) *The Dawn of Conscience*, New York: Charles Scribner's Sons.

Budge, E.W. (trans.) (1960) *The Book of the Dead*, New Hyde Park, N.Y.: University Books.

Budge, E.W. (1961) *Osiris: The Egyptian Religion of Resurrection*, New Hyde Park, NY: University Books.

Bynum, LaTaunya Marie. (1980) *Black Feminist Theology: A New Word About God.* Unpublished master's thesis, School of Theology, Claremont.

Cannon, Katie G. (1988) *Black Womanist Ethics*, Atlanta: Scholars Press.

Cannon, Katie G. (1983) *Resources for a Constructive Ethic for Women with Special Attention to the Life and Work of Zora Neale Hurston.* Unpublished dissertation, Union Theological Seminary, New York.

Carson, Claybourne. (1991) *Malcolm X: The FBI File*, New York: Carroll and Graf Publishers, Inc.

Carruthers, Jacob H. (1984) *Essays in Ancient Egyptian Studies*, Los Angeles: University of Sankore Press.

Clarke, John H. (1969) *Malcolm X: The Man and His Times*, New York: Macmillan.

Cleage, Albert Jr. (1972) *Black Christian Nationalism*, New York: William Morrow and Co.

Cleage, Albert Jr. (1968) *The Black Messiah*, New York: Sheed and Ward.

Cone, James. (1969) *Black Theology and Black Power*, New York: Seabury Press.

Cone, James. (1970) *A Black Theology of Liberation*, Philadelphia: Lippincott Co.

Cone, James. (1984) *For My People: Black Theology of the Black Church*, New York: Orbis Books.

Cone, James. (1975) *God of the Oppressed*, New York: Seabury Press.

Cone, James. (1991) *Martin and Malcolm and America: A Dream or A Nightmare*, Maryknoll, New York: Orbis Books.

Cone, James. (1983) *My Soul Looks Back*, Nashville: Abingdon Press.

Deng, Francis. (1973) *The Dinka and Their Songs*, Oxford: Clarendon Press.

Diop, Cheikh Anta. (1991) *Civilization or Barbarism: An Authentic Anthropology*, New York: Lawrence Hill Books.

Diop, Cheikh Anta. (1981) *Civilization ou Barbarie*, Paris: Présence Africaine.

Diop, Cheikh Anta. (1974) *The African Origin of Civilization: Myth or Reality*, Westport, CT: Lawrence Hill & Co.

Dodson, Jualynne. (1983) *Women's Collective Power in the African Methodist Episcopal Church.* Unpublished dissertation, University of California, Berkeley.

Drewal, Margaret T. (1992) *Yoruba Ritual*, Bloomington: Indiana University Press.

Essien-Udom, E.U. (1964) *Black Nationalism*, New York: Dell Publishing Co.

Eure, Joseph and Richard Jerome (1989) *Back Where We Belong: Selected Speeches by Minister Louis Farrakhan*, Philadelphia: DC International Press.

Evans, James. (1981) "Black Theology and Black Feminism," in *Journal of Religious Thought*, 38, Spring/Summer, pp. 43-53.

Evans-Pritchard, E.E. (1965) *Theories of Primitive Religion*, London: Oxford University Press.

Evanzz, Karl (1992) *The Judas Factor: The Plot to Kill Malcolm X*, New York: Thunder Mouth Press.

Faulkner, R.O. (1973) *The Ancient Egyptian Coffin Texts*, Warminister, England: Aris & Phillips, Ltd.

Faulkner, R.O. (1969) *The Ancient Egyptian Pyramid Texts*, Oxford: University of Oxford Press.

Fauset, H. (1944) *Blacks Gods of the Metropolis*, Philadelphia: University of Pennsylvania Press.

Frankfort, Henri. (1948) *Kingship and the Gods*, Chicago: The University of Chicago Press.

Frazier, E. Franklin. (1974) *The Negro Church in America*, New York: Schocken Books, Inc.

Gleason, Judith. (1975) *Santería*, Bronx, NY: Atheneum Press.

Gonzales-Wippler, Migene. (1982) *The Santería Experience*, Bronx, New York: Original Publications.

Grant, Jacquelyn. (1979) "Black Theology and The Black Woman," in Gayraud Wilmore and James Cone (eds.) *Black Theology*, New York: Orbis Books.

Grant, Jacquelyn. (1989) *White Women's Christ and Black Women's Jesus: Feminist Christology and Womanist Response*, Atlanta: Scholars Press.

Griaule, Marcel. (1978) *Conversations with Ogotemmeli*, New York: Oxford University Press.

Griaule, Marcel and Germain Dieterlen. (1965) "The Dogon," in Daryll Ford (ed.) *African Worlds*, London: Oxford University Press, pp. 83-110.

Griffith, F.L. (1926) "The Teachings of Amenophis," *Journal of Egyptian Archeology*, XII, 191-231.

Gutierrez, Gustavo. (1974) *The Mystical and Political Dimensions of the Christian Faith*, New York: Hurder & Hurder.

Gutierrez, Gustavo. (1973) *A Theology of Liberation*, Maryknoll, New York: Orbis.

Gyekye, Kwame. (1987) *An Essay on African Philosophical Thought: The Akan Conceptual Theme*, New York: Cambridge University Press.

Haley, Alex. (1976) *Roots*, New York: Dell Publishing Co.

Harding, Vincent. (1969) "The Religion of Black Power," in *The Religious Stratum*, 1968, (ed) Donald Cutler, Boston: Beacon Press.

Harris, J.R. (ed.) (1971) *The Legacy of Egypt*, Oxford: Oxford University Press.

Hoover, Theressa. (1979) "Black Women and the Churches: Triple Jeopardy" in Gayraud Wilmore and James Cone (eds.) *Black Theology*, New York: Orbis Books.

Idowu, E. Bolaji. (1975) *African Traditional Religion*, Maryknoll, New York: Orbis Books.

Jackson, John (1972) *Man, God and Civilization*, New Hyde Park, New York: University Books.

James, George. (1976) *Stolen Legacy*, San Francisco: Julian Richardson Associates.

Johnson, Joseph. (1978) *Proclamation Theology*, Shreveport: Fourth District Press.

Johnson, Joseph. (1971) *The Souls of the Black Preacher*, Philadelphia: United Church Press.

Jones, Major J. (1971) *Black Awareness*, Nashville: Abingdon Press.

Jones, Major J. (1974) *Christian Ethics for Black Theology*, Nashville: Abindgon Press.

Jones, William R. (1973) *Is God a White Racist?* Garden City, New York: Anchor Press/Doubleday.

Karenga, Maulana. (1988) *The African American Holiday of Kwanzaa: A Celebration of Family, Community, and Culture*, Los Angeles: University of Sankore Press.

Karenga, Maulana. (1981) *Afro-American Nationalism: An Alternative Analysis*, unpublished manuscript.

Karenga, Maulana. (1990a) *The Book of Coming Forth By Day: The Ethics of the Declarations of Innocence*, Los Angeles: The University of Sankore Press.

Karenga, Maulana. (1980) *Kawaida Theory: An Introductory Outline*, Inglewood, Ca: Kawaida Publications.

Karenga, Maulana. (1982) "Malcolm and the Messenger: From Psychological Assumptions to Political Analysis," *The Western Journal of Black Studies*, 6, 4, (Winter)pp. 193-201.

Karenga, Maulana. (1993) *The Moral Ideal in Ancient Egypt: A Study in Classical African Ethics*. Unpublished dissertation, University of Southern California, Los Angeles.

Karenga, Maulana. (1990) *Reconstructing Kemetic Culture*, Los Angeles: University of Sankore Press.

Karenga, Maulana. (1986) "Restoration of the Husia: Reviving a Sacred Legacy" in Maulana Karenga and Jacob H. Carruthers (eds.), *Kemet and the African Worldview*, Los Angeles: University of Sankore Press.

Karenga, Maulana. (1990) "The Rescue and Reconstruction of Ancient Egypt: The Spiritual Dimension of the Project" in Maulana Karenga (ed.) *Reconstructing Kemetic Culture*, Los Angeles: University of Sankore Press.

Karenga, Maulana. (1984) *Selections From the Husia: Sacred Wisdom of Ancient Egypt*, Los Angeles: University of Sankore Press.

Karenga, Maulana. (1979) "The Socio-Political Philosophy of Malcolm X," *Western Journal of Black Studies*, 3, 4 (Winter) 251-262.

Karenga, Maulana. (1989) "Towards a Sociology of Maatian Ethics: Literature and Context," in Ivan Van Sertima (ed.), *Egypt Revisited*, New Brunswick, NJ: Transaction Publications.

Karenga, Maulana and Jacob H. Carruthers, (eds.). (1986) *Kemet and the African Worldview*, Los Angeles: University of Sankore Press.

King, Martin Luther, Jr. (1963) *Strength To Love*, New York: Harper & Row.

King, Martin Luther, Jr. (1958) *Stride Toward Freedom*, New York: Harper & Row.

King, Martin Luther, Jr. (1964) *Why We Can't Wait*, New York: Harper & Row.

King, Martin Luther, Jr. (1967) *Where Do We Go From Here: Chaos or Community*, New York: Harper & Row.

Lichtheim, Miriam. (1975) (1976) (1980) *Ancient Egyptian Literature: A Book of Readings, Vol. I, Vol. II, Vol. III*, Los Angeles: University of California Press.

Lincoln, C. Eric and Lawrence H. Mamiya. (1990) *The Black Church in the African American Experience*, Durham, NC: Duke University Press.

Lincoln, C. Eric. (1974a) *The Black Church Since Frazier*, New York: Schocken Books, Inc.

Lincoln, C. Eric. (1974b) *The Black Experience in Religion*, Garden City, New York: Anchor Books.

Lincoln, C. Eric. (1961) *The Black Muslims in America*, Boston: Beacon Press.

Lomax, Louis. (1963) *When The Word Is Given...*, New York: World Publishing Co.

Lucas, J.O. (1948) *The Religion of the Yoruba*, Lagos: C.M.S. Bookshop.

Malcolm X. (1965a) *The Autobiography of Malcolm X*, New York: Grove Press.

Malcolm X. (1970) *By Any Means Necessary*, New York: Pathfinder Press.

Malcolm X. (1983) *The End of White Supremacy*, New York: Seavers Books.

Malcolm X. (1992) *February 1965: The Final Speeches*, New York: Pathfinder Press.

Malcolm X. (1965b) *Malcolm X Speaks*, New York: Merit Publishers.

Malcolm X. (1968) *Speeches of Malcolm X at Harvard*, New York: William Morrow & Co.

Malcolm X. (1989) *The Last Speeches*, New York: Pathfinder Press.

Marx, Karl and Frederick Engels. (1964) *On Religion*, New York: Schocken Books, Inc.

Massey, Gerald. (1970) *Egypt Light of the World*, New York: Samuel Weiser, Inc.

Mbiti, John S. (1970) *African Religions and Philosophy*, Garden City, NY: Anchor Books.

Mbiti, John S. (1991) *Introduction to African Religion*, (2nd edition), Oxford: Heineman International Literature and Textbooks.

Mends, E. H. (1976) "Ritual in the Social Life of Ghanaian Society," in J. M. Assimeng, (ed.) *Traditional Life, Culture and Literature in Ghana*, New York: Cinch Magazine Limited.

Mohammed, Imam W. Deen. (1991) *Al-Islam, Unity and Leadership*, Chicago: The Sense Maker.

Morenz, Siegfried. (1984) *Egyptian Religion*, Ithaca: Cornell University Press.

Moorish Science Temple of America, Inc. (1991) *Moor Sense 2000 Journal: Righting of a National Resurrected*, Augusta, WV: Seven Circles Publishing Co.

Morrison, Silburn M. (1992) *Rastafari: The Conscious Embrace*, Bronx, NY: Itality Publishing House.

Muhammad, Elijah. (1973) *The Fall of America*, Chicago: Muhammad's Temple of Islam No. 2.

Muhammad, Elijah. (1965) *Message to the Black Man in America*, Chicago: Muhammad's Temple of Islam No. 2.

Muhammad, Elijah. (1992) *The Theology of Time*, Hampton, VA: U.B. & U.S. Communication Systems, 1992.

Muhammad, Wallace D. (1980) *As the Light Shineth From the East*, Chicago: Wallace D. Muhammad Publishing Company.

Murphy, Joseph. (1988) *Santería: An African Religion in America*, Boston: Beacon Press.

Murray, Pauli. (1979) "Black Theology and Feminist Theology: A Comparative View," in *Black Theology*, (eds.) Gayraud Wilmore and James Cone, New York: Orbis Books.

Overbea, Luix. (1978) "Leader Quits Black Muslims," *Christian Science Monitor* (June 13).

Paris, Peter J. (1985) *The Social Teaching of the Black Churches*, Philadelphia: Fortress Press.

Petrie, W. M. Flinders. (1914) "Egypt in Africa," *Ancient Egypt*, 3, 115-127.

Ray, Benjamin C. (1976) *African Religions*, Englewood Cliffs, N.J.: Prentice-Hall, Inc.

Richards, Dona Marimba. (1976) "A Community of African Descendants; The Afro-Bahian Candomblé, *The Proceedings of the Conference on Yoruba Civilization, 26-31 July*, Ife, Nigeria: University of Ife.

Richards, Dona Marimba. (1989) *Let the Circle Be Unbroken, Implications of African Spirituality in the Diaspora*, New York: Dona Marimba Richards.

Roberts, J. DeOtis. (1974) *A Black Political Theology*, Philadelphia: Westminister Press.

Roberts, J. DeOtis. (1971) *Liberation and Reconciliation*, Philadelphia: Westminister Press.

Rogers, J.A. (1972) *World's Great Men of Color*, Volume 1, New York: MacMillan.

Sagan, Carl. (1979) *Broca's Brain-Reflections on the Romance of Science*, New York: Random House.

Temple, Robert. (1976) *The Sirius Mystery*, New York: St. Martin's Press.

Thompson, Robert F. (1983) *Flash of the Spirit*, New York: Random House.

Torres, Sergio. (1981) *The Challenge of a Basic Christian Community*, Maryknoll, N.Y.: Orbis Books.

Torres, Sergio. (1976) *Theology in the Americas*, Maryknoll, N.Y.: Orbis Books.

Walton, Hanes Jr. (1976) *The Political Philosophy of Martin Luther King, Jr.* Westport, Conn.: Greenwood Press.

Washington, James M. (ed.) (1986) *A Testament of Hope: The Essential Writings of Martin Luther King, Jr.*, San Francisco: Harper and Row.

Washington, Joseph. (1964) *Black Religion*, Boston: Beacon Press.

Washington, Joseph. (1967) *The Politics of God*, Boston: Beacon Press.

West, Cornel. (1982) *Prophesy Deliverance: An Afro-American Revolutionary Christianity*, Philadelphia: Westminster Press.

West, Cornel. (1988) *Prophetic Fragments*, Trenton, NJ: African World Press.

Williams, Delores. (1975) *The Black Woman Portrayed in Selected Black Literature and Some Questions for Black Theology*. Unpublished master's thesis, Columbia University and Union Theological Seminary, Columbia and New York.

Wilmore, Gayraud S. (ed.) (1989) *African American Religious Studies*, Durham, N.C.: Duke University Press.

Wilmore, Gayraud S. (1983) *Black Religion and Black Radicalism*, (2nd Edition), Garden City, N.Y.: Anchor Books.

Wilmore, Gayraud S. (1979) "The Role of Afro-America in the Rise of Third World Theology: A Historical Reappraisal," in *African Theology En Route*, (eds.) Kofi Appiah-Kubi and Sergio Torres, pp. 196-208.

Wilmore, Gayraud S. and James H. Cone (eds.). (1979) *Black Theology*, Maryknoll, N.Y.: Orbis Books.

Woodson, Carter G. (1945) *The History of the Negro Church*, Washington, D.C.: Associated Publishers.

Wright, Richard A. (1984) *African Philosophy: An Introduction*, (3rd edition), New York: University Press of America.

Yinger, Milton. (1970)   *The Scientific Study of Religion*, N.Y.: Macmillan.

Zahan, Dominique. (1979) *The Religion, Spirituality, and Thought of Traditional Africa*, Chicago: The University of Chicago Press.

BLACK SOCIOLOGY

4
BLACK SOCIOLOGY

4.1 INTRODUCTION

Black sociology is essentially the critical study of the structure and functioning of the Black community as a whole, as well as the various units and processes which compose and define it, and its relations with peoples and forces external to it. This includes study of family, groups, institutions, views and values, relations of race, class and gender and related subjects. Moreover, Black sociology directs itself to the study of Black social reality from a Black perspective. The need for a Black perspective evolves inevitably from the fact that U.S. society is a society divided and organized along racial lines, that the ideology and/or social theory which rules in academic and social circles is the ideology of the ruling race/class, and that this ideology or social theory is more of an apologia for the established order than a critical analysis of it. Therefore, it becomes important that Blacks who are concerned with political, economic and cultural emancipation have an emancipatory social science which is Afrocentric. As Staples (1973:168) argues, "if white sociology is the science of oppression, Black sociology must be the science of liberation."

As an emancipatory social science, Black sociology offers both critiques and correctives. Continuing the tradition of DuBois (1967), Frazier (1957), Cox (1970), and Hare (1965), Black sociology has set for itself several basic aims: 1) to rescue Black life from the racist interpretations which pose it as pathological and pathogenic, and redefine it in its multidimen-

269

sionality and variousness; 2) to create new concepts, categories, analytical frameworks and bodies of data that enhance understanding of both Black reality and the larger reality of U.S. society; 3) to make ongoing critical analyses of the structure and functioning of U.S. society, especially in terms of race, class and power; 4) to join severe criticism of internal forces negative to Black progress and liberation with criticism of negative external forces; and 5) to discover, develop and reveal possibilities of social change inherent in both the Black community and the larger society (Ladner, 1973; Staples, 1976; DuBois, 1975).

Since Black sociology is so inclusive a social science, only a small selection of its concerns can be treated in this chapter. Other major concerns such as politics, economics and social psychology of the Black community will be treated in the other appropriate chapters. The selected concerns which follow are fundamental to understanding Black social organization and are also reflective of issues and problems which are directly related to Black subordination and oppression in U.S. society and Black struggle to end this condition.

The Problem of Ghettoization

The Black community, like other communities, is defined by its sharing of common space, experiences, view and value systems, social institutions and self-consciousness. Its common space, however, is a bounded area of living, i.e., a ghetto, which not only closes Blacks in the community, but simultaneously shuts them out from the access and various opportunities available in the larger society. It is what Wilson (1989:61) calls ghetto *social isolation which is further aggravated now by middle-class and working class out migration, strengthening the structures of constraint on inner-city residents.* Even when Blacks move beyond the original bounded areas and form what is called "gilded ghettos" in integrated areas, these outskirt communities "also become linked to the central Black area," as whites leave and other Blacks move in (Glasgow, 1981:34). Moreover, even outside the ghetto physically, Blacks are defined and treated as the majority who are still in the ghetto with allowable variations. Benjamin (1991) argues forcefully that racism, both as an institutional and individual expression, affects the lives of all African Americans regardless of class. She (1991:97) argues that even in the corporate world "there is a sense of ghettoization of Black professionals...."

W.E.B. DuBois (1967) pioneered the scientific study of Black urban life with a major work, *The Philadelphia Negro*, in 1899 and in 1945. St. Clair Drake and Horace Cayton (1962) produced the first major study which was a systematic and scholarly investigation of the Black ghetto itself. During the 60's Kenneth Clark (1965) contributed *Dark Ghetto: Dilemmas of Social Power* which gave an incisive overview of the problems of ghetto life using Harlem as a model.

What appears, then, from DuBois', Drake's and Cayton's, and Clark's analyses, along with others, is a social reality defined by six basic dimensions. First, the ghetto is territorial, i.e., residential, bounded and segregated. In spite of Wilson's (1979) findings of increased suburbanization, Rose (1976) shows that in five major cities, it was simply the expansion of the central city areas or increase in the Black population already in the suburbs. Moreover, Clay (1981:89) reports that suburban migration is limited essentially to the middle class and generally "produces a resegregation pattern where Blacks are concentrated in a few suburban enclaves." Also, racism in housing traps even those who perhaps could afford to move from the ghetto (Momemi, 1986). Secondly, the ghetto is racial/ethnic, i.e., essentially Black and a product of a racist society which poses race as a central criteria for determining life-chances, opportunities, social status and human worth (Bullard and Feagin, 1991). Thirdly, the ghetto is socio-economic, i.e., marked by what Clark (1965:27ff) calls economic and social decay. Clark lists, as symptoms of ghetto life, poor education, poor housing, unemployment, drug addiction and alcoholism, frequent illness and early death, and crime, all accented by "the primary affliction of inferior racial status in a racist society."

Fourthly, the ghetto is institutional, i.e., it has a complex of community institutions, organizations and enterprises which are both a positive and a negative (Spear, 1967). The positive aspect of them is that they are structures necessary for self-determined maintenance and development. But the negative aspect is that they are often not strong enough to fulfill their function or fail to use their strength adequately for social advancement and change. This becomes even clearer with the loss of a large segment of the middle and working class which built and sustained the institutional base and social networks (Wilson, 1987:56).

Fifthly, the ghetto is clearly political, i.e., both an expression and product of Black powerlessness to prevent its establishment or end its existence. This powerlessness is obviously related to the ghetto's structural incapacity to define, defend and develop its interests as alluded to above. For without strong community structures to resist imposition and advance Black interests, external interests will most likely be imposed. Thus, the ghetto is controlled from outside and it is this external control joined with other factors of ghetto life which have led some to argue that it is an internal colony (Cruse, 1968; Clark, 1965). This powerlessness is clear in the inner-city's inability to protect itself from what Robert Bullard calls "environmental racism," i.e., turning the ghetto into a toxic waste dumping ground (1990).

Finally, the ghetto is psycho-cultural, i.e., defined by views, values and self-consciousness negative to its development and transformation into a free, proud and productive community (Clark, 1965; Karenga, 1980). Although the psychological aspect will be discussed at length in the chapter on psychology, the cultural dimensions which are directly related will be discussed below. In conclusion, then, it is this fact of ghetto life, the negatives which emerge from it and the solutions posed to correct them and develop a higher level of life that form the core of sociological inquiry and prescription.

The Race/Class Question

One of the most pressing questions in Black sociology is the significance of race and class in Black life. The significance of the question rests not only in its relevance to understanding Black oppression, but also in its relevance in developing strategies for liberation. For depending on the weight each or both are given, the Black community correctly or incorrectly grasps the character of its oppression and the theoretical and practical requirements necessary to end it. Thus, since the late Seventies the debate has intensified concerning which is the most important -- race oppression or class oppression and how the two interact and relate (Wilson, 1987, 1978; Willie, 1979).

The focus on class as the fundamental unit of social analysis and the key determinant in social life has been provided most definitively by the sociology of Marxism (Bottomore and Rubel, 1964). Marx argued essentially that the shape and functioning of society was determined by its economic foundation and that class, as a socio-economic category, was basic to the understanding of society and history. Furthermore, he contended that productive systems establish given economic roles -- farmer, trader, industrialists, worker -- and that each group of persons which stands in the same relationship to the means of production (raw materials, factories, machines,etc.) form a class. As a class, each did the same work, had the same basic interests ("real" as opposed to "perceived") and often engage in conflict with other classes. This conflict between classes, he argued, is the motive force of history. Finally, he contended that the economic foundation was the base from which the superstructure (law, religion, politics, ideology, etc.) rose and upon which it rested.

From this materialistic (economic) interpretation of society and history evolved two basic Marxist interpretations of the interaction of race and class, the orthodox Marxist theory

(Cox, 1970; Reich, 1981) and the split labor-market theory (Bonacich, 1972). Orthodox Marxist theory argues that racism is a reflection of the manipulation of workers by the capitalist class to divide them along racial lines and reduce their capacity to struggle against the system. This results in encouraging discrimination against Blacks, arguing their inferiority, use of Blacks as a surplus, marginal low-paid working force, and establishing a privileged better-paid racist white labor force. Thus, racism is a function of class struggle, not an independent variable itself. The split labor-market theory argues that racial antagonism begins in the labor-market split along racial lines when business promotes worker competition to displace higher paid labor. If the labor-market split is along racial lines with whites being the higher-paid and Blacks being the lower-paid labor, class antagonism is transformed into racial antagonism in which whites fight to neutralize or eliminate occupational competition with Blacks.

Both of these class theories of race fail to perceive that race and class interact dynamically as variables in social conflict and position. Although the orthodox Marxist view blames the capitalist and split labor-market theory places the essential burden on the white worker, there are clearly cases where both white capitalists and white workers join to oppress or discriminate against Blacks and other Third World people. Moreover, sometimes it is done for reasons of race and others times for reasons of class and still at other times for both reasons of race and class. Also, in a racist society the class position of a person is greatly determined by his/her race. This is what Fanon (1968:40) meant when he wrote that in a racist context, i.e., the colony, race is the key determinant.

Blauner (1972:31) also calls attention to the fact that often in a racist society, racial exploitation and/or control becomes "an end itself, despite its original limited purpose as a means to exploitation and privilege." Finally, Turner (1979:31) argues that racism has become so endemic and historically rooted in U.S. society and its institutions that "it exists apart from and in some cases in spite of, the social attitudes of the people who administer these institutions." Thus, the factor of "covert or institutional racism has a dynamic of its own, despite the vagaries of prejudice and bigotry, real as they are." Given all the above contentions concerning race and class and their interaction and relation, it is clear that racism cannot be reductively translated as a function of class or class struggle. Such a position obscures the complexity and variousness of their interplay and their separate relevance as factors in a racist-capitalist society (Franklin, 1991; Staples, 1987; Turner, 1979).

Moreover, recent literature argues the persistence of race as a major determinant in life-chances and life-conditions (Bell, 1992, 1987; Hacker, 1992). Hacker (1992:13) notes that even those Blacks "who aspire to careers in white institutions, and emulate white demeanor and diction, find that white America lets them only partly past the door." It is in this context of the historical and continuing denial of racial justice to Blacks and others of color that Derrick Bell (1992:ix) concludes, "racism is an integral, permanent and indestructible component of this society" at least in its present form.

There are other positions on race and class, but they will be covered in chapter VI on economics. However, it is important to note in conclusion that one of the problems many social scientists and others have in identifying racism is that their definition is deficient. Marxists and non-Marxists tend to see racism as simply attitudes or ideology rather than as multi-faceted involving ideology, structure and practice (Allen, 1974).

Racism is essentially a system of denial and deformation of the history and humanity of Third World people (people of color) and their right to freedom based exclusively or primarily on the specious concept of race (Karenga, 1981). Stripped of all its cultural and scientific mystification, race is a bio-social category designed to assign human worth and social status, using Europeans as the paradigm of humanity and social achievement. Racism, then, which begins with the creation and mystification of race, is social thought and practice which expresses itself in three basic ways, i.e., as: 1) imposition, i.e., conquest of a people, and interruption, destruction and appropriation of a people's history and productive capacity in racial terms; 2) ideology, i.e., an elaborate system of pseudo-intellectual categories, assumptions and contentions negative to Third World peoples and serving as justification of the imposition and reinforcement of the institutional arrangement; and 3) institutional arrangement, i.e., a system of political, economic and social structures which insure white power and privilege over Third World peoples (Karenga, 1985).

The Issue of Culture

Although the question of culture had been raised during the Harlem Renaissance in the 20's, it was during the 60's that the Black community became increasingly concerned about the possession, meaning, reappropriation and reconstruction of their culture. The shift away from integration as the main Movement goal and the resurgence of Black nationalism brought with it a renewed interest in Black culture, its role in life and struggle and a profound and pervasive commitment to revitalize, reconstruct and construct it. Expressive of this thrust were the struggle for Blacks Studies which demanded recognition of Black contribution to society and the world, the look to Africa for inspiration and models and the proliferation of creative artist groups, study groups, literature and institutions which focused on culture. This thrust was both reactive and proactive, defensive and developmental. It sought not only to halt and reverse the racist attempt to negate Black culture, but also to rebuild and build a system of views and values which aided Blacks in their struggle for liberation and a higher level of human life.

Many racist, liberal and Marxists social scientists argued that Blacks had no real culture, that slavery destroyed it, and that what passed as Black culture was simply a pathological reaction to whites, a duplication of them or an expression of lower-class culture rather than a specific Black culture (Liebow, 1967;

Berger, 1967). Myrdal (1944:927-930) argued that the Black person is "an exaggerated American" and essentially a "pathological" reaction to whites. Ellison (1966:316:317) responding to Myrdal, stated that Myrdal misjudges Blacks' creativity and adaptive vitality. He posited that Blacks could not possibly "live and develop for over three hundred years simply by reacting." On the contrary, Blacks have made self-conscious and self-constructive efforts which have contributed to American culture, not simply borrowed from it.

Glazer and Moynihan (1963:52) argued that the key to understanding Blacks is to recognize they cannot view themselves as other ethnic groups who have a culture. For the Black person "is only an American and nothing else. He has no values and culture to guard and protect." Such a contention was challenged by the Black Cultural Revolution of the 60's which not only reaffirmed Black culture and its difference from white culture in terms of life-goals, worldview and values, but also the need to draw on its African and mass sources to recreate and revitalize it and use it as a weapon in the Black struggle (Karenga, 1967, Gayle, 1971).

Harold Cruse (1967) in his massive study of culture and politics in Harlem, made a profound contribution to the focus on cultural revitalization and struggle. He maintained that cultural oppression is tightly interlocked with political and economic oppression. For cultural control facilitates political control which in turn insures economic control. Thus, he argued instead of placing higher priority on any one of the three factors of culture, politics and economics, the three must be welded together into a dynamic synthesis and social strategy. Stressing the essentiality of culture to political and economical struggle, Cruse (1967:12) maintained that "as long as the (African Americans') cultural identity is in question or open to self-doubt, then there can be no positive identification with the real demands of his political and economic existence." Therefore, Cruse (1967:45) argues that "there can be no real Black revolution in the U.S. without a cultural revolution as a corollary to the scheme of 'agencies for social change'." He concludes, calling on the Black intellectuals to solve their historical crisis, i.e., alternating between integrationist fantasies and nationalist demands when rejected by whites, and guide the masses to liberation and a higher level of human life.

As argued in chapter II in the section on the Sixties, Kawaida Theory stood out as the most structured and influential theory of the Black Cultural Revolution. Kawaida (Karenga, 1980, 1978b) contends that the key crisis in Black life is the cultural crisis, i.e., a crisis in views and values. This crisis was caused by several factors, among which are enslavement and deculturalization, the ideological hegemony (dominance in the realm of ideas and values of the ruling race/class) and the growth of popular culture at the expense of national culture.

The need, then, is for a cultural revolution which will prepare the Black masses for a political struggle to end the social conditions which deny and deform their history and humanity. The cultural revolution, Kawaida states, precedes and makes possible the political revolution and also sustains it. By cultural revolution is meant "the ideological and practical struggle to transform persons and people and to build structures to insure, maintain and expand that transformation" (Karenga, 1982:2). Whereas political revolution is the struggle to seize and reorder the unequal power and wealth in society, cultural revolution is the process which makes it possible and sustains it with transformed self-conscious participants, i.e., self-conscious agents of their own liberation.

Cultural revolution, according to Kawaida, can be defined as the ideological and practical struggle to: 1) transform the cultural context in which people live; 2) transform them in the process, making them self-conscious agents of their own liberation; and 3) build the institutional base to sustain and constantly expand that transformation. It implies and necessitates revitalizing, creating and recreating culture (Karenga, 1967). *Kawaida defines culture as the totality of a people's thought and practice by which a people creates itself, celebrates, sustains and develops itself and introduces itself to history and humanity.* This occurs in seven basic areas: religion, history, social organization, economic organization, political organization, creative production (art, music and literature), and ethos (collective self-definition and consciousness). It is on these seven levels, Kawaida contends, that Black people must rebuild themselves by rebuilding their culture, so that each area is in both their image and interests. This in turn necessitates a struggle against oppression to define, defend and develop that distinct culture. For it is a political fact that the greater the difference between the culture of the oppressed and the oppressor, the greater the difficulty of dominance and the capacity for resistance (Cabral, 1973).

Finally, Kawaida, in the tradition of DuBois (1969), Frazier (1973), and Cruse (1967), posits that the cultural and political struggle must be led by a self-conscious vanguard who commits class suicide and identifies with the aspirations of the masses (Karenga, 1985). This vanguard will build on the strengths of Black culture, i.e., its adaptive vitality, strong emphasis on expressive values, empathetic sharing, durability, humanism and creativity, and expand them. Moreover, the vanguard must create an Afrocentric ideology or social theory which negates the ruling race/class ideology and provides the basis for a critical Afrocentric conception of reality and the possibilities and methods of changing it. Kawaida contends that this vanguard must also urge the self-conscious creation of a national culture which not only distinguishes Blacks from their oppressor, but also aids them in their rescue and reconstruction of their history and humanity and enables them to contribute to human history and achievement in their own unique way.

4.2   THE BLACK FAMILY

At the heart of social organization is the way a people organizes its relationships. In fact, another way to define social organization is as "ways of teaching, structuring, validating, changing and expanding social behavior and relationships" (Karenga, 1980:35). Thus, an important focus of sociology is on the socialization process, i.e., the value and vision orientation designed to instruct and enhance personal and collective behavior and relationships. Nowhere is this more clear than in the discussion of the Black family. For if the Black family is the smallest example of the nation, i.e., Black people, its strength and weakness greatly determine the capacity of Black people to achieve the social tasks they pose for themselves.

The assessment of the Black family's strength and weakness pervade social science literature (Staples and Johnson, 1993; Parker, 1991; Cheatam and Stewart, 1990; Willie, 1988, 1986; Jewell, 1988; Hare and Hare, 1984). In fact, much of the literature, if not most, can be assigned to either one school of thought and research or the other (Willie, 1970; Staples, 1991, 1978; McAdoo, 1981). These two approaches to the Black family may be termed the pathological-pathogenic and the adaptive-vitality approaches. The first is predicated on the assumption that the Black family is either pathological or pathogenic or both. That is to say, it is not only a dysfunctional and sick social unit, but produces sick and dysfunctional members of society.

Frazier (1939) unwittingly helped lay the basis for the pathology school in his research on the Black family. He believed that enslavement, urbanization and racism prevented perpetuation of the African family relations and forms and imposed severe strains on the Black family's ability to function effectively. Thus, it developed negative situational adaptations to handle this legacy of oppression and exploitation. From this, he notes, came the matriarchal character of the Black family with its strong women and ineffective and marginal men; its unstable marriages; the prevailing norm of casual sex, and the loss of folk culture cohesiveness in the urbanization process.

Daniel Moynihan (1965), using largely census data, tried to confirm Frazier's conception by statistics. Although Frazier had pointed to the social causes of Black family problems, Moynihan blamed social problems on the Black family. Making

a generalized indictment of Black families, he (1965:5) argued
that "at the heart of the deterioration of the fabric of (Black)
society is the deterioration of the (Black) family." Citing Frazier
as if to escape the charge of racist sociology, Moynihan charged
that the Black community was plagued by pathological and
pathogenic families marked by and conducive to matriarchy,
broken and ineffective males, delinquency, economic dependency,
poor academic performance, unwed motherhood, etc.

The adaptive-vitality school contends that adaptation by
Blacks to socio-economic pressures and limitations must not be
seen as pathology, but as strength, i.e., adaptive vitality. Billingsley (1993, 1968), Blassingame (1972), Young, (1970), Hill (1989,
1972), Nobles (1987, 1985, 1984, 1978), Staples (1991, 1978), and
Staples and Johnson (1993) et al represent this school. Among
the propositions they argue are the following: 1) that the Black
family is unique and cannot be fitted into a white formula for
analysis; 2) that it was not totally destroyed in slavery; 3) that it
has proved its durability and adaptive vitality in the face of
severe oppression, and thus, is a strong and functional social unit.

Staples (1971:133) notes that one of the major problems
with the traditional approaches to the study of the Black family
has been their tendency to fit it in a white-middle class formula.
He argues that the result of this subjective approach "has been
that the Black family continues to be defined as a pathological
unit whose unique way of functioning sustains the conditions of
its oppression." He and Johnson (1993) reaffirm this contention
in a later work, arguing that the problems of Black families are
essentially attributable to social conditions of oppression in which
they find themselves. Billingsley (1993, 1970) also criticized
white social science for focusing almost exclusively on lower
income families and ignoring the majority of stable Black families
and blaming lower-class families for their victimization by society.
Although, he concedes lower-class family negatives while praising
upper-class positives, he nevertheless argues these negatives are
socially rooted. Moreover, he stresses that many misunderstood
features of the Black family are sources of strength and raises

questions concerning politically suspect conclusions which have social policy implications.

Although proponents of the adaptive vitality approach do not agree on the degree of African influence on African American culture and family, there is agreement that enslavement did not destroy all. Early studies by DuBois (1969) and Carter G. Woodson (1936), as well as Herskovits (1941) showed a legacy from Africa as well as from enslavement in African American culture and social institutions. Twenty years ago, Blassingame (1972) found African survivals in courtship practices, dance, familial roles, folktales, language, music, names, proverbs, and religious beliefs and practice. Blassingame asserted that it is important to realize that "Whatever the impact slavery had on (Blacks') behavior and attitudes, it did not force them to concentrate all their psychic energy on survival." On the contrary, they showed remarkable adaptive vitality in the system and in spite of the end of contact with Africa when the slave trade ended, the enslaved African "was able to retain many cultural elements and (for a while) an emotional contact with his motherland."

Nobles (1985, 1984, 1981, 1978) posits that Africanity or Africanness is clearly evidenced in African American families. He (1978:22) cites "the actuality of black kinship bonds and the sense of extended family" as an example of this as well as an egalitarian quality to relationships and a profound commitment to the survival of the family (ethnic group). Moreover, he sees Africanity in Blacks' affective rather than economic approach to family life and their sense of collectivity rather than the individualism which is endemic to European culture. Thus, Nobles (1985) argues that viewing the African American family from an Afrocentric perspective is not only key to understanding them, but also indispensable in assisting them in self-strengthening.

Finally, Sudarkasa (1980, 1981) asserts that both African and enslavement legacies exist. She (1981:37) states that "just as surely as Black American family patterns are in part an outgrowth of the descent into slavery, so too are they partly a reflection of the archetypical African institutions and values that informed and influenced the behavior of the Africans who were enslaved in America." Also she (1981:39) notes, that although there are "relatively few 'traces' of direct *institutional transfer* from Africa to America," there are "numerous examples of the *institutional transformation* from Africa to America." Thus, she tends to support Blassingame's contention that Africans were able to build viable and creative synthesis out of African and European culture. Sudarkasa essentially poses the concept and force of consanguinity strength or bloodtie kinship as an enduring Africanism as well as the extended family of which it is an expression. "The extended family networks that were formed during slavery by Africans and their descendants were based on the institutional heritage which Africans had brought with them to this continent," she (1981:45) contends. And the specific forms they assumed depend on the cultural, economic and political circumstances in which Blacks found themselves. Martin and Martin (1978) also identify this extended family tradition and reaffirm its relevance to Black family life.

The proponents of the adaptive-vitality model and approach are concerned also that the Black family be viewed and studied as a distinct institution with its own historical tradition and characteristics, not as a pathological or defective variation on the European theme. Although some make a distinction between *alternative* and *adaptive* strategies and forms developed by Black families to meet the challenges of an oppressive social life, that distinction is not made here. As Sudarkasa (1981:37) has noted, the two characterizations of Black families are not mutually exclusive and represent false dichotomies. For adaptive strategies and behavior contribute to the development of alternative formations as the history of the Black family shows. I have used the term adaptive vitality which is the "ability to adjust structurally and ideologically in confrontation with society without losing one's distinct character," to absorb stress and strain and bounce back with vigor (Karenga, 1980:51). It is the ability to push past simple survival and develop continuously. It is in the context of the above clarification that the strengths of Black families which proponents of the adaptive-vitality school are presented and have meaning.

Although Staples, Ladner (1971), Billingsley, Nobles and others have listed various strengths of Black families, the classic study on this is Robert Hill's (1972) book of the same title, *The Strengths of Black Families*. Hill (1972:3) defines family strengths as "those traits which facilitate the ability of the family to meet the needs of its members and the demands made upon it by systems outside the family unit." Having done this, he lists five strengths which examination of literature on Black families reveal as having been "functional for their survival, development and stability" (1972:4): 1) strong kinship bonds which is stronger among Blacks than whites and expresses itself by absorption of relatives, especially minors and the elderly in various families; 2) strong work orientation, i.e., "the Black poor still are more likely to work than the white poor"; 3) the adaptability of family roles, i.e., male and female can assume each other's household roles in the event of absence, illness, etc.; 4) high achievement orientation, i.e., the majority of low-income students and their parents have college aspirations; and finally, 5) religious orientation.

In criticism of the adaptive-vitality proponents, Nathan Hare (1976) contends the strength-of-the-family school may have unwittingly created their own negatives while challenging the negatives of the pathology-pathogenesis school. First, he (1976:9) states that strength-of-the-family orientation "prohibits any recognition of pathological consequences of our oppression" and thus, undermines the thrust of corrective action. Secondly, Hare (1976: 10) argues that such an approach "fails to incorporate a power-conflict model appropriate to advocates of social change." Finally, Hare (1976:11) contends that the strength-of-the-family approach helps "make it easier for an oppressive society to ignore the heinous conditions it imposes on the Black family." He stresses that he is not advocating victimology, but he has problems with claiming all is well with the Black world at the expense of social criticism.

Hare's contentions point to a serious dilemma of Black scholarship, i.e., how does one prove strength in oppression without overstating the case, diluting criticism of the system and absolving the oppressor in the process? Likewise, the parallel dilemma is how does one criticize the system and state of things without contributing to the victimology school which thrives on litanies of lost battles and casualty lists, while omitting victories and strengths and the possibilities for change inherent in both Black people and society? The answer to these questions is not easily done. The tasks of an emancipatory social science are to develop a critical and balanced analysis which reveals Blacks' strengths and weaknesses as well as a prescription for self-conscious action to free themselves and to shape reality into their own image and interest. Such, then, is the central task of an emancipatory Black social science.

4.3   BLACK MALE/FEMALE RELATIONS

Womanist/Feminist Discourse

One of the earliest and most important texts of Black womanist or feminist discourse is Anna Julia Cooper's *A Voice From the South* (1892). In this seminal volume she criticizes racism, sexism and classism and argues that "there is a feminine as well as masculine side to truth, that these are related, not as inferior or superior, not as better or worse, not as weaker or stronger, but as complements -- complements in one necessary and symmetric whole." Moreover, Cooper (1892:29) argues against elevation of the personal over the collective saying, "we too often mistake individual honor for race development and are so ready to substitute petty accomplishments for sound sense and purpose." She (1892:134) recognized and noted the dual character of her oppression and possibilities as both Black and woman and the essential role women must play in defining "an ideal manhood and womanhood" free from racist, classist and sexist flaws. Maintaining that the women's cause in this epoch of crisis and struggle is a universal one which will free not only Africans, but Native Americans and other oppressed peoples, she (1892:144) says "To be a woman in such an age carries with it a privilege and opportunity never implied before. But to be a woman of the (African) race in America and to grasp the deep significance of the possibilities of the crisis is to have a heritage, it seems to me, unique in the ages." Finally, Cooper (1892:71) challenges Black men to build a partnership of equals in love and struggle for liberation and a higher level of human life for "nature never meant the ideals and standards of the world should be dwarfing and minimizing ones, and men should thank us for requiring of them the richest fruits they grow." It is this equal partnership in love and struggle that Afrocentric womanists would later pose as the key and priority focus in male/female relationships and womanist discourse.

      As mentioned in the chapter on Black History, the 70's marked a flourishing of discourse around the issue of Black male/female relations. The discourse originally rose from within the ranks of activist women who had worked in the Black Freedom Movement and who, in looking back on their experiences, remembered painful encounters with sexism, marginalization and disappreciation of their contributions. Writings and narratives by key women in the Black Movement such as Toni Cade Bambara (1970a, 1970b), Frances Beale (1970), Ella Baker (Cantarow, 1980) and Septima Clark (Brown, 1986) bear important witness to these problems. In an essay titled "On the Issue of Roles," Toni Cade (Bambara) (1970b) outlined some of the basic criticisms of sexism in the Movement: 1) assignment of silencing and servile roles to women; 2) focusing on problematic notions of manhood and womanhood rather than progressive concepts of "Blackhood"; and 3) talking revolutionary rhetoric about "picking up the gun" rather than facing "the task of creating a new identity, a (new) self" which synthesized the best of both woman and man "via commitment to struggle."

Inherent in Bambara's concerns is a set of charges and challenges which have consistently informed Black women's discourse concerning men's approaches to male/female relationships and relations. Among the major points of focus are: 1) the tendency to define roles which are unequal, exploitative, oppressive, and unresponsive to the demands of equality, reciprocity and mutual benefit; 2) the tendency to subordinate gender issues to racial (people) issues and using calls to unity to suppress difference, critique and challenge; 3) failing to define the terms and goals of the struggle, so that freedom is a collective project and practice and current relations prefigure the new society and community struggled for; 4) resistance to redefining and reconstructing Black masculinity and Black femininity in and for the liberation struggle; 5) inadequate sensitivity to Black women's pain -- current and historical -- and the need to bear witness to it and have it acknowledged and ended; and 6) frequent unwillingness to be self-critical and self-corrective and to practice partnership in equality rather than relationship in dominance.

The ongoing dialogue around these issues in the 60's was not always conducted in a full, free, frank and principled manner and it began to take an ominous turn in the 70's. Key developments in this dialogue were the publication and resultant discourse around Ntozake Shange's play, *For Colored Girls Who Have Considered Suicide When the Rainbow is Enuff* (1977) and Michele Wallace's *Black Macho and the Myth of the Super Woman* (1979). Major publications in the Black community such as the *Black Scholar*, *Black Books Bulletin* and *Freedomways* provided ample space for the ongoing debate; and the debate was wide-ranging in the community. Toni Morrison's *The Bluest Eye* (1970) and *Beloved* (1987) and Gloria Naylor's *Women of Brewster Place (1982)* among other works by African American women in the 80's not only continued to express the painful and intense conflict between Black men and women, but also revealed the development of Black women's literature as a major, perhaps the primary, way in which this conflict was defined and pursued.

Black men writers like Ishmael Reed in *Reckless Eyeballing* *(1986)* and Trey Ellis in *Platitudes (1988)* responded strongly to this genre of literature and its negative representation of Black men. Other men, on campus and in the community, joined in the criticism and challenge. Thus, the debate around Wallace's work had essentially yielded a series of issues and a pattern of public and private encounters that would repeat themselves in the 80's and 90's (*Black Scholar,* May/June 1979; Karenga, 1979; Staples, 1979). Such exchanges intensified and expanded in the debate around Alice Walker's *The Color Purple (1982)* and culminated in a very bitter and difficult discourse around the Clarence Thomas-Anita Hill confrontation in 1991 (*Black Scholar,* 1992; Morrison, 1992; Karenga, 1992). Terry McMillan's *Waiting to Exhale* (1992) however, tends to take a different turn and appeared to many men as a call to responsible and principled partnership between Black women and men rather than the condemnatory project they perceived much of other Black women's literature to be.

As it was possible to glean from Toni Cade Bambara's (1970b) concerns a basic set of charges and challenges posed by Black women concerning men's approaches to male/female relations, it is also possible to extract a similar set of concerns from the discussion by Black male writers and other Black men around Black women's literature. Among the major points of focus are: 1) the tendency towards monolithic and reductive characterizations of Black men; 2) the failure to contextualize the problem and critique race, class and gender relations in the context of oppression; 3) subordination of race, community and collective issues to gender and personal ones rather than linking them in a mutually beneficial way; 4) consciously or unconsciously providing the established order and racists in general with negative images of Black men, women and families which they appropriate and use to their advantage against all; 5) the failure to develop an Afrocentric approach to the question of male-female relations and thus an over-reliance on white feminists for both essential categories and concepts; and 6) the unwillingness to be self-critical and self-corrective, moving from an over-abundant discourse on victimization and oppression to one of agency and the practice of freedom. It is important to note here that within the Black women's study project and the Black Women's Movement in general, there exist two intellectual and political tendencies. The first is the Afrocentric womanist tendency which as Stewart (1992:4) notes "embraces the field's (Black Studies') long-standing cultural nationalist ideology" and focuses on "forging a new partnership between Africana men and women in pursuit of previously articulated intellectual and political objectives." Moreover, this body of scholars and activists consider alliances with white feminists problematic at best and use of their theories and practices inappropriate in defining the Black woman's experience and approaching Black male/female relations. On the contrary, they pose rootedness in Black culture as indispensable to creating the new partnership between women and men, free of racist, classist and sexist assumptions and practices (Gordon, 1987; Hudson-Weems,1989; Hare and Hare, 1989; Rodgers-Rose and Rodgers,1985; Henry and Foster, 1982).

The other tendency which may be called either Black womanist or Black feminist "elevates feminism to a higher ideological status than cultural nationalism...tends to be more directly connected to traditional academic disciplines...and, more specifically, they are clustered in the areas of literary criticism and creative writing" (Stewart, 1992). Moreover, they are both critical of and collaborative with white feminists, often building alliances with them, but usually trying to maintain a measure of distinctiveness. In fact, the category womanist introduced by Alice Walker (1983:xi) is an expression of this desire for distinction. However their priority focus on gender issues and criticism of race focus often finds them unable to establish a clear distinction conceptually between Black and white feminism (Collins, 1991; Carby,1987; Christian 1989; Hull, Scott and Smith, 1982).

The Question of Quality Relations

Perhaps, then, a definition of the importance of quality Black male/female relations is in order. Many others have discussed this importance (Aldridge, 1989; Gordon, 1987; Hare and Hare, 1989; Staples, 1978, 1981; hooks, 1990, 1992). Building on these insights, male/female relationships can be seen as a fundamental and enduring concern and has importance for several reasons: 1) they have a species character, i.e, they are indispensable to the maintenance and development of the species; 2) they are a measurement of our humanity, i.e., how far humans are from the animal world; 3) they are a measurement of the quality of social life of any given society, i.e., the treatment of women in relationships and by extension in society becomes as Toure (1959:72) notes, "...a mirror that reflects the economic and social conditions, the level of political, cultural and moral development of a given country," 4) they are a measurement and mirror of personal development and identity, i.e., a revelation of who persons really are; and finally, 5) they are a measurement of a people's capacity for struggle and social construction, for as a fundamental unit of the nation, their strengths and weaknesses determine the nation's capacity to define, defend and develop its interest (Karenga, 1978a; Aldridge, 1989; Rodgers-Rose and Rodgers, 1985).

No one can honestly deny that there are substantive problems concerning Black male/female relationships (Karenga, 1979). This is true whether one focuses on sexism (hooks, 1990; Collins, 1991) or the scarcity of men (Jackson, 1978), or the games one plays to begin and sustain relationships (Staples, 1981), or the self-destructiveness and racist targeting of Black men (Wilson, 1990; Madhubuti, 1990; Gibbs, 1988; Gary, 1981). For in the final analysis, it is the quality of relations that is a key and continuing question and challenge. And this challenge requires serious and sober reassessment and reconstruction of and by both men and women in order to lay the basis for more proactive and mutually beneficial exchanges and relationships.

However, in discussing the problems of Black male/female relationships, it is important to keep in mind at least four fundamental facts. First, Black male/female relationships, like Black families, are no more problem-ridden or pathological than white families and male/female relationships, but given our moral claims and liberational struggle, we are morally compelled to create a context for maximum human flourishing. Secondly, it is important to recognize that real life unavoidably involves problems and problem-solving. The point, then, is not to be without problems, but to be resourceful in devising solutions. Thirdly, it is important to recognize that not all Black male/female relationships are in turmoil and trouble. However, there are enough relationships in turmoil and trouble and enough persons without relationships to make the question of Black male/female relationships necessary for discussion. Finally, it is of equal importance to realize that any criticism of Black male/female relationships is at the same time and in equal measure a criticism of U.S. society which has shaped them to fit and function "properly" in it. For social conditions create both social consciousness and social conduct and failure to recognize this can lead one to see racial defects where social ones are more real and relevant.

It is this final contention that serves as a key point of departure for any serious analysis of Black male/female relationships. For to say we are products of our social conditions is to say the same thing about our relationships. Analyses of the major defects in Black male/female relationships clearly reveal their social rather than genetic or purely personal basis. Thus, to understand the negatives of our relationships we must understand the negative characteristics of society which have shaped them.

These negatives of U.S. society are defined by and derived from three major structural and value systems: capitalism, racism and sexism. *Capitalism is a socio-economic system defined by private ownership of the means to satisfy human needs and the ruthless and continuous pursuit of profit which turns virtually everything into a commodity, i.e., an object for sale and purchase. Racism is a system of denial and deformation of a people's history and humanity and right to freedom based primarily or exclusively on the specious concept of race and racial hierarchies. Sexism is the social practice of using gender or sex as the key determinant in establishing, maintaining and explaining relationships and exchanges.* In other words, it is a system of assumptions and acts, theories and practices which imply and impose unequal, oppressive and exploitative relationships based on gender or sex.

Capitalism, then, turns relationships and parts of relationships into commodities and utilitarian arrangements. Racism engenders self-hate, self-doubt and pathological fixation on the white paradigm. And sexism encourages artificial personal power over women as a substitute for real social power over one's destiny and daily life. The result of these three structural and value strains on Black male/female relationships expresses itself as a transformation of the relationships into what can be best described as connections. A connection is a short-term or tentative association which is utilitarian and alienated and is designed primarily for the mutual misuse of each other's body. A quality relationship on the other hand is a long-term, stable association defined by its positive sharing and its mutual investment in each other's happiness, well-being and development.

The Connections

There are four basic connections which plague male/female relationships in the U.S. and by logical extension Black male/female relationships: 1) the cash connection; 2) the flesh connection; 3) the force connection; and 4) the dependency connection (Karenga, 1978a). The cash connection grows out of the commodity character of society. It is informed by several capitalistic assumptions among which are: 1) everything and everyone has a price; 2) anything you can't buy ain't worth having anyhow; 3) what you invest money or material assets in is yours; and 4) money is the measure of and solution to everything.

In such a context, mothers tell their daughters to look for and marry someone who can "take care" of them, as if they were disabled; women sell themselves to men, exchanging sex for economic security and call it marriage; teenage men invest materially in young women with a movie and a Mac burger and demand their bodies in exchange; and male idiots claim the right to rule and ruin the lives of their wives and children on the basis of the money they bring in. Money and material consideration, then, form the basis for the cash connection and diminish the chances for a quality relationship which is conscious of, but not ruled by, material consideration. It often leads to women collaborating in their own oppression.

The flesh connection grows out of the pornographic character of society and is defined as an association based purely or predominantly on the pursuit of sex. This connection focuses on the body and all the perverse things one can do with all or selected parts of it. Pornography, as a definite social thought and practice and as the essence and source of the flesh connection, expresses itself in five basic ways: 1) as species alienation, i.e., one alienated from and oblivious of his/her species half; 2) objectification of the species half, turning a natural partner into an object of use and disuse; 3) fragmentation of the body, i.e., hacking the body into usable pieces and rejecting the wholeness of the human personality; 4) brutalization, most viciously expressed in the sadomasochistic vulgarities society at its most violent and alienated level has produced; and 5) a sexual commodity form, i.e., the joining of the cash and flesh connection through the packaging and peddling of the human body.

A third connection is the force connection which rises out of the violent and oppressive character of society. Historically, men have used their greater physical strength to subdue women and win arguments they would otherwise lose. Moreover, the flesh and force connection merge in the act of rape which is not so much sexual as it is psycho-cultural and physical. For above all, it is an act of domination practiced by husbands, friends and strangers (Karenga, 1978a:15).

Also, there is social or ideological coercion which forces women, through censure and labelling, into roles which degrade and silence. As Vivian Gordon (1987:18,19) notes, "we are all familiar with the denigrating labels which confront the Black woman who strikes out and dares to maintain a valued self; such women are variously viewed to be: domineering, aggressive, probably non-threatening to the man, bad looking/bad acting women that no man wants." The tragedy, she says is that many Black women have accepted these stereotypes but fortunately "the majority of Black women have managed to maintain positive self-identities". The force connection also expresses itself in economic coercion. This operates on the principle that whoever controls the means to satisfy human needs controls at the same time the humans with those needs.

The fourth and final connection which challenges and often prevents quality Black male/female relationships is the dependency connection. This connection is the logical and inevitable result of the others. After a woman has been transformed into a commodity, reduced to parts of her body and physically or ideologically whipped into compliance, she can only be dependent. Like all enslaved persons and servants, she becomes a set of reactions to her slaveholder, a defender of his definitions and treatment of her (Ali, 1989; Madhubuti, 1990). Thus, interdependence, a key value in quality relationships, becomes impossible and the connection becomes the model rather than the deviance (Nobles, 1978).

Toward Solutions

Given the seriousness of the problem, it is only logical to ask, what is the solution? The solution like the problem has both a personal and social dimension and requires transformation on both levels. Although one can argue that conditions create consciousness, consciousness and the social practice that it engenders can and often do create conditions. Certainly, capitalism, racism and sexism shape our relationships, but they are systems created and maintained by humans and they can be changed and rebuilt by humans. Without such a proactive conception of human possibility, neither personal nor social change is possible (hooks, 1990, 1992).

But the struggle to change systems must begin with the struggle of a people to change themselves, i.e, their own views and values and the negative and non-productive ways they have organized and live their daily life. Only then can they self-consciously rebuild their relationships and begin to change the social conditions which deform and deny these relationships.

The solution to deficient relations, then, is rooted in the creation, acceptance and practice of a new value system. Both Ladner (1971:269) and Staples (1981:231-232) argue the need for a value system which rejects and counters the standards of the dominant society. "We must seek other alternative and more viable standards," Ladner (1971:269) asserts. For the U.S. model "which purports to be the exemplary one" is not only negative to Black interest, but also "is in the process of internal destruction, and there is little within it which seems worthy of salvaging." This requires an alternative value system which calls for a redefinition of reality in Blacks' own interest and image, for a new definition of man and woman and the kind of relationship they ought to have.

Real relationships must begin with terms clearly stated, and then grow and are reinforced by common values, common interests and aspirations, quality commitment, support structures, continuous renewal, and common struggle for liberation and a higher level of human life (Karenga, 1980:47-48). For in the final analysis, the call for an end to deformed and defective relationships must be a call for an end to the social conditions which created and sustain them. One must begin with a *moral minimum* that cannot be compromised, a set of values which are resistant to revision because they are at the very roots of the relationship. Prohibition against violence; full, free and frank discussion; egalitarian exchange; collective decision-making; and shared responsibility in love and struggle must be a part of that moral minimum, if a relationship is to be real and mutually beneficial. Moreover, it is important that women continue to define and fight for the freedom, equality and the kind of relationships they need and want, that they reconstruct their supportive links with each other and speak their own African truth of what it means to be a woman-in-community. Likewise, men must stand upright, assume a moral posture on the personal and the political level and reconstruct themselves in relationship with and in consideration of women.

It is important to repeat that any solution that evolves must be a collective and community-affirming solution, one that honors the moral demands of equality, mutual respect and reciprocity. It is this conception of person-in-community, being of equal worth, rights and respect that stands at the center of any Afrocentric conception of man/woman relations. Rodgers-Rose (1980:12, 13) in her early work on the Black woman reaffirmed this location and rootedness in community, saying the authors of articles in her book "stress the point that the history and lives of Black women cannot be separated from the history and lives of Black men and Black children." Thus, the need became one of studying and reconstructing relations among them to achieve maximum human flourishing.

When Alice Walker (1983:xi) says in her definition of womanist that a womanist is one "committed to the survival and wholeness of an entire people, male and female," she repeats this theme of person-in-and-for-community. Also Vivian Gordon (1987:13) reaffirms this when she states that "African women are in a partnership struggle with Black men for the emancipation of their communities." Defining a fundamental aspect of Afrocentric feminism, Clenora Hudson-Weems (1989:187) argues that "The Africana womanist...perceives herself as the companion to the Africana man, and works diligently toward continuing their established union in the struggle against racial oppression." But the community cannot stifle, cannot impose silence or abusive conformity. On the contrary, if it stifles voices, it stifles itself and will wither and decay morally and culturally. Maximum freedom is the basis for maximum human flourishing, and social freedom as well as social oppression are ultimately expressed or exposed in the quality of human relations.

This, however, is just a beginning and an outline of possibilities. The realities will be built by those *New Africans* in U.S. society who dare to be other than their immediate and social conditions encourage them to be. Staples (1981:232) has correctly observed that, "Now we stand at the crossroads of a major decision about which way we will proceed to order our lives." The choice is clearly between the continuation of the current social and personal state of things or self-conscious intervention to change it and build a better society and more life-affirming, moral and meaningful relationships. And as Staples concludes, "Whatever the decision may be, we should not be deluded into believing that the consequences are individual ones. The future of the race may be at stake."

STUDY QUESTIONS

1. Define social organization.
2. What are some basic aims of Black sociology as an emancipatory social science?
3. What are the basic characteristics of the ghetto?
4. What are the possible resource structures and some pro-posed solutions to problems of the ghetto?
5. Discuss the race/class controversy.
6. What is racism? Discuss its three basic aspects.
7. Discuss Kawaida's position on cultural revolution.
8. What are the two basic approaches to the study of the Black family? What are their basic concerns and contentions?

9.   What are Hare's contentions about the strength-of-the-family advocates and the problems these pose for a critical and emancipatory social science?
10.   Discuss womanist/feminist concerns about Black male/female relationships.
11.   Discuss the men's concerns with the womanist/feminist approach to male/female relationships.
12.   Define and discuss the differences and commonalities between the Afrocentric womanists and other Black womanists/feminists.
13.   What are the reasons male/female relationships are so important?
14.   What four fundamental facts must be kept in mind when discussing Black male/female relations?
15.   What three structural and value tendencies of U.S. society help shape male/female relations?
16.   What are the four basic connections in male/female relations?
17.   What are some basic solutions to the problem of male/female relations?

REFERENCES

Aldridge, Delores. (ed.) (1989) *Black Male - Female Relation ships: A Resource Book of Selected Materials,* Dubuque, IA: Kendall/Hunt Publishing Co.

Ali, Shahrazad. (1989) *The Blackman's Guide to Understanding the Blackwoman,* Philadelphia: Civilized Publications.

Allen, Robert. (1974) *Reluctant Reformers,* Washington, D.C.: Howard University Press.

Bambara, Toni Cade. (1970a) "On The Issue of Roles," in *The Black Woman: An Anthology,* Toni Cade Bambara (ed.), New York: Signet, 101-110.

Bambara, Toni Cade. (1970b) *The Black Woman: An Anthology,* New York: Signet.

Beale, Frances. (1970) "Double Jeopardy: To Be Black and Female," in *The Black Woman: An Anthology,* Toni Cade Bambara (ed.), New York: Signet, 90-100.

Bell, Derrick. (1987) *And We Are Not Saved: The Elusive Quest for Racial Justice,* New York: Basic Books.

Bell, Derrick. (1992) *Faces at the Bottom of the Well: The Permanence of Racism,* New York: Basic Books.

Benjamin, Lois. (1991) *The Black Elite: Facing the Color Line in the Twentieth Century,* Chicago: Nelson-Hall Publishers.

Berger, Bennett. (1967) "Soul Searching," *Trans-Action,* (June) 54-57).

Billingsley, Andrew. (1970) "Black Families and White Social Science," *Journal of Social Issues,* 26, 3 (Summer) 127-142.

Billingsley, Andrew. (1968) *Black Families in White America,* Englewood Cliffs, NJ: Prentice-Hall, Inc.

Billingsley, Andrew. (1993) *Climbing Jacob's Ladder: The Enduring Legacy of African-American Families,* New York: Simon & Schuster.

Blassingame, John. (1972) *The Slave Community,* New York: Oxford University Press.

Blauner, Robert. (1972) *Racial Oppression in America,* New York: Harper & Row, Publishers.

Bonacich, Edna. (1972) "A Theory of Ethnic Antagonism: The Split Labor Market," *American Sociological Review,* 37 (October), 547-559.

Bottomore, T.B. and Maximilien Rubel. (1964) *Karl Marx: Selected Writings in Sociology and Social Philosophy,* New York: McGraw Hill.

Branch, Taylor. (1988) *Parting the Waters: America in the King Years,* New York: Simon & Shuster.

Brown, Cynthia Stokes. (ed.) (1986) *Ready From Within: Septima Clark and the Civil Rights Movement,* Navarro, CA: Wild Trees Press.

Bullard, Robert. (1990) *Dumping in Dixie: Race, Class and Environmental Quality,* Boulder, CO: Westview Press.

Bullard, Robert and Joe Feagin. (1991) "Racism in the City," in Mark Gottdiener and C.V. Pickvance (eds.) *Urban Life in Transition*, Newbury Park, CA: Sage Publications.

Cabral, Amilcar. (1973) *Return To The Source*, NY: Monthly Review Press.

Carby, Hazel. (1987) *Reconstructing Womanhood: The Emergence of the Afro-American Woman Novelist*, New York: Oxford University Press.

Carson, Claybourne et al. (1987) *Eyes on the Prize Reader*, New York: Penguin Books.

Cantarow, Ellen. (1987) *Moving the Mountain: Women Working for Social Change*, Old Westbury, NY: Feminist Press.

Cheatham, Harold and James Stewart. (1990) *Interdisciplinary Perspectives*, New Brunswick, NJ: Transaction.

Christian, Barbara. (1989) "But Who Do You Really Belong To-Black Studies or Women Studies?", *Women Studies*, 17, 1/2, 17-23.

Clark, Kenneth. (1965) *The Dark Ghetto*, New York: Harper & Row Publishers.

Clay, Phillip. (1981) "Housing and Neighborhoods," in *The State of Black America-1981*, New York: National Urban League.

Collins, Patricia Hill. (1991) *Black Feminist Thought: Knowledge, Consciousness, and the Politics of Empowerment*, New York: Routledge, Chapman and Hall.

Cooper, Anna Julia. (1892) *A Voice From the South*, Xenia, OH: Aldine Printing House.

Cox, Oliver C. (1970) *Caste, Class and Race*, New York: Monthly Review Press.

Cruse, Harold. (1967) *The Crisis of the Negro Intellectual*, New York: William Morrow.

Cruse, Harold. (1968) *Rebellion or Revolution?* New York: William Morrow.

Drake, St. Clair and Horace R. Cayton. (1962) *Black Metropolis*, New York: Harper & Row Publishers.

DuBois, W.E.B. (1969) *The Negro American Family*, New York: New American Library.

DuBois, W.E.B. (1967) *The Philadelphia Negro*, New York: Schocken Books.

DuBois, W.E.B. (1959) "The Talented Tenth," in *The Negro Problem*, (ed.) Ulysses Lee, New York: Arno Press and New York Times, pp. 31-76.

DuBois, W.E.B. (1975) *W.E.B. Dubois on Sociology and the Black Community*, (eds.) Dan Green and Edwin Driver, Chicago: University of Chicago Press.

Ellison, Ralph. (1966) *Shadow and Act*, New York: New American Library.

Fanon, Frantz. (1968) *The Wretched of the Earth*, New York: Grove Press.

Farmer, James. (1985) *Lay Bare the Heart: An Autobiography of the Civil Rights Movement*, New York: Arbor House.

Foster, Frances S. (1990) *A Brighter Coming Day: A Frances Ellen Watkins Harper Reader*, New York: The Feminist Press and City University of New York.

Franklin, Raymond S. (1991) *Shadows of Race and Class*, Minneapolis: University of Minnesota Press.

Frazier, E. Franklin. (1973) "The Failure of the Negro Intellectual," in *The Death of White Sociology*, (ed.) Joyce A. Ladner, New York: Vintage Books, pp. 52-66.

Frazier, E. Franklin. (1939) *The Negro Family in America*, Chicago: University of Chicago Press.

Frazier, E. Franklin. (1957) *The Negro in the United States*, New York: Macmillan Company.

Garrow, Paul. (1986) *Bearing the Cross: Martin Luther King, Jr. & the Southern Christian Leadership Conference*, New York: Morrow.

Gary, Lawrence E. (ed.) (1981) *Black Men*, Beverly Hills: Sage Publications.

Gayle, Addison. (1971) *The Black Aesthetic*, New York: Doubleday & Co.

Gibbs, Jewelle Taylor. (1988) *Young, Black, and Male in America: An Endangered Species*, Dover: Auburn House.

Glasgow, Douglas. (1981) *The Black Underclass*, New York: Vintage Books.

Glazer, Nathan and Daniel P. Moynihan. (1963) *Beyond the Melting Pot*, Cambridge: M.I.T. and Harvard University Press.

Gordon, Vivian. (1987) *Black Women, Feminism and Black Liberation: Which Way?*, Chicago: Third World Press.

Hacker, Andrew. (1992) *Two Nations: Black and White, Separate, Hostile, Unequal*, New York: Charles Scribner's Sons.

Harding, Vincent. (1987) *Hope and History: Why We Must Share the Story of the Movement*, Maryknoll, NY: Orbis.

Hare, Bruce R. (1988) "Black Youth at Risk," in National Urban League *The State of Black America 1988*, New York: National Urban League, Inc.

Hare, Nathan. (1965) "The Challenge of a Black Scholar," in *The Death of White Sociology*, (ed) Joyce A. Ladner, New York: Vintage Books, pp. 67-78.

Hare, Nathan. (1976) "What Black Intellectuals Misunderstand About the Black Family," *Black World*, (March) 5-14.

Hare, Nathan and Julia Hare. (1989) *Crisis in Black Sexual Politics*, San Francisco: The Black Think Tank.

Hare, Nathan and Julia Hare. (1984) *The Endangered Black Family*, San Francisco: Black Think Tank.

Henry, C. and F. Foster. (1982) "Black Women's Studies: Threat or Challenge?" *The Western Journal of Black Studies*, 6, 1, 15-21.

Herskovits, M. (1941) *The Myth of the Negro Past*, New York: Harper & Row, Publishers.

Hill, Robert. (1989) "Critical Issues For Black Families By The Year 2000," in Janet Dewart (ed.), *State Of Black America 1989*, New York: National Urban League, pp. 41-61.

Hill, Robert. (1972) *The Strengths of Black Families*, New York: Emerson Hall.

hooks, bell. (1990) *Yearning: Race, Gender and Cultural Politics*, Boston: South End Press.

hooks, bell. (1992) *Black Looks: Race and Representation*, Boston: South End Press.

Hudson-Weems, Clenora. (1989) "Cultural and Agenda Conflicts in Academia: Critical Issues for Africana Women's Studies, "*Western Journal of Black Studies*, 13, 4, 185-189.

Hull, Gloria, Patricia Bell Scott and Barbara Smith. (eds.) (1982) *All the Women are White, All the Blacks are Men, but Some of Us are Brave*, Old Westbury, NY: Feminist Press.

Jackson, Jacqueline. (1978) "But Where Are the Men?" in *The Black Family: Essays and Studies*, (ed) Robert Staples, Belmont, Ca: Wadsworth Publishing Company, pp. 110-117.

Jewell, K. Sue. (1977) *Survival of the Black Family: The Institutional Impact of American Social Policy*, New York: Praeger.

Karenga, Maulana. (1985) "The African Intellectual and the Problem of Class Suicide: Ideological and Political Dimensions," in Molefi Kete Asante and Kariamu Welsh Asante (eds.) *African Culture: The Rhythms of Unity*, Westport, CT: Greenwood Press.

Karenga, Maulana. (1978a) *Beyond Connections: Liberation in Love and Struggle*, New Orleans: Ahidiana.

Karenga, Maulana. (1992) "Under the Camouflage of Color and Gender: The Dread and Drama of Thomas-Hill," in Robert Chrisman and Robert L. Allen (eds.) *Court Of Appeal*, New York: Ballantine Books.

Karenga, Maulana. (1978b) *Essays on Struggle: Position and Analysis*, San Diego: Kawaida Publications.

Karenga, Maulana. (1980) *Kawaida Theory: An Introductory Outline*, Inglewood: Kawaida Publications.

Karenga, Maulana. (1979) "On Wallace's Myths: Wading Thru Troubled Waters," *The Black Scholar*, 10, 8 (May/June) 36-39.

Karenga, Maulana. (1981) "The Problematic Aspects of Plural
    ism: Ideological and Political Dimensions" in *Pluralism,
    Racism and Public Policy: The Search for Equality*. (eds.)
    Edwin G. Clausen and Jack Bermingham, Boston: G.K.
    Hall & Co., pp. 223-246.
Karenga, Maulana. (1967) *The Quotable Karenga*, (eds) Clyde
    Halisi and James Mtume, Los Angeles: Saidi Publi-
    cations.
Karenga, Maulana. (1982) "Society, Culture and the Problem of
    Self-Consciousness: A Kawaida Analysis," in *Philosophy
    Born of Struggle: Anthology of Afro-American Philosophy
    From 1917*,(ed.) Leonard Harris, Dubuque, IA: Kendall-
    /Hunt; pp. 212-228.
Kluger, Richard. (1976) *Simple Justice: The History of Brown v.
    Board of Education and Black America's Struggle for
    Equality*, New York: Knopf.
Ladner, Joyce. (1973) *The Death of White Sociology*, New York:
    Vintage Books.
Ladner, Joyce. (1971) *Tomorrow's Tomorrow: The Black Woman*,
    Garden City, N.Y.: Anchor Books.
Lewis,Diane K. (1988) "A Response to Inequality: Black Wo-
    men, Racism, and Sexism," in Micheline Malson et al,
    (eds.) *Black Women in America*, Chicago: University of
    Chicago Press.
Liebow, Elliot. (1967) *Tally's Corner*, Boston: Little, Brown &
    Co.
McAdam, Doug. (1983) *Political Process and the Development of
    Black Insurgency 1930-1970*, Chicago: Chicago University
    Press.
McAdoo, Harriette P. (ed.) (1981) *Black Families*, Beverly
    Hills: Sage Publications.
Madhubuti, Haki. (1990) *Black Men: Obsolete, Single, Danger-
    ous?*, Chicago: Third World Press.
Madhubuti, Haki. (ed.) (1990) *Confusion By Any Other Name*,
    Chicago: Third World Press.

Madhubuti, Haki. (1980) "Not Allowed to Be Lovers," *Black Books Bulletin*, 6, 4, pp. 48-57, 71.

Martin, E.P. and J. M. Martin. (1978) *The Black Extended Family*, Chicago: University of Chicago Press.

Momemi, Jamshid (ed.). (1986) *Race, Ethnicity and Housing in the United States*, Westport, CT: Greenwood Press.

Morris, Aldon.l (1984) *The Origins of the Civil Rights Movement* New York: Free Press.

Morrison, Toni. (ed). (1992) *Race-ing Justice, En-gendering Power*, New York: Pantheon.

Moynihan, Daniel. (1965) *The Negro Family*, Washington, D.C.: Office of Planning and Research, U.S. Dept. of Labor.

Myrdal, Gunnar. (1944) *An American Dilemma*, New York: Harper & Row Publishers.

Nobles, Wade. (1987) *African American Families: Issues, Ideas and Insights*, Oakland, CA: Black Family Institute.

Nobles, Wade. (1981) "African-American Family Life," in *An Instrument of Culture*, (ed) Harriette P. McAdoo, Beverly Hills: Sage Publications.

Nobles, Wade. (1985) *Africanity and The Black Family*, 2nd Edition) Oakland, CA: Black Family Institute Publishers.

Nobles, Wade. (1978) "Africanity: Its Role in Black Families," in *The Black Family: Essays and Studies*, (ed.) Robert Staples, Belmont, Ca: Wadsworth Publishing Co., pp. 19-25.

Nobles, Wade and L. L. Goddard. (1984) *Understanding the Black Family: A Guide to Scholarship and Research*, Oakland, CA: Black Family Institute Publishers.

Parker, Matthew. (1991) *The Black Family: Past, Present and Future - Perspectives of Sixteen Black Christian Leaders*, Grand Rapids: Zondervan Publishing House.

Pinderhughes, Dianne M. (1988) "Civil Rights and the Future of the American Presidency," in National Urban League *The State of Black America 1988*, New York: National Urban League, Inc.

Reich, Michael. (1981) *Racial Equality*, Princeton: Princeton University Press.

Rodgers-Rose, La Frances. (ed.) (1980) *The Black Woman*, Beverly Hills, CA: Sage Publications.

Rodgers-Rose, La Francis and James T. Rodgers. (1985) Strategies *for Resolving Conflict in Black Male and Female Relationships*, Newark: Traces Institute Publications.

Rose, H.M. (1976) *Black Suburbanization*, Cambridge, MA: Ballinger.

Shange, Ntozake. (1977) *For Colored Girls*, New York: Emerson Hall.

Sowell, Thomas. (1981a) *Ethnic Minorities*, New York: Basic Books.

Sowell, Thomas. (1981b) *Markets and Minorities*. New York: Basic Books.

Sowell, Thomas. (1975) *Race and Economics*, New York: David McKay Company.

Spear, Allen H. (1967) *Black Chicago*, Chicago: University of Chicago Press.

Staples, Robert, (ed.) (1978) *The Black Family: Essays and Studies*, Belmont, Ca: Wadsworth Publishing Company.

Staples, Robert. (1976) *Introduction to Black Sociology*, New York: McGraw Hill.

Staples, Robert. (1979) "The Myth of Black Macho: A Response to Angry Black Feminist," *The Black Scholar*, 10, 6, 24-33.

Staples, Robert. (1971) "Toward A Sociology of the Black Family: A Theoretical and Methodological Assessment," *Journal of Marriage and Family*, 33, 1 (February) 119-138.

Staples, Robert. (1973) "What is Black Sociology: Towards a of Black Liberation," in *The Death of White Sociology*, (ed) Joyce A. Ladner, New York: Vintage Books, pp. 161-172.

Staples, Robert. (1987) *The Urban Plantation: Racism and Colonialism in the Post Civil Rights Era*, San Francisco: Black Scholar Press.

Staples, Robert. (1981) *The World of Black Singles*, Westport, CT: Greenwood Press.

Staples, Robert and Leanore Boulin Johnson. (1993) *Black Families at the Crossroads: Challenges and Prospects*, San Francisco: Jossey-Bass Publishers.

Stewart, James B. (1992) "Reaching for Higher Ground: Toward an Understanding of Black/Africana Studies," *The Afrocentric Scholar, 1, 1, 1-63.*

Sudarkasa, Niara. (1980) "African and Afro-American Family Structure: A Comparison." *The Black Scholar*, 11 (November/December) 37-60.

Sudarkasa, Niara. (1981) "Interpreting the African Heritage in Afro-American Family Organization," in *Black Families*, (ed.) Harriette P. McAdoo, Beverly Hills: Sage Publications.

Toure, Sekou. (1959) *Toward Full Re-Africanization*, Paris Présence Africaine.

Turner, James. (1979) "The Political Sociology of Racism and Systematic Oppression: Internal Colonization as a Paradigm for Socio-Economic Analysis," *Studia Africana*, 1, 2 (Fall) 294-314.

Tushnet, Mark. (1987) *The NAACP's Legal Strategy Against Segregated Education 1925 - 1*, Chapel Hill: University of North Carolina.

Walker, Alice. (1983) In Search of Our Mothers' Gardens, New York: Harcourt Brace Jovanovich.

Wallace, Michelle. (1979) *Black Macho and the Myth of the Superwoman*, New York: Dial Press.

Willie, Charles. (1988) "The Black Family: Striving Toward Freedom," in National Urban League *The State of Black America 1988*, New York: National Urban League, Inc.

Willie, Charles. (1979) *The Caste and Class Controversy*, New York: General Hall, Inc.

Willie Charles. (1970) *The Family Life of Black People*, Columbus, OH: Charles Merrill.

Wilson, Amos N. (1990) *Black-on-Black Violence: The Psychodynamics of Black Self-Annihilation in Service of White Domination*, New York: Afrikan World Infosystems.

Wilson, Franklin. (1979) *Residential Consumption, Economic Opportunity and Race*, New York: Academic Press.

Wilson, William J. (1978) *The Declining Significance of Race*, Chicago: University of Chicago Press.

Wilson, William J. (1989) *The Ghetto Underclass: Social Science Perspectives*, Newbury Park, CA: Sage Publications.

Wilson, William J. (1987) *The Truly Disadvantaged: The Inner city, The Underclass and Public Policy*, Chicago: Chicago University Press.

Woodson, Carter G. (1936) *The African Background Outlined*. Washington, D.C.: Association for the Study of Negro Life and History.

Young, Virginia. (1970) "Family and Childhood in a Southern Negro Community," *American Anthropologist*, 72:269-288.

BLACK POLITICS

5
BLACK POLITICS

5.1 INTRODUCTION

Politics can be defined as the art and process of gaining, maintaining and using power. Whether one uses system-oriented literature (Apter, 1977) or studies on revolutionary structures and processes (McAdam, 1983; Gross, 1974), the focus is on power, the process of its acquisition, maintenance and utilization. Thus, the essence of politics is *power which can be defined as the social capacity of a group to realize its will, even in opposition to others* (Karenga, 1980:65). Social capacity is used here to stress both the *collective* and *structural* character of power as well as to indicate that power as a political concept and fact must be achieved in a societal context as opposed to a family or personal context.

Social capacity, then, is rooted in collective (group) capacity and is expressed in a group's structural capacity, i.e., its organizational and institutional ability to realize its will - even in opposition to others. Also, it is important at this point to make the distinction between influence and power which are often used interchangeably though technically they are very different. For whereas power is the capacity to act and achieve, influence is simply the ability to affect. It is having influence with people in power that often passes in Black leadership circles as having power itself.

It is in the context of these assumptions about the pervasiveness and centrality of power to politics that Mack Jones (1972:8) defines Black politics as "a manifestation of one

311

dimension or extension of the universal struggle for power." This
stress on power, then, is the beginning concept in establishing
and developing a fundamental framework for the study of Black
politics.   However, there are other concepts key to a critical
grasp of Black politics as both a study and a social process.
These key concepts are *conflict, interest, change,* and *the state*
which are also alternative and related ways of defining and
understanding politics and its central concept, power.

The stress on the struggle for power presupposes the real
and continuing presence of conflict in society as another basic
aspect of politics. As Hanes Walton Jr. (1972b:1) states, "Politics
is born of societal conflict." This conflict is defined not only by
the struggle for power but also, as Samuel D. Cook contended,
for "values associated with and derived from the possession of
power" (Walton, 1972b:xv). In other words, power, although the
key social value in politics, is sought not simply for itself but for
other key values or treasured things, which power can provide
and protect, i.e., rights, resources, status, etc. The assumption
here then, is that the presence of conflict in society, especially an
oppressive one, is normal rather than abnormal and that its most
severe forms are rooted in the struggle for power and the values
it provides and protects. Therefore, system theory which poses
conflict as abnormal is not so much an analysis as it is a political
projection and description of utopia (Parsons, 1951).

Another key concept of Black politics is interests. In fact,
another way to define *power is a group's capacity to define, defend
and develop its interests.* To define them is to articulate and
establish them; to defend them to is protect them against
challenge and to develop them is to promote and expand them.
Interests can be defined as social stakes, claims or concerns
(Balbus, 1974). They may be subjective (simply perceived) or
objective, (existing independent of perception). In a society
divided and defined by race and class, interests and the conflict
around them assume a race and class character (Browning,
Marshall and Tabb, 1990; Marable, 1985; Scott, 1980; Drake,
1971). Thus, another way of viewing social conflict is as the

struggle between differing, competing and often antagonistic interests.

A fourth key concept in Black politics is social change which is linked to and rooted in social conflict. The assumption here is that the U.S. political system is defined by contradictory interests not simply by consensus as the pluralists (Apter, 1977; Dahl, 1967) contend. Consensus or universal agreement on values is clearly impossible in a society racked by severe race and class division. Thus, constraint through coercion becomes a way to institutionalize and regulate interests and conflicts or suppress them. The political struggle to break through constraints and reorder society in a group's interest becomes the key impetus for social change.

Finally, it is important in understanding politics to realize that "power in society is ultimately determined by a people's relationship to the state" (Karenga, 1980:65). The state here is defined as "the totality of institutions which facilitate governance and insure social control." Within the general framework of these functions, two sets of institutions stand out as most definitive. These are the institutions of dominance, i.e., coercion (armed forces, police, courts, etc.) and political socialization (the educational system and other structures used to advance the ideas and values of those who rule). The instruments of political socialization represent the right and ability to define social reality and the instruments of domination represent the power of the state to make its definition stick. Given this awesome power of the state, and the fact that ultimately power is determined by a group's relationship to the state, an essential political question is how does one check, challenge, seize control of or effectively participate in the exercise of state power?

Walton (1985; 1972b:2-4), however, is correct in his criticism of the exclusive or predominant emphasis on electoral politics in the study of Black politics. The political studies of Gosnell (1967) and Wilson (1960) in Chicago, Ladd's (1966) study of Black leadership in two North Carolina cities, and the readings on the Black electorate on the national level by Bailey

Jr. (1967) all reflect this unbalanced focus on electoral politics. However, power and the struggle for it which are the essence of politics are much more multidimensional than electoral activity.

Essentially there are eight areas or bases of political power: 1) key positions in government; 2) voting strength; 3) community control; 4) economic capacity; 5) community organization; 6) possession of critical knowledge; 7) coalition and alliance; and 8) coercive capacity (Preston, Henderson and Puryear, 1987). Key offices in government at the national, state or local levels place a group in the position to determine or share in the determination of public policy. These positions may be appointed (cabinet members, advisors, bureaucratic appointments) or elected (Congresspersons, mayors, council persons, etc.) Voting strength is key to electing one's own representatives or allies or in penalizing or threatening penalty. Community control is translated as command of an authority over the economic, political and cultural institutions and processes of the community as a result of community organization, institutional penetration and development. Economic capacity is transformed into political power through financing campaigns and lobbies, control of a city's economics, determining public opinion through control of the media, and buying votes and/or officials.

Community organization means a highly mobilized, organized political force which makes possible all the others. For if power is collective and structural capacity, organization of the people itself is the *sine qua non* of this. Another source of power is the possession of critical knowledge, especially given the social tendency toward specialized knowledge. Possession of such knowledge whether in science, technology, finance or politics makes processes and structures dependent on the possessors and often puts the possessors at the very center of the social power process. Coalitions and alliances are also ways to create and augment power. Effective unity strengthens weak groups and increases the power of strong ones.

Finally the ultimate power is coercive power, the capacity to impose one's interest, to physically factor out opposition under the cover of law, to raise class or race will and interest to the status of law and to establish authority through the strength of the gun. In the final analysis, the ultimate power is state power and state power is above all rooted in control of the coercive apparatus, i.e., army, police, etc. There is, however, the alternative power of violence, i.e., urban guerilla strikes, revolt and revolution against the state or social disruption in other forms.

Below is a discussion of three basic areas and expression of Black politics. Each represents Blacks' struggle to define, defend and develop their interests as a people in and outside of government. Hopefully, the discussion of these will give added meaning to Mervyn Dymally's (1972:21) statement that:

> Because of the Black man's (and woman's) situation which is radical by any definition, and because of the nature of American politics, which is moderate to conservative by any definition, the Black man (and woman) in America has been condemned to seek radical ends within a political framework which was designed to prevent sudden and radical social and economical changes.
>
> The radicalness of the situation is not always by choice, but by the fact that Blacks' social location - in terms of both race and class - is such that an effective end to their oppression must and will require the fundamental restructuring of society, i.e., its power and status relations. The history of Blacks in the U.S. offers ample proof of this contention and their future will undoubtedly reaffirm it.

5.2   PARTY POLITICS

Rationale

The rationale for party politics begins with the fact that a party is the key political structure in the acquisition and exercise of state power (Sorauf, 1976; Gross, 1974). By definition, *a party*, revolutionary or system-oriented, *"is a political structure specifically designed to seize, control or effectively participate in state power"* (Karenga, 1980:66). Within the framework of the party's focus on the exercise of state power, Blacks, like other party members and/or supporters, seek to use the party to achieve their group and personal interests (Key, 1962). Among the perceived benefits of participation in Democratic and Republican party politics are: 1) a vital, even if tenuous, link to state power; 2) a vehicle through which one's interests are represented, i.e., advanced and protected; 3) a means of becoming one's own group representative, i.e., an elected or appointed official; 4) an opportunity to determine or help determine public policy; 5) a share of party patronage (appointments, jobs, funds, etc.).

In addition to participation in the two-party system, Blacks have also participated in non-Black third parties such as the Socialist, Progressive, Communist, Populists, Liberty and the Peace and Freedom parties (Walton, 1969). Although these parties did not usually win and had little or no patronage to offer, Blacks supported them for various other reasons, as Walton (1972a) notes. These include: 1) dissatisfaction with the two dominant parties' level of lack of commitment to Black interests; 2) a sense of exclusion and alienation from the two major parties, as in Southern racist branches; 3) perception that opportunities to voice and fight for Black interests exist in alternative parties; 4) the ideological appeal of third parties; and 5) strong recruitment efforts by third parties.

Finally, Black parties have also emerged as an alternative to the two-party system (Walton, 1972a). Given the fact that Black parties are third parties, they tend to rise for similar reasons as other third parties. Hardy Frye (1980:5) states that "independent Black parties tend to rise when (1) Black participation in one or the other party is denied," or (2) when "political leaders decide that aspects of their social, political and economic grievances cannot or will not be met by existing parties." He cites the founding of the Mississippi Freedom Democratic Party and the National Democratic Party of Alabama as examples of the first and the founding of the United Citizens' Party in South Carolina and the Lowndes County Freedom Organization in Alabama as examples of the latter. In addition, to these reasons for formation, Black parties also rise as a result of: 1) increased levels of Black consciousness; 2) the desire for an independent politics which not only wins a share of the political power, but also makes a statement concerning their capacity for independent action; and 3) perception that party-building and electoral activities are ways of politically educating, mobilizing and organizing the masses of Blacks around vital issues (Walters, 1988: Chapter 6).

The Republican Experience

The first electoral activity of Blacks was in the context of the Republican party. During Reconstruction, Blacks joined the Republican party in great numbers and held various offices on the national, state and local levels. The reasons for the Black affiliation with the Republican party were both by choice and the political situation in the U.S. at the time. First, Blacks joined and supported the Republican party because it was the party of Lincoln. Secondly, Republicans actively recruited Blacks in an effort to build a Black electorate in their struggle with the Democrats. Thirdly, they financed Black candidates for office. Finally, the Democratic party was closed to Blacks, thus, eliminating an alternative option. Milton Morris (1975:19), in discussing Republican motivation for involvement of Blacks, cites three basic reasons: 1) their desire to solidify Republican control by developing a solid base of support among Blacks in the South; 2) their desire to punish the South by imposing a strong Black electorate on it; and 3) the struggle between the legislative and executive branches, with each needing to prove its predominance. In such a context, Morris concludes, Blacks and Republicans entered into a mutually beneficial relationship which, however, was short lived.

The decisive year was 1876 when Republican presidential candidate, Rutherford B. Hayes, agreed to withdraw federal troops and adopt a hands-off policy toward the South in exchange for Southern electoral votes needed to win the election. This "Compromise of 1877" led to massive violence against Blacks at the hands of white terrorist societies such as the KKK and to a division of the party into two factions, the lily-white Republicans and the Black and Tan Republicans (Walton, 1975). Thus, in their efforts to accommodate white racists, Republicans lost the Black electorate which began to transfer to the Democratic Party in 1932 with the election of Franklin D. Roosevelt.

Not until the late 70's did Republicans make a significant effort to challenge the Democratic monopoly on the Black vote and to reinvolve Black people in the Republican party process (Karenga, 1982). Their strategy had two basic aims: 1) to win a significant share of the Black vote in various elections and failing this; 2) to minimize the size and effect of the Democrats' share.

In 1978, it looked as though Republicans would at least make significant inroads in the Democratic monopoly on the Black vote, given the rise of a new middle class with interests which seemed to coincide with some Republican positions. As an indication of their seriousness in wooing Blacks, the GOP appropriated monies for recruitment and campaign finance for suitable Black candidates and invited leaders like Jesse Jackson of PUSH and Benjamin Hooks of the NAACP to open the dialogue on possible mutually beneficial cooperation.

However, beginning in 1980 with the election of Ronald Reagan, the push seemed to have been deemphasized. Blacks voted overwhelmingly Democratic in that election even when other ethnic and interest groups shifted (Williams and Morris, 1981). Reagan, being a model conservative and not exactly sensitive to or mindful of Black needs and interests, set about cutting the budget and advancing negative policy in areas most detrimental to Blacks, other peoples of color and the poor (Barker, 1987:30-31). Given this, it was difficult for either Black or white Republicans to seriously suggest a reinvolvement of Blacks in the party.

Nevertheless, even if all this had transpired and Reagan had not turned out to exhibit so much of what is called now "social meanness" in his brutal attacks on social welfare programs, there still would have been formidable problems for the Republicans to overcome in their quest for Black support. Among these are: 1) the historical tendency of Blacks to vote Democratic regardless; 2) the ideological orientation of the Republican Party which stands for objectives and principles opposite to Black interest, i.e., it stands against social welfare, government intervention and African liberation movements; and 3) the conservative internal resistance to courting Blacks and making the kind of concessions this requires with no guarantee of positive results (Karenga, 1982).

The Democratic Experience

It was during the Roosevelt Administration beginning in 1932 that Black support for the Democratic party began. Before this, Blacks were repelled by the open racism advocated and practiced by the party. It not only opposed the vote for Blacks, but used terror and violence against them to discourage their voting. But during the New Deal era, the Roosevelt Administration drew Blacks to the party through economic initiatives which benefitted Blacks and later through Roosevelt's anti-discrimination measures. Roosevelt also reinforced his position with Blacks

by creating the "Black Cabinet," an advisory group of skilled
Blacks, and by issuing Executive Order 8802 which created a Fair
Employment Practice Commission and banned discrimination in
industries with federal contracts.

Since the Roosevelt Administration, Blacks have maintained a steadfast loyalty to the Democratic party even though
Roosevelt and subsequent presidents did not always live up to
their commitment or even promise Blacks substantial gains. Ron
Walters (1975) has continuously called attention to this impolitic
loyalty for the Democratic party, arguing that "there is no
bargaining leverage in a situation where a Black vote for the
Democratic party is expected and delivers." Such a blind and
impolitic loyalty is clearly disadvantageous to Blacks in the
political arena and it becomes important to raise the question of
why the persistence.

From available evidence, it seems that Blacks' party
identification with the Democrats persists for several reasons.
First, the Democrats have historically tended to be more
favorable to socio-economic issues facing Blacks. Secondly, the
party had been supportive of civil rights since the Roosevelt
administration. Thirdly, the factor of group cohesiveness tends
to reinforce existing patterns once they are established. Fourthly,
socialization into a given party tends to persist. Finally, the
Republican party offers no real alternative given its stance on
socio-economic and civil rights issues (Morris, 1975; Barker and
McCorry, 1976).

Although Milton Morris (1975), Lucius Barker and Jesse
McCorry (1976) and Eddie Williams (1979) see indicators of
rising independent registration and voting, evidence does not
suggest a substantial shift in party participation patterns. In fact,
in the 1980 presidential election, Blacks gave 90% of their vote
to Carter in spite of their severe criticism of him (Karenga, 1977)
and in spite of shifts by Jews, labor and others to Reagan. And
in the election of Bill Clinton, the Black vote remained virtually
as high. Williams and Morris (1978: 227ff) suggest that the
consequence of this vote might be an impetus to a more sophisti-

cated and pragmatic approach to party politics. But again, as of this writing, there are no such indicators. This is not to say that the shift will not come, but only to emphasize its difficulty and the need for a new and bolder politics than traditional approaches suggest (Walters, 1988; Marable, 1985; Strickland, 1972).

Black Party Initiatives

Black Party initiatives have been on both the national and state levels, but the most successful efforts have been on the state level (Frye, 1980; Walton, 1972a). Moreover, these parties have been two basic types - parallel and independent parties (Walton, 1972a:80-81). Black party initiatives began as early as 1904 with the founding of the National Liberty Party. In that year delegates from 36 states met in a national convention in St. Louis and developed a platform dedicated to complete enfranchisement and the restoration of Black civil rights which were lost after the Compromise of 1877 (Walton, 1972a:51). This party, however, was short lived and in its place rose a series of non-partisan political organizations, beginning with the National Negro American Political League in 1908 and culminating in the National Negro Congress in 1936.

The 60's saw the rise of three independent Black parties: 1) the African American Party in Alabama (1960); 2) the National Civil Rights Party (1963); and 3) the Freedom Now Party (1964). However, the electoral activity of these parties was also minimal and unsuccessful and they too eventually faded from the political scene. Although Walton considers the Peace and Freedom party a Black party, its integrated character and predominant white membership contradict this classification. Moreover, even he (1972b:128) states that "it was a coalition of Black militants and white liberals," i.e., between the Panthers and their white allies, an arrangement which clearly pushes it outside any meaningful definition of Black.

Also, the 60's saw the rise of four major parallel Black parties: 1) the Mississippi Freedom Democratic Party (MFDP)

(1964); 2) the Lowndes County Freedom Organization or the Black Panther Party of Alabama (1966); 3) the National Democratic Party of Alabama (NDPA) (1968); and 4) the United Citizens' Party of South Carolina (1969) (Walton, 1927a). The MFDP led the way and left valuable lessons for subsequent parallel parties. It taught the method and possibilities of challenge to the established parties at national conventions, the value of using elections to dramatize basic issues and politically educate the masses, and the possibilities and problems of being a parallel party (McLemore, 1971; Walton, 1972a: Chapter 3). The NDPA has clearly been the most successful Black party in terms of both votes received and offices won (Frye, 1980; Walton, 1972a:1957). Although it declined in the late seventies, it too, by both achievements and losses, left valuable lessons on the problems and possibilities of Black parties in the political arena.

        The most recent example of the Black party thrust is the founding of the National Black Independent Political Party (NBIPP) in 1980 (Walters, 1988:148ff). The ideological origins of the party are rooted in the National Black Political Convention held in Gary in 1972 (Gilliam, 1975; Chapter 6). William Strickland (1972), who helped develop a National Black Political Agenda at Gary which set forth political goals for Blacks in the U.S., summed up the basic concerns for a new Black politics and a new party to initiate this process and give it an ongoing practical expression. He (1972:25-26) argued that the point was not to create just any party and certainly not the kind "that white folks have or talk about." Nor could it be one which is "simply an electoral party" or "simply a party that is dedicated to jobs and patronage or the election of individuals as a first concern." What was needed, Strickland posited, was a party which self-consciously strove to "advance the interests of the Black masses" and was fundamentally concerned with institution-building and institutional control, the assumption of power and ultimately the shaping of the destiny and daily lives of Black people. Without such a bold and multidimensional approach, i.e., electoral and non-electoral politics, he concluded, the party would be neither new nor viable.

Thus although the Gary Convention did not produce a mandate for a new party, it did raise and thoroughly discuss the question. Moreover, it did produce a mandate for a new politics and a National Black Political Assembly (NBPA). Ron Daniels (1980:3), who served as chairman of NBPA and later of NBIPP, posed the "principal role" of NBPA as "the shaping, projecting and institutionalization of an independent progressive Black politics of social transformation, economic democracy and self-determination." It is thus out of such a mandate, structure and political focus that the Black party merged (Elam, 1981a; Marable, 1980).

NBIPP has not assumed an electoral significance yet on the national or state level, but it has had some local victories, i.e., in northern California. Thus, its relevance resides not so much in its achievements, but in the multidimensionality and ambitiousness of its goals and the possibilities suggested by these. Like all third parties, NBIPP has general and specific problems (Walton, 1969). Among these are: 1) building bases in local communities and a viable effective national structure; 2) developing a financial base; 3) developing non-material incentives in the absence of monies and patronage and in furtherance of a new politics; 4) building and maintaining an effective unity among the diverse tendencies in it, especially avoiding the disruptive struggles between nationalists and Marxists which have undermined so many other Black united efforts; and 5) making significant and ongoing gains which demonstrate its viability and possibilities (Walters, 1988:148ff).

Daniels (1971) poses both socio-psychological and structural constrains on Black party building. Among the former are Black "feelings of inferiority and of political inefficacy," a negative definition of politics, previous party identification and belief in integration. The structural constrains include the institutionalized cooptation process which absorbs real and potential Black challengers; single member districts which prohibit a numerical minority from winning; rigid built-in qualifying rules and gerrymandering of political districts. In addition and reinforcement of the above problems and constraint, I (1980:71) have also posed the following constraints: political underdevelopment of the Black community; ideological hegemony of the system which argues that only two parties are viable and realistic; fear of penalty, i.e., loss of benefits from the Democratic or Republican party; fear of failure; and lack of an historical model which worked well for a considerable time.

But in spite of these constraints and problems, Black party advocates still argue that the Black party is both possible and necessary. For if a party is impossible, they argue, then so is liberation and an effective relation to state power. In fact, Harold Cruse (1974:10) has summed up their position quite well in his assertion that "if such a party is premature, then so is all talk of 'revolution' and "if an independent Black political party is unwise and unfeasible so is revolution unwise and unfeasible." In a word, if the party is key to state power, those without one can never hope to seize, control or effectively participate in it.

5.3 BLACK ELECTED OFFICIALS

In the early seventies, a prevalent assumption was that mass political struggle was somewhat passe and that electoral politics was the key to power and the future. In fact, James Conyers and Walter Wallace (1976:6) state that "...the presence of Blacks in elected government positions...is not only a manifestation of the Black community's political advance but a principal guarantee that advance will continue." Such faith is perhaps understandable but easily an overstatement. As Matthew Holden (1973:193) observed, "the electoral process is neither sufficient in itself nor has any politically sophisticated population regarded it as sufficient by itself." He states that "The basic rationale for electoral politics, insofar as policy is concerned, is that desirable policies will emerge when there is a clear identity between the

interests and values of the elected and of those who elect them."
But he notes, "This rationale also required, of course, that those
elected come into command of the appropriate public resources."
Moreover, it presupposes a strong enough political force to
assume command or at least share in it.

There have been many studies on the limitations of the
electoral process and on the various constraints imposed on
Black elected officials or BEO's. Speaking in general, Michael
Preston (1978:196-197) lists eight basic constraints: 1) lack of
"permanent political machinery;" 2) lack of "tradition and power;"
3) "little economic clout;" 4) tendency of votes to be taken for
granted by Democrats; 5) "lack (of) power to implement program
or policies;" 6) limited influence because of the structure of
government and fragmentation; 7) reluctance of national policy
makers "to deal with the issues of Blacks and the poor," and 8)
"minority status in a majority culture and the race variable." He
notes that these eight constraints are in addition to the obvious
fact of limited numbers and their inheriting long-term problems
which have plagued the country for over two hundred years.

In his important study of Black politics in Gary and his
subsequent study with Philip Meranto on electing Black mayors
in Gary, St. Louis and Cleveland, William Nelson (1972; 1977)
also found constraints on BEO's inside and outside the Black
community. Among those internal are the low-level of political
mobilization in the Black community, its position as an economic
colony, its competition over resources, its "mosaic" of ideological
positions and approaches, "social class tensions" and a pervasive
distrust of Black leadership and alienation from the political
system (Nelson and Meranto, 1977). In terms of political
alienation, they advance William Gamson's (1971) theory of
"stable unrepresentation" in which they argue that Blacks occupy
a status essentially outside the area of political decision-making
on a more or less permanent basis.

Moreover, Nelson and Meranto (1977:382) assert in their
study that "the election of a Black mayor does not automatically
mean that the colonized position of the Black community will be

significantly changed." For "constraints placed on the administrative authority of Black mayors by a host of economic, political, social and psychological factors make it impossible for their administrations to effectively satisfy the quest for Black liberation," i.e., material, education and cultural benefits which "would encourage the development rather than the oppression of Black people." Among these constraints are: white racist resistance, bureaucratic obstruction, the political need to represent all the people, the tendency toward over-dependence on the federal government for the limited urban reform resources available, inability to successfully challenge the hold of the economic elite (especially corporations) on the decision-making process of the cities and finally, the "inability to attack the fundamental character of the economic and the political order" (Nelson and Meranto, 1977:385).

In a more recent piece, Nelson (1987:195) argues that in spite of a new Black politics, "the key assumption that the movement for social and economic freedom is always progressive has not been substantiated by the pattern of political activity occurring in many Black communities over the past two decades." He concurs with James Jennings (1986:176) that political activities can either support or change the established order. And it is his assumption that "in the 70's and 80's, Black political activities in local communities have been heavily weighted toward the maintenance of existing social economic and political arrangements." This he attributes to a problem of theory and practice, i.e., the abandonment of "theories of political independence and self-determination" which characterized the quest for freedom and social justice in the 60's. In their place a vulgar pragmatism of traditional power structures has emerged.

Also, W. Avon Drake and Robert Holsworth (1993:104) identify a similar pragmatism which they call "calculated cooperation" and which they say does not "necessarily strengthen the quality of democracy in the city" and "ultimately serve(s) to widen the gap between development oriented elites and rank and file African Americans." Finally, Georgia Persons (1993b) has designated this problematic as a key dilemma in Black politics. She (1993a:62-63) focuses on the problematic of "race-neutral" cross-over politics which changes the process of Black politics from "system-challenging action" to emphasis on the "positive symbolism of race." This in turn leads to the "delegitimizing of insurgent-style politics." In such a process, she concludes, whites are provided "an opportunity to embrace demonstrably the principles of full participatory equality for Americans regardless of race; for Blacks it provides major symbolic gratification and necessary opportunities to take pride in the achievements of Blacks to more and higher offices."

In spite of these new developments and continuing constraints, there are studies which show the value of BEO's and of Black participation in the electoral process. Leonard Cole (1976), in his study of BEO's in New Jersey, found several important functions they serve. First, they are able to formulate and influence the formulation of policies which affect Black life. This is, of course, more effective on the local level where voting blocs along racial lines are not often found. Secondly, BEO's are instrumental in the increasing number and level of Black appointments to governmental positions. Thirdly, they tend to influence white associates' sensitivity to Black issues and interests as well as demonstrate to whites their capacity to govern. Fourthly, Cole argues, BEO's provide a necessary link between government and Black citizens white elected officials could not possibly provide. And finally, he contends that BEO's serve an important function as a role model for the Black community demonstrating Black capacity to govern and challenging the concept of white superiority and their monopoly on government.

In sum then, as I (1980:76) have argued elsewhere, BEO's have the following positive functions: 1) introduce and advance African American interest on the level of law, policy, appropriation, allocation, etc.; 2) expose contradictions and criticize the established order from a position of "legitimacy;" 3) create and propose alternatives to the existing order; 4) make appropriate alliances and coalitions; 5) serve as a symbol of the possibility of

Black political power; 6) monitor use of social wealth and struggle for Blacks's just share; and finally 7) gain historical experience in electoral politics which could be transferred to building a Black party.

The Jesse Jackson Campaigns

Of all the electoral campaigns Black have waged, won and lost, none has captured their imagination and cultivated their sense of history as the Jesse Jackson campaign. Doug Wilder's winning the governorship of Virginia and the mayoral victory of David Dinkins of New York both in 1989 were seen as mile-stones (McCormick and Jones, 1993). As John Jacobs (1990:4) described these events they "were another step in the long process of removing America's racial barriers, indicators that we have come a long way as a nation since the 1965 Voting Rights Act" (see also Holden, 1990).   Also Harold Washington's skillfully achieved victory as Mayor of Chicago in 1983 became another indicator of electoral progress and the possibilities of principled democratic leadership (Starks and Preston, 1990; Preston, 1987).

But it was Jesse Jackson whose historical campaigns, the first major and wide-reaching campaigns by an African American, captured the hearts and minds of African Americans on a national scale and in a special way (Henry, 1991; Collins, 1986; Karenga, 1984; Walters, 1989; Barker, 1988). In spite of his critics, Jackson's campaigns were important not only to the Black community but to the country (Reed, 1986; Faw and Skelton, 1986; Landess and Quinn, 1985).

The significance of the Jesse Jackson campaigns revolves around and is rooted in several factors. First, Jackson redefined the racial parameters of U.S. politics. He was the first African American or person of color to mount a major campaign which in the second run garnered over seven million votes. He thus confronted the system with an anomaly reflected in his media treatment in which white reporters and commentators continued to ask "What does Jesse want?" even though he was clearly running for the presidency. At the same time it caused a kind of cognitive dissonance for some whites; it was a politically motivating boundary crossing for African Americans and others.

Secondly, Jesse reopened the social justice dialog missing since the Sixties, again crossing boundaries, especially in the first campaign and moving beyond the safe center of standard politics (Henry, 1991; Walters and Barker, 1989; Barker, 1988). He spoke to such issues as homelessness, the oversized military budget at the expense of social programs, the inner city problematic, the farm problems of monopoly and foreclosure, and peace and justice in the Middle East (Hatch, 1988; Jackson, 1987). Thirdly, in raising these and other critical issues, Jackson reaffirmed the African American legacy of setting the moral and progressive agenda (Cavanaugh and Foster, 1984; Collins, 1986; Henry, 1991).

Fourthly, Jackson opened the party process for people of color and other marginalized persons and reaffirmed the value and vision of the democratic process (Barker, 1988; Cavanaugh and Foster, 1984). It can be argued that it was this opening and involvement that made possible the gains for African Americans and others formerly marginalized (Collins, 1986). Fifthly, Jackson contributed to the redefinition of relations between the African American community and the Democratic Party. Ron Walters (1989) argues that Jackson was successful in his attempt to increase Black leverage through his operating and organizing resources within the Democratic Party. But as Walters notes, Jackson also lost leverage by refusing to build an independent campaign and then bargaining (Henry, 1991:132). He thus never really developed the Rainbow Coalition as an independent option (Collins, 1984).

Sixthly, Jackson's significance rests in his reaffirmation of the value of electoral politics (Henry, 1991; Walters and Barker, 1989). The campaign proved to be an important way to raise critical issues and to mobilize and organize people around their own interest. Finally, Jackson laid the basis for a new coalition politics. Charles Henry contends that Jackson's campaign in California and his impressive showing among Latinos, Asians and whites as well as Blacks "reflects his understanding of coalition politics, in which three concepts are crucial: interest, reciprocity and leverage." Jackson, Henry continues, "believes that America's rejected hold the keys to progressive political change." And thus, their interest must be respected and reciprocity rather than domination must be a central principle." Jackson posited that a Rainbow Coalition based on such principles can, in fact, exercise effective leverage on national politics.

5.4 INTEREST GROUP POLITICS

As Lucius Barker and Jesse McCorry (1976:207) contend, "Interest groups are a dominant feature of American life." This is true and necessary because of the conflicting and competing interests which, as mentioned above, shape and define U.S. life. An interest group may be defined as a group organized to define, defend and advance common claims and/or stakes in society, i.e., common interests. Interest groups realize that "political organization and political power are inextricably intertwined" and that "An unorganized mass of people can have little impact on the governmental allocation of social and economic values" (Bailey, 1968:27). Moreover, interest groups tend to be aware that organizational power not only means the ability to help shape government policy, but also private policy, i.e., that of other groups and organizations, enterprises, institutions and persons. Finally, interest groups, in this case Black ones, embrace Jewel Prestage's (1968:460) contention that "any meaningful gains for Blacks will come as a result of demands, supported by evidence of Blacks' willingness to cause great inconvenience to the community at large if these legitimate demands are ignored."

Black interest groups use varying strategies and tactics to achieve their goals or policy objectives. Essentially, strategies are broad plans for the achievement of goals and tactics are specific methods of action used to carry out the strategy. Interest group tactics include electoral participation, i.e., voting, campaigning, donations, etc., influencing public opinion, verbal protests, lobbying governmental and non-governmental sources, negotiations, litigation, threats, mass action, i.e., strikes, demonstrations, marches, etc., disruption, violence and focus on internal development. Black interest group strategies can be categorized according to their goals and the methods used to achieve them. Given this, there are three major interests groups strategies among Blacks: liberal, conservative and radical.

Liberal Strategy

The liberal strategy is reflected in the leadership offered by such middle-class groups as the Urban League and NAACP, but it is prevalent among many sectors of Black people. This strategy, like the leadership which proposes and pursues it, is characterized by several factors. Among these are: 1) assumption that the system is flawed but salvageable; 2) stress on integration; 3) focus on goal pursuance through non-confrontational means where possible, i.e., litigation, elections, lobbying, etc.; 4) rejection of violence; 5) reliance on white political and financial support; 6) strong reliance on government intervention; 7) general confusion on influence with power, i.e., personal persuasion with structural capacity; and 8) focus on minimal goals rather than maximum goals, i.e., jobs vs. ownership, participation in major parties vs. building a Black one, etc. (Bailey, 1968; Thompson, 1963).

Out of these basic dimensions of liberal strategy, three seem to pose more problems than others. First, is the over-emphasis on what Pinderhughes (1980) calls electoral lobbying, i.e., attempts to use the Black vote in sanction or support in order to affect decision makers. Pinderhughes sees this as problematic in that the liberal interest groups do not yet have the

(1970) and others' suggestion to use the Black vote as a swing vote becomes impossible even if the election were close enough to allow it.

Moreover, such a heavy focus on electoral lobbying and the attendant posing of it almost as a panacea has caused liberal Black interest groups to abandon the mass action tactics which served them so well in the past. In fact, the assumption developed is that these methods are passé and less than sophisticated. The expression used to advance this position is "Blacks must move from protest to politics." This seem to suggest protest and the pressure which accompanies it are not politics, but rather some unclassified or unsophisticated kind of action.

Secondly, liberal Black interest groups rely heavily on white philanthropic support and are thus vulnerable to its political pressure. In such a position, independence is also threatened by the belief that whites are indispensable for Black success as well as the patron-recipient relation which Charles Hamilton (1979) rightly criticizes. Such positions clearly damage initiative and make self-determination highly problematic, if not impossible. Finally, liberal Black interest groups face the problem of over-reliance and governmental support. One can easily see the positive role government intervention has played in the Black struggle for rights and development during Reconstruction and the Civil Rights era. But one can also see the vulnerability of over-reliance on government in the "benign neglect" of the Nixon administration or even the last years of the Carter Administration when it was clear that even a favorable Administration might be unable to act in Black interests, if the political climate is against it and if interest groups who are more powerful oppose Black interests or simply push their own at Blacks' expense (Karenga, 1977; Robinson, 1982).

Conservative Strategy

Although the liberal strategy was temporarily challenged by the Black Power Movement, it reigned unchallenged in the civil rights era and resurged in the early Seventies. However, it now faces a challenge from Black conservatism (Henry, 1982; Daniels, 1981, Willingham, 1981). Black conservative interest-group strategy is defined by: 1) opposition to government intervention and regulation on behalf of Blacks; 2) distaste for mass action tactics; 3) emphasis on individual self-reliance and achievement; 4) stress on group self-help; 5) tendency to blame Blacks for their social problems; 6) a belief in the free-enterprise system as it was, i.e., without its current monopoly and with chances for Black and white miraculous success stories (Fairmont Papers, 1980; Sowell, 1981). Among the Black conservative strategists are Thomas Sowell, an economist at the Hoover Institute; Martin Kilson and Glen Lowry, political scientists at Harvard; Walter Williams, an economist at George Mason University in Virginia; and J.A.Y. Parker, president of Lincoln Institute and the Educational Foundation in Washington. More recently, Shelby Steele (1991) has emerged as a major spokesperson for this tendency.

The conservative strategy clearly mirrors the philosophy of Booker T. Washington who rejected Black protest, stressed economic developments and power and argued the need for self-help. Likewise, the liberal counter to this adds the DuBoisian dimension to the debate with his emphasis on protest, political rights and the government's obligation to facilitate and insure the freedom, justice and equality for all. Although the conservatives do not have the historical record or structural capacity the liberals enjoy, the conservative character of U.S. politics tends to give them an increased relevance they would otherwise lack. The election of Bill Clinton however, may pose problems for them and give liberal Black interest groups a renewed boost.

As I (1982:18-20) have argued elsewhere, the increased relevance of conservatives was based on several factors. First, Black conservatives were tied to the party in power -- politically and/or philosophically -- and thus benefitted in stature and influence from that position, i.e., in appointments, resource allocation and consultation. Secondly, Black conservatives benefitted from the country's shift to the right. In addition to patronage from the Reagan and Bush administrations, Congressional support was more likely as well as private support from "resource-rich white conservatives who (had) never been comfortable with the Black Civil Rights Leadership" (Daniels, 1981:21). Thirdly, given their philosophical and political link with the Republican administrations and the general rightward shift, they were considered more "media worthy" and thus were given more time to introduce and argue their position.

Fourthly, their relevance as an oppositional strategy to liberal strategy dominance was more apparent the more they were used: to lessen the charge of racism by their inclusion at some level in policy decisions; to support and justify public policies negative to Black interests; and to break the monopoly on Black leadership which liberal interest groups usually enjoy. The irony of this is that liberal administrations and other liberal whites use Black liberals for similar purposes, i.e., to push and justify their version of what the social order and social policy should be.

The Radical Strategy

The radical interest-group strategy is basically nationalist although Pan-Africanist and socialist themes also inform it (Karenga, 1978b: Pinkney, 1976). *Black nationalism is a social theory and practice organized around the concept and conviction that Blacks are a distinct historical personality and they should therefore "unite in order to gain the structural capacity to define, defend and develop their interests"* (Karenga, 1980:15). It expresses itself in three basic ways. It is first a redefinition of reality, a redefining of the world in Black images and interests, i.e., from an Afrocentric perspective. Secondly, it is a social corrective, i.e., a thrust to build alternative structures, which check the deprivation and deformation of European institutions and house and advance Black aspirations and interests. Finally, nationalism is

a collective vocation, a call and active commitment to liberate
Black people, restore them to their traditional greatness and
"make African presence both powerful and permanent throughout the world." It is this last aspect of collective vocation which
points to the link between nationalism and Pan-Africanism.

There are two basic kinds of Pan-Africanism - continental
and global. *Continental Pan-Africanism is essentially thought and
practice directed toward the liberation and unity of the African
continent* (Ajala, 1973; Padmore, 1971). *Global Pan-Africanism
is essentially thought and practice directed toward the liberation,
unity and mutual support of African peoples throughout the world*
(Garvey, 1977; Chrisman and Hare, 1974). African Americans
are essentially global Pan-Africanist, but among them are two
tendencies. The first tendency accepts and works within the
general framework of the definition above and is represented by
groups as diverse as TransAfrica, the Black lobby for Africa and
the Caribbean, Ahidiana, the RNA and Us. The second tendency argues not only for the unity and liberation of Africa, but also
the return of all Africans to the Continent. This tendency is
represented most definitively by the All African People's
Revolutionary Party which sees nationalism as a component part
and a beginning level of Pan-Africanism (Carmichael, 1971).
Also, the radical strategy includes a socialist dimension,
either as a separate thrust or as a component part of nationalism
(Cruse, 1967; Allen, 1970). Moreover, some socialists see
nationalism as a state in socialist development (Boggs, 1974) and
some nationalists see socialism as a contribution to nationalist
development (Karenga, 1980). Given these qualifications, the
radical interest-group strategy is defined by: 1) profound
alienation from and what Barker and McCorry (1976:217) call
"low-integration" into the established political system; 2) call and
struggle for fundamental change in the economic and political
structure of society; 3) willingness to use any means necessary to
achieve ultimate goals; 4) preference for confrontational and
mass action politics; 5) focus on the Black masses as the ultimate

power with simultaneous stress on the role of a Black vanguard to organize, educate and lead them; 6) stress power, self-development and self-determination; 7) emphasis on history, heritage and the distinctness this expresses; and 8) emulation of and solidarity with African and other Third World peoples and struggles.

The radical interest groups include among others, the Republic of New Africa (RNA), All African People's Revolutionary Party (AAPRP), the East, Ahidiana, the NOI, Us, Council for Independent Black Institutions (CIBI), and Institute of Positive Education (IPE). Once SNCC, CORE and the Panthers were included in this category, but these groups have either disbanded or been transformed into less than radical models. For a review of these and other radical groups ideologies, tactics and achievements, see "Civil Rights and Revolts" in Chapter 2. The problems radical interest groups face are many. First, they face the severe and sustained hostility of the system reserved for those who challenge its legitimacy. Secondly, they are actively opposed by the established liberal and conservative interest groups who consider their strategy rhetoric, irrational and negative to their and Black interests. Thirdly, except for possibly the NOI, they lack the financial resources available to the liberal and the conservative groups. Fourthly, they have less institutionalized bases than the liberals and conservatives. Fifthly, they are upstaged by the liberals in their thrust for mass leadership. However, in crisis and with the continuing failure of the liberals to produce resources or viable plans, they get the opportunity to advance alternatives and win greater respect. Finally, the radical interest groups have not yet firmly established the kind of viable working alliance that the liberals had in the Sixties with its Big Six leadership grouping, i.e., SNCC, CORE, SCLC, NUL, NAACP and NALC (Barker and McCorry, 1976:216ff) and now have in the National Black Leadership Forum.

The radical interest groups have, however, begun to build such a group, the National Black United Front. Given the essentiality of such a structure of combined strength and resources and collective planning, it can be safely argued that their success or failure in building it certainly helps determine their success or failure in achieving the objectives they have set for themselves. Also, key to their success will be the development of an intellectual vanguard which can give both a critical and substantive theoretical and practical dimension to their strategy with both rooted in the social reality of U.S. society (Strickland, 1975; Cruse, 1967). Without such a theoretical and practical rootedness in U.S. social reality, their thought and practice will be less than effective and the alternative strategies will reign unchecked and unchallenged. Even worse, the alternative to building internally and calling on Blacks to develop and use their own resources instead of depending on external sources will be reduced by critics to rhetoric and denied its deserved status as a viable and critical alternative.

5.5   THE PROBLEM OF COALITIONS

Another key concern and problem of Blacks politics is the problem of coalition. Central to the problem is the definition, character and results of those coalitions. As Stokely Carmichael and Charles Hamilton (1967:59-60) noted, "all too frequently, coalitions involving Black people have been only at the leadership level, dictated by terms set by others, and for objectives not calculated to bring major improvements in the lives of the Black masses." Historically, Black middle class leadership, i.e., the liberal interest group leadership, has depended on white coalition partners -- Jewish and Gentile -- for financial, legal and political support. In fact, there is or seems to be a basic assumption among this leadership that Blacks would not have come as far as they have, if it were not for whites of goodwill. Such a conception is problematic on at least three levels and speaks to the crisis which currently plagues Black middle class leadership.

First, it has been an underlying theme for misconceptions created about Black/white coalitions. Secondly, it has led to a confusion of patronage with coalition. And thirdly, it has tended to encourage denial and reductive translation of Blacks' contribution to their own struggle.

Two of the coalitions on which Blacks have relied on heavily are the Jewish and Democratic coalitions. These coalitions have produced their share of misconceptions and at the same time revealed the nature of the problem of coalitions faced by Blacks, especially the Black middle class leadership. The misconceptions which surround coalitions are many. Carmichael and Hamilton (1967:58ff) have cited three myths of coalitions which are important to understanding their weakness and unworkability. Agreeing with and incorporating some of their contentions, I have developed five misconceptions of coalitions which clearly create a problem for the coalitions in which Black middle class leadership involved itself.

First, there is a clear misconception that the basis of coalition is long-term common interests and principles rather than short-term specific goals. This is a confusion between alliance and coalition. Alliance is a long-term ongoing unity based on common interests and common basic principles, whereas a coalition is a short-term working association based on specific short-term goals. Failure to make and observe this basic distinction has created situations in which Blacks have assumed too much about their relationship with their more powerful coalition partners and left themselves vulnerable to joint actions not mutually beneficial and to withdrawal of expected support at crucial time. The Andrew Young affair with the Jews and Carter's poor performance on his behalf are good examples (Fuller, 1969; Karenga, 1977).

A second misconception is that common goals on one level or in one area are bases for unity in the other. For example, Jews might support Blacks against one kind of racism (new-Nazi or KKK attacks) but oppose them in correctives for racism (Affirmative Action). Thirdly, there is a misconception that moral unity, assumed or real, is a substitute for unity around concrete goals and self-interests. This is clear in the case of the assumed Black/Jewish unity based on common or similar suffering. But no unity is automatic, neither political nor personal; each one must be built around concrete goals and interests which change or disappear and therefore, must be reinforced and renewed or replaced by others.

A fourth misconception is that a genuine coalition between the powerful and the powerless (or clearly less powerful) is always possible, rather than always problematic and often pure patronage politics. In fact, one of the problems of the Jewish and Democratic coalitions is that they often deteriorate into patronage politics, i.e., dependence by Blacks on Jewish and Democratic patrons which may be unable or unwilling at various times, to give the largesse or support Blacks request or need (Hamilton, 1979). And the problem is that Blacks cannot effectively penalize or reward these partners in any significant way to compel compliance. The Jewish withdrawal of support from SNCC and CORE as they transformed into Black power structures and their opposition to Affirmative Action are examples of the disenchantment and disengagement without penalty from coalition partners. So are the Democratic Party's unwillingness to support fully Black social justice and social welfare goals under Carter and their unwillingness and inability to produce substantive beneficial alternatives under the Reagan/Bush administrations.

In such a coalition, the less powerful partner can lessen or eliminate such politically unhealthy arrangements in three basic ways. It can: (1) unite with other less powerful partners in the coalition to increase its power; (2) build other coalitions to offset negative effects of the problematic one; and (3) shelter no misconception about the problems of coalitions between the powerful and clearly less powerful. Black middle class leadership does not seem to have achieved any of these alternative options.

A final misconception about coalitions is that coalition action is a substitute for a people's or group's own initiative.

Such a misconception leaves a group hopelessly and slavishly dependent on forces outside its control and often beyond its influence. There is, in fact, no substitute for the structural capacity to define, defend and develop one's interest. For regardless how numerous or sincere one's allies are, a people that cannot save itself is lost forever.

The Black/Jewish coalition is a classic study in the problems of coalitions. Not only does it reflect commitment to the misconceptions which characterize coalitions in general, it also carries its own particular myths or misconceptions held mainly by its Black members. Among these are first, the myth that Jews are not white in spite of visual reality, self-definition and social acceptance of this fact. A second myth is that Jews are Blacks' best friend, a myth which Harold Cruse (1967:467) argues is misphrased. It would be far more accurate to say, he states, that "certain Jews have been best friends of certain (Blacks) which in any case is nothing unusual." Thirdly, there is a myth of moral affinity between Blacks and Jews based on similar suffering - historical and current.

These myths suggest or seek to foster a unity and commonality of interests that do not exist and thus produce a political practice and thought based on false premises problematic to Blacks interests. The first myth seeks to redefine Jews into the Third World to achieve unity through a contrived similarity. The second makes a claim more true for the Black middle class leadership than the Black masses and the third assumes an automatic unity and commonality of interest and implies that moral affinity, if it exists, can substitute for concrete interests and goals as a basis for a viable coalition.

As Stephen Isaacs (1974:160-181) and Robert Weisbord and Arthur Stein (1970) point out, concrete differences of interests and goals not only separate Blacks and Jews, but also often place them in active opposition to each other. The Andrew Young Affair; Affirmative Action; the 1966 New York City referendum on a civilian review board; the fight over the Forest Hills housing project in Queens, New York; and the struggle for

Black community control in Brooklyn's Ocean-Hill Brownsville School District, all clearly reflect this. This is due to the fact that Jewish power, wealth, social achievement and status, and white skin privilege objectively give them a different set of priorities and interests than Blacks whose race and general class character assign them a marginal and subordinate role and status in the social process. (Shorris, 1982).

Since Roosevelt's New Deal in the 30's, Blacks have aligned themselves with the Democratic Party. But the alliance was never of equals or semi-equals. On the contrary, like the other alliances, it was essentially a question of patronage, an alignment based on influences not power, and thus subject to the interests and aspirations of the persons who control it. The party, as a political structure, after all is out to win votes and to do so will no doubt cater to the cutback, cut-off and trim-down attitudes dominant now among white voters. Black middle class leadership finds itself, then, locked into the Democratic Party, with no structural or financial ability to significantly reward or punish it to induce it into compliance with the demands of Black interest. Moreover, it has developed no party alternative either with the Republican Party or through the building of a national Black independent party.

As mentioned above, there was talk in 1978 of Blacks moving in significant numbers to the Republican Party as a way of increasing their bargaining power and political options, but as also noted above, nothing serious has come of it. There is no developed strategy to enter or construct, conduct or benefit from the proposed relation with the Republicans, to pressure the Democrats or demand and get from each party a minimum set of legislative and financial concessions. It could well be that both will decide Blacks are dispensable, that given their overall structural incapacity to reward or punish with organized, self-conscious voting or financial and campaign labor contributions, they are neither needed nor worthy of serious consideration. This obviously presents a practical problem for Black middle class leadership which counts so much on the Democratic coalition and talked so much about the Republican option.

The question of alliances also must be answered. And although coalition and alliance are used interchangeably in most political science literature, I would like to maintain the difference. Essentially, alliances are internal first and then among others whose long term goals and principles coincide or mesh with those of African Americans. These are usually other Third World people. Two examples of internal alliances are the Black Leadership Forum (BLF) among the liberal middle class leadership and the National Black United Front (NBUF) among the radical leadership.

The Black leadership Forum, formed in 1977, is a national coalition of 16 Black civil rights groups and leaders. The Forum focuses on political and economic issues vital to Blacks and tries to influence public policy in support of Black interests. To achieve this, members meet and lobby with presidents and Congresspersons and make joint position statements. However, it is not well-known or visibly active in the daily problems confronting Blacks as was the Big Six.

The National Black United Front, as noted in Chapter 2, was founded in 1980 and has regional and local networks. Unlike the BLF, NBUF is visibly involved in the daily struggles of Black people. Like NBIPP, it is dedicated to "defense of social service programs and civil rights laws; the fight against the upsurge in racist violence, and opposition to the imperialist war danger" (Elam, 1981b:5). It is also engaging in political education, mass rallies, demonstrations, strikes, and boycotts as well as various expressions of support for continental African and Third World Liberation struggles.

The second kind of alliance has been established at various times with various Third World people, most notably Puerto Ricans in the East and Mexicans in the Southwest. In late 1978, Blacks and Hispanics formed a coalition called "Working Committee on Concerns of Hispanics and Blacks" to ensure that the two constituencies "not bear the brunt of a restrictive economic, social and political climate" (Williams, 1979:74). Participating in the formation of this coalition were Black, Puerto Rican, Mexican and Cuban organizations.

As I (Karenga, 1980:77) have argued elsewhere, there are concrete bases for alliances among Third World people growing out of their situational similarity in that they are oppressed and exploited on the bases of race and class. In order for such alliances to work, however, clear principles of unity must be established and observed. Among these should be: "1) mutual respect for each people's political, economic and cultural interest; 2) non-interference in each other's internal affairs; 3) a clear conception of each other's interests; 4) independent power bases; 5) a clear conception of possibilities and problems in unity; 6) clear and concrete goals around which to unify; 7) a clear statement and agreement on principles of cooperation; and 8) a clear statement and agreement on methods of cooperation and struggle" (Karenga, 1980:77-78). Although acceptance and agreement on these principles will not eliminate all obstacles and problems to Third World alliances, it will lay a necessary basis for them.

Charles Henry (1980:230) notes that although there are admittedly obstacles confronting such alliances, they nevertheless "appear to be less formidable than those facing Black-white coalitions..." Moreover, given the existence of over 50 million Blacks and Hispanics in the U.S., the importance of exploring and building such an alliance is clear and compelling. For if the essence of politics is power, and power rests in structural capacity, an alliance becomes a way not only to increase one's own strength, but to deprive the opposition of allies. This is especially true in an oppressive and conflict-laden society where competing sides seek allies constantly, and neutrality is objectively supportive of the established order. For it deprives smaller power blocs of possible added strength and spares the established order a united challenge from the oppressed. Black politics,then, as argued at the beginning, has been and must remain multidimensional in both theory and practice. After all, given the multidimensional character of the problem of liberation and a higher level of human life, anything less would certainly be unsuccessful.

STUDY QUESTIONS

1. What is politics? Discuss some of its core concepts.
2. What are eight areas of power?
3. What is the rationale for party politics?
4. Discuss the Democratic party experience.
5. Discuss the Republican party experience.
6. Discuss the Black party initiatives in terms of problems and possibilities.
7. Discuss the significance of the Jesse Jackson campaigns.
8. Cite and discuss constraints on BEO's.
9. What are some of the valuable functions BEO's serve in spite of constraints?
10. What is an interest group and what are three basic Black interest group strategies?
11. What are some misconceptions about coalitions?
12. Discuss two basic coalitions Blacks have been in and the problems of each.
13. Discuss two kinds of alliance giving examples of each.

REFERENCES

Ajala, Adekunle. (1973) *Pan-Africanism: Evolution, Progress and Prospects*, New York: St. Martin's Press.

Allen, Robert. (1970) *Black Awakening in Capitalist America*, Garden City, New York: Doubleday.

Apter, David. (1977) *Introduction to Political Analysis*, Cambridge, MA: Winthrop Publishers, Inc.

Bailey, Harry, Jr. (1968) "Negro Interest Group Strategies," *Urban Affairs Quarterly*, 4, 1 (September).

Bailey, Harry, Jr. (ed.) (1967) *Negro Politics in America*, Columbus, OH: Charles Merrill Books.

Balbus, Isaac. (1974) "The Concept of Interest in Pluralist and Marxian Analysis," *Politics and Society*, (eds.) Ira Katznelson, et al, New York: David McKay Co., Inc. pp. 278-304.

Barker, Lucius and Jesse McCorry, Jr. (1976) *Black Americans and the Political System*, Cambridge, MA: Winthrop Publishers, Inc.

Barker, Lucius. (1988) *Our Time Has Come*, Urbana: University of Illinois Press.

Barker, Lucius. (1987) "Ronald Reagan, Jesse Jackson and the 1984 Presidential Election: The Continuing American Dilemma of Race," in Michael Preston et al (eds.), *The New Black Politics*, New York: Longman.

Boggs, James. (1974) *Revolution and Evolution in the Twentieth Century*, New York: Monthly Review Press.

Broh, C. Anthony. (1987) *A Horse of A Different Color.* Washington, DC: Joint Center for Political Studies.

Browning, Rufus, Dale Rogers Marshall and William Tabb. (1990) *Racial Politics in American Cities*, New York: Longman.

Carmichael, Stokely. (1971) *Stokely Speaks*, New York: Vintage Books.

Carmichael, Stokely and Charles V. Hamilton. (1967) *Black Power: The Politics of Liberation in America*, New York: Random House.

Cavanaugh, Thomas and Lorn Foster. (1984) *Jesse Jackson's Campaign: The Primaries and Caucuses*, Washington, D.C.: The Joint Center for Political Studies.

Chrisman, Robert and Nathan Hare. (1974) *Pan-Africanism*, Indianapolis, NY: Bobbs-Merrill Co., Inc.

Chrisman, Robert and Robert L. Allen. (eds.) (1992) *Court of Appeal*, New York: Ballantine Books.

Cole, Leonard. (1976) *Blacks in Power*, Princeton, NJ: Princeton University Press.

Collins, Sheila D. (1986) *The Rainbow Challenge: The Jackson Campaign and the Future of U.S. Politics*, New York: Monthly Review Press.

Conyers, James and Walter Wallace. (1976) *Black Elected Officials*, New York: Russell Sage Foundation.

Cruse, Harold. (1967) *Crisis of the Negro Intellectual*, New York: William Morrow.

Cruse, Harold. (1974) "The National Black Convention at Little Rock," *Black World*, 24, 1 (November) 4-21.

Dahl, Robert. (1976) *Pluralist Democracy in America*, Chicago: Rand McNally.

Daniels, Johnnie. (1971) "The Development of an Independent Black Political Party," *African American Studies*, 2, pp. 95-105.

Daniels, Lee A. (1981) "The New Black Conservatives," *New York Times Magazine* (October 4) Section 6:20, 54, 58.

Daniels, Ron. (1980) "The National Black Assembly" *The Black Scholar* 11, 4 (March/April) 32-42.

Dewart, Janet (ed.) (1990) *The State of Black America 1990*, New York: National Urban League.

Drake, W. Avon and Robert Holsworth. (1993) "Richmond and the Politics of Calculated Cooperation", in Georgia Persons, (ed.) *Dilemmas of Black Politics: Issues of Leadership Strategy*, New York: Harper Collins College Publishers, pp.87-108.

Drake, St. Clair. (1971) "The Social and Economic Status of the Negro in the United States," in Edward Greenbert et al (eds.) *Black Politics*, New York: Holt, Rinehart and Winston.

Dymally, Mervyn. (1972) "The Black Man's Role in American Politics," in Lenneal Henderson, Jr., (ed.) *Black Political Life in the United States*, San Francisco: Chandler Publishing Company.

Elam, Frank. (1981a) "NBIPP: Problems and Prospects," *Guardian*, (October) 7ff.

Elam, Frank. (1981b) "NBUF Action Plan Targets Budgets Cuts, Racism, War," *Guardian,* (July 15) 5.

Elliot, Jeffrey M. (1986) *Black Voices in American Politics,* Orlando, FL: Harcourt Brace Jovanovich.

The Fairmont Papers, *Black Alternatives Conference.* (1980) San Francisco: Institute for Contemporary Studies (December).

Frye, Hardy. (1980) *Black Parties and Political Power,* Boston: G.K. Hall & Co.

Faw, Bob and Nancy Skelton. (1986) *Thunder in America,* Austin: Texas Monthly Press.

Fuller, Hoyt. (1969) "Black Leadership and the Black-Jewish Debacle," *First World, 2, 3.*

Gamson, William. (1971) "Stable Unrepresentation in American Society," in *Black Politics,* Edward S. Greenberg, et al (eds.) New York: Holt, Rinehard and Winston.

Garvey, Marcus. (1977) *Philosophy and Opinions of Marcus Garvey, I & II,* New York: Atheneum.

Gilliam, Reginald, Jr. (1975) *Black Political Development,* Port Washington, NY: Dunellen Publishing Company, Inc.

Gosnell, Harold (1967) *Negro Politicians: The Rise of Negro Politics in Chicago,* Chicago: University of Chicago Press.

Gross, Feliks. (1974) *The Revolutionary Party: Essays in the Sociology of Politics,* Westport, CT: Greenwood Press.

Hamilton, Charles. (1979) *"The Patron-Recipient Relationship and Minority Politics in New York City,"* Political Science *Quarterly,* 95, 2, pp. 211-227.

Hatch, Roger. (1988) *Beyond Opportunity,* Philadelphia: Fortress.

Henry, Charles. (1980) "Black-Chicano Coalitions: Possibilities and Problems," *The Western Journal of Black Studies,* 4, 4 (Winter) 222-231.

Henry, Charles. (1982) "Black Neo-Conservatism," a paper presented at the Annual Meeting of the National Conference of Black Political Scientists, New Orleans, LA (April 21-24).

Henry, Charles. (1991) *Jesse Jackson: The Search for Common Ground,* Oakland, CA: The Black Scholar Press.

Holden, Matthew, Jr. (1973) *The Politics of the Black Nation,* New York: Chandler Publishing Company.

Holden, Matthew, Jr. (1990) "The Rewards of Daring and the Ambiguity of Power: Perspectives on the Wilder Election of 1989," in *The State of Black America, 1990,* Janet Dewart (ed.) New York: National Urban League, Inc. pp. 121-142.

Isaacs, Stephen. (1974) *Jews and American Politics,* Garden City, NY: Doubleday.

Jackson, Jesse. (1987) *Straight From the Heart,* Philadelphia: Fortress.

Jacobs, John. (1990) "Black America, 1989: An Overview" in *The State of Black America, 1990,* Jane Dewart (ed.) New York: National Urban League, Inc. pp. 1-8.

Jennings, James. (1986) "Black Politics in America: From Access to Power," in James Jennings, et al (eds.), *From Access to Power: Black Politics in Boston,* Cambridge, MA: Schenkman Books.

Jones, Mack. (1972) "A Frame of Reference for Black Politics," in Lenneal Henderson Jr. (ed.) *Black Political Life in the United States,* San Francisco: Chandler Publishing Co. 7-20.

Karenga, Maulana. (1977) "Carter and His Black Critics: The Dialogue and Its Lessons," *The Black Scholar,* 9,3 (November) 52-54.

Karenga, Maulana. (1982) "The Crisis of Black Middle-Class Leadership," *The Black Scholar,* 13,6 (Fall) 16-36.

Karenga, Maulana. (1978b) *Essays on Struggle: Position and Analysis,* Inglewood, CA: Kawaida Publications.

Karenga, Maulana. (1984) "Jesse Jackson and the Presidential Campaign: The Invitation and Oppositions of History," *The Black Scholar,* 15,5 (Sept/Oct) 57-71.

Karenga, Maulana. (1980) *Kawaida Theory: An Introductory Outline,* Inglewood, CA: Kawaida Publications.

Key, V.O. Jr. (1962) *Politics, Parties and Pressure Groups,* New York: Thomas Y. Crowell Company.

Ladd, Everett. (1969) *Negro Political Leadership in the South,* New York: Atheneum.

Landess, Thomas and Richard M. Quinn. (1985) *Jesse Jackson and the Politics of Race,* Ottawa, IL: Jameson Books.

Marable, Manning. (1985) *Black American Politics: From the Washington Marches to Jesse Jackson,* London: Verso.

Marable, Manning. (1980) From the Grassroots, Boston: Southend Press.

Marable, Manning. (1985) *Race, Reform and Rebellion,* Jackson: University Press of Mississippi.

McAdam, Doug. (1983) *Political Process and the Development of Black Insurgency 1930-1970,* Chicago: Chicago University Press.

McCormick, Joseph and Charles E. Jones. (1993) "The Conceptualization of Deracialization: Thinking Through the Dilemma," in *Dilemmas of Black Politics,* Georgia A. Persons (ed.) New York: Harper Collins College Publishers, pp. 66-84.

McLemore, Leslie B. (1971) "Mississippi Freedom Democratic Party," *The Black Politician,* 3,2 (October) 19-22.

Morris, Milton. (1975) *The Politics of Black America,* New York: Harper & Row Publishers, Inc.

Nelson, William Jr. (1972) *Black Politics in Gary: Problems and Prospects,* Washington: Joint Center for Political Studies.

Nelson, William Jr. (1987) "Cleveland: The Evolution of Black Political Power," in *The New Black Politics,* Michael B. Preston, Lenneal J. Henderson, Jr. and Paul L. Puryear (eds.) New York: Longman, pp. 172-199.

Nelson, William and Philip Meranto. (1977) *Electing Black Mayors,* Columbus, OH: Ohio State University Press.

Padmore, George. (1971) *Pan-Africanism or Communism,* Garden City, NY: Doubleday.

Parsons, Talcott. (1951) *The Social System,* New York: Free Press.

Persons, Georgia A. (1993a) "Black Mayoralities and the New
    Black Politics: From Insurgency to Racial Reconciliation,"
    in *Dilemmas of Black Politics*, Georgia A. Persons (ed.)
    New York: Harper Collins College Publishers, pp. 38-65.

Persons, Georgia A. (1993b) *Dilemmas of Black Politics: Issues
    of Leadership Strategy*, New York: Harper Collins College
    Publishers.

Pinderhughes, Dianne. (1980) "The Limits of Electoral Lobby-
    ing," a paper presented at the Annual Meeting of the
    National Conference of Black Political Scientists, Atlanta,
    GA, (March 19).

Pinkney, Alphonso. (1976) *Red, Black and Green: Black Na-
    tionalism in the United States*, New York: Cambridge
    University Press.

Pohlmann, Marcus D. (1990) *Black Politics in Conservative Ameri-
    ca*, New York: Longman.

Prestage, Jewel. (1968) "Black Politics and the Kerner Report:
    Concerns and Directions," *Social Science Quarterly*, 49,3
    (December) 453-464.

Preston, Michael. (1978) " Black Elected Officials and Public
    Policy," *Policy Studies Journal*, (Winter) 196-201.

Preston, Michael et al (eds.) (1987) *The New Black Politics: The
    Search for Political Power*, New York: Longman.

Reed, Adolph Jr. (1986) *The Jesse Jackson Phenomenon*, New
    Haven: Yale University Press.

Robinson, Pearl T. (1982). "Black Political Power - Upward or
    Downward," in *The State of Black America* (ed.).
    James Williams, New York: National Urban league.

Scott, Joseph W. (1980) "Capitalism, Socialism and Libertarian-
    ism: Race, Class and Power in the Black American
    Experience," *Western Journal of Black Studies*, 4,2 (Sum-
    mer) 78-83.

Shorris, Earl. (1982) "The Jews of the New Right," *The Nation*,
    234, 18 (May 8) 543, 557-561.

Sorauf, Frank. (1976) *Party Politics in America*, Boston: Little,
    Brown & Company.

Sowell, Thomas. (1981) *Ethnic Minorities,* New York: Basic Books.

Starks, Robert and Michael Preston. (1990) "Harold Washington and the Politics of Reform in Chicago: 1983-1987," in *Racial Politics in American Cities,* Rufus Browning, Dale Rogers Marshall and William Tabb (eds.) New York: Longman, pp. 88-107.

Steele, Shelby. (1991) *The Content of Our Character: A New Vision of Race in America,* New York: Harper Perennial.

Stone, Chuck. (1970) *Black Political Power in America,* New York: Dell Publishing Company.

Strickland, William. (1975) "Black Intellectuals and the American Social Scene," *Black World,* 25,1 (November) 4-10.

Strickland, William. (1972) "The Gary Convention and the Crisis of American Politics," *Black World,* 21,12 (October) 18-26.

Thompson, Daniel. (1963) *The Negro Leadership Class,* Englewood Cliffs, N.J.: Prentice Hall, Inc.

Walters, Ron. (1988) *Black Presidential Politics in America: A Strategic Approach* , Albany: State University of New York Press.

Walters, Ron. (1980) "Black Presidential Politics in 1980: Bargaining or Begging? *The Black Scholar,* 11, 4 (March/April) 22-31.

Walters, Ron. (1975) "Strategy for 1976: A Black Political Party" *The Black Scholar,* 7 (October).

Walters, Ron. and Lucius Barker. (eds.) (1989) *Jesse Jackson's 1984 Presidential Campaign,* Urbana: University of Illinois Press.

Walton, Hanes, Jr. (1972a) *Black Political Parties,* New York: Free Press.

Walton, Hanes, Jr. (1972b) *Black Politics,* Philadelphia: J.B. Lippincott Co.

Walton, Hanes, Jr. (1975) *Black Republicans,* Metuchen, NJ: The Scarecrow Press.

Walton, Hanes, Jr. (1985) *Invisible Politics: Black Political Behavior*, Albany: State University Press.

Walton, Hanes. Jr. (1969) *The Negro in Third Party Politics* Philadelphia: Dorrance & Co.

Weisbord, Robert and Arthur Stein. (1970) *Bittersweet Encounter: The African American and the American Jew*, Westport, CT: Negro Universities Press.

Williams, Eddie. (1979) "Black Political Participation in 1978, *The State of Black America*, New York: National Urban League.

Williams, Eddie and Milton Morris, (1981) "The Black Vote in a Presidential Election Year," *The State of Black America*, New York: National Urban League.

Willingham, Alex. (1981) "The Place of the New Black Conservatives in Black Social Thought: Groundwork for the Full Critique," unpublished paper, Philadelphia, PA, (October).

Wilson, James Q. (1960) *Negro Politics*, New York: Free Press.

BLACK ECONOMICS

6
BLACK ECONOMICS

6.1 INTRODUCTION

Economics is generally defined as the study and process of producing, distributing (or exchanging) and consuming goods and services. Such a definition, however, in part hides the fact of how economics penetrates every aspect of social life. Whether one talks of poverty, income, jobs, housing, class, racial discrimination, education, religion, the arts or social status, all at one level imply and necessitate a concern with economics. Even the major ideologies and social systems of today which compete for the minds of peoples i.e., capitalism, socialism, nationalism, etc., have been shaped in significant part by important economists of the past, i.e., Adam Smith, Karl Marx, and John Maynard Keynes, etc. (Heilbroner, 1972; Fusfeld, 1977).

Moreover, it would be relatively impossible and certainly unwise and irregular for national leaders to make political decisions without economic considerations. In fact, politics and economics are unavoidably linked on several levels. First, wealth and power are mutually engendering and supportive. The possession of one implies and leads to the possession of the other. Likewise, the lack of one implies the lack of the other. Secondly, those with power and wealth tend to strive to monopolize both. Thirdly, those with wealth and power tend to shape society in their own image and interests at the expense of those without it, especially Blacks and other Third world peoples whose relative possession of both wealth and power are at low levels. It is thus difficult to imagine corporations not having political

355

power, i.e., significant and greater control and influence over public policy, especially as it relates to their own interests. Finally, the struggle for distributive justice or an egalitarian distribution of social wealth is both an economic and a political struggle. In fact, the decision of who gets what and how much is both an economic and political decision, made by those whose wealth and political power enable them to control directly or indirectly the decision-making process.

It is this interrelatedness of politics and economics which prompts some Black and radical economists to insist that the science of economics is best categorized as *political economy*. As the staff of the *Review of Black Political Economy* explained in their inaugural issue (Spring/Summer, 1970), the term seems a more accurate one. For it "includes within its scope the political realities of economic relations" and thus describes "the necessary focus of Black economic development." Moreover, given the political dimension of economics, "for Black people to affect any significant alteration in their economic position, they will first be obliged to develop a sound political strategy."

Political economy, then, can be defined as the study of the interrelationship between politics and economics and the power relations they express and produce. It focuses not simply on the economic process, but also on economic policy and the race and class interests and value judgments this suggests. Thus, the study of Black economics of necessity includes a study of the politics which shape economics in both positive and negative ways. This will become clear as the problems and solutions posed are discussed.

6.2   POLITICAL ECONOMIC STATUS

The ghettoization of the African American community is both an economic and political reality as argued in Chapter IV. Even allowing for class differences, the general state of political and economic subordination is obvious and unarguable. The only question is the character and process of the subordination. The race and class character and process of the exploitation and oppression of the Black community has been summed up by many as domestic colonialism. As early as 1962, in an article reprinted in a later book, Harold Cruse (1968) used the category "domestic colonialism" to discuss Black-white relations in the U.S. society. He (1968:77) argued that "from the beginning (the African American) has existed as a colonial being...The only fact which differentiates the (African American's) status from that of a pure colonial status is that his position is maintained in the 'home country' in close proximity to the dominant racial group." Kenneth Clark (1964) argued the colony analogy two years later using the political, economic and social structure of Harlem to demonstrate it. Although, he (1965) did not pursue the analogy in *Dark Ghetto*, he used the category and most of his analysis pointed to the same conclusion.

Two years later, Stokely Carmichael and Charles Hamilton (1967:6ff) advanced the internal colony analogy in their book on Black power. Admitting that "the analogy is not perfect," they argued that regardless of the difference between the classical colony and the ghetto, there are still enough significant similarities to justify calling the ghetto an internal colony. Among these similarities were: 1) economic exploitation of the colony as a cheap supply of labor and a captive market; 2) external control of the colony by the ruling country, usually by indirect rule through political puppets; and 3) the socio-psychological results of racist humiliation and assignment of Blacks to "subordinate, inferior status in society." Robert Allen (1970) also discussed the Black community in terms of the internal colony analogy. He (1970:7ff) maintained that "Black communities are victims of white imperialism and colonial exploitation." Colonialism, he suggested, can be defined as direct and overall subordination, administration, economic exploitation and cultural destruction of a nation, people or country by another whose power is enshrined in law and backed by coercive bodies, i.e., armies and police. Thus, he concludes, the status of the Black population in the United States shows a striking similarity to this colonial situation.

Allowing for limitation of the analogy, one still is unavoidably struck by the political oppression and economic exploitation of the Black community which stand at the heart of any form of colonialism. The ghetto economy stands out at the center of urban poverty. Its unemployment is so high that if it occurred in the overall economy, it would be defined as symptomatic of a depression. Its labor is superexploited in both racial and class terms, being employed mainly in the low-wage sector of the economy and with unequal power in unions in spite of proportional representation (Harris, 1982).

Moreover, the ghetto economy is marked by a continuous drain of financial, physical and human resources. The savings are placed in financial institutions whose loans are primarily made to enterprises outside the inner city. The approximately $287 billion annual purchasing power is spent mainly outside the ghetto. Andrew Brimmer (1982:30) had noted that Black firms are continuously losing ground in growing competition by white firms for Black consumer dollars. "In 1969 receipts of Black firms were equal to 13.5 percent of total Black income. By 1980 the share was down to 8.9 percent, and his projection for 1990 was a decline to 7 percent. Furthermore, products sold in the ghetto and outside it are made outside the ghetto, most of the businessmen live outside the ghetto, and the enterprises which service the retail business, i.e, wholesale, shipping, advertising, etc., also are located outside the ghetto (Browne, 1971).

Finally, there is a lower level of repairs and renewal of physical plants in the ghetto, and better educated Blacks with higher salaries tend to move out, thus, depriving the ghetto of persons whose education, income, and initiatives would be valuable to its revitalization and organized efforts to free itself. It is in such context of oppression, exploitation and relative powerlessness, that the colonial analogy seems to be the definitive one (Tabb, 1970; Fusfeld, 1970; Browning, Marshall and Tabb, 1984).

6.3   DATA OF ECONOMIC DISADVANTAGE

Summing up this situation, David Swinton (1990, 1991, 1992) has argued that the African American community is above all marked by *economic disadvantage* in varied and essential ways. In his reports to the National Urban League on the economic *State of Black America*, Swinton (1992:61) states that "in comparison to Americans of European descent, African Americans experience substantially lower economic status throughout the income distribution." Moreover, he continues, " (a)s we have noted on several occasions, relatively well-off Blacks are much less well off than well-off whites, and relatively poor Blacks are much poorer than poor whites." He concludes saying "all standard measures of central tendency have consistently revealed the relatively low economic status of the population as a whole."

Income Inequality

Swinton (1992:74) shows a clear pattern of inequality between Blacks and whites. As he notes, "African American per capita income in 1990 was $9,017 compared to $15,265 for whites." This translates as Blacks' having "only 59.1 percent as much income per capita as whites had during 1990." Moreover, data show the Black male median income to be $12,868 for 1990 compared to white male income of $21,170. This equals only 60.8 of white male median income. The Black female median income of 1990 was $8,328 compared to $10,317 of the white female's median income or 85 percent.

Poverty Rates

Swinton (1992:88) also states that "income disadvantages for Blacks lead directly to higher rates of poverty. In 1990, 31.9 percent of Blacks were in poverty as compared to 10.7 percent of whites. This means that "for Blacks 9.8 million persons were in poverty, up by 500 thousand over 1989." This picture is made bleaker by the fact that the rate of poverty among Black children was 44.8 percent compared to 15.9 percent for white children. Thus over 44 out of every 100 Black children are in poverty compared to 16 of every 100 white children. This picture of child poverty is explained in part and at the same time made more severe by the fact that over 50 percent of all persons living in female-headed Black families (6,005,000) live in poverty compared to 30 percent of persons in white female-headed households. Female-headed Black families are 45 percent of all Black families compared to 12 percent of white families. Swinton (1992:91) concludes that "the problem of female-headed poverty is of much larger magnitude for Blacks." Finally, Swinton (1992:95) states that 13 percent of the African American community received public assistance (6.5 percent) or supplemental security income (5.3 percent) compared to 3.33 percent of the white population.

Employment Status

The economic disadvantage of the African American community appears also in employment data and labor market trends. Employment for Blacks fluctuates between 54.1 and 55.7 percent. This low employment rate, however, is higher than the historical average and "is primarily due to the increasing participation and employment of Black women" (Swinton, 1992:97ff). The "employment rates for Black women have risen from mid-40 percent range to 54 percent of the (African American community) over the past two decades." Overall unemployment fluctuates also and ranges between 11.8 and 13.1 percent for the Black community as a whole. For the first three quarters of 1991, the unemployment rate average was 12.4. The past two decades have yielded data of high unemployment among Black men, Black women and Black teenagers. "Adult Black men have had unemployment rates above 10 percent for every year since 1980 and adult Black women have had unemployment rates above 10 percent in every year except 1989 and in 1990 when their employment rate was 9.8 percent" (Swinton, 1992:102). Moreover, "the lowest unemployment rate experienced by Black teenagers since 1980 was 31.1 percent in 1990." The unemployment rate of Black teenagers, however, fluctuates between 30 and 50 percent and there is the likelihood it will rise higher given the fact they will "comprise an increasing proportion of the youth population; and probably will continue to be concentrated in areas of limited job opportunities" (Anderson, 1982:5). Furthermore, Black youth unemployment will be more difficult to reduce due to increased competition for jobs and the problems of preparation (Freeman and Holzer, 1986).

There are several reasons offered for Black unemployment: low educational levels and lack of job skills, the recurring recession, unwillingness to take menial jobs; displacement, the move of industry from the central city; shutdowns in industries where Blacks are in heavy numbers; lack of viable social networks and above all, continuing discrimination (Wilson, 1987; Jaynes and Williams, 1989:315-324). In his analysis of racism, Alexis (1980) challenges Becker's (1957) often quoted study on discrimination for its focus on personal rather than collective discrimination and the problem this poses for employment. He (1980:338) argues that Becker's focus on personal discrimination fails to see that "discrimination is against Blacks as a group, not as individuals" and that hiring or not hiring is a political decision as well as an economic one. In what he calls the "malice-envy approach," the economic discriminator (employer, employee, government or consumer) interprets the relative well-being of Blacks as a decrease in his/her own welfare. Blacks are thus viewed as opponents and under such competitive conditions, the white employer "might be willing to reduce (his/her) own welfare, if by doing so, (he/she) could reduce the welfare of (his/her) competitor by more." Given this political aspect of economic discrimination, Alexis maintains that the "remedy to the economic plight of Blacks is not to be found in economic activity alone." Thus, "until and unless Blacks achieve some degree of effective power, (i.e., command over institutions --

public and private -- that establish the rules of the game and determine the payoffs) they will continue to suffer from second-class economic citizenship."

The problem of preparation indeed remains a problem of employment. Brimmer (1982:32) predicted correctly in the 80's that science and technology with heavy reliance on computers would be the area of the fastest growing occupations. Thus, he stated, "if Blacks are to get a fair share of the new jobs, they will have to accelerate and upgrade their basic preparation in mathematics and communication skills." Secondly, Brimmer argued that the private sector will expand more rapidly than the public sector. He also projected that this decline will cost Blacks jobs given their large share of public jobs.

Not only will most of the jobs be in the private sector, he predicted correctly, but they will demand a high degree of skill. In fact, corporate requirements for entry and promotion are the typical skills needed, as Brimmer suggested they would be. For many of these professional and managerial positions are in production, marketing, distribution and financial controls (i.e. accounting). Clearly, Black preparation is necessary to be eligible for these positions. But whether they will get them depends not only on their availability, but also the willingness of firms to hire Blacks. Without a concern for the problems of the economy and the problems of discrimination in it, job possibilities are not a realistic assumption.

Nevertheless, as Margaret C. Simms of the Joint Center for Political and Economic Studies argues, "the key to creating a productive work force is quality education and training" (McCoy, 1992:202). For "increased real incomes are closely related to education." She maintains that for Blacks, especially higher educational levels are associated with greater employment. As other African American economists, she advocates a comprehensive strategy for improving the productivity of the U.S. workforce which will, of necessity, include African Americans. She notes that such a comprehensive strategy "will provide: adequate preparation of new entrants to the labor force; the upgrading of low-skilled workers; and the retraining of adult workers for new jobs and improved technology."

Occupational Distribution

Swinton (1991:62) reports that African Americans are further disadvantaged by unfavorable occupation distribution. "Employed Black males (are) only about half as likely as white males to be employed in managerial, sales or professional occupations, and only about three-quarters as likely to be employed as technicians or craft workers." These occupational categories are the top-paying ones for males and, of course, Blacks are restricted in these areas and highly represented in the lowest paying occupational categories. Similarly, Black women were less likely to be employed in the top paying jobs. "In 1990 40.8 percent of white women and only 28.1 percent of Black women were employed in these good jobs" (Swinton, 1992:106). On the other hand, "37.3 percent of Black women compared to 22.9 percent of white women were more likely to be employed in household or other service, laborer and operative occupations."

Finally, although education is noted as central to the possibility of better paying jobs, Swinton (1992:114) argues that in general "racial inequality does not decline with education." For both males and females, racial inequality in wages are about the same across educational levels. "For females, racial inequality increased slightly with education up to a college degree (whereas) females with four years of college have equal wages."

Darity and Myers (1992:136-137) list several factors for earning inequality: 1) increase in female-headed families who earn less; 2) "the continued decline in the relative earnings and educational prospects of young Black males"; 3) the unevenness of educational gains within the Black community; and 4) a continuing gap between Blacks and whites in higher education. For example, "in 1990 46 percent of whites had some college education compared to only 37 percent of Blacks."

Introduction to Black Studies

6.4   PROBLEMS OF RACE AND CLASS

The race and class question serves as a problem for Black economics on two levels. First, both race and class are the bases of Black exploitation and oppression. And secondly, the development of sharp class divisions among Blacks tend to impede an overall solution to the problem of Black economic development (Turner, 1976). In fact, the interpretation of the source of and solution to Black oppression can in fact end up as a class focused interpretation rather than an overall Black one.

For example, one could take the interpretations of Thomas Sowell (1975, 1981a, 1981b). Sowell essentially argues that race is not as important a factor as often suggested and that the attitudes and skills of Blacks may be as important to social achievement and social status as racism. Moreover, he maintains that demographics rather than racism explain differences in income among ethnic groups. Thus, the source of Blacks' differential income can be found for example in the fact of age, i.e., they are disproportionately younger and still climbing the income ladder, and in the fact of residence, i.e., they live more often in the South where wages are usually lower. He also rejects affirmative action as insulting treatment and gratuitous government intervention in an admittedly flawed though essentially workable system. Finally, Sowell argues that racism, where it exists, can be explained by economic motivations and interests and that once racism becomes economically unprofitable, racists will no longer practice it. Therefore, he argues that market forces are much more effective mediators of racial inequities than non-market forces like the collective Black struggle and government intervention.

Much of the criticism of Sowell has been ad hominem and unworthy of repetition. But his argument tends to support and dovetail William Wilson's ideas which will be covered below. Thus, criticism of Wilson's contentions will for the most part answer Sowell's. However, it is important to note that Sowell, like Wilson, tends to blame the victim, overlook or minimize the active force and result of racism, and while blaming Blacks for defective attitudes and habits, seems reluctant to indict racist attitudes and practices of whites. Moreover, his contention that racism ends when it is no longer profitable is not always true. Reich (1981:311-312) discovered that although "racism works against most whites' economic interest, it is being reinforced today" by a series of social, cultural and personal factors. Also, Malveaux (1992; 1987) has shown that both racial and gender discrimination are deep-rooted persistent problems for African Americans in their quest for economic justice and parity.

Certainly, one of the most provocative works in recent sociological literature is William Wilson's (1978) *The Declining Significance of Race*. Wilson's work, while attempting to de-emphasize the significance of race, also points to the problem of uneven development among African Americans and the accompanying class divisions. Essentially, Wilson argues that race has declined in significance and been replaced by class as the key determinant affecting life-chances and institutional access in U.S. society. He contends that this shift on the basis of social stratification is due to government intervention and support, the current predominance of service industries (transportation, government and social service, public utilities, finance, social welfare, etc.) over productive industries (manufacturing, mining, etc.), and the substitution of class characteristics for racial ones as criteria for employment. Moreover, he maintains that this declining significance of race has created a new middle class insensitive to "lower" class Black needs and is increasingly used by the whites to control Blacks in the working class and undercl-ass. Furthermore, he (1978:152) argues that "the traditional racial struggles for power and privilege have shifted away from the economic sector and are now concentrated in the sociopoliti-cal order."

The arguments against Wilson's thesis are numerous and cogent and Wilson, himself, found it necessary to clarify further his ideas in a more recent work (Willie, 1979; Pinkney, 1984; Wilson, 1987). First, Wilson's use of the advancing middle class as an index of the declining significance of race is impoverished data, showing not that race has declined, but suggesting that racism against the middle class has declined. Furthermore, Black and white middle class income are still not the same and evidence of "catching up" does not eliminate the fact that significant differences still exist. Also, there are not enough African Americans in these new positions or significant power positions to claim such a momentous event as the decline of the significance of race. They are not in ownership positions or significantly represented in high level management. And even when they arrive, they continue to suffer severe discrimination (Benjamin, 1991). Finally, it could be argued that allowing certain sectors of the Black middle class access to new status is also based on race and a political calculation. For it tends to legitimize and reinforce the system and win it new Black allies which, even Wilson admits, can and may be used against the interests of the Black masses.

Secondly, Wilson concentrated only on the narrow data of income increase to prove his thesis, as if income discrimination were an inclusive category of the various forms of racism. A modicum of acquaintance with the various open and covert expressions of racism tends to disprove such a contention. Thirdly, he commits a gross conceptual error by attempting to separate the economic arena from the socio-political one. A holistic conception of society shows that all areas of society interact, and policies in one area tend to affect and often determine conditions and behavior in others. Affirmative action legislation had impact on the economic and educational spheres. And the Supreme Court decision outlawing segregation, *Brown vs. Board of Education*, affected virtually every area of social life (Kluger, 1977).

Fourthly, Wilson's contention that the discrimination against the Black poor is only because of their low level of education and few marketable skills, overlooks the fact that it is racism which imposed this condition on them and continues to exclude them (Harris, 1982; Cotton, 1988). Thus, a system which is responsible for inadequate acquisition of education and skills by African Americans and other Third World peoples cannot escape the charge of racism simply by saying that their lack of qualifications is the reason for their occupational rejection. Finally, Wilson's position suggests that now Blacks are responsible for their non-access and non-achievement, as if wealth and power were equitably distributed and equally available. This personalization of blame for social evils could be and perhaps already is being used as a justification for an end to public and private policies and programs designed to end racist and socio-economic inequities in U.S. society.

Regardless of Wilson's flawed interpretation of the declining significance of race, his charge of increasing class division and middle class insensitivity to the interests of the Black masses requires discussion. For if he and others are correct, then rather than being a resource for Black liberation and economic development, the Black middle class will serve the opposite function of retarding development and the social struggle for a higher level of social life (Wilson, 1987).

6.5   THE MIDDLE CLASS

The problem of the middle class was first raised extensively by E. Franklin Frazier (1962) in his classic work, *Black Bourgeoisie*. In it, he posed the middle class as essentially living in a world characterized by make-believe, self-hate, conspicuous consumption, rejection of the Black masses and fruitless and frustrating quest for white status and acceptance.

Nathan Hare (1965), a student of Frazier, reinforced Frazier's view of the middle class in his book, *Black Anglo-Saxons*, which posed "aping of the white man as their overriding concern." Cruse (1967:312) in his seminal work on the African American intellectual also reinforced Frazier's stress on the theme of personal self-interest of the middle class, arguing that "No matter how you view it, the integration movement is run by the middle class who, even when they are militant and sometimes radical, twist the meaning of integration to suit their own aspirations." If these assessments are correct, then the problem of class division and distance become not simply a problem of economics, but also a problem of politics. For if middle class interests are pushed at the expense of the masses of Blacks, then, rather than being a resource in terms of capital and leadership for economic development, the middle class will become an obstacle in both the political and economic sense.

The above claims do not go without challenge. There is evidence to suggest that the claims of a growing middle class are exaggerated and must be seen in the light of several related facts. First, although "professionals and managers" is the standard census category for middle class, it also includes modest status jobs as dental technicians and night managers, along with doctors, lawyers and other traditional professionals. Moreover, growth in the professional occupations is concentrated at the lower end of the income scale with technicians, counselors and health technologists. Secondly, Anderson (1982:7) notes that many of these occupational gains were in the public sector in social welfare. This public sector concentration makes the Black middle class highly vulnerable to a reduction-in-force policy which calls for heavy layoffs at social service agencies which employ large numbers of Blacks as was the case during the Reagan Administration.

In addition, Robert Hill (1978) argues that the advocates of the new middle class are confusing "middle income" with "middle class." "Income only indicates how much money a person has, while class helps determine how that money is spent." In a word, a class is not simply defined by income but by wealth, status, "styles of life, living standards, values, beliefs." Also Hill (1980:40) contends that although middle class classifications usually include all persons holding white collar jobs or moving into higher status jobs, movement into higher status jobs does not necessarily mean higher paying jobs. In fact, he (1980:37) states, "only a small minority of Black white collar workers have middle class incomes." He concludes that instead of a spectacular growth of the Black middle class, one has statistics that show 25% of Blacks belong to the middle class as compared to 50% of whites.

Finally, in terms of middle class insensitivity, the argument can be made that the leadership of the civil rights movement and their constant struggle to maintain gains of the 60's contradict the insensitivity and selfishness suggested by Frazier and reinforced by those after him (Morris, 1984). Moreover, it can be argued that a distinction must be made between the radical or socially conscious and active segment of the middle class and the "tomish" sector. The former, it can be said, led the struggle, and the latter served the traditional role of buffer between the masses and the rulers of society. The radical, Cabral (1969:110) argues, has committed "class suicide" and identified with the aspirations of the masses whereas the toms have thrown their lot in with society's rulers. The problem, then, becomes one of how to initiate and sustain the process which radicalizes a significant sector of the middle class and causes them to assume the "Talented Tenth" role of leadership Dubois (1969) and others posed for them. Working for this community consciousness is, of course, the fact that in spite of middle-class advancement, racism still restricts their movement and reminds them of their limitations in a racist society (Benjamin, 1991; Landry, 1987).

6.6   THE UNDERCLASS

The problem of class also figures in the ongoing discourse around the question of the *underclass*.   Douglas Glasgow (1981:3,5) offered one of the earliest studies of this group and defined underclass as "a permanently entrapped population of poor persons, used and unwanted...unemployed, welfare dependent and without sufficient income to secure a decent quality of life." Such an entrapped sector of the population, Glasgow maintains, not only poses a threat to the broader social order, but more importantly to the safety, survival and development of the African American community. For such a state of things creates not only the potential and reality of violence turned inward and crime, but also diminishes the life chances of those so trapped.

More recently, William J. Wilson (1987) has also contributed an important study of this class which he calls "the truly disadvantaged." He (1987:8) defines the underclass as "...the most disadvantaged segments of the Black urban community, that heterogeneous grouping of families and individuals who are outside the mainstream of the American occupations system." Defining this class more extensively, he goes on to say that "included in this group are individuals who lack training and skills and either experience long-term unemployment or are not members of the labor force, individuals who are engaged in street crime and other forms of aberrant behavior, and families that experience long term spells of poverty and/or welfare dependency."

Wilson sees the evolution of this class as being shaped by both internal and external factors in a context of both historic and contemporary discrimination. These factors include: 1) the flow of migrants which created a large concentration of the disadvantaged; 2) the increasing number of young people among inner city residents which is associated with major problems, i.e., out-of-wedlock births, crime, female-headed households and welfare dependency; 3) structural changes in the economy "such as the shift from goods-producing to service-producing industries, the increasing polarization of the labor market into low-wage and high-wage sectors; technological innovations and the relocation of manufacturing industries out of the central cities" to the suburbs and low-wage foreign countries (Wilson, 1987:45); and 4) concentration of poverty in the inner city which as a result of middle class exodus creates both extreme social isolation and an institutional inability to effectively intervene in community problems or build on role models of possibility and achievement.

Moreover, Wilson argues that key to the solution of the problem of the underclass is to first concede its existence and problematic character and then develop a comprehensive public policy to solve it. He (1987:163) concludes that this comprehensive program must be one "that combines employment policies with social welfare policies and that features universal as opposed to race- or group-specific strategies." This would include stress on generation of a tight labor market, industrial competitiveness, increased skills for the labor force and social welfare policies of child support, family allowance and child care. His stress on the universal programs rather than race-specific ones is called a "hidden agenda" which will appeal to the larger public while simultaneously solving specific problems of the disadvantaged in a general framework.

There are arguments against both the identification of an underclass and Wilson's "hidden agenda" strategy to solve problems of the underclass. First, the term underclass is rejected as stigmatizing and indicting ghetto residents. It is argued that not only does such conceptualization of problems give racist categories with which to indict ghetto residents, but it also tends to blame the victims of the system rather than the system itself (Katz, 1986). A second problem with the term is its tendency toward imprecision, lumping together different peoples with different problems for different reasons and with differing capacities to solve them. Thirdly, such a formulation can easily deny or diminish the importance of racism in the very factors Wilson cites as shaping the formation of the underclass.

Fourthly, it is argued that underclass arguments are uncomfortably close to the culture-of-poverty arguments which stress the interconnection between cultural traditions, family history and individual character and values (Auletta, 1982: Chapter 2). The conservatives who argue these points tend to see the situation of the underclass as self-perpetuating and a reflection of the pathological character of both the subculture and the persons who compose it (Murray, 1984; Gilder, 1981). Although Wilson clearly rejects this stress on cultural tradition, family history and individual values and instead stresses structural factors which shape the formation and maintenance of the class, it is argued that focus on the problems of the group rather than society's oppressive character still leave open the door for racist manipulation.

Finally, Wilson's approach to solving the problems associated with the underclass has been questioned. The issue revolves around his "hidden agenda" strategy which suggests that one must disguise the real and greater needs of the poor and vulnerable and offer advantaged groups a public policy proposal which is universal and caters to their moral insensitivity to the truly disadvantaged. As I (Karenga, 1992:70) have argued, "the question is: do we cater to the advantaged group's insensitivity to issues involving the poor and vulnerable by disguising or hiding our real agenda and offering them similar benefits or do we challenge them to grow morally and recognize and respond positively to the priority of the poor and the vulnerable?" To search for common ground in public policy, as Wilson suggests, is imperative, but to find or fashion it at the expense of the disadvantaged is both morally untenable and politically counter-productive.

6.7   THE PROBLEM OF BUSINESS

The problem of economic development is also tied to the problems of Black business. Although Frazier's (1962) contention that Black business was a "social myth" was extremely harsh, one cannot disagree that it has certainly found itself fragile and marginal to the larger economy (Swinton, 1992; Coles, 1975; Tabb, 1970). In fact, African Americans "own 424,000 business firms out of a total of 17.5 million for the entire country: (Swinton, 1992:65). First, among the problems of Blacks businesses is undercapitalization which insures smallness and inefficiency, prevents acquisition of managerial competence and often leads to failure. It is estimated that Black firms in 1987 generated receipts of 22.8 billion or one-tenth of one percent of the total U.S. 11.4 trillion dollars generated (Swinton, 1992:67).

Secondly, African American businesses in spite of some diversification are essentially concentrated in personal services as in the past. *Black Enterprise's 1992 Top 100 Black Businesses* report (June, 1992) reaffirms this. Thus, the essential process of production escapes them and is not a fundamental part of government or private proposals for Black economic development. Thirdly, as mentioned above, Black businesses are losing in the grossly unequal competition for Black consumer dollars. Fourthly, low-level of managerial competence continues to plague Black businesses. Most are self-owned and too small to hire any other employee, let alone skilled managers which insure correct business decisions. Hacker (1992:108) reports that "only 70,000 of the 425,000 (Black businesses) have any paid employees. In other words, almost 85 percent are one person enterprises or family-run firms."

Fifthly, Black businesses essentially operate in a restricted market which is marked by small savings, high debt, low income, high unemployment and an environment shunned by possible large investors although the top 100 Black firms do not have these problems to the same degree (McCoy, 1992). Finally, the shift in the politics and economics of the country to the right with a focus on the rich at the expense of the poor and stress on less government assistance to the Black community in general and Black businesses in particular had an ill effect on Black business. For government assistance had been an important source not only of loans but also of support for affirmative action contracts for Black business and hiring (Lee, 1982).

The *Black Enterprise*'s assessment of Black businesses' future in the 90's links it to a variety of continuing practices. In order to sustain growth and avoid falling on the fatality list, Black businesses will have to, among other things: 1) acquire increased amounts of capital from other sources than the government; 2) diversify and work to get a greater share of the approximately $265 billion income of Blacks; 3) locate in industries such as telecommunications, cable, high technology and manufacturing; 4) engage in collective community planning; and 5) participate in building political bases among Blacks through service, donation and investment which come back in higher levels of Black support as consumers, investors, and partners in political and economic development of the Black community (McCoy, 1992).

6.8　SOLUTIONS

Introduction

Given the severity of the political-economic problems of the inner city, the question of what is to be done and who is to do it are necessarily raised. Three basic resource structures are identified as fundamental to reversing the tendency and fact of ghettoization: 1) government; 2) the private sector; and 3) the Black community itself (Barnett and Hefner, 1976; Williams, 1982; Karenga, 1980; Jaynes and Williams, 1989; Swinton, 1990, 1991, 1992). Governmental intervention and assistance are proposed for four basic reasons (Franklin and Norton, 1987). First, the problems are of dimensions beyond the means of any one or combination of community structures. Secondly, the problems are socially rooted and the result of racist discrimination and the government is obligated to assist in providing necessary correctives for these problems. Thirdly, Blacks helped create the social wealth of America and deserve an equitable share of it, not in the sense of sympathetic welfare, but in the sense of *distributive justice*, i.e., that share which is rightly theirs by their contribution and by just reasoning. Finally, it is objectively in the interest of the whole society to solve these problems, for as long as they remain unsolved, their negative effect will impact on the larger society also. For example, acquisition crime, generational poverty, socially incompetent members of society, and violently aggressive alienation all merit societal attention.

Secondly, the private sector is proposed because 1) there is a sense that businesses, especially larger corporations, have drained and exploited the community and thus, owe it support in its revitalization efforts; 2) that businesses will benefit in tax credits, public relations, and even make a profit on their investment in the ghetto; and 3) they too should be concerned about the negative impact of unsolved ghetto problems on the larger society.

Undoubtedly the most important resource structure, however, in solving Black problems is the Black community itself. Regardless of external goodwill, a people must initiate and lead the struggle for its own liberation. However, this necessitates the structural capacity -- an institutional and organizational network -- to wage such a struggle. As noted above, one of the greatest, if not the greatest, problems Blacks face is structural incapacity to define, defend and develop their interests. This, therefore, must be a priority. Each year in its *State of Black America*, the National Urban League gives recommendations for the struggle for Black freedom, justice and equality, placing heavy emphasis on governmental intervention and assistance. However, the tasks proposed and the struggle to be waged presupposes and necessitates a self-conscious organized people to execute them. After all, one cannot expect the government to respond simply because recommendations are published or verbally proposed yearly. The government is a political structure, organized around the holding, using and respect of power. Thus, African Americans must politically educate and organize themselves and become a self-conscious social power with which to reckon.

Often, it is pointed out that the problems of the ghetto are too large and deep-rooted for Blacks to solve and that talk of community self-help is utopian. There are several things wrong with this "reasoning" which are immediately observable. First, no one offers such a position to Jewish or Gentile communities or any other Third World communities except the African American community. Secondly, as noted above, resources from the government or others still require organization, knowledge of policy, collective strategy and the power to have an impact on policy. Thirdly, given Black structural incapacity, the government and the private sector are not likely to run to the rescue with the immediately necessary resources, as history has shown. Moreover, given the shift to the right in and out of government, the unlikelihood of this is even greater. Fourthly, given the above reality, it would seem sensible and contributive to survival and development if Blacks developed structures which, even on a limited scale, helped improve conditions of the ghetto.

Finally, Blacks have already built structures to deal with their deprivations imposed by discrimination; the point then would be how to expand and strengthen them. And here again, the Sixties provide a model, as I have argued in Chapter II. For not only were structures built to provide services, politically educate and organize the community, pressure was also put on the system to produce legislation, judicial decisions and programs which improved conditions in a significant way. The problem often faced is the one of dismissing Black strategies that do not produce the maximum goals or results and making alternative suggestions that theoretically produce maximum gains, but practically are less than effective or realistic. It is obvious that three resource structures must be tapped and utilized for whatever gains are possible. But it is equally obvious that without a *structural base* of its own, the Black community will not only be unable to effectively demand from government and the private sector what is rightfully theirs, but will also be unable to provide for itself what is possible in the meantime. Black history is full of examples of Black self-help and struggle to win their rightful share of social wealth and social space. Not to honor this history by continuing it, seems not only an avoidable loss, but also an irrational and self-defeating position.

In terms of proposals for each resource structure, several recommendations for government and the private sector (businesses) are most often quoted   (Barnett and Hefner, 1976; Williams, 1982; Franklin and Norton, 1987; Simms, 1989). Recommendations for the state and federal governments to assist in economic development are: 1) continued and reinforced employment training programs;   2) more federal government revenue for domestic programs and less for an inflated defense budget;   3) less layoffs of government workers which affect Blacks, other Third World people and women disproportionately;

4) perception of federal Third World business programs as economic programs rather than social welfare programs and improvement of delivery services to them; 5) encouragement of majority-owned and operated business to assist and use services of Third World businesses; 6) encouragement of employment and training of Blacks by private industry and small and medium business through tax incentives, wage subsidies, work study, etc.; 7) rejection of altered minimum wage for youth; 8) serious efforts toward full employment; 9) a reduction of budget cuts which affect monies and services vital to Blacks, other Third World peoples and the poor; and 10) continued application and support of Affirmative Action. Recommendations for the private sector are: 1) location of plants in the inner city; 2) job training and employment for Blacks; 3) use of Black business services and products; 4) provision of resources to insure expansion of alternative educational programs.

Politically, government, especially federal, is asked to: 1) resume and reinforce its traditional defense of civil rights; 2) monitor white terrorist and racist organizations like the Klan and neo-nazi groups; 3) appoint qualified Blacks in the government structure; 4) support the Voting Rights Act; and 5) oppose reapportionment schemes that dilute Black voting power or dissolve districts represented by Blacks. Educationally, govern-ment should: 1) oppose the voucher education system which is detrimental to public education; 2) increase support for histori-cally Black colleges; 3) continue federal resources for quality education for the disadvantaged; and 4) insist that post-secondary institutions receiving federal monies maintain effective affirma-tive action programs for faculty and students.

In terms of the Black community, is clear as stated above, that their primary focus must be on building the *structural* capacity to define, defend and develop their interests. This essentially means building an organizational, institutional and enterprise network that not only provides social services, but politically organizes and educates the community to its interests and possibilities. This requires strengthening existing structures and building new ones, building economic enterprises on the individual and cooperative level, alternative educational institutions, Black united fronts for collective planning and actions, and eventually, a Black political party which is dedicated exclusively to organizing Blacks for political power and effectively participating in the exercise of state power.

Broad Strategies

There are obviously several eclectic approaches to Black economic development which are initiated and controlled by Blacks (Coles,1975; Cash and Oliver,1975; Browne,1976; America,1977; Woodson, 1987; Wilson, 1987; Simms, 1989). Approaches can also be defined by their rootedness in or advocacy of three broad developmental strategies: capitalism, socialism and cooperative economics. Although it is theoretically possible to combine these developmental strategies, advocates of each usually tend to praise one and condemn or severely question the others. However, cooperative economic and socialist strategies are often linked and capitalist advocates have been known to tolerate parallel cooperative strategies. The discussion below seeks to give the basic contentions of each of these strategies with explanatory comments where warranted.

Black Capitalism.   Black capitalism which gained popularity as a strategy during the Nixon Administration attempted to reduce the "perceived cycle of Black dependency" on governmental intervention. The alternative was to expand Black ownership which would stress private efforts, profit pursuit and free marketism for Blacks using the model of capitalism on a societal level (Cross, 1969). Black capitalism as a strategy contains several basic principles which define it and also lay the basis for its criticism.

First, it argues that increase in Black private ownership and control will enhance Black independence and pride, employ Blacks and help ease unemployment, increase the availability of services for the community and expand the wealth in the community. Secondly, Black capitalism argues for market protectionism that would shield Black enterprises from competition with larger more competitive outside enterprises. Thirdly, it advocates Black self-help and solidarity which would support Black business and benefit from its expansion. Fourthly, Black capitalism demands subsidization from the dominant society, i.e., government and the private sector. Subsidization may take the form of loans, grants, property equipment or training and is seen as a contribution to capital formation as well as a moral and economic debt U.S. society owes African Americans for long-term discrimination and deprivation.

Criticism of Black capitalism is severe and from many quarters. First, Boggs (1970) argues that it is an irrational strategy which poses itself as a collective strategy, but is in fact a class strategy to further enrich a few at the expense of the many. Secondly, Allen (1970) and Zweig (1972) argue that the political economy of subsidization is negative to Black self-determination and will mean creation of a manipulated class still dependent on outside sources. Thirdly, Ofari (1970) calls attention to the fact that the strategy is overweighed toward service rather than *production*, the key process in economics. And finally, Brimmer and Terrell (1971), as well as Ofari, point to its nonviability given the small amount of capital available to Black enterprises, their low expansion possibility, low efficiency, marginal existence, high mortality rate, and restricted and problematic market, i.e., the ghetto economy.

Socialism. Black advocates of socialism see Black capitalism as a myth and hindrance to serious Black economic development and political emancipation (Ofari,1970; Allen,1970). Their focus is essentially on Black labor rather than Black capital. As Harris (1978:14) argues, "Blacks cannot be adequately understood except as an integral part of the capital labor relation as a whole in U.S. capitalism." Given the fact that the Black working class is approximately 90% of the Black population, a strategy which does not focus on problems and possibilities of Black labor is both deficient and self-deluding.

Secondly, Black socialists argue that regardless of the temporary and partial measures that Blacks institute for economic betterment, a real and full solution depends on the transformation of society from capitalism to socialism. Given this reality, Black socialists argue for greater stress on the political dimensions of the economic process, and stress the need for organizing Black workers and the Black community into a self-conscious political force which challenges and transforms the established order (Alkalimat and Johnson,1974).

Fourthly, the Black socialist strategy involves seizure of power and institution of: 1) collective ownership and control of the productive apparatus; 2) an egalitarian distribution of wealth; 3) a planned economy; 4) a political and economic democracy; and 5) an end to class, race and sexual alienation (Karenga, 1980:61-61). Essentially this is seen as a long-range strategy, and the organization of the Black workers (and the Black community) as a fighting force for democratic rights, higher wages, better work and living conditions and greater participation in political and economic decision-making are posed as immediate goals.

This stress on the working class, especially by orthodox Marxists, however, often poses a problem for a specifically Black solution. For not only does it tend to play down racism as a simple function of capitalism (Harris,1978), but it also ends up with no ethnic-specific program for African Americans -- only for workers in general. Thus, as Browne (1976:153) contends, given Marx's and Lenin's failure to "directly address the unique situation in which American Blacks find themselves...there are very real limits on the extent to which that analysis speaks to our racial situation, irrespective of how eloquently it may dissect our economic dilemma." Moreover, the failure of communism to establish humanist societies and the recent collapse of the Soviet Union and communism in Eastern Europe have made both communists and socialists reevaluate the problematics and possibilities of socialist society, especially in a multicultural context (Davis, et al, 1987).

Cooperative Economics.   As Ofari (1970:89) states, the theory and practice of cooperative economics has an early history in the mutual aid societies in northern Black communities which pooled resources and dedicated themselves to social service and community development.   Stewart (1984) has also written concerning the challenge of building a cooperative economy and the lessons which evolve from the Black experience in this ongoing historical project. The idea of cooperative economics among African Americans, however, was eventually submerged with the emergence of a Black elite which developed a capitalist merchant class orientation (Harris, 1936). But in 1940, DuBois (1968) had proposed a comprehensive theoretical framework and rationale for cooperative economics as a viable and necessary alternative to capitalism.

He (1968:216-219) stressed the need for a communal, Black-focused solution which would emphasize and establish: 1) social ownership; 2) strong family and group ties; 3) consumer unions; 4) economic planning; 5) socialized medicine; 6) cooperative organization of Black professionals for social service; 7) the elimination of private profit; 8) a Black controlled educational system; and 9) the essentiality of collective self-reliance. This solution he called "a cooperative commonwealth," a communal social system which built new relations among African Americans and gave them the internal strength to resist the corrupting influence of capitalism and the collective values necessary for cooperative community development.

Although DuBois' program was never implemented, it did yield an important model and since the 60's cooperatives have been posed as an important mode of Black economic development, especially in the South (Marshall and Godwin,1971). Over one hundred were formed during the 60's in the South and ninety of those were organized in the Federation of Southern Cooperatives. Although they have been resisted by hostile forces, they nevertheless have provided food, jobs, and capital otherwise unobtainable and have thus helped raise the overall standard of living among the rural population.

Ofari (1970:89), though a socialist, admits that in spite of its problems, the Black cooperative proposal is "by far the most positive proposal that has been offered." Likewise, Allen (1970) who is also socialist, concedes the limitations of cooperative economics, but maintains that given the distance of the socialist revolution and the problems of integrating into a capitalist economy, a transitional program of cooperative economics is necessary." Led by an independent Black party, this transitional program, he (1970:278) states, should involve "a struggle to create an all encompassing, planned communal social system on a national scale and with strong international ties."

Finally, as I (1980:62-64) argued elsewhere, cooperative economics proves its validity in that it: 1) aids in increasing capital capacity, necessary for economic development; 2) increases the beneficiaries, unlike Black capitalism; 3) teaches the value for shared social wealth, egalitarianism, collective work and decision-making, the priority of the person over profit and the centrality of the community; and 4) establishes cooperative thought and practice which can be transferred to other areas, i.e., political struggle and social construction. Again, then, it is clear that politics and economics are unavoidably linked and any strategy for one must have as a major focus concern for the other.

STUDY QUESTIONS

1.   Define economics.
2.   Discuss the relation between politics and economics and why political economy is a more accurate word for economics.
3.   Discuss the political economic status of the ghetto as an internal colony.

4. Discuss Sowell's and Wilson's contentions and arguments against them.
5. Why is the middle class both a resource and problem in Black economic development and political emancipation?
6. Discuss the employment problem of the African American community.
7. What are some basic problems of Black business?
8. Discuss the three basic resource bases for Black economic development and the rationale for each.
9. What are the basic principles and criticism of Black capitalism?
10. What are the basic contentions and objectives of socialism?
11. What were DuBois' cooperative economic proposals?
12. What are the arguments for cooperative economics?

REFERENCES

Alexis, Marcus. (1980) "Race and Social Organization: An Economic Perspective," *The Review of Black Political Economy*, 10,4 (Summer) 334-353.

Alkalimat, Abdul H. and Nelson Johnson. (1974) *"Toward the Ideological Unity of the African Liberation Support Committee,"* a position paper, South Carolina (June-July).

Allen, Robert L. (1970) *Black Awakening in Capitalist America*, Garden City, N.Y.: Anchor Books.

America, Richard. (1977) *Developing the Afro-American Economy*, Lexington, Mass.: Lexington Books.

Anderson, Bernard C. (1982) "Economic Patterns in Black America," (ed) James D. Williams, *The State of Black America*, 1982, New York: National Urban League, pp. 1-32.

Auletta, Ken. (1982) *The Underclass*, New York: Random House.

Barnett, Marguerite and James Hefner. (1976) *Public Policy for the Black Community*, New York: Alfred Knopf Publishing Company.

Becker, Gary. (1957) *The Economics of Discrimination*, Chicago: University of Chicago Press.

Benjamin, Lois. (1991) *The Black Elite*, Chicago: Nelson-Hall Publishers.

Boggs, James. (1970) "The Myth and Irrationality of Capitalism," *The Review of Black Political Economy*, 1, 1 (Spring/Summer) 27-35.

Brimmer, Andrew. (1982) "Economic Growth and Job and Job Opportunities: The Long-Term Outlook," *Black Enterprise*, 12,7 (February) 32.

Brimmer, Andrew and Henry S. Terrell. (1971) "The Economic Potential of Black Capitalism," *The Black Politician*, 2,4 (April) 19-23, 78-88.

Browne, Robert S. (1976) "The Black Community and Contemporary Economic Dynamics," *The Review of Black Political Economy*, 6,2 (Winter) 145-160.

Browne, Robert S. (1971) "Cash Flow in a Ghetto Economy," *The Review of Black Political Economy*, (Winter/Spring).

Browning, Rufus, Dale R. Marshall and David H, Tabb. (1984) *Protest Is Not Enough: The Struggle of Blacks and Hispanics for Equality in Urban Politics*, Berkeley: University of California Press.

Cabral, Amilcar. (1969) *Revolution in Guinea*, New York: Monthly Review Press.

Carmichael, Stokely and Charles Hamilton. (1967) *Black Power*, New York: Random House.

Cash, William L., Jr. and Lucy R. Oliver (eds). (1975) *Black Economic Development*, Ann Arbor: The University of Michigan Press.

Clark, Kenneth. (1965) *Dark Ghetto*, New York: Harper & Row.

Clark, Kenneth. (1964) *Youth in the Ghetto*, New York: Haryou Associates.

Coles, Flournoy A. (1975) *Black Economic Development*, Chicago: Nelson Hall.

Cotton, S. (1988) "Discrimination or Favoritism in the U.S. Labor Market: The Cost to a Wage Earner of Being Female and Black and the Benefit of Being Male and White," American Journal of Economic Sociology, 47, (January) pp. 15-28.

Cross, Theodore L. (1969) *Black Capitalism*, New York: Atheneum.

Cruse, Harold. (1967) *The Crisis of the Negro Intellectual*, New York: William Morrow & Co.

Cruse, Harold. (1968) *Rebellion or Revolution*, New York: William Morrow & Co.

Darity, William Jr. and Samuel Myers, Jr. (1992) "Racial Earnings Inequality into the 21st Century," in Billy Tidwell (ed.) *The State of Black America*, New York: National Urban League, pp. 119-139.

Davis, Mike. et al (1987) *The Year Left 2, Towards a Rainbow Socialism*, Lorder: Verse.

DuBois, W.E.B. (1968) *Dusk of Dawn*, New York: Schocken Books.

DuBois, W.E.B. (1969) "The Talented Tenth," (ed.) Ulysses Lee, *The Negro Problem*, New York: Arno Press and The New York Times, pp. 31-76.

Franklin, John H. and Eleanor Holmes Norton. (1987) *Black Initiative and Governmental Responsibility*, Washington, D.C.: Joint Center for Political Studies.

Frazier, E. Franklin. (1962) *Black Bourgeoisie*, New York: Collier Books.

Freeman, Richard and Harry Holzer. (1986) *The Black Youth Employment Crisis*, Chicago: University of Chicago Press.

Fusfeld, Daniel. (1977) *The Age of the Economist*, Chicago: Scott, Foresman and Co.

Fusfeld, Daniel. (1970) "The Basic Economics of the Urban and Racial Crisis," *The Review of Black Political Economy*, 1, 1 (Spring/Summer) 58-83.

Gilder, George. (1981) *Wealth and Poverty*, New York: Basic Books.

Glasgow, Douglas. (1981) *The Black Underclass*, New York: Vintage Books.

Hacker, Andrew. (1992) *Two Nations, Black and White, Separate and Hostile*, New York: Macmillan.

Hare, Nathan. (1965) *The Black Anglo-Saxons*, New York: Marzani and Munsell, Inc.

Harris, Abram. (1936) *The Negro as Capitalist*, Philadelphia: American Academy of Political Science.

Harris, Donald J. (1978) "Capitalist Exploitation and Black Labor: Some Conceptual Issues," *The Review of Black Political Economy*, 8, 2 (Winter) 134-151.

Harris, William H. (1982) *The Harder We Run*, New York: Oxford University Press.

Heilbroner, Robert. (1972) *The Worldly Philosophers*, New York: Oxford University Press.

Hill, Robert B. (1980) "Black Families in the 70's." in (ed.) James D. Williams, *The State of Black America*, 1980, New York: National Urban league, Inc., pp. 29-58.

Hill, Robert B. (1981) "The Economic Status of Black Americans." (ed.) James D. Williams, *The State of Black America*, 1981, New York: National Urban League, Inc.

Hill, Robert B. (1978) *The Illusion of Black Progress*, Washington, D.C: National Urban League Research Department.

Hogan, Lloyd. (1984) *Principles of Black Political Economy*, London: Routledge and Kegan Paul.

Jaynes, Gerald D. and Robin Williams, Jr. (eds.) (1989) *Common Destiny: Blacks and American Society*, Washington, D.C.: National Academy Press.

Karenga, Maulana. (1992) "African Americans and the Reconstruction of Social Policy." *Harvard Journal of African American Public Policy, Vol. I*, pp. 55-74.

Karenga, Maulana. (1980) *Kawaida Theory: An Introductory Outline*, Inglewood, CA: Kawaida Publications.

Katz, M.B. (1986) *In the Shadow of the Poorhouse*, New York: Basic Books.

Kluger, Richard. (1977) *Simple Justice*, New York: Vintage Books.

Landry, Bart. (1987) *The New Black Middle Class*, Berkeley: University of California.

Lee, Elliot. (1982) "The BE Board of Economics Look at the Future" *Black Enterprise*, 12,11 (June) 191-200.

Malveaux, Julianne. (1992) "The Poverty Initiative: Civil Rights, Economic Justice and the New American Dilemma" in Billy J. Tidwell (ed.) *The State of Black America, 1992*, New York: National Urban League, pp. 281-303.

Malveaux, Julianne. (1987) "The Political Economy of Black Women" in Mike Davis et al *The Year Left 2 - Towards A Rainbow Socialism: Essays on Race, Ethnicity, Class and Gender*, London: Verso, pp. 52-73.

Marshall, Ray and Lamond Godwin. (1971) *Cooperatives and Rural Poverty in the South*, Baltimore: The John Hopkins Press.

McCoy, Frank. (1992) "A Decade in Review," *Black Enterprise*, 22, 11 (June) 195-202.

Morris, Aldon. (1984) *The Origins of the Civil Rights Movement: Black Communities Organizing for Social Change*, New York: The Free Press.

Murray, Charles (1984) *Losing Ground: American Social Policy, 1950-1980*, New York: Basic Books.

Ofari, Earl. (1970) *The Myth of Black Capitalism*, New York: Monthly Review Press.

Pinkney, Alphonso. (1984) *The Myth of Black Progress*, Cambridge: Cambridge University Press.

Reich, Michael. (1981) *Racial Equality*, Princeton, NJ: Princeton University Press.

Simms, Margaret C. (1989) *Black Economic Progress: An Agenda for the 1990's*, Washington, DC: Joint Center for Political Studies.

Sowell, Thomas. (1981a) *Ethnic Minorities*, New York: Basic Books.

Sowell, Thomas. (1981b) *Markets and Minorities*, New York: Basic Books.

Sowell, Thomas. (1975) *Race and Economics*, New York: David McKay.

Stewart, James. (1984) "Building a Cooperative Economy: Lessons from the Black Experience," *Review of Social Economy*, XVII, pp. 360-268.

Swinton, David H. (1992) "The Economic Status of African Americans: Limited Ownership and Persistent Inequality," in Billy Tidwell (ed.) *The State of Black America*, New York: National Urban League, pp. 61-117.

Swinton, David H. (1991) "The Economic Status of African Americans: 'Permanent' Poverty and Inequality," in Janet Dewar (ed.) *The State of Black America*, New York: National Urban League, pp. 25-75.

Swinton, David H. (1990) "Economic Status of Black Americans During the 80's: A Decade of Limited Progress," in Janet Dewar (ed.) *The State of Black America*, New York: National Urban League, pp. 25-52.

Tabb, William K. (1970) *The Political Economy of the Black Ghetto*, New York: W.W. Norton and Company.

Turner, James. (1976) "Implications of Class Conflict and Racial Cleavage for the U.S. Black Community," *The Review of Black Political Economy*, 6, 2 (Winter) 133-144.

Williams, James D. (ed.) (1982) *The State of Black America*, 1982, New York: National Urban League, Inc.

Willie, Charles. (1979) *The Caste and Class Controversy*, New York: General Hall, Inc.

Wilson, William J. (1978) *The Declining Significance of Race*, Chicago: University of Chicago Press.

Wilson William J. (1987) *The Truly Disadvantaged*, Chicago: University of Chicago Press.

Woodson, Robert. (ed.) (1987) *On The Road To Economic Freedom*, Washington, DC: Regency Gateway.

Zweig, Michael. (1972) "The Dialectics of Black Capitalism," *The Review of Black Political Economy*, 2 (Spring) 25-37.

BLACK CREATIVE PRODUCTION

7
BLACK CREATIVE PRODUCTION

7.1 INTRODUCTION

Defining Art

Although the category creative production can be used more generally to include various other forms of creative work, it will focus in this chapter on Black Art, Music and Literature. These are definitive of Black aesthetic creations and can, for the purpose of this chapter, be categorized as Black Arts or Art in the general sense. By *Art*, I mean *"cultural production informed by standards of creativity and beauty and inspired by and reflective of a people's life-experiences and life-aspirations"* (Karenga, 1980:80). The focus here is on the collective base of art, for as Mari Evans (1979:37) contends concerning Black art, "...it is Black art because it is saturated in the experience and behavior patterns of the people for whom it is created and because its substance is functional."

W.E.B. DuBois (1925) also stressed the collective source of Black art in his discussion of its social origin. He (1925:53) stated that even though Black art has both a personal and universal aspect, these are "combined with a certain group compulsion...meaning that the wishes, thoughts and experiences of thousands of individuals influence consciously and unconsciously the message of the one who speaks for all." This "social compulsion," DuBois continues, was shaped by Black experience in enslavement and emancipation, and the struggle Blacks waged to liberate themselves and strive upward.

It is this struggle for freedom, dignity and self-definition in a hostile and challenge-filled world that shaped African American art and gave it its relevance and reality. Black art, therefore, *"as an expression of Black life experiences and aspirations, is the conscious and unconscious aesthetic contribution of Black people to their struggle to rescue and reconstruct their history and humanity in their own image and interest"* (Karenga, 1980:80). Thus, Alain Locke (1969:266), a key figure in the Harlem Renaissance of the 1920's, argued for the development of an African American mode of Black artistic expression which spoke directly to the Black need for self-expression in their own terms. "We ought and must have a school of (Black) art," he asserted, "a local and racially representative tradition." The impetus and inspiration for this, he maintained, would come from African Americans' recognition, respect and use of their African heritage.

The Black Aesthetic

Although this question was raised and debated during the Harlem Renaissance and after, it received its most critical and enthusiastic attention during the Sixties in the debate revolving around the Black aesthetic (Gayle,1971). The Black aesthetic had two distinct but interrelated meanings. First, it was used to mean a distinctive mode of aesthetic expression by which Black art could be identified. Secondly, it meant a criteria by which Black art could not only be judged in terms of its creativity and beauty, but also in terms of its social relevance.

If one combines these two interrelated definitions, *the Black aesthetic* can be defined as *a distinctive mode of artistic expression and a distinctive standard by which Black art can be identified and judged in terms of its creativity and beauty as well as its social relevance.* From the debate around this question which continues even now, two schools of thought evolved, the detached-art school and the committed-art school. Writers such as Ralph Ellison (1966) and J. Saunders Redding (1966) argued the primacy of art rather than race or politics, suggesting art was universal and personal but not Black. They asserted that the artist does a disservice to himself/herself and his/her profession by being overly concerned with race and politics.

Langston Hughes, Richard Wright and the creative artists and critics of the 60's all argued against such a view. Hughes (1970:262) stated that he was "ashamed for the Black poet who says 'I want to be a poet not a (Black) poet', as though his own racial world were not as interesting as any world." Also, he expressed shame for the Black artist who paints sunsets instead of Black faces "because he fears the strange un-whiteness of his features." Wright, as Addison Gayle (1970:xiii) notes, "argued, in essence, that conditions in America had not changed to the degree that the (African American) could desert the race question, engage in an art for art's sake endeavor or wander free in the sunny utopia of abstraction in attempt to desert the harsh reality of being Black in the twentieth century."

In the 60's Hoyt Fuller, Larry Neal, Mari Evans, Haki Madhubuti (Don L. Lee), Carolyn Rodgers, Rhonda Davis, Addison Gayle, Amiri Baraka, Sonia Sanchez, Woodie King, Ron Milner, Dudley Randall, Maulana Karenga and others contributed to the discussion and definition of the Black aesthetic (Gayle 1971). Neal (1971:272) posited essential contentions of the committed-art school when he rejected "any concept of the artist that alienates him from the community," posed Black art as "the aesthetic sister of the Black Power concept" and argued that the Black artist's primary duty is to speak to the spiritual and cultural needs of Black people. Moreover, the *Negro Digest* (later named the *Black World*) under the editorship of Hoyt Fuller (1971) who helped establish it in 1967, ran over a year of continuous commentary and discussion on the Black aesthetic from September 1968 through November 1969. In the January 1968 issue, a wide spectrum of views was presented on the question of the Black aesthetic. Most of these commentaries reaffirmed the need for African Americans to create and employ an aesthetic in their own image and interest.

In the 70's, the discussion continued. Elizabeth Catlett (1975:13) reaffirmed the need for art being linked to Black struggle, stating that, "(o)nly the liberation of Black people will make the real development of Black art possible. Therefore, it is to our advantage as artists as well as Blacks to lend all our strength to the struggle." She notes that art "...will not create authentic social change, but it can provoke thought and prepare us for change, even helping in its achievement. For art can tell us what we do not see consciously, what we may not realize, and that there are other ways of seeing things-maybe opposite ways."

John Killens (1975:46) also reemphasized that culture and literature were weapons for liberation and "words are the writer's ammunition." And Haki Madhubuti (Don L. Lee) (1972:39) continued his stress on the social role of art and the artist, and the need to develop a people-focused art stating that, "(t)o be able to define one's self from a historically and culturally accurate base and to follow through in your work keeping the best interest of your history and culture in mind, is to-actually-give direction to the coming generations." In addition, Mari Evans (1979:37) reaffirmed the political character and role of Black art, contending that, "It is political since its intent is to speak to the Black community about the quality of life in that community and the ramification of individual responsibility for the community both within and outside the systems of the larger society."

Finally, Chestyn Everett (1975:34,35) reasserts the need for respect of Black tradition. For any art "which denies *tradition* removes the necessary cultural cohesion of the form, sensibilities and integrity" of the art itself. Artists, he continues, "enrich themselves and their works when they bring to themselves and to their writing a clear perspective and appreciation for the *cultural and historical tradition* of Black life and (art). The need, then, is to "advance the best of this tradition and 'standing on the shoulders of our forefathers' set our rainbow in the sky!"

It is in the context and support of the committed-art school, that Maulana Karenga (1971, 1980:34ff;) offered suggestions for a Black aesthetic, first in the *Black World* series of commentaries and afterward in an outline of *Kawaida Theory*. Essentially, he (1980:84ff) argued that, "(f)or Black Art to truly be in the image and interest of Black people to whom it owes its existence and inner thrust, it must be informed, inspired and judged by social criteria as well as an aesthetic criteria." This social criteria which evolved within the framework of Kawaida Theory was based on 1) the traditional role of art in African society; 2) the discussions by advocates of the committed-art school during and before the 60's; and 3) a Kawaida perception of the demands of Black life and struggle (Ransaw, 1979).

Therefore, Karenga (1980:84ff) contended that for Black art to be real and relevant, it had to have three basic characteristics, i.e., it had to be functional, collective and committing. For art to be functional it has to be useful. And if art is not useful, it is by definition useless. To be functional, art must self-consciously have and urge social purpose, inform, instruct and inspire the people and be an unashamed partisan for them. "In a word, to be functional, Black art must be an aesthetic translation of our will and struggle for liberation and a higher level of life," searching for and creating new forms and styles to speak our truth and possibilities. To be collective, Black art must be done for all, drawn and synthesized from all, and rooted in a life-based language and imagery rich in everyday relevance. It must be understandable without being vulgarly simplistic, that is, so pedestrian and impoverished that it does damage to art as a discipline and to the social message it attempts to advance.

Finally, Black art, must be committing. It must not simply inform and inspire Blacks, but also commit them to the historical project of liberation and a higher level of human life. To do this, "(i)t must demand and urge willing and conscious involvement in struggle and building of a new world and new men, women and children to inhabit it." And it must move beyond protest and teach possibilities, beyond victimization and teach Blacks to dare victory. Art, then, "must commit us to what we can become and are becoming and inspire us to dare the positive in a world defined and deformed by the negative."

Moreover, "(c)ommitting art is nationally self-conscious art, i.e., consciously a fundamental contribution to the definition, defense and development of the national Black community." This is not to deny art's human character, but to endow it with a concrete human reality by giving it a people-specific expression. For "our art, like our lives, is great not because it's defined as more human than Black, but because we have explored the richness of our own life experience and aspirations and discovered and offer life-lessons from which the whole world can benefit--not only aesthetically, but culturally in the wide sense of the word." It is in the framework of these assumptions that the following summaries of Black artistic achievement are offered and explained. This also maintains the stated thrust of this text to present a proactive and positive view of African American life and struggle in their current and historical unfolding.

7.2 BLACK ART

The Continental African Dimension

African American art has its origins in Africa where art and artistic production, like religion, manifested itself in all aspects of communal life. African art was functional as well as aesthetic, being created for and used in various religious and social activities (Adler and Barnard, 1992; Niangoran-Bouah, 1984; Gillon, 1984; Porter, 1970; Smith, 1981). African artists were carvers in wood, ivory and bone, sculptors in stone, clay, bronze, gold and iron, and created one of the oldest and most skilled traditions of functional and aesthetic art in the history of humankind (Locke, 1936; Butcher, 1956; McLeod, 1980; Wilkinson, 1992). Although there is continuing controversy over how much of the African artistic tradition was transferred to the U.S., the fact cannot be denied that there are clear evidences of the African motif in early African American art (Porter, 1943; Dover, 1960; Thompson, 1983).

Even though slaveholders often condemned and destroyed Black art to destroy Black communication and culture, enslaved Africans nevertheless produced impressive works of art (Driskell, 1976:12ff). These included not only personal art objects but public works as Samella Lewis (1978):9ff) asserts. Among the personal art objects, Robert F. Thompson (1969) lists ceramics, basketry, earthenware, grave decorations, woodcarvings and weavings. Examples of these are in the works of Elsa Fine (1973:12ff) and David Driskell (1976:12ff). James Porter (1943) contends that the Janson House, built on the Hudson River in 1712 for a Dutch patron, exhibits a clear African motif in its construction and ornamentation, i.e., hand forged hinges and detailed-work fireplace. He also cites their art work in silver, gold and iron. Driskell (1976:22ff) shows remarkable similarities between African and African American art and architecture, among which are wrought iron balconies in New Orleans, plantation houses in African motif, a cylindrical quarter for enslaved Africans in Virginia which resemble Tembu houses in South Africa, and carved mantels with an African mask motif in North Carolina.

In addition, there is impressive evidence of African building and masonry skill in the Chapel of Cross in Chapell Hall, N.C., the Virginia State Capital building, the Torrence House of Mecklingburg County, the Harvey Castle near New Orleans, St. Andrew's Episcopal Church in Prairieville, Alabama and the famous Melrose plantation, near Natchitoches, Louisiana. (Dozier, 1974; Newton, 1977). James Newton concludes that there were at least 90 different areas of arts and craft in which African American exhibited skillful workmanship.

Professional Emergence

Lewis (1978:12-13) marks the emergence of the professional artist before Emancipation with painters Scipio Moorhead and G.W. Hobbs in the 1770's, and Josua Johnston who "was the first artist of Black ancestry to gain public recognition in the

United States as a portrait painter." After these were Julien Hudson (active 1830-40); Robert Douglass (1809-87); an abolitionist and painter, Patrick Henry Reason (1917-50); an engraver, William Simpson (active 1854-72); and later Robert Duncanson, Edward Bannister, Grafton Brown and Nelson Primus.

Edmonia Lewis (1843-1900) was the first Black woman in the U.S. to gain widespread recognition as an artist and the first Black to gain national reputation as a sculptor. Her *Forever Free*, a Black couple looking upward with broken chains, is in Howard University's Gallery of Art. Also, one of the most impressive early Black artists is Henry O. Tanner (1859-97), famous for his oil on canvas pieces such as *Banjo Lesson* and *The Thankful Poor*. However, having suffered much from racism, Tanner went to Paris and although he helped young Black artists who came to Paris, he refused to return to the U.S. and establish the Black Art School Alain Locke advocated.

The Harlem Renaissance

The Harlem Renaissance produced race and socially conscious artists who reached back to Africa and the Black masses for a distinctive Black motif. As mentioned above, Locke (1968:267) had challenged Black artists to turn to their "ancestral arts of Africa" in order to develop a race art. He argued that if African art had influenced Pablo Picasso, Modigliani, Matisse and other white artists, it was surely "not too much to expect...its influence upon the culturally awakened (Black) artist of the present generations." Three artists in particular--Palmer Hayden, Archibald Motley, Jr., and Aaron Douglass--focused on developing styles that reflected the Black aesthetic.

Hayden in his *Fetiche et Cleurs (Fetish and Flowers)* used African print to emphasize Africanness and later painted subject matter which stressed the life and custom of the Black masses as in *John Henry on the Right, Stem Drill on the Left* and *The Janitor Who Paints*. Motley also used African and African American themes. His *Old Snuff Dipper, The Barbecue* and *Chicken Shack* are clear examples of his focus on Black life. Douglass was a "pioneer Africanist," using the ancestral legacy to develop an original style which "combined modernism and Africanism in an astonishing (and original) synthesis" (Driskell, 1976:62). Focusing on the beauty and strength of Black life, he employed geometric figures reflecting an African motif in his illustrations for Locke's (1968) *The New Negro* and James Weldon's Johnson's *God Trombones* and in his major work, a series of murals for the Countee Cullen branch of the New York library which portrays the history of African Americans.

Post Renaissance

Hale Woodruff also reflected a race and social consciousness in his art. In 1939, he painted a series of three socially conscious oil on canvas pieces entitled *The Amistad Murals* in honor of the Amistad Mutiny. This creation for Talladega College in Alabama reflects the influence of socially conscious Mexican muralists Jose C. Orozco, Diego Rivera, and David Siqueiros on him and other Black artists during the 30's and 40's (Lewis, 1978:67-68). Richmond Barthe (b.1901) is clearly one of African Americans' leading sculptors. His sculptural figures are technically immaculate and graceful and focus on Black life, strength and dignity. Among these are *Blackberry Woman, Wetta, African Dancer,* and the *Negro Looks Ahead*. He also produced two marble reliefs, *Exodus* and *Dance*.

The 40's continued the tradition of race and socially conscious art, and mural art stood out as a major mode of expression. This, as mentioned before, was influenced by the Mexican muralists Rivera, Orozco and Siqueiros, but also Lewis (1978:110) notes, "mural art is a major aspect of African architectural tradition." Charles Alston was one of the most important Black muralists during this time. Using a cubist style, his mural, *Magic and Medicine* for the Harlem Hospital in 1937, depicts a contrast between African and American life, the former being nature-oriented and warm, and the later, mechanical and cold. Alston also produced with Hale Woodruff a joint mural documenting Black contributions to the founding of California for Golden State Mutual Life Insurance Company of Los Angeles. Alton's panel is entitled *Exploration and Colonization (1527-1850)* and Woodruff's is *Settlement and Development (1850-1949)*.

Charles White is by all estimates one of the most gifted race and socially conscious Black artists. Early in his art he announced that he was interested in the social role and function of art and sought to express it in his own. He showed Black people in various roles in history as worker, soldier, mother, father, scientist, civic leader, and musician. Drawing from the muralists school, his works are monumental, bold and defiant. Some of his most famous murals are *Five Great American Negroes* and *The Contribution of the Negro to American Democracy*. His lithographs, *Frederick Douglass* and *Harriet Tubman*, and his crayon *Mother and Child* are also impressive pieces.

James Porter, who wrote *Modern Negro Art*, and was appointed head of Howard University's art department and art gallery in 1953, also painted. Essentially between 1954 and 1964, he painted African and African American themes and as an art critic and art historian. He, like Alain Locke, played a vital role in the early establishment and development of Black art (Lewis, 1978:102).

Lois Mailou Jones and Elizabeth Catlett were two important Black women artists during this period. Although Jones painted the French countryside in an earlier period, she evolved into a self-conscious Black artist, visited 11 African countries and incorporated African imagery in her subsequent painting. Her *Moon Mask* from her African series reflects this consciousness. Catlett, a sculptor and printmaker, was involved in the Civil Rights Movement as a student and teacher, and assigned art a social role in the struggle against oppression. Some of her strongest works are *Black Unity*, in honor of Pan-Africanism; her lithograph *Negro Es Bello* (Black is Beautiful), a gentle rendition of the profile of a Black child; and *Malcolm Speaks For Us*, a strong linocut in her series on Black heroes.

The Sixties and Beyond

The Sixties and Seventies saw an impressive growth of race conscious and socially conscious art. The Black Art Movement of the 60's which demanded that art serve Black people and their struggle recruited many artists who reflected in their art not only a commitment to their heritage but also a commitment to use their medium to support and achieve Black liberation. Murals again became a way to make art serve and express the people. Among these are *Mural at Massachusetts* in Boston by Dana Chandler and Gary Rickson, Eugene Edna's *Howard University Mural*, John Outterbridge's *Something From Nothing* in Compton, California, Dana Chandler's *Knowledge is Power: Stay in School* in Boston, and in Chicago, William Walker's *Peace and Salvation Wall*, Mitchell Caton's *Universal Alley Wall* and *Wall of Respect* by Eugene Edna, William Walker, Jeff Donaldson and other members of the Organization of Black American Culture, a group of artists and community workers dedicated to bringing art to Black people.

Paintings with Black themes of struggle, repression and daily life are also found in the works of David Hammonds, Cliff Joseph, Faith Ringgold, Alvin Hollings, Benny Andrews, Milton Johnson, Joe Overstreet, Daniel Johnson, Ben Jones, Murray De Pillars, Malcolm Bailey, Ernest Trove, Lovett Thompson, Ernie Barnes and Mikelle Fletcher. Herman Kofi Bailey's *Unity*, Varnette Honeywood's *Gossip in the Sanctuary*, David Driskell's *Shango Gone*, John Bigger's *The Time of Edge, Nigeria* and *Web of Life "Ananse,"* Jacob Lawrence's *The Worker*, Vernell DeSilva's *Chicago Pool Hall* and *Harriet Tubman*; and Murray De Pillars' *People of the Sun* are definitive period pieces also.

Mixed media assemblages include Noah Purifoy's *Sir Watts*, Bettye Ann Saar's *Nine Mojo Secrets*, John Outterbridge's *Shoeshine Box*, and Kay Brown's *Take It Now*. In sculpture,

Margaret Burrough's *Head* and Doyle Foreman's *Corner* with their African projections stands out. And in graphic processes, Ruth Waddy's *The Key*, Jeff Donaldson's *Victory in the Valley of Eshu*, and Carol Ward's *Foloyan* are strong examples of African and African American focus. Examples of these and all others listed above can be found in Lewis (1978), Driskell (1976) and Fine (1973).

7.3 BLACK MUSIC

African Origins

The African origins and character of Black music are well-documented (Southern, 1971; Meadows, 1979; Maultsby, 1979). Not only did Africans bring songs and dances but also brought and reconstructed musical instruments played in Africa such as the banjo, the balafo (xylophone), the musical bow, flutes, the elephant tusk horn, a kind of bagpipe, types of clarinets (dududen), trumpets made of wood and ivory, gongs, rattles, castanets, the quill or panpipes, the sansa or thumb piano and, of course, the drum. Harold Courlander (1963) gives a detailed discussion of Africa-derived instruments played by African Americans. Moreover, as Eddie Meadows (1979:185) notes, "the performance practices, melodies, rhythms, and aesthetic musical practices of today's Black Americans are only a mirror of the practices of their African forefathers and mothers."

None of this means that Africans in the U.S. did not borrow from their new environment, for they did (Levine, 1977). But as Portia Maultsby (1979:200-21) states, "these elements were recycled through the concepts and aesthetic principles that defined the musical tradition of the Africans." For example, melodies, rhythms, texts, and tempos were changed and shouts, calls, words, clapping, footstomping and body movements were added to give them an African character. The first music Blacks sang in the U.S., then, were songs from Africa. These included war songs and holiday songs in their own languages. However, fearing rebellions and plots, the slaveholders moved to prohibit both African songs and languages as well as instruments like drums which could be used for communication.

The Spirituals

Following African tradition, early African Americans distinguished many different types among their songs according to how they were used (Southern, 1971:175). Given the religiousness of Africans, the largest number of songs in the antebellum or pre-Civil War period were religious songs or spirituals. DuBois (1969) in 1903 was the first scholar to pay deserved attention to the beauty and significance of the spirituals. He saw these "sorrow songs" of enslaved and disappointed Africans as a message to the world in their expression of "faith in the ultimate justice in the world."

There are three basic approaches to the interpretation of the spirituals, i.e., that they are: 1) essentially social; 2) essentially religious; and 3) a synthesis of both the social and religious. John Lovell (1969) and Mark Fisher (1953) see them as essentially expressions of social strivings and struggle whose themes are: 1) the desire for freedom, justice and penalty for the oppressor; 2) criticism of the existing order; and 3) coded messages of escape, meetings and struggle. "Go Down Moses," "Swing Low Sweet Chariot," "Oh Freedom, Oh Freedom," "Before I'd Be A Slave I'd Be Buried In My Grave," "If I Had My Way I'd Tear This Building Down," "Oh Mary Don't You Weep, Don't You Mourn," "My Lord Delivered Daniel," and "No More Auction Block For Me," etc. are examples of social themes within the spirituals.

Secondly, Howard Thurman (1947) and Benjamin Mays (1968) saw the spirituals as essentially religious. Thurman (1947:12) contended that "The clue to the meaning of the spirituals is to be found in religious experience and spiritual discernment." He saw them as a religious expression of the enslaved African's struggle to maintain his/her dignity, personality and human spirit and transcend the context dedicated to their destruction. Mays (1968:21) argues that the spirituals are rooted in the "compensatory idea that God will bring His own out victoriously in the end." The compensatory aspect, then is rooted in a religious force and outcome, not social ones.

Finally, James Cone (1972) sees the need for a synthesis for the two interpretations. He (1972:20) contends that "no theological interpretation of the Black spirituals can be valid that ignores the cultural environment that created them." The enslaved African found him/herself in a violent, brutal and dehumanizing environment and he/she offered both social and religious resistance. Spirituals, Cone concludes, are a religious expression of resistance. They are reinforcement of identity and dignity, an expression of the use of religion as a "source of strength in a time of trouble" and "a vibrant affirmation of life and its possibilities in an appropriate aesthetic form" (Cone, 1972:32-33).

Songs of Work and Leisure

Work songs, as Eileen Southern (1971:177) notes, grew out of work activity in the fields, in prisons, on roads, on the waterfront, on railroads, and other worksites. Essentially, this was not only psychic relief from tedium, but also depicted graphically the worker's situation and built on a sense of shared responsibility and fate (Roberts, 1974:140ff). Especially relevant were heroic work songs like "John Henry" which showed Blacks defeating "white society on its own terms" by smashing its expectations and the stereotypes, by insisting that their lives transcend the traditional models and roles established for them and their people by the white majority" (Levine, 1977:420)

Southern (1971:182) also lists dance songs and play songs often called "fiddle songs," "devil songs," etc. As the names suggest, these were recreational songs. In addition, there were also narrative songs, satirical songs and field and street cries. All these reflected Blacks' aesthetic expression created in the midst of giving beauty and color to a hostile and challenge-filled world.

The Blues

It is important to stress here how each kind of Black music, both religious and secular, reaffirms and reinforces the functional, collective and committing character of Black art forms. All truly African art was/is rooted in and reflective of life-situations, aspirations and possibilities. Thus, Black music, as an art form, expresses these characteristics. This is clear in blues which began to take form in the late nineteenth century and "by the twentieth century had become a major form of Black expression" (Maultsby, 1979:203).

Cone (1972:112) argues that blues are secular spirituals; secular in their focus on this world, the body and spiritual in that "they are impelled by the same search for the truth of the Black experience." According to Leroi Jones (1963:18), "the immediate predecessors of blues were the African American...work songs which had their origins in West Africa." Maultsby contends that Blues is rooted in both secular and religious musical traditions, citing the training blues singers had in church, their singing of both hymns and blues, the tendency to call on the Lord while expressing deep sorrow, etc.

Blues, then, is rooted in the totality of the Black experience in the U.S. and the historical and social burden of being Black in a racist society which this implied, i.e., exploitation and oppression, loss of love, "hard rows to hoe," bad news and worse dreams, drinking and loving hard, resignation, reaffirmation and above all durability. In an earlier article on Black art, I (Karenga, 1971) criticized blues as being essentially focused on resignation, but as my critics have rightly observed, blues is much more multidimensional than that (Neal, 1972).

Thus, blues speaks of: Black beauty; woman so good looking "make a bulldog break his chain and a snail to catch a train; being down and out, "sometimes I feel like nothing, somethin' th'owed away, Then I get my g'itar and play the blues all day;" defiant dignity, "I'd rather drink muddy water, sleep in a hollow log, dan stay in this town and be treated like a dirty dog;" sexual betrayal, "went out this morning left my gate unlatched, come back home, found that boy in my potato patch;" plea bargaining, "come back baby, please don't go, cuz the way I love you baby, you'll never know," and social criticism, "Uncle Sam ain't no woman, but he sure can take yo' man. Boys der got'em in the service, doin something I cain' understand."

Some of the more important names in blues are William C. Handy, considered the "Father of the Blues," who first published "Memphis Blues," in 1912 and in 1914, "St. Louis Blues" which made Blues a household word around the world; Ma Rainey, the first professional Blues singer, considered "Queen of the Blues;" Billie Holiday; John Lee Hooker; Leadbelly; Muddy Waters; Sara Martin; Blind Lemon Jefferson, B.B. King; Bobby Blue Bland; Nina Simone; Lightnin Hopkins; Aaron T-Bone Walker, "Sonny Boy" Williamson; Bessie Smith; Alberta Hunter; Josh White and Ray Charles.

Ragtime

Ragtime, like blues and spirituals, was another early manifestation of distinct African American music. Because it was associated primarily with the piano, it evolved after enslavement when Blacks had access to the instrument. It was especially designed for Black consumption and was played by Black musicians anonymously and known in eating places, saloons, riverside dives, honky tonk spots and later clubs. Ragtime composers were many. Among the earliest were Irving Jones and Cris Smith. Others were Scott Joplin, the "King of Ragtime," whose music was made popular in the 70's by the movie *Sting*; Thomas Turpin, "Father of St. Louis Ragtime," Joe Jordan; Eubie Blake; James Scott; Scott Hayden and Louis Chauvin.

Gospel Music

Gospel music rose out of the late 19th century and early 20th century folk church as opposed to the 20th century middle class church (Williams-Jones, 1975; Heilbut, 1975)). Essentially, it is created in a context of individual and collective spontaneity, improvisation for church service and are thus called "church songs." Methodist minister Charles Albert Tindley, the pioneer gospel song creator, wrote his first songs in the early 1900's. And Thomas Dorsey, another pioneer, contributed to the gospel idiom "a ragtime, boogie woogie piano style, his blues-based melodies, harmonies and an interest in religious spirit and faith" (Maultsby, 1979:204). From this instrumentation, chants, calls, handclapping and footstomping were added in the free creativity and expression characteristic of folk environments. Some of the most notable gospel singers are Mahalia Jackson, James Cleveland, Clara Ward, Marion Williams, Rosetta Tharpe, Sallie Maetin, Mother Smith, Bessie Griffin, Golden Gate Quartet, the Sensational Nightingales, the Dixie Humming Birds, Ruth David and the Staple Singers.

The Emergence of Jazz

Eileen Southern (1971:374) states that "the fusion of blues and ragtime with brass band and syncopated dance music resulted in a music called Jazz, a music with its own characteristics." Jazz started in New Orleans with pioneers like King Oliver and his Creole Band; Jelly Roll Morton and his Red Hot Peppers, Louis Satchmo Armstrong with his Hot Five and Hot Seven and clarinetist John Dodds. From New Orleans, jazz moved in the 20's to the Chicago Southside. In addition, big bands like those of Chick Webb, Jimmie Lunceford, Cab Calloway, Erskine Hawkins, Lionel Hampton, Count Basie and Duke Ellington also emerged in the 20's.

With jazz several styles developed among which were: swing in the 30's associated with Duke Ellington and big bands;

bop in the early 40's which evolved into hardbop or soul jazz in the 50's represented by Dizzy Gillespie, Thelonius Monk, Kenny Clarke, Charlie Christian, Lester Young, Jimmie Blanton, Charlie Parker, Bud Powell, Miles Davis, Earl Hines, Max Roach, Art Blakey, Horace Silver, Nat and Cannonball Adderley, Sonny Rollins, avant garde in the late 50's exemplified by Ornette Coleman, John Coltrane, Cecil Taylor, Charles Mingus and Eric Dolphy. In addition, Sun Ra, Pharoah Saunders, Albert Ayler, Don Ayler, Marion Brown and Archie Shepp have shown impressive originality.

There are obviously too many Black musicians to be listed in this short overview, but it is important to mention musical greats like jazz singers Ella Fitzgerald, Billie Holiday, King Pleasure, Dinah Washington, Lena Horne, Joe Williams, Sarah Vaughan, Nancy Wilson, Arthur Prysock and pianists Fats Waller, Errol Garner, Hazel Scott and trumpeter Donald Byrd.

Rhythm and Blues

Rhythm and blues emerged during the 40's and 50's, but reached its height in the 60's. Essentially an urban product, it reflected a self-conscious identity, cohesiveness and focus on love, combining elements of pop, gospel and blues traditions. In the 60's rhythm and blues became "Soul" music, a further indication of its identification with the Black Power thrusts of the 60's. Stress was placed on distinctiveness from white music, Black self-respect and self-celebration of soul. This is by far the most popular music among Blacks, although it is constantly challenged by commercial attempts to absorb and dilute it and deprive it of its distinctiveness as in the case of disco.

Some of the notable names in the 60's were James Brown *I'm Black and I'm Proud*, Mr. Soul; Aretha Franklin *Respect*, Ms. Soul; Otis Redding *Sitting on the Dock of the Bay*; Chuck Berry; The Four Tops; Curtis Mayfield; The Impressions *We're A Winner*; Marvin Gaye and Tammy Terrell *Ain't No Mountain High Enough*; The Supremes *Love is Like An Itchin In My Heart*;

Gladys Knight and the Pips; The Temptations *My Girl*; *Message From A Black Man*; Al Green *Let's Stay Together*; Sam Cooke *Change Gon' Come*; Smokey Robinson *I'll Try Something New*; Nina Simone *Young, Gifted and Black*; Ray Charles, Les McCann and others. (Current artists are assumed to be familiar so there is little need to list them.)

Given the influence music has on Black life, there is a continuous discussion on how to make it better serve the interests of Blacks. This questions becomes especially urgent in terms of rhythm and blues which is the most popular music among Blacks, and which has not only lost its social consciousness for the most part but is losing its distinctiveness as Black music (George, 1988). One cannot help but notice the contrast between the race and socially conscious quality music of the 60's and the insipid, socially irresponsible, raw sex-focused music of today. What one is witnessing, as disco most vividly showed, is the merciless drive of the music industry to make money, reducing all music to a homogenized packageable sound, regardless of its effect on social life, aesthetics or a rich Black heritage (Byrd, 1978). In the early 20's, Alain Locke (1969:45) had argued, Black music had become "tarnished with commercialism and the dust of the market place," and that Black musicians were "in commercial enslavement to the Shylocks of Tin Pan Alley and in artistic bondage to the cash of...dance halls and vaudeville stages." If this were true then, it is obviously even more so now (Byrd, 1978; Ashburne, 1977).

Few artists are strong or politically conscious enough to oppose the tide of commercialism and create the race-and socially-conscious model and music which so marked the 60's. Paul Robeson stands as a model in the past of the socially conscious artist who excelled aesthetically and refused to compromise politically (Dent, 1976). Most recently, Terry Callier "Be A Believer," "African Violet" and "Martin Street Martin," and especially Gil Scott-Heron stand out as models of artists who have a high level of aesthetic achievement and social consciousness. As Kalamu ya Salaam (1982:12) states, "Scott-Heron represents the most socially conscious element of (the message-music) tradition." His hits, among which are "The Revolution Will Not Be Televised," "The Bottle," an attack on alcoholism, "We Almost Lost Detroit," a criticism of nuclear power, and "Angel Dust," an appeal to youth to avoid it, all demonstrate a commendable aesthetic and socially conscious quality.

The Challenge of Rap

This concern for socially conscious music led African Americans in the 70's to embrace and support reggae for its social commentary and criticism and then turn to socially conscious rap to celebrate community and reaffirm the necessity of the struggle (George, 1988:188f; Spencer, 1991; Eure and Spady, 1991). Although rap emerges in the 70's, it is in the 80's that it becomes a wide-spread definitive statement of new Black music. Ronald Stephens (1991) is correct, however, to put the origins of rap back even further within the context of Black musical history as well as the African cultural tradition of Nommo or oratory (Asante, 1987:59ff; Toop, 1984:19; Smither-man, 1973). The form clearly evolves in the tradition of oratorial modes such as "signifying" and "playing the dozens" as well as "rapping" in both the sense of political discourse and romantic "programming," in a word, the sense of skilled word use to achieve given ends.

Artists like King Pleasure, Eddie Vinson and Joe Williams created modes of singing-talking that already prefigured rap in the pre-60's period. Later, the Last Poets, Gil Scott-Heron and the Watts Prophets in the 60's and 70's continued the tradition adding to it their own unique contribution (Williams, 1992). Thus, as Ceola Ross Baber (1984:104) notes, "Master rappers of today are keeping alive and visible the tradition of African American artistry in communication, like all those unnamed Blacks who toasted B'rer Rabbit, Stagolee, or some other fictitious character; like the authors and lyrics who have praised Black perseverance in poem and song; and like all the average Black Americans who speak poetically and poignantly of their experiences, and who give rhythm and sense to their daily existence through music of rhyming speech."

Rap, then, evolved from an ancient tradition passing through modern forms of that tradition and emerging in night clubs and the streets of New York in the mid-seventies. Names of major figures include D.J. Hollywood, Kurtis Blow, Eddie Cheebu, D.J. Lovebug, Starsky, Junebug Starski, Grandmaster Flash and the Furious Five, Afrika Bambaataa, Melle Mel, Whodini, Russell and Joey. Rap gets its definitive push on the national and international scene with Sylvia and Joe Robinson's recording of the Sugar Hill Gang's "Rapper's Delight" in 1979, which sold over 2 million copies. From this point on rap becomes a major and engaging African American music form.

It is important here to note that there are various schools of rap music defined by their self-definition and lyrical stress (Powell, 1991). The first kind is a teacher-rap or nation-conscious rap which stresses social consciousness, social commitment and struggle (Eure and Spady, 1991). This includes rap by KRS-One, Arrested Development, Def Jef, Poor Righteous Teachers, X-Clan, Sister Souljah, Queen Latifah, Kool Moe Dee, Prince Akeem, Boogie Down Productions, and perhaps the premier nation-conscious group, Public Enemy, as well as many others. A second major form of rap is 'gangsta rap' represented by rappers like NWA, Ice Cube, Ice T and BWA. Thirdly, there is a player/lover rap represented by LL Cool J, Salt n' Pepa et al. Fourthly, there is porno rap as reflected in the lyrics of 2 Live Crew et al. Although these are the major forms of rap, there are other forms which can be categorized differently, and even these forms are not always clear cut. On the contrary, they often overlap and resemble each other.

Rap, unlike any music before it, initiates a passionate discourse of supporters and critics. Essentially this is because of its dual character and mixed messages and its relevance to both youth culture and the Black musical tradition (*Black Collegian*, 1990). Rap's relevance begins with its providing a much-needed challenge to the crossover tendency of many Black artists such as Prince and Michael Jackson (George, 1988). This tendency included denial of Blackness, servile attempts to appeal to white audiences through both alteration of music and physical features and claiming a desperate and vague universality which denied African authenticity. This created the basis for white co-optation of Black music in sound and market, and the initiation of a trend which Nelson George calls "the death of rhythm and blues." And, although rhythm and blues did not die, it was for a brief period rendered less vigorous. Ironically, however, as crossover artists abandoned their rootedness in Black music, white artists, especially those from Britain, began to sing Black music, reviving old songs and making them popular. Also, rap artists, while often denying their debt to predecessors in rhythm and blues, nevertheless add depth and color to their rap by using R & B music as background.

Rap's relevance begins with its reaffirming the creativity and distinctiveness of Black music. Moreover, it carved out a space for independent Black artists and companies though eventually most succumbed to capitalist cooptation. Thirdly, rap rebuilt an eroding sense of community among Black youth, spoke to them in a special way and at its best, i.e., nation-consciousness rap, contributed in a significant way to conscious raising. Fourthly, rap helped rebuild an equally eroding sense of community among Black musicians who, since the introduction of mechanization of music, began to lose both the opportunity and ability to build community along the model of the earlier jazz community which was so interactive, mutually supportive and creatively challenging. Fifthly, rap's relevance lies also in its reintroducing in its nation-consciousness form a political discourse in African American music which was missing since the sixties. It thus became a way to both criticize and understand U.S. society.

Rap, however, because of its varied forms brings mixed messages which divides its history into both the relevant and positive and the problematic and negative. The first problem rap poses is its sexist character (Peterson-Lewis, 1991). It demeans the Black woman, reducing her to her genitals and an objectified instrument of male gratification, and preaches violent domination of the woman. Moreover, closely related to this is the widespread vulgar character of 'gangsta' and porno rap, rejecting all boundaries under the amoral observation that people want it. Thirdly, 'gangsta' and porno rap are too often violent in a vulgarly individualistic way, pretending strength by symbolically claiming the power to destroy, injure, and maim. Also, such rap is extremely nihilistic, tending to destroy and dominate rather than propose creative or life affirming solutions. Fourthly, these negative forms of rap offer an easy vocabulary and image to stereotype Blacks and give license to racists to use anti-Black images and vocabularies. It is, at this level, the height of self-disrespect and self-mutilation, reducing oneself to mindless sexual and physical beings and calling each other and oneself "niggers," "bitches," "'ho's," "nasty," "freaks," etc.

Also, negative forms of rap pretend a *sui generis* origin for rap, dismissing a rich cultural history and drawing generational lines so typical of the European society these rappers claim to reject. Finally, even political rap has a tendency to claim a knowledge it does not have, a link with struggle it does not demonstrate, and a political relevance it still must prove. The point is that a song is not a revolution, and as Gil Scott-Heron says, "the revolution will not be televised," nor will it be the result of a song or series of songs. In the final analysis, Sekou Toure is instructive. For he says, "(t)o take part in the African revolution, it is not enough to write a revolutionary song; you must make the revolution with the people. If you make it with the people the songs will come by themselves and of themselves" (quoted in Fanon, 1968:167). What rap offers, then, is a promise, and this promise can only be realized in positive social practice.

The continuing need is for the *cultivation* and *support* of the positive in rap and in every other form of African American music. For in the final analysis, a people saves itself from social danger and disintegration or there is no hope for it. Moreover,

Blacks are for the most part Black artists' main customers and have the capacity to give or withhold support. Thus, if the records and concerts of negative artists were not bought or attended, raw sex, sexist labelling and assaults on Black women, the reductive translations of love and other negatives could not survive. And in place of much of the current music which has neither socially or aesthetically redeeming value, a music marked by race and social consciousness and solid aesthetic quality can and will re-emerge, and a rich distinctive Black heritage will be preserved and expanded. The success of such a project, however, will depend upon the success of the revival of the cultural and political development and struggles which characterized the Sixties. For without a cultural struggle to transform consciousness and the political struggle to acquire control of Black destiny and daily life, neither Black music nor Black lives will be shaped in their own image and interest.

7.4 BLACK LITERATURE

The Early Period I

Black literature does not begin with written aesthetic expressions but with oral ones. Although some African literature was written, much of it was not and still none of what was written was brought by enslaved Africans when they were brought to the Americas. Debate still rages on how much oral literature survived from Africa but every serious writer concedes a significant amount of African survivals (Courlander, 1976; Dorson, 1965). Moreover, as Arna Bontemps and Langston Hughes (1958) noted, in addition to Africanization, there was a parallel process of Americanization which translated as Africans' modifying characters and themselves in their literature to reflect more accurately their new experience in the U.S. Thus, the African animals--jackal, hare, tortoise and hyena--are translated in an American environment as the fox, rabbit, turtle or terrapin and wolf.

African American folklore is often associated with animal stories like B'rer Rabbit, made familiar to American audiences through Joel Chandler Harris' collection and publication of them in his *Uncle Remus: His Songs and Sayings* and Walt Disney who made them into a movie, *Song of the South*. But as Sterling Brown (1970) contends, it is important to note that there are much more kinds of folklore than the animal stories. Zora Neale Hurston (1935) in her collection, *Mules and Men*, Charles Chestnutt in the *Conjure Woman* (1889), Arthur Huff Fauset, Thomas Talley, and J. Mason Brewer all give an idea of the rich variousness of Black folklore.

From the above, several kinds of folklore emerge: 1) animal stories; 2) legendary hero stories; 3) human trickster stories; 4) exaggeration stories; 5) why stories; and 6) tales of satire. In animal stories, there is the theme of weakness overcoming strength through intelligence, skill and cleverness. B'rer Rabbit, B'rer Squirrel and other small animals outwit the larger slower ones. In legendary men stories, like those of Stagolee, African Americans are posed as defiant and rebellious or in colloquial terms "a bad, crazy nigger that don't take no shit from nobody, Black or white." In the ones like John Henry, they are posed as beating the white man at his own game, breaking stereotypes and winning against all odds. The human trickster is ol' John that outwits the white man playing on his ego--saying, "I went on the rid light cuz the whites were going on the green and I knew then it wasn't for me." The exaggeration stories in Hurston's collections have mosquitos sing like alligators, eat up the cow and then ring the bell for the calf or a man so fast he shoots at a deer, runs and catches the deer and holds him till the bullet hits him. Why stories give explanations of the origin of the world, races, division of labor, etc. And tales of satire lampoon the slaveholder and white man in general who figure with a crooked pencil, that "ought's a ought, figger's a figger, all for de white man, none for de nigger."

Although blues, spirituals and work songs can be considered folklore also, their treatment in the music section will be considered sufficient. It is important to note here that folklore though originally oral, took on a written form in the works of Charles Chestnutt, Paul Lawrence Dunbar, Earnest Gaines, George Henderson, Langston Hughes, Zora Neale Hurston, Claude McKay, Jean Toomer, Margaret Walker and Sarah Wright, J. Mason Brewer, Arthur Huff Fauset, Thomas Talley et al.

The Early Period II

A second early period of Black written literature began in 1746 with Lucy Terry's (1730-1821) poem on a Native American raid in Massachusetts which was the first known piece of literature by an African American (Whitlow, 1974:15). After her came Jupiter Hammond, poet and essayist and Phyllis Wheatley, who wrote the first Black book of poems by an African in English, *Poems on Various Subjects, Religious and Moral*, (1773). Narratives of enslaved Africans, Briton Hamon in 1760 and Oladah Equiano (Gustavus Vassa) in 1789, followed with Equiano's narrative being the most popular and detailed on life in Africa and during enslavement. These early writings are marked by a "redeemed Christian" mentality which is racially self-effacing and apologetic for enslavement, seeing it as God's way of rescuing them from savagery.

The 1800's

The 1800's marks a third period and the rise of what is commonly called "protest" literature, i.e., the speaking out strongly against the established state of things--enslavement, oppression, exploitation, racism. It is set in the midst of the revolts by enslaved Africans and other forms of resistance like abolitionism. Thus, almost all Black writers who published during this period wrote in the spirit of protest (Whitlow, 1974:29). George Moses Horton's (1797-1883) *Hope of Liberty*, James Whitefield's *America and other Poems*, Lucy Delany's

From Darkness Cometh the Light or *Struggles for Freedom* and
Frances Harper's *Poems on Miscellaneous Subjects* all indict the
slave system for its injustice and brutality. In this period also
autobiographies were written by Frederick Douglass (1817-1895),
Life and Times, a brilliant well-written autobiography with strong
political content; Harriet Jacobs, *Incidents in the Life of a Slave
Girl*, and by William Wells Brown, the *Narrative of William Wells
Brown*. Also, Brown wrote three novels and three plays. The first
novel *Clotel: or the President's Daughter* was written in 1853 and
was the first Black novel. The earliest novel by a Black woman
was *Our Nig; or Sketches from the Life of a Free Black* (1859)
written by Harriet Wilson. Other novelists were Frank Webb,
The Garies and Their Friends; Frances Harper, *Iola Leroy*, which
criticizes the failure of Reconstruction and the racism which
followed; and Martin Delaney, *Blake*. Delaney also wrote a major
political work, *The Condition, Elevation, Emigration* and *Destiny
of the Colored People of the United States*. Also included in this
period are the classic feminist writings of Anna J. Cooper, *A
Voice From the South* (1892).

The Pre-Harlem Renaissance Period

The pre-Harlem Renaissance period begins with publication of poetry by one of Afro-America's most gifted poets, Paul
Lawrence Dunbar. Dunbar is well-known for his poetry in
African American idiom like when "Malindy Sings," "The
Antebellum Sermon" and "Keep A Plugging Away." But he also
wrote short stories and a novel. His works were, however,
consciously unpolitical to accommodate the fact that his main
audience was white. The Black middle class was embarrassed by
his use of folk language instead of standard English.

Charles Chestnutt is know for his *Conjure Woman* and
Other Tales, based on folklore heard in North Carolina and
narrated by Uncle Julius, a shrewd African who was formerly
enslaved and now manipulates his employer with these tales.
However, he also wrote short stories and three novels. James

Weldon Johnson spans two main periods in African American literature. He wrote his novel, *Autobiography of An Ex-Colored Man in 1912, God's Trombones, Seven Negro Sermons* in verse in 1927, *Black Manhattan*, an excellent study of Black culture in 1930 and his autobiography *Along This Way* in 1933. His poetic sermon, "The Creation," is considered a classic. Also Johnson wrote the Black National Anthem, "Lift Every Voice and Sing" along with his brother, John Rosamond Johnson. Ida B. Wells joined literature with political activism, writing essays critical of lynching and racism in general. She is most known for her essays *Southern Horror* and *A Red Record*. W.E.B. DuBois wrote in this period also. In addition to his social and political writings, he wrote five novels and a volume of poetry. His most known piece during this period was his *Souls of Black Folk* in 1903. Finally, Pauline Hopkins wrote four novels and many short stories in this period. Her first novel was *Contending Forces* (1900). She was also founding editor of the *Colored American Magazine*, the first monthly magazine dedicated to African American art and literature, with a readership extending to China, Hawaii, Manila and the West Indies (Carby, 1987:125ff).

The Harlem Renaissance

The Harlem Renaissance was one of Black writers' most prolific periods (Huggins, 1979). It was a time when Harlem became the capital of Black America; African Americans looked to their African roots for revitalization; Marcus Garvey issued the call for Black self-respect and power and the rescue and reconstruction of Africa (Garvey, 1977); and Alain Locke (1969), the main interpreter of the Renaissance, announced the coming into being of the "New Negro." In fact, Garvey's and Locke's influence on the Harlem Renaissance cannot be overestimated. Garvey's ideological and political push for respect, African heritage and race pride, coincided with Locke's stress on the need for examination and use of the African ancestral legacy. And although Garvey was misunderstood and often maligned by the writers of this period, it is safe to assume he and his movement are significantly responsible for their stress on Black culture and consciousness (Martin, 1983).

Locke's *The New Negro* is a classic and his most known work, but he wrote and edited other works on Black culture, i.e., *Four Negro Poets*, *The Negro in Art*, and *The Negro and His Music*. Claude McKay was one of the most militant writers of the Renaissance. His "If We Must Die" in 1917 which calls for Blacks not to die like dogs but to fight the "murderous cowardly pack" is definitive and is considered by some to be the beginning of the Renaissance. His *Home to Harlem* is also well-known. Jean Toomer's *Cane*, a collection of prose and poems; Countee Cullen's collection of poems, *Copper Sun*; Nella Larsen's novel *Quicksand*; and Langston Hughes classic poem, "The Negro Speaks of Rivers," his dozen books of poetry and two autobiographies, *The Big Sea* and *I Wonder as I Wander*, stand out as definitive of the period. Also included in this period is Jessie Fauset's *There is Confusion* and *Plum Bun*. Later she would also write *The Chinaberry Tree* and *Comedy American Style*.

The Depression of 1929 marked the slowing of the prolific writing of the Renaissance. New writers emerged such as Zora Neale Hurston, *Mules and Men* (folktales), three novels and a satire on America race relations--*Jonah's Gourd Vine, Their Eyes Were Watching God, Tell My Horse, Moses, Man of the Mountain* and *Dust Tracks on a Road* (autobiography); and Arna Bontemps' three novels, *Black Thunder, Drums at Dusk* and *God Sends Sunday*.

In the period of 1940-1960, Richard Wright stands out as a giant with his classic novel, *Native Son*, and his autobiography *Black Boy*. He established a school of writing called Urban Realism, a rough unadorned exposure and critical depiction of urban Black life. Among the writers who were included in this school were Chester Himes, *If He Hollers Let Him Go*, and Ann Petry, *The Street*. Ralph Ellison's work *Invisible Man* (1952), is another Black classic of this period in which he poses Blacks as invisible in a racist society and in search of a solid identity.

James Baldwin is a multi-talented essayist, novelist and play-
wright of this period. Among his works are the novel, *Go Tell It
On the Mountain* (1953); an essay, *The Fire Next Time* (1963); a
play, *The Amen Corner* (1967); and his latest novel *Just Above My
Head* (1982).

Gwendolyn Brooks emerges in this period also. She is
obviously one of the most gifted poets in the U.S. having won the
Pulitzer Prize for Poetry for her collection, *Annie Allen in* 1950.
She was the first Black to receive the award. Moreover, she
wrote *Maud Martha* (1953). She continues to write, lecture
around the country and aid young aspiring poets. Margaret
Walker is known for classic poem, *For My People* and her novel,
Jubilee. Her poem written in free verse is a praise poem to the
life, struggle, adaptive vitality, durability, strength and achievement of Blacks. It is also a call for struggle and a new social
order. Robert Hayden has published five volumes of poems,
among which are *A Ballad of Remembrance* and *Words in the
Mourning Time*. Lorraine Hansberry's play, *A Raisin in the Sun*,
was a successful Broadway production and marked a high point
in critical achievement and recognition for Black drama.

The Sixties

The Sixties is considered by many a Second Black Renaissance (Bigsby, 1979). It produced and was produced by both
literary and political diversity and multiplicity. It was, as argued
in Chapter II, Blacks' most significant decade in terms of self-
conscious goals and achievements. The Harlem Renaissance was
in part fostered by white patrons and declined with their
withdrawal after the Crash of '29. But the Sixties was self-
generating, self-determining and self-sustaining. Its literary
personalities are often known in political as well as literary
circles, for the decade demanded a merging of the political and
the literary. Larry Neal, Askia M. Toure, Ishmael Reed, Amiri
Baraka, Sonia Sanchez, Nikki Giovanni, Mari Evans, Etheridge
Knight, A.B. Spellman, Johari Amini, June Jordan, Quincy

Troupe, Lucille Clifton, Stanley Crouch, Joe Goncalves (Dinga-an), Carolyn Rodgers, Yusef Iman, Ed Bullins, James Randall, Stephany, Conrad Rivers, Eugene Redmond, Haki Madhubuti and Kalamu ya Salaam are but a few examples of Black socially conscious writers (Randall, 1971). Many of the above wrote poetry, drama and prose.

Definitive of this period are Sonia Sanchez's *We a Badd-DDD People*; Amiri Baraka's *Black Magic Poetry 1961-67* and *Four Revolutionary Plays*; Johari Amini's *Black Essence*; Haki Madhubuti's *We Walk The Way of the New World*; June Jordan's *Who Look at Me*; Ishmael Reed's *Yellow Back Radio Broke-Down*; Ed Bullins *New Plays From the Black Theatre*; Larry Neal's and Leroi Jones' (Baraka) *Black Fire*, Mari Evans' *I'm A Black Woman*, Etheridge Knight's *Poems from Prison*; Nikki Giovanni's *Black Feeling Black Talk*; and John Williams' *The Man Who Cried I Am*.

The Seventies

The Seventies saw the emergence of Alice Walker whose credits include novels, *Meridian*, poetry, *Revolutionary Petunia* and short stories, *In Love and In Struggle*; novelist Toni Morrison who had then written four novels and whose *Song of Solomon* won the Best Novel of the Year Award in 1977; and a long list of Black poetesses and poets who have published in the Black literature issues of the Black scholar, '71, '75, '78 and '81. Notable also are the new poetry of Sonia Sanchez, *I've Been A Woman*, Mari Evan's *Night Star*; Bell's, Parker's and Guy-Sheftalls, *Sturdy Black Bridges: Visions of Black Women in Literature;* Gwendolyn Brooks' anthology of new Chicago poets, *Jump Bad*, Maya Angelou's *I Know Why the Caged Bird Sings*, Kalamu ya Salaam's *Revolutionary Love*, and Eugene Redmond's *Drum Voices: The Mission of African American Poetry*.

Although these writings do not have the self-conscious urgency and fire of the 60's, they, nevertheless, like the literature of the 60's and other periods, speak the truth of Black people, i.e., their hopes, aspirations, love and constant struggle to have a full and free life. Thus, by teaching beauty in the midst of ugliness and strength and durability under stress and strain, they inspire and teach possibilities which, as argued at the outset, is the fundamental function of African American literature.

The Eighties and Nineties

Literature in the 80's and 90's is marked by several distinguishing features. The first of these is the overwhelming predominance of works by and about Black women. This surge begins in the 70's and reaches its height in the 80's. In the 80's this process seems to be defined by Alice Walker's *The Color Purple* (1982) which won a Pulitzer Prize and initiated a rather passionate discourse which ran the gamut of topics from the quality of Black male-female relations to the political use of the book by the dominant society to indict the Black community and reaffirm its racist conceptions and practices. Drawing both avid supporters and critics, the book nevertheless was a kind of literary omen of both the predominant women-focused character of the coming literature and the larger society's interest in or preference for publishing it.

Other notable works were Toni Morrison's *Beloved* (1987) which also received a Pulitzer Prize; Gloria Naylor's *Women of Brewster Place* (1982), Ntozake Shange's *Betsy Brown* (1985); Paule Marshall's *Praise Song for the Widow* (1983); Sonia Sanchez's *Home Girls and Hand Grenades* (1984) and *Under a Soprano Sky* (1987); June Jordan's *Passion: New Poems, 1977-1980* (1980) and *Living Room: New Poems 1980-1984* (1985); Audre Lorde's *Chosen Poems: Old and New* (1982) and *Our Dead Behind Us* (1986); Sherley Anne Williams *Dessa Rose* (1986); Maya Angelou's *All of God's Children Need Travelling Shoes* (1986); and Rita Dove's *The Yellow House on the Corner* and *Thomas and Beulah* (1986) for which she won a Pulitzer Prize and became the only Black woman since Gwendolyn Brooks' award to win the Pulitzer Prize for Poetry. Certainly notable also is Henry Louis Gates, Jr.'s editing of the *Schomburg Library of Nineteenth Century Black Women Writers* (1988), a forty-volume set of prominent texts by Black women from 1890-1910.

Finally, among women writers no one has emerged as quickly and distinctively as Terry McMillan. Her *Waiting to Exhale* became both a tremendous commercial success and a major literary achievement which, while resembling other major women writers' approach, differed in significant ways. First, McMillan, although critical of Black male-female relations as Walker, Naylor, Shange et al, nevertheless maintains an open-textured posture toward reconciliation and reconstruction. Secondly, her women characters are more self-critical and her criticism of Black men appears more as a challenge to them to self-correct than a condemnation. Thirdly, she writes in a popular style and has created a mass reading audience which differs from the academic style and audience many other Black women writers have cultivated.

Black men continued to write, of course, but were less prominent and less published, causing some authors and critics to suggest the publishing industry was both disinterested in and hostile to works by and about Black men. Nevertheless, important works by Black men did emerge. Among these were John Edgar Wideman's *Brothers and Keepers* (1984); August Wilson's *Fences* (1985) for which he won a Pulitzer Prize; Ishmael Reed's *Reckless Eyeballing* (1986); Henry Dumas' *Goodbye Sweetwater* (1988); Jay Wright's *The Double Invention of Komo* (1980); Haki Madhubuti's *Earthquakes and Sunrise Missions* (1984), *Killing Memory, Seeking Ancestors* (1987) and *Say that the River Turns: The Impact of Gwendolyn Brooks* (1987); and Etheridge Knight's *Born of a Woman: New and Selected Poems* (1980). Worthy of note also are the anthologies by Terry McMillan, *Breaking Ice* (1990); Henry Louis Gates, Jr. *Reading Black, Reading Feminist* (1990); and Frank McGill, *Master Plots of African American Literature* (1992).

A second defining characteristic of the Eighties and early Nineties is the continuing expansion of African American literary criticism. This includes both a general criticism as well as a specific womanist or Black woman's criticism. Among works in this genre are: Mari Evans' *Black Women Writers: A Critical Introduction* (1984); Gloria Wade-Gayles' *No Crystal Stair: Visions of Race and Sex in Black Women's Fiction* (1984); Barbara Christian's *Black Feminist Criticism: Perspectives on Black Women Writers* (1985); Hazel Carby's *Reconstructing Womanhood: The Emergence of the Afro-American Woman Novelist* (1987); Henry Louis Gates, Jr.'s *Figures in Black: Words, Signs and the 'Racial' Self* (1987) and *Loose Cannons: Notes on Cultural Wars* (1992); Charles Johnson's *Being and Race: Black Writing Since the 1970's* (1988); Houston Baker, Jr.'s and Patricia Redmond's *Afro-American Literary Study in the 1990's* (1989); Fred Lee Hord's *Reconstructing Memory: Black Literary Criticism* (1991); Houston Baker Jr.,'s *Workings of the Spirit: The Poetics of Afro-American Women's Writing* (1991); and Toni Morrison's *Playing in the Dark* (1992).

A third feature of the writing of this period is a tendency for the authors to distance themselves from the long literary tradition of social engagement as members of the African American community. This problematic distancing is achieved in several ways. First, there is a tendency to privilege the vaguely universal and human at the expense of the particular and the African. This is done first in the spirit and language of deconstructionism with critiques of racial essentialism and calls for focus on the specificity of the texts," which is supposed to "reveal a depth and range of culture details far beyond the economic exploitation of Blacks by whites" (Gates, 1992:101). From these "close readings of the text," it is argued, one learns to invent oneself and the other and rejects the preconstituted racial self." For Gates (1992:151) the project of the new generation of writers "is about affinities, unburdened by an ideology of descent; it speaks about blackness without blood" and sees race as a trope, i.e., a mere problematic figure of speech.

A second mode of distancing and creating what Trey Ellis calls "a new Black aesthetic" is to privilege gender over racial or ethnic concerns. Such a posture, while giving necessary voice to Black women, can and often does treat gender concerns as exclusive of and often hostile to ethnic concerns. In fact, appeals to ethnicity are often seen as ways to stifle women's voices and equate the race with men. As an important text states in its title, *All the Women are white, All the Blacks are Men, But Some of Us are Brave*, (Hull, Scott, Smith, 1982). And as Deborah McDowell (1989:59) contends, focus on race "is often almost tantamount to focus on maleness." Thus, she advocates a women's literature free from race conscious concerns and transcending social and linguistic boundaries. It is important to note that not all women writers separate race and gender struggle, but those who do contribute to the transformation of the tradition of engaged literature.

A third way of distancing from the historical tradition of an engaged Black literature is to declare literature and text exempt from the burden of history and community and essentially an individual author's context for invention and reinvention of self, a self no longer "shocked," "surprised" or "enraged" by racism as Trey Ellis states (McMillan, 1990:xxi). Self-focus is privileged here over collective concerns or self-in-community. For these writers, speaking deconstructionist language, the self is fluid, ambiguous, contradictory and hardly a candidate for the unchanging essence of race or ethnicity. Loyalties and relationships to various social groups are ambiguous, complex and constantly shifting. What is key, then, is not the community or group, but "self."

Deborah E. McDowell (1989:55) notes that "...Afro-American literary criticism has finally seen the beginnings of a paradigm shift, one that has extended the boundaries and altered the terms of inquiry." She goes on to say that "falling in step with recent developments in contemporary critical theory, some critics of Afro-American literature have usefully complicated some of our most common assumptions about self, and about race as a meaningful category in literary study and critical theory." This paradigm shift, of course, is not only in literary criticism, but also in the literature itself. And thus, self, in the making and constantly in transition and contradiction, becomes the replacement for the person-in-community, and one who is socially conscious and committed to liberation and a higher level of human life. According to this argument, the focus on struggle is limited and limiting. Indeed, the self must have no boundaries, no fixed identities and thus cannot be concerned with defense of cultural borders it does not recognize, nor with ethnic loyalties it does not feel compelled to maintain.

A final development in the literature of the 80's and early 90's is the assumption of a relevance for literature equal or even superior to social science in understanding the Black experience. Many writers and their supporters have argued that literature can and often does yield a more accurate portrait of Black life than the social sciences. Such a claim can best be seen in the discourse around *The Color Purple* which became a text that for many offered a more accurate assessment of the Black family than the works of sociologists such as Harriet McAdoo, Nathan and Julia Hare, Robert Staples, Andrew Billingsley et al.

Moreover, in major universities this same text becomes, for various interrelated reasons, the central text to explain Black culture and history in multicultural classes. Thus literature, even as fiction and personal imagination, is used as an alternative to a social scientific understanding of Black life rather than as a contribution to a holistic understanding of it. In other words, personal subjectivity is privileged over social science study and a novel or short story becomes the most important and at times only way one understands Black life.

This privileging of literature over social science data takes place in a context where humanities discourse in general becomes more important and frequent than discussion of real life. In such a context of privileging humanities, history is reduced to a Rap song, relationships to imaginative revelations of a novel or short story, and the complexity and achievement of a world historical man reduced to the banality of a comedic movie. This is clearly a problematic deserving a creative solution. For although one can easily concede the importance of literature to life, given its personal and subjective character, it cannot serve as an alternative to an objective study of life nor as a substitute for the social struggle to enrich and expand it. A sociology of this problematic development suggests that its life and tenure fit well within the interests and ideology of the established order. For emphasis on the personal at the expense of the social, and discussion of literature rather than its source, i.e., concrete life, is less likely to pose a threat to the existing social power and wealth relations. In fact, this discourse is by its own definition detached from its social source, and instead is rooted and developed essentially in and through the text itself. Such a discourse, then, is not a social analysis but rather the imaginative product of authors and audiences constantly reinventing themselves in the context of ambiguity, contradiction and shifting loyalties.

In such a context, art is no longer a reflection of life, it becomes its surrogate or substitute. And discourse on literature becomes a myth of social action, relieving its participants of the responsibility of seeking social solutions. In their place one seeks personal understanding and personal gratification. The point, therefore, is not to heal the world, but to heal oneself, not to concern oneself with the issues of human flourishing in community but of personal expansion and enjoyment in the context of shifting loyalties and ambiguous and contradictory callings.

The problematic posed by such a paradigm shift in African American literature is clearly one worthy and demanding of further discourse. It is thus, posed here to provoke and expand the discussion, not to close or avoid it.

STUDY QUESTIONS

1. What is art?
2. What is the Black aesthetic and what are the two schools of thought which developed around the issue? Discuss their views.

3.   What is the Kawaida social criteria for art? Discuss the three criteria.
4.   Give examples of African art survivals.
5.   Discuss the artists of the Harlem Renaissance period and of the 40's.
6.   Discuss some of the main Black women artists.
7.   What are the main themes of African American art in the 60's and 70's?
8.   What are three basic approaches to interpretations of the spirituals?
9.   Discuss the multidimensionality of blues as a reflection of the Black experience.
10.   Discuss the origin of gospel and ragtime and some of the pioneers.
11.   Discuss the evolution of jazz and the different styles.
12.   What are the origins of rhythm and blues and the problems it poses?
13.   What are the several forms of African American folklore?
14.   Discuss the evolution of African American literature from narratives through the 70's including themes and focus.
15.   What are the relevances and problematic aspects of rap?
16.   Discuss fundamental developments in the literature of the 80's and 90's.
17.   What are some basic aspects of the new aesthetic among some African American writers.

REFERENCES

Adler, Peter and Nicholas Barnard. (1992) *African Majesty: The Textile Art of the Ashanti and Ewe*, London: Thames and Hudson.

Asante, Molefi K. (1987) *The Afro-centric Idea*, Philadelphia: Temple University Press.

Ashburne, Michael R. (1977) "Black Music: A Financial Perspective," *Western Journal of Black Studies*, 1, 4 (December) 263-269.

Baber, Ceola Ross. (1984) "The Artistry of Artifice of Black Communication," in Geneva Gay and Willie Baber (eds.) Expressively Black: The Cultural Basis of Ethnic Identity, New York: Praeger.

Bigsby, C.W.E. (1980) *The Second Black Renaissance*, Westport, CT: Greenwood Press.

Black Collegian. (1990) "Rap Music, Positive or Negative? Passing Fad or Cultural Force? Censored or Uncensored? 21, 2, (November-December 181-183).

Bontemps, Arna and Langston Hughes. (1958) *The Book of Negro Folklore*, New York: Dodd, Mead.

Brown, Sterling A. (1970) "Negro Folk Expression" in *Black Expression*, (ed.) Addison Gayle, Jr., New York: Weybright and Talley.

Butcher, Margaret J. (1956) *The Negro in American Culture*, New York: Knopf.

Byrd, Donald. (1978) "Music Without Aesthetics: How Some Non-Musical Forces and Institutions Influence Change in Black Music," *The Black Scholar* (July-August 2-5).

Catlett, Elizabeth. (1975) "The Role of the Black Artist," *The Black Scholar*, 6, 9 (June) 10-14.

Cone, James. (1972) *The Spirituals and the Blues*, New York: The Seabury Press.

Courlander, Harold. (1963) *Negro Folk Music*, U.S.A. New York: Columbia University Press.

Courlander, Harold. (1976) *A Treasury of American Folklore*, New York: Crown Publishers, Inc.

Dent, Roberta Y. (ed.) (1976) *Paul Robeson Tributes and Selected Writings*, New York: Paul Robeson Archives, Inc.

Dorson, Richard M. (1965) *American Negro Folktales*, Greenwich, CT: Fawcett.

Dover, Cedric. (1960) *American Negro Art*, New Haven: York Graphic Society.

Dozier, Richard K. (1974) "Black Architects and Craftsmen," *Black World* (May) 5-7.

Driskell, David C. (1976) *Two Centuries of Black American Art*, New York: Los Angeles County Museum of Art and Alfred A. Knopf.

DuBois, W.E.B. (1925) "The Social Origins of American Negro Art," *Modern Quarterly*, 3, 1 (October-December) 53-55.

DuBois, W.E.B. (1969) *The Souls of Black Folk*, New York: The New American Library.

Ellison, Ralph. (1966) *Shadow and Act*, New York: Signet Books.

Eure, Joseph D. and James Spady. (1991) *Nation Conscious Rap*, New York: PC International Press.

Evans, Mari. (1979) "Political Writing as Device," *First World*, 2, 3:34-39.

Everett, Chestyn. (1975) "Tradition in Afro-American Literature," *Black World*, 25, 2 (December) 20-25.

Fanon, Frantz. (1968) *The Wretched of the Earth*, New York: Grove Press.

Fine, Elsa H. (1973) *The Afro-American Artist*, New York: Holt Rinehart and Winston.

Fisher, Mark M. (1953) *Negro Slave Songs in the United States*, New York: Citadel Press.

Fuller, Hoyt W. (1971) "Introduction: Towards a Black Aesthetic," in *The Black Aesthetic*, (ed.) Addison Gayle, Jr., Garden City: Doubleday.

Garvey, Marcus. (1977) *Philosophy and Opinions*, New York: Atheneum.

Gates, Henry Louis. (1992) *Loose Canons: Notes on the Culture Wars*, New York: Oxford University Press.

Gayle, Addison, Jr. (ed.) (1971) *The Black Aesthetic*, Garden City: Doubleday.

Gayle, Addison, Jr. (1970) *Black Expression*, New York: Weybright and Talley.

George, Nelson. (1988) *The Death of Rhythm and Blues*, New York: Pantheon Books.

Gillon, Werner. (1984) *A Short History of African Art*, New York: Viking Penguin.

Heilbut, Tony. (1975) *The Gospel Sound*, Garden City: Anchor Books.

Huggins, Nathan I. (1979) *Harlem Renaissance*, New York: Oxford University Press.

Hughes, Langston. (1970) "The Negro Artist and the Racial Mountain," in *Black Expression*, (ed.) Addison Gayle Jr., New York: Weybright Talley.

Hull, Gloria, Patricia Bell Scott and Barbara Smith, (eds.) (1982) *All Women Are White, All Blacks are Men, But Some of Us Are Brave*, Old Westbury, NY: Feminist Press.

Jones, Leroi (Amiri Baraka). (1963) *Blues People*, New York: William Morrow,

Karenga, Maulana. (1971) "Black Cultural Nationalism," in *The Black Aesthetic*, (ed.) Addison Gayle, Jr., Garden City: Doubleday.

Karenga, Maulana. (1980) *Kawaida Theory: An Introductory Outline*, Inglewood, CA: Kawaida Publications.

Killens, John O. (1975) "The Image of Black Folk in American Literature," *The Black Scholar*, 6, 9 (June) 45-52.

Levine, Lawrence W. (1977) *Black Culture and Black Consciousness*, New York: Oxford University Press.

Lewis, Samella. (1978) *Art: African American*, New York: Harcourt Brace Jovanovich.

Locke, Alain. (1969) *The Negro and His Music*, New York: Arno Press, New York Times.

Locke, Alain. (1936) *Negro Art*, DC: Association in Negro Folk Education.

Locke, Alain. (1968) *The New Negro*, New York: Atheneum.

Lovell, John. (1969) "The Social Implications of the Negro Spiritual," in *The Social Implications of Early Negro Music in the United States*, (ed.) Bernard Katz, New York: Arno Press.

Madhubuti, Haki (Don L. Lee). (1972) "The Achievement of Gwendolyn Brooks," *The Black Scholar*, 3, 10, (Summer) 32-41.

Martin, Tony. (1983) *Literary Garveyism: Garvey, Black Arts and the Harlem Renaissance*, Dover, MA: The Majesty Press.

Maultsby, Portia K. (1979) "Influences and Retentions of West African Musical Concepts in U.S. Black Music," *Western Journal of Black Studies*, 3, 3 (Fall) 197-215.

Mays, Benjamin. (1968) *The Negro's God*, New York: Atheneum.

McDowell, Deborah. (1989) "Boundaries: Or Distant Relations and Close Kin" in Houston Baker, Jr. and Patricia Redmond, (eds.), *Afro-American Literary Study in the 1990's, Chicago: University of Chicago Press, pp. 51-70.*

McLeod, Malcolm. (1980) *Treasure of African Art*, New York: Abbeville Press.

McMillan, Terry. (1990) *Breaking Ice: An Anthology of Contemporary African American Fiction*, New York: Penguin Books.

Meadows, Eddie S. (1979) "African Retentions in Blues and Jazz," *Western Journal of Black Studies*, 3, 3 (Fall) 180-185.

Neal, Larry. (1972) "The Ethos of the Blues," The Black Scholar, 3, 10 (Summer) 42-48.

Neal, Larry. (1971) "Some Reflections on the Black Aesthetic," in *The Black Aesthetic*, (ed.) Addison Gayle, Jr., Garden City: Doubleday.

Newton, James E. (1977) "Slave Artisans and Craftsmen: The Roots of Afro-American Art," *The Black Scholar*, 9, 3 (November) 35-44.

Niangoran-Bouah, G. (1984) *The Akan World of Gold Weights: Abstract Design Weights*, Abidjan, Ivory Coast: Les Nouvelles Editions Africaines.

Porter, James. (1970) "African Art From Prehistory to Present," The Negro Impact on Western Civilization, (eds.) Joseph S. Roucek and Thomas Kiernam, New York: Philosophical Library, 467-487.

Porter, James. (1943) *Modern Negro Art*, New York: Dryden Press.

Powell, Catherine. (1991) "Rap Music: An Education with a Beat from the Street," *Journal of Negro Education*, 60, 3 (Summer) 245-259.

Randall, Dudley. (1971) *The Black Poets*, New York: Bantam Books.

Ransaw, Lee A. (1979) "The Changing Relationship of the Black Visual Artist to His Community," *Black Art*, 3,3:44-56.

Redding, Lee A. (1966) "The Negro Writer and American Literature," *Anger and Beyond*, (ed.) Herbert Hill, New York: Harper & Row.

Redding, J. Saunders. (1966) "The Negro Writer and American Literature," in Herbert Hill, (ed.), *Anger and Beyond*, New York: Harper & Row.

Roberts, John Storm. (1974) *Black Music of Two Worlds*, New York: William Morrow.

Salaam, Kalamu ya. (1982) "Hit Records in an Old Tradition," *In These Times*, (May 19-25) 21.

Smith, L.A. (1981) *Art and Architecture of Ancient Egypt*, New York: Penguin.

Smitherman, Geneva. (1973) "The Power of Rap: The Black Idiom and the New Black Poetry," in Twentieth Century Literature, 19,4 (October).

Southern, Eileen. (1971) *The Music of Black Americans*, New York: W.W. Norton.

Spencer, Jon Michael, (ed.) (1991) "The Emergency of Black and the Emergence of Rap," in Special Issue of *Black Sacred Music*, Durham: Duke University Press.

Stephens, Ronald J. (1991) "Three Waves of Contemporary Rap Music," in Jon Spencer (ed.) *The Emergency of Black and the Emergence of Rap*, Durham: Duke University Press.

Thompson, Robert F. (1969) "African Influence on the Art of the United States," *Black Studies in the University*, Robinson, A.L. (eds.) Connecticut: Yale University Press, 122-70.

Thompson, Robert F. (1983) *Flash of the Spirit*, New York: Random House.

Thurman, Howard. (1947) *The Negro Spiritual Speaks of Life and Death*, New York: Harper & Row.

Toop, David. (1984) *The Rap Attack: African Jive to New York Hip Hop*, Boston: South End Press.

Wade-Gayles, Gloria. (1984) *No Crystal Stair: Visions of Race and Sex in Black Women's Fiction*, New York: The Pilgrim Press.

Whitlow, Roger. (1974) *Black American Literature*, Totowa, NJ: Littlefield, Adams & Co.

Wilkinson Richard (1992) *Reading Egyptian Art*, London: Thames and Hudson, Ltd.

Williams, Todd (Ty.) (1992) "The Last Poets and Gill Scott-Heron are Pioneers of Rhythm and Spoken Word," in *The Source*, (May) 42-44, 59.

Williams-Jones, Pearl. (1975) "Afro-American Gospel Music: A Crystallization of the Black Aesthetic," *Journal of the Society for Ethnomusicology*, XIX (September).

BLACK PSYCHOLOGY

8
BLACK PSYCHOLOGY

8.1   INTRODUCTION

Psychology is essentially the science that systematically studies behavior in its relationship to the complexity of mental, emotional, physical and environmental factors which shape it. Although there is a tendency to include the study of animal behavior as part of the definition of psychology (Kagan and Haveman, 1976), I have purposely omitted it in order to maintain focus on the human personality as the core and motive force of psychological study.   In fact, even the study of animal behavior in psychology is only relevant in its use to deepen and expand understanding of human behavior.   Otherwise, such study of animals is better defined as zoology rather than psychology.

Furthermore, all science is ultimately systematic study and knowledge to enhance human grasp of and effective encounter with themselves and their environment. Psychology, then, as a person-focused discipline, stands out as a key science in this historical project of overall human understanding of self, society and the world. For at its most relevant level, it not only focuses on the structure and functioning of the human personality, but equally important, points to the possibilities of its unlimited expansion and thus the realization of a higher level of human life on the personal and social level (Karenga, 1978).

The concerns of Black psychology revolve around the development of a discipline which not only studies the behavior of Black persons, but seeks to transform them into self-conscious agents of their own mental and political liberation. This is achieved through: 1) a severe critique and rejection of white psychology, in terms of its methodology, conclusions and the ideological premises on which it rests; 2) provision of Afrocentric models of study and therapy; and 3) self-conscious intervention in the social struggle for a more Black and human environment (Jones, 1980; Jackson, 1982).

Black psychology has its origins in the 1920's when Francis Sumner became the first Black Ph.D. in psychology in 1920, and subsequently Blacks began to publish research to disprove racists charges of Black inferiority, to push for stronger departments of psychology in Black schools, and to attempt to provide better psychological services to the Black community (Guthrie, 1976). It gained greater strength as an educational thrust when in 1938 Herman Canady of West Virginia State College began to organize Black professionals interested in psychology. Although he was unable then to organize an independent Black psychologist association, he did establish a Black psychologists' caucus within the American Teachers Association, the main professional structure for Black educators. Among the goals they set for themselves were: 1) to promote the teaching and application of psychology, especially in Black schools; 2) to stimulate study, research and exchange; and 3) to set up qualifications for teachers of psychology and assist Black institutions in training and selecting psychologists (Guthrie, 1976:115ff).

However, it was not until the 60's as Jackson (1979:27) notes, "that Afro-American psychologists made a concerted and sustained effort to expand their concerns into a distinct system of thought and not until the 70's that publications appeared in the form of a Black Psychology." In the 60's, the resurgence of Black nationalism, and its Black Power expression, encouraged and demanded Black caucuses within traditionally white-controlled and white-oriented professional organizations as well as independent Black organizations. In 1968 the Association of Black Psychologists (ABP) was founded in the midst of criticism of the American Psychological Association (APA) for its limited vision and conscious and unconscious support of the racist character of American society.

Pledging themselves "to the realization that they are Black people first and psychologists second," the ABP vowed not to "ignore the exploitation of the Black community" and expressed urgent concern "about its role and that of the APA in Black people's struggle for dignity and equality in this country" (Williams, 1974:11-12). The suggestion that the APA had a role in the Black struggle and the subsequent 10-point program for correctives of the APA's thought and practice shows that Black psychologists were still in transition toward an Afro-centric psychology. However, in 1974 when Williams wrote a brief history of the ABP, it was his assessment that traditional psychology was out and Black psychology coming into being. "Black psychologists," he (1974:24) asserted, "have finally broken the symbiotic relationship with white psychology." Black psychology must now, he continued, "be about the business of setting forth new definitions, conceptual models, test theories, normative behavior, all of which must come from the heart of the Black experience."

The history of the Association of Black Psychologists reflects the consolidation and development of distinct but overlapping schools of Black psychology. These are the traditional, reformist and radical schools. Although these approximate Jackson's (1979) reactive, inventive and innovative categories of Black psychology components, I find the categories "inventive" and innovative" close enough in redefinition to warrant alternative categories. Thus, I have offered "reformist" and "radical" as alternative categories. It is important to state here that I suggest no pejorative meaning to reform or the reformist school. I recognize it as a transitional and middle posture between the traditional and the radical schools and as having exhibited necessary and significant development from the traditional school. Moreover, the reformist school not only often borrows from the radical school, but also often leads to the assumption of a radical posture.

The traditional school is defined by: 1) its defensive and/or reactive posture; 2) its lack of concern for the development of a Black psychology and its continued support of the Eurocentric model with minor changes; 3) its concern with changing white attitudes, and 4) its being essentially critical without offering substantive correctives (Guthrie, 1970).

The reformist represents a period of historical evolution as well as a current posture. It maintains some of the concern for white attitudes and behavior, but focuses more on change in public policy than on simply attitudinal change. Furthermore, this school begins to advocate an Afrocentric psychology but still combines it with traditional focus on appeal for change that would ostensibly benefit Blacks and whites and thus U.S. society (Thomas, 1971; Cross, 1971).

The radical school makes no appeal to whites and directs their attention instead to Black people in terms of analysis, treatment and transformation. Moreover, they insist on and are developing a psychology that has its roots in the African worldview which is opposite of and opposed to the European worldview (Jackson, 1982; King, et al, 1976; Baldwin, 1992). Moreover, the members of this school are socially conscious theorists and practitioners who advocate self-conscious participation of Black psychologists and Black people in the transformation of social reality through cultural and political struggle. This, of course, is in the Fanonian tradition which influenced many of them (Fanon, 1968, 1967).

8.2   PERSPECTIVES

The Traditional School

Kenneth Clark.   Clark, who is the first and only Black to be president of the APA, early established himself with the citation of his work on the damaging effects of segregation by the U.S.

Supreme Court in its historical *Brown vs. Board of Education* (1954) decision. The author of several books and articles, his work, *The Dark Ghetto: Dilemma of Social Power* (1965) stands out as a seminal work on the sociology and psychology of the ghetto. In chapter IV of his book, entitled the "Psychology of the Ghetto," he essentially gives a "traditional" analysis of segregation. He (1965:63) argues that "racial segregation, like all other forms of cruelty and tyranny, debases all human beings-- those who are its victims, those who victimize, and in quite subtle ways those who are merely accessories."

The victims, Blacks, are essentially portrayed with little or no strengths, i.e., as fantasy-oriented, sexually excessive, matriarchal, irresponsible, etc. However, Clark does not attribute these negatives to Black inferiority, but to an insensitive and brutally segregated society which imposes these patterns of thought and behavior on Blacks. Clark argues that social (white) insensitivity is "a protective device" and criticizes some of its "primitive examples," i.e. labeling of Blacks as inferior and "subhuman persons who cause and perpetuate their own difficulties" (1965:75-76).

In addition, he criticizes those social scientists whose "preoccupation with trivia...leads to the irrelevance of much of social science research," and "detached professionalism," which, in reality is a false objectivity and masked insensitivity. And finally, he (1965:77, 80) criticizes the "professional perspective which constricts social vision to the impulses, strengths and weakness of the individual 'client' as if these can be isolated from the injustices and pathologies of his life." Such a detached and alleged objectivity, he concludes, serves "not to enlarge truth but to constrict it."

William Grier and Price Cobbs. Grier and Cobbs are best known for their work *Black Rage*. Although it was written in a popular style, it nevertheless reflects some of the basic contentions of the traditionalist school. Like Clark, Grier and Cobbs are concerned with whites knowing what they're doing to

Blacks in order to change their attitudes and behavior. Concerned with the implication of the mutual racial hostility, they (1968:2) assert that "if racist hostility is to subside and if we are to avoid conflict on a nationwide scale, information is the most desperate commodity of our time." And, they continue, "of all the things worth knowing, none is more important than that all Blacks are angry"--in a word enraged.

Having established the fact of Black rage, Grier and Cobbs then set out to explain its origins and expressions. They establish the effects of what they call the shadows of the past, i.e., slavery, arguing that through this oppression and its sequel, "The psyche of Black men has been distorted." But, they assert "their genius is that they have survived" through adaptations of both positive and negative dimensions (1968:31). Unwilling and/or unable to see significant distinctness in Black life, they (1968:29) contend that "the psychological principles first understood in the study of white men are true, no matter what the man's color." And they (1968:86) maintain that "all that is uniquely (Black) found its origins on these shores, and provides a living document of Black history in America."

In what seems to be a contradiction to the denial of Black uniqueness, Grier and Cobbs then set down some principles of a "Black norm" which they claim distinguish black psychological postures from others but which are essentially a list of unsubstantiated and self-indicting negatives (1968:149ff). Among these are: 1) Blacks' understandable and necessary cultural paranoia; 2) their cultural depression and cultural masochism rising out of "sadness and intimacy with misery;" and 3) cultural anti-socialism, i.e., disrespect for white laws which are designed to protect whites not Blacks. They (1968:124) conclude their "dismal tone is deliberate" in an attempt to stir the feelings of the reader to the "depression and hopelessness" Blacks feel daily.

Alvin Poussaint. Poussaint's major work is his *Why Blacks Kill Blacks*. In his work, he covers a series of topics including Black Power, Black suicide, Black sexuality, and suggestions to white parents on how to raise their children free of prejudice. Criticizing the racial and socio-economic bias of traditional white psychiatry, Poussaint (1972:49ff) shows sensitivity to Black "suspicion of its concepts and practice" and their tendency to label it the "white man's psychology." He (1972:51) states that not only have white psychiatrists preferred to treat members of their own race and class, but their "short-sighted training...has made it impossible for them to distinguish deviant behavior from what is in fact *different* behavior." In this regard, he (1972:54) argues for "understanding special cultural adaptations or interests" of Blacks, if white psychiatrists are to be effective clinicians. For he (1972:55) believes that "despite obvious handicaps, some white psychiatrists are sensitive to the Black experience and have helped all types of Black patients."

In his chapter on "Why Blacks Kill Blacks," Poussaint (1972:69-70) begins by criticizing deficient modeling of Blacks as "culturally deprived" and "socially disadvantaged" and "culturally paranoid." These labels would fit the racist more than the Black, he argues. Likewise, the "creation of self-serving theories by some white academicians" about how Blacks hate themselves is not only exaggerated, but "another subtle attempt to maintain the oppressor's false sense of superiority." In fact, "it is likely," he maintains, "that whites have more self-hate and insecurity than we do, since they need racism to maintain a sense of self."

Recognizing, however, that there are negatives among Blacks and that crime and violence by Blacks against each other is a serious problem, he posits several reasons for it. Among these are: 1) the American cultural experience that teaches "crime and violence as a way to success and manhood;" 2) the fact that "Americans respect violence and often will not respond to just demands except through violence" as with the revolts; 3) the sense of power that violence gives the oppressed; and 4) dehumanizing transformation in incarceration which perpetuates the cycle of violence. Poussaint, however, rushes to say that regardless of the blame white society must shoulder for the Black condition, Blacks, in the final analysis, must move to intervene in and transform their own lives and life-conditions. This essentially means development of community programs which check the negatives and support development of "deep self-love that ends the self-defeating behavior among ourselves."

The Reformist School

Charles Thomas. Thomas is one of the founders and first co-chairpersons of the ABP and was instrumental in shaping the early moves of Black psychology from the negatives of the traditional school. He and others of the school stand as bridges between the traditional and radical school, attempting a synthesis of the social and discipline criticism of the traditional school and the demands for and development of new models and professional engagement from the radical schools. Thomas' book *Boys No More* and subsequent articles represent this attempt toward synthesis.

Thomas (1979, 1971) begins by assigning Black psychologists the fundamental task of "instructive intervention" which leads to change in Black attitudes, self-mastery, social competence and personal fulfillment. He asserts that social scientists have an ethical responsibility for changing the Black condition "by defining, defending and developing information systems that will give Blacks increased socio-political power" (1979:7). Thus, he rejects the simple treatment-centered therapy and urges community engagement for the psychology.

Secondly, Thomas (1974) argues the significance of the Ethnocentrism factor. By ethnocentrism or ethnicity, he means, focus and pride in one's bio-social identity--in this case, one's Blackness. For Thomas, ethnicity not only provides the "frame of reference...for the development of countervailing social forces and institutions, it encourages self-activated behavior and breaks down patterns of self-hate and self-denial." Thomas contends that within the context of Black oppression four major social roles were generated to meet it: "hybrid or bad niggers, conformists or good negroes, marginalists or white middle class negroes and rebels or Black 'militants.'" Each group not only represents a search for identity but, except for the last one, they also represent "modes of escape which are ineffective." This is so, for the flight from oneself essentially means a flight from one's humanity. Ethnicity as a proactive alternative, then, poses and cultivates "the renewed thrust toward self-esteem, environmental mastery, definition of self in terms of potential and a variety of other concerns around intervention or prevention of pathological cognition..."

Also, Thomas (1978:11ff) is concerned about the damage done by white or other social scientists who "have confused knowledge about a people with knowledge of a people." The first is superficial learning from without and imposing a conceptual framework; the latter is learning from within the group and sharing its conceptual framework. The bio-socialists who deny cultural differences, the cultural pathologists who are "preoccupied with the victim of oppression rather than with oppressive institutions," and the integrationists which limit social options on the assumption that Blacks "ought to be white or placed in situations where they can be treated as if white," all fit in this category of deficient and damaging social science.

Finally, Thomas (1978, 1971) poses deficient-deficit modeling as a major problem of Black psychology as well as for Blacks in terms of its implications for public policy and self-actualization. Examples, of this are terms such as *minority*, and all its variations, i.e., *minority status and culture*, etc., *disadvantaged*, *culturally deprived*, *negro*, etc. He (1978:21-22) states that "if 'Blackness' came into existence as a healthy support state, it cannot be logically used as a symptomatology of maladaptive behavior." The need, then, is for imaginative cross-cultural conceptual models which press for para-cultural (equal rather than sub-cultural) frames of reference.

Joseph White. Although White has written other articles and a book (White and Parham, 1990) his "Toward A Black Psychology," written in 1970, is seen as an important piece of

literature in the early criticism of and move from the traditional
school of psychology.   In fact, he (1980:5) begins his article
arguing that "it is very difficult, if not impossible to understand
the life styles of Blacks people using the traditional theories
developed by white psychologists to explain white people."
Furthermore, "when these traditional theories are applied to the
lives of Blacks folks, many incorrect, weakness-dominated, and
inferiority-oriented conclusions come about."

     White maintains that traditional psychology's use of "an
Anglo middle-class frame of reference" gives it a distorted view
of the adaptive vitality of Black children and the Black family.
Instead of a correct and positive view, hypotheses of cultural
deprivation and matriarchal families are advanced.   His
contention is that a Black frame of reference is necessary which
will enable Black psychologists and others "to come up with
more accurate and comprehensive explanations" of Black life, as
well as enable them "to build the kinds of programs within the
Black world which capitalize on the strengths of Black people"
(White, 1980:8).

     He also argues "That not all traditional white psychology
theory is useless." The existentialists' stress on pain and struggle
as unavoidable and the self-theorists' stress on understanding
one's experiential background to understand a person are
examples of useful theories. The need, then, in building a Black
psychology is to incorporate what is useful and reject the rest.
White (1980:11) suggests the value of Black/white dialogue and
exchange in encounter groups, suggesting they give whites a
better chance to experience Blackness "outside the protective
group setting."

William Cross.   Concerned with the prevalence and negatives
of Western thought and science and the need for "psychological
liberation under conditions of oppression," Cross (1971:13)
offered a model suggesting the stages persons go through in the
process of the "Negro-to-Black conversion."   In a subsequent
article, comparing this model to one Thomas developed, he

(1980) terms these models of "nigrescence," i.e., the process of becoming Black. The first stage of nigrescence is the *pre-encounter* (or prediscovery) stage in which the person is out of touch with himself/herself racially and the "the person's worldview is dominated by Euro-American determinants" causing him/her to act in manners which degrade and deny Blackness (Cross 1971:15ff).

The second or *encounter* (discovery) stage involves a shocking personal or social event which pushes the person past his/her old conceptions of Black and Black conditions to an intense search for Black identity. The third stage is one of *immersion-emersion.* In the first phase, there is an intense involvement in being and demonstrating Blackness and rejection and condemnation of white people and culture. In the second phase, there is a levelling off and emergence from either/or and racist positions and the oversimplified aspects of Blackness, as well as acceptance of white humanity. Stage four is one of *internalization*, a sense of security, receptivity to discussion, and action and resolution of the conflict between the old and the new. The final state is *internalization--commitment* in which one "becomes the new identity and pro-Black attitudes become more expansive, open and less defensive."

In focusing in on and criticizing Blacks for high levels of racial identity and severe rejection of whites and white values in the immersion phase, Cross seems to demonstrate again the reformist school's concern for relations with whites. This is not to say or imply that this represents servility, but to make the point that this is clearly an issue the radical school would neither raise, be concerned with, nor agree with. On the contrary, the radical school would see questioning of white humanity and total rejection of their values as positive.

In a more recent work, however, Cross (1991) has revised his original theory of nigrescence in order to bring it in line with new discoveries in his research. He begins his revision by noting that understanding Black mental health is more complex than his original theory of nigrescence suggested. Such complexity begins with recognition of the fact that any identity change is mixed, not pure, and thus involves carryovers from previous identity, transformation of old into new and incorporation of things new. Also Cross argues that given the distinction between personal identity and group identity or reference group orientation, one can be mentally healthy without the need to relate strongly to a distinct cultural group. Finally, he contends that the aspects of the personality remain stable and healthy even while ideologies are changing, thus revealing a greater diversity of attitudes, behaviors and possibilities than he first suggested. Thus, he (1991:xiv) maintains that at the heart of the identity conversion in the 60's "was not so much the dynamics of self-hatred as the metamorphosis of a Eurocentric worldview into an Afrocentric one."

The Radical School

Na'im Akbar.   Akbar's (1991, 1981, 1976, 1974) critique of the traditional psychology model begins with the historical fact that African Americans have been victims of intellectual as well physical oppression. "Intellectual oppression," he asserts (1981: 18), "involves the abusive use of ideas, labels and concepts geared toward the mental degradation of a people." And, he states, "there is no area in which mental or intellectual oppression is more clearly illustrated than...the area of mental health judgement." In such a context not only are white oppressors' sanity not questioned, but Black mental health is not linked with the social conditions which shaped it.

   The white oppressor, Akbar (1981:18,49) states, uncertain as to "what constituted a normal human being," established a kind of "democratic sanity" model of mental health. This was a kind of "majority rule application to mental health judgement, i.e. insane behavior was determined "on the basis of the degree to which it deviated from the majority's behavior in a given context." This approach had the tragic consequence of judging sane and competent "entire communities of raving inhuman lunatics...

because the majority of people in that particular context either participated in the questionable behavior or refused to question (it)." It is, Akbar maintains, clearly necessary to raise questions about the mental health standards and mental competence of a people who enslaved, terrorized and murdered numerous non-hostile peoples throughout the world.

Secondly, Akbar (1981:20) criticizes white scientists for "acquiring great scholarly renown for documenting deficits of Afro-Americans," a pathology perspective based on the norm and context of the people who uphold the "democratic sanity" standard. Thirdly, he (1981:20) criticizes Black traditionalists like Clark and Grier and Cobbs for "following the lead of Caucasian scholars in both conceptualizing and analyzing problems." He especially criticizes Grier and Cobbs for their "guide to the neurotic Negro," *Black Rage*, and their overgeneralization and use of the pathology model in it. Moreover, he concludes that the traditional school: 1) equates mental health with imitation of white middle class behavior; 2) assumes similarity of sources of Black and white behavior; and 3) assumes "democratic sanity" standards are "reflective of human standards documented by thousands of years of human history."

Fourthly, he argues that these and other traditional psychologists fail to take into consideration "two essential variables in determining the adequacy of human behavior:" 1) the historical antecedents or determinants of the behavior; and 2) the effects of inhuman conditions on the human being. As a result of these failures, there are attempts to eliminate or diminish many behaviors in African Americans "which are essential to their survival and development."

Having critiqued the traditional school, Akbar defines mental health in proactive terms as a state "reflected in those behaviors which foster mental growth and awareness (i.e., mental life)." Mental illness, then, is posed as reflected in "ideas and forces within the mind that threaten awareness and mental growth." It also can mean, from an extended self-concept, disorders reflected in "behaviors or ideas which threaten the survival of the collective self," i.e., one's people. Given these definitions, one can understand the reasoning of an insane parasitic people which justified domination as a model of survival and the reasoning of the dominated people which poses liberation as a mode of survival and development.

Finally, within the framework of his definitions, Akbar (1981) poses four kinds of disorders which threaten Black life and development, i.e., "anti-life forces." These are the alien-self disorder, a socialization to be other than oneself on a race, class and sex level; the anti-self disorder, which expresses "overt and covert hostility towards the group of one's origin and thus one's self"; the self-destructive disorder, a destructive retreat from reality, i.e., drugs, etc.; and organic disorders, physiological, neurological or biochemical malfunctions. He (1981:25) concludes by noting that these four disorders, it must be remembered, all emanate from "a psychopathic society typified by oppression and racism," a situation which must be changed for Blacks to "realize the full power of their human potential."

In a recent work, Akbar (1991) offers an analysis of the problematic of maleness and the challenge of manhood. He explains this as a process concerning, "the transformation of African consciousness" (Akbar, 1991:3). For him, the essence of the transformation is moving from the biologically bound in both the physical and mental sense. This requires first external discipline then internal discipline. "The thing that moves us from the male to the boy is discipline and that frees the boy from being slave to his male" (Akbar, 1991:18). Likewise that which transforms a boy into a man is knowledge. "Consciousness is a natural possibility or potential, but it must be tended and guided in order for it to develop properly."

Manhood for Akbar (1991:32), which is at first defined by discipline and then knowledge, is also expressed by self-definition. "Men must define themselves. It is their definitions that give them power." Finally, Akbar (1991:61) argues that manhood must ultimately be grounded in a proactive spirituality. "In order to establish authority over our lives, you must call upon that ruling force of 'will power' within your make-up. That will be the representative of the 'Divine Kingship' within our being...You can do it once you begin to utilize the power that is naturally yours. You are the ones who first came into human mastery," therefore, he concludes, "you can do it again."

Joseph Baldwin (Kobi Kazembe Kalongi Kambon). Within the context of his contribution to Black psychology, Baldwin (1992, 1980, 1976) focuses on the function of definitional systems in liberation and oppression. Definitional systems are key, he (1980:96) posits, for they "determine how we experience (perceive and respond to) the various phenomena that characterize the ongoing process of everyday existence." Moreover, the definitional system or worldview represents the ideological or philosophical base of a social system or a people and thus determines the meanings or values a people attach to their experience including their experience of themselves and how they will react.

The problem, however, arises, Baldwin argues, when an alien worldview is imposed on and/or accepted by people, leaving the people at the mercy of definitions negative to their image and interests. Such is the case of Blacks under white domination. According to Baldwin, race, i.e., biogenetic commonality, "constitutes the principal binding condition underlying the evolution of definitional systems which "in their most basic fundamental nature have a 'racial character'."

Given this, what passes and is pushed as a universal worldview turns out to be nothing more than a European definitional system. This system is not only diametrically opposed to Black interests, but reinforces a distorted reality in the image and interest for the Europeans. Thus, African Americans "operate in a space dominated primarily by a definitional framework which does not and cannot give legitimacy to our African social reality" (1980:108). Complicating resistance to this state of things, Baldwin (1980:101) contends, is that the "Europeans control the formal process of social reinforcements," i.e., economics and political power. This gives them power to impose their "definitions and the experiential confirmations on the experiences of Black people in society."

Although there has been some Black resistance to this imposition, it has "not necessarily been of a highly conscious form," that is to say, "it has not generally taken the form of a carefully planned or necessarily intentional collective resistance" (1980:106). Thus, if Blacks are to liberate themselves and validate and expand their own African definitional system and social reality, "*conscious, collective resistance* is ultimately required." This of necessity requires a "clear frame of reference from which to ultimately examine the psychological nature of (Black) oppression" (1980:107). This in turn demands a Black psychology, Baldwin concludes, which not only explains the "ongoing process of psychological genocide," but contributes to a critical understanding of Euro-American society by which African people can "ultimately achieve the fullness of psychological and physical liberation from it."

Continuing his concern with the distinctness of a worldview for the African person, Baldwin (1992) develops an Africentric theory of the Black personality. Essentially he argues that a healthy functioning African personality has a bio-genetic tendency to affirm rather than deny Black life, makes group a priority, including survival of culture and institutions, and engages in activities that promote this survival as well as the dignity and mental health of Black people.

He (1992:41) also makes four critical "assumptions about the nature of the African personality which derive from an Africentric approach." They are : 1) a bio-genetically or innately determined character of the personality; 2) the intra-psychic integrity of the personality which cannot be separated or analyzed from the context of the whole; 3) the social or collective character of the personality and the need to understand it in a "social-collective context"; and 4) the racial distinctiveness of the personality which is affirmed in its own context and negatively affected outside of it. Finally, Baldwin identifies two major psychological components of the core African personality: 1) The African Self-Extension Orientation (ASEO); and 2) African Self-Consciousness (ASC) which derives from the ASEO and engages it in a mutually interactive process.

Linda James Myers.   The key concepts in Myers' (1992, 1988, 1987, 1985) contribution to an Afrocentric psychology are optimality and suboptimality.   Her thrust is to define and implement, as a critical framework for understanding and achieving maximum mental health, a theory of psychology rooted in and reflective of   African culture.   This begins with a definition of the optimal Afrocentric belief system.   For Myers such an Afrocentric worldview is characterized by at least three basic concepts: 1) holistic-spiritual/unity; 2) communalism; and 3) proper consciousness.   For Myers (1988:12) this optimal worldview first of all "assumes that reality is spiritual and material."   Thus, the first aspect of it is a spiritual/material unity (Myers, 1988:41ff).   This arises from the concept of the unity of being through assumption that "all is spirit individually and uniquely expressed" (Myers, 1988:19).   When one adheres to this principle, she states, one "loses the sense of the individualized ego/mind and experiences the harmony of collective identity of being one with the source of all good" (Myers, 1988:12).

Secondly, the African worldview is communalistic.   It originates from the concept of the extended self.   "Self in this instance is extended to include all the ancestors, the yet unborn, all nature and the entire community" (Myers:1988:12).   Thirdly, Myers argues that proper consciousness or self-knowledge is another aspect of the Afrocentric worldview.   She states that "the role of consciousness is primary in this conceptual system; in fact consciousness is identifiably that permeating essence or pervasive energy and spirit."   This centrality is reflected in African concepts of Maat (truth); Mdw Ntr (divine speech) and Nommo (word power).

Myers contrasts this African worldview to the Eurocentric worldview with the former representing an optimal psychology and the latter a suboptimal psychology. The latter is racist, sexist, materialist and ultimately unworkable. Its fatal flaw is the socialization of its adherents to seek the key values in life, i.e. self-worth, peace, happiness, etc. through externals. But the reality is "identity and self-worth are intrinsic" and peace and happiness are generated from within. This in turn requires self-realization of the spirit within.

Secondly, she (1988:14) asserts that "the suboptimal conceptual system oppresses all its adherents. It makes the racist/sexist the oppressor acting out and projecting the negativity and insecurity he/she feels within." The oppressed however, are "doubly oppressed" when they absorb, "adapt and assimilate the conceptual system of the oppressor." In the end they suffer from all kinds of mental health and social problems.

Myers (1992:6) also defines the suboptimal or Eurocentric worldview in terms of its tendency to fragment and segment not only reality but peoples (racism) and genders (sexism). Although racism is clearly a problem for the African American community, "sexism is a serious problem that we have not as a people really addressed or solved" (Myers, 1992:8) It is her contention that "in a suboptimal/fragmented culture like this one, womanhood and motherhood (the central role of woman) are disdained rather than revered. But she (Myers 1992:9) notes "In a patriarchal society, anything feminine is inferior." Moreover, "In a sexist environment, women tend to hate themselves," Myers states and they tend to "think that men are superior just like many Blacks (in a racist society) tend to think whites are superior."

The need then is to come into African consciousness "to begin forging a relationship with ourselves so that we can come into right relationship with our counterpart." She (1988:15) concludes, arguing that Black intervention in their liberation from oppression is key and compelling in the struggle for an optimal psychology and a positive social context. The "charge then is to learn more about our choices through increased awareness of the nature of that which is us" and then act accordingly (Myers, 1988:15).

Wade Nobles.   Clearly Nobles (1986, 1985, 1980, 1976) is the pioneer and most quoted in the area of using African philosophy as a foundation for Black psychology. In his seminal essay on the subject, Nobles (1980:23) begins by arguing that Black psychology is more than the psychology of the underprivileged, the ghettoized or the enslaved and more than the 'darker' dimension of general psychology. In a word, "Its unique status," "is derived not from the negative aspect of being Black in white America," he argues, "but rather from the positive features of basic African philosophy which dictates the values, customs, attitudes and behavior of Africans in Africa and the New World."

Nobles argues that what we have here is a commonality of consciousness based on guiding beliefs, an ethos which is at the core of African philosophy. This ethos determines two operational orders--the notion of oneness with nature and the survival of one's people. Given its distinctiveness from the white ethos and its place at the center of African philosophy, African philosophy easily and effectively serves as the foundation for Black psychology. A study of African philosophy shows several fundamental themes which not only explain African philosophy, but also African (Black) psychology.

First, one sees the rootedness of philosophy in religion. Religion, in turn, was life-practice, not sect or church or Sunday or proselytizing. "Traditional Africans made no distinction between the act and the belief" (1980:25). Secondly, the notion of unity of humans with God and the whole universe is key to African philosophy. A third key concept is the concept of time which is/was essentially "a composition of events" in two dimensions, the past and present, which are experienced rather than calculated. A fourth fundamental concept is that of death and immortality through recognition and remembrance. A final concept is one of kinship or collective unity which created a sense of collective identity, i.e., an extended self.

What this explanation of African philosophical themes does is demonstrate a distinctiveness of philosophy and psychology. The point now, Nobles (1980:31) contends is to "'prove' that Africans living in the Western world and in contemporary times still have or maintain an African philosophical definition." Thus, there is a need for demonstration of links and ways that Blacks express an African perception of reality. Nobles argues that several Africanisms did survive slavery and contemporary times. The first is the stress on the survival of the people which expressed itself in a mentality and structures like benevolent societies and the church. Also the idea of a man being inseparable, one with nature and the community, is a surviving Africanism. Oral tradition in the form of folktales, the dozens, rappin, etc., have also survived. Finally, the concept of time as phenomenal, potential and flexible rather than mathematical as expressed in CP time is also a surviving Africanism. These, Nobles (1980:35) states, are some examples which demonstrate a distinctiveness of Black consciousness rooted in and reflective of African philosophy. "The task of Black psychology, (then), is to offer an understanding of the behavioral definitions of African philosophy and to document what, if any, modifications it has undergone during particular experiential periods" in the U.S.

Frances Cress Welsing.   Cress Welsing (1991,1980,1970), a noted psychiatrist, advances one of the most controversial and discussed theories in the area of Black psychology, "The Cress Theory of Color-Confrontation and Racism (White Supremacy)." Cress Welsing builds on the contentions of Neeley Fuller in his *Textbook of Victims of White Supremacy* (1969). Fuller essentially argued that: 1) white supremacy was the only functional racism; 2) all Third World people are victims of it; 3) racism is not merely an individual or institutional phenomena, but a universal system of domination; and 4) that European theories and systems of political and economic organization are designed to establish, insure and expand white domination.

Having accepted these essential contentions, Cress Welsing developed them further and advanced other ones. First, she (1970:5) argued that the white supremacy drive is in fact like other neurotic drives for superiority or domination "founded upon a deep and pervading sense of inadequacy and inferiority." Secondly, she contends that the basis for this neurotic disorder is found in the "quality of whiteness (which) is indeed a genetic inadequacy or a relative genetic deficiency, state or disease based upon the genetic inability to produce the skin pigments of melanin which are responsible for all skin coloration."

Whiteness as the absence of color or "the very absence of any ability to produce color" is the minority in the world given that "the massive majority of the world's people are not so afflicted." Thus, the color normality in the majority throws light on the abnormality of the colorless minority. Moreover, given that "color always annihilates phenotypically and genetically speaking, the non-color, white," and given their numerical minority status, whites are faced with the constant fear of genetic extinction (1970:6). Therefore, Cress Welsing continues, "an uncontrollable sense of hostility and aggression developed defensively which has continued to manifest itself throughout the entire historical epoch of mass confrontations of the whites with people of color."

Cress Welsing contends that this "sense of numerical inadequacy and genetic color inferiority" led whites not only to dominate, destroy and deform Third World peoples, but also to alienation and self-hatred as well as defense mechanisms to handle these feelings. Among these are: 1) repression of the inadequacy inferiority feeling by denying it; 2) discrediting and despising Black and other colors of skin; 3) suntanning and making up to acquire color; 4) elaborating myths of white genetic superiority as with Jensen's and other racist theories; 5) projection of their hate and sexual desires on Third World peoples, pretending it is they who hate and lust after white; 6) obsessive focus on the body yet alienated from sex because of inability to produce color; 7) dividing Third World people into factions to make them minorities; and 8) imposing birth control on Third World people to limit or reverse their majority number. Cress Welsing (1970:10) concludes that if Third World people are armed with the above insights, this will indeed reduce their vulnerability to manipulation and messages of white supremacy and contribute to their psychological liberation from the white racist ideology which so dominates their lives.

In her latest work, Cress Welsing (1991) reaffirms her theories in earlier literature adding emphasis in two basic areas: decoding symbols of white supremacy and the crisis in male/female relations. She (1991:xi) states that there are many symbols "in the system of white supremacy that reveal its roots in the struggle for white survival." These include the cross, the gun, smoking objects, boxing, paper money and various sizes and colors of balls. Cress Welsing (1991:54) contends that "the process of decoding a power system and its culture is a necessary first step to achieve behavioral mastery over that system/culture." As she concludes, "the attainment of such mastery is an essential step in the process of total liberation for the victims who wish to end that oppression and regain their self-respect and mental health." Without this, there is a failure to understand the system which is being confronted, low levels of self and group consciousness and respect and the pervasive presence of mental illness.

Cress Welsing (1991:277) also turns attention to the crisis in Black male/female relationships. She argues that most discussions on the subject focus on the wrong issue. The key to understanding Black male/female relationships is analysis of "the white supremacy dynamic" which puts "disproportionate pressure on Black males (and) ...produces a grave imbalance between the Black male and female, even though both are victimized by white supremacy." The thrust is to incapacitate Black males in a white struggle for survival so that the "Black female must confront a white male-dominated power system alone" (Cress Welsing, 1991:278). But, Black males and females can defeat this, if they together "take up the struggle for justice against white supremacy" as "their number one priority." For in this move they are strengthened and "are united in a common effort against injustice and simultaneously, they express the strongest possible statement about respect and love for themselves as individuals" (Cress Welsing, 1991:280).

Amos Wilson.   Focusing on the psychological development of the Black child, Wilson (1991a, 1991b, 1981, 1978), contributes to the projects of defining the tasks and parameters of Black psychology.   Wilson (1981:8) argues, as do Nobles and others, that an understanding of the psychology of Blacks, adults and children, demands that the study of Blacks begin in Africa, not in slavery.   Moreover, he (1981:10) maintains that Black psychology must be extremely careful about the application of European based psychology and the use of its models.   In fact, he suggests white psychology does not even adequately explain white people who "seem bent on destroying themselves as well as the rest of the world."

Drawing on the growing interest in melanin and its properties, Wilson (1981:10) contends that the study of melanin is important in the study of Black people.   Arguing that the history of Blacks are in their genes, he suggests Black superiority in the areas of mental development, neurological functioning and psychomotor development of the Black child which are all related to the possession of a high level of melanin.   Melanin, he contends, is not simply a coloring agent, but "an integral part of the body system itself operating in the brain."   In fact, the ability of the Black child to survive and the comparative long life of Blacks are related to their Blackness.

Wilson (1981:12) is also concerned that Blacks have been reduced to use only one side of their brain.   This right side, he states "processes information...deals with the world in a holistic fashion and (also) processes music and art."   The left side is the analytical side which develops technology, mathematics and so forth.   But "the side of the brain an individual uses is determined by experience," therefore, if we look at the history and experience of Blacks in America, we see essentially that the European has rewarded Blacks for using the right brain," i.e., singing, dancing, music and sports. On the other hand, because whites "are afraid of intellectually assertive Black people," Blacks are discriminated against and discouraged from using the left side of the brain, i.e., the linguistic and analytical. The need is thus for a balance, for "the ultimate human being is the one who can balance between the use of both sides of the brain."

Finally, Wilson (1981:12) maintains that one of the major problems of Black child development "is determining how we can maintain the intellectual and psychological advance that nature has give our children." It is here, he states, that we see the inadequacy of white child psychology for "the issues and questions that the Black psychologist must address are distinctively different." This essentially demands the development of an educational psychology and methodology directed toward "the reconstruction of the personality and the orientation of our children" (Wilson, 1981:13; 1991a).

Such a thrust would be directed toward educational and cultural change which not only stimulates the brain, but teaches children how to think, not simply prepares them for jobs but also facilitates and encourages high levels of self-development and service to their people. For "Blacks who are not conscious of their Blackness, who have no sense of destiny, and then go through (white systems of education) ultimately end up serving their own oppressors and become a means of oppressing their own people."   Therefore, Black liberation depends on an educational system for Black children based on a psychological model which builds on and develops Black strength in order "to create an intelligent, independent thinking, interpretive and critical person committed to working tirelessly in the interest of Black people."

In one of his latest works, Wilson (1991b) discusses the social psychology of violence among young Black men. It is his (1991b:2) contention that Black male adolescent criminality is the principle outcome of three things: 1) white-on-Black violence since enslavement; 2) the deliberate creation of white American-dominated racist society; and 3) "unrelenting and collective ego defensive and political economic needs for white America to criminalize, denigrate and degrade Black America." Moreover, he states that he is not arguing that Blacks have no responsibility in this problem. Rather he is arguing that white America sets the context and sustains it. But he (1991:31) argues that "such a regime can only hold sway over African Americans and Africans in general as long as their consciousness and identity are not African centered." The need then, is to bring that consciousness to them in order to end their destructive alienation from self and community and enable them to escape the criminality and anti-social conduct which plagues them.

Bobby Wright. Although Wright (1981;1975) has written other pieces in Black psychology, his fundamental and most-known work is *The Psychopathic Racial Personality*. In this essay, he poses whites as the mortal danger to Black people and seeks to analyze their behavior to demonstrate this. The urgency of such an analysis, he suggests, is due to the fact that this period in history is critical to Blacks' future. Using the analogy of a bull fight in which the bull finally stops charging the cape blindly, sees the "matador" and faces "the moment of truth," he (1975:3) argues that "this is indeed Blacks' moment of truth and it is time for them to look at the matador."

According to Wright, European "matadors" have for hundreds of years held up various banners to distract and delude Black people, i.e., "such concepts as democracy, capitalism, Marxism, religion and education." But now these banners, Wright contends, have been reduced to one--genocide, as evidenced in the development of genetic, chemical, electrical surgical and other behavioral control strategies. This emerges from the fact that due to technological development and the worldwide struggle for resources, "Blacks are now a threat and a liability to the white race." It is in such a context that the understanding of the white "matador" becomes imperative.

Wright (1975:3) states at the outset that the basic premise of his work "is that in their relationship with the Black race Europeans (whites) are psychopaths." Moreover, he states that this "behavior reflects an underlying biologically transmitted proclivity with roots deep in their evolutionary history." He defines a psychopath as "one who is constantly in conflict with others,...unable to experience guilt, completely selfish and callous and has total disregard for the rights of others."

Expanding his analysis, Wright focuses on evidence of behavior traits which he reasons proves his contentions and demands Black consideration. He (1975:5) asserts that key to understanding the psychopathic personality is its "almost complete absence of ethical or moral development and an almost total disregard for appropriate patterns of behavior." This is expressed in the fact that whites have "historically oppressed, exploited and killed Black people--all in the name of their God Jesus...and with the sanction of the churches"(Wright, 1975:6). The activities of the KKK, a white Christian organization, and the Pope blessing Italian planes and pilots on their way to bomb Ethiopia without provocation are cited as examples.

Secondly, Wright maintains, the psychopath is also defined by the lack of "concern or commitment except to their own interest" and becoming indignant and angry when they are exposed or questioned. The unkept promises of the 60's by whites and their attitude toward Black liberation and progress are examples of this. Also, Wright argues that "the psychopath is usually sexually inadequate with a very limited capacity to form interpersonal relationships." This is exhibited in whites in their constant projection of excessive sexuality on Blacks, although it is they "who streak, mate swap, participate in orgies, etc."

Fourthly, the psychopath has a marked "inability to accept blame (or) to learn from previous experience." Whites "never accept blame for Blacks' environmental conditions which is clearly the result of white oppression" (1975:7). Instead, Blacks are held responsible. Also, attempts to sensitize and change them fail because of their inability to feel guilt. Finally, the psychopath rejects authority and discipline. Even when their own laws are the authority, they reject them if it is not in their interest, as Blacks "who seek legal solutions to their problems" discover (1975:8).

Given this kind of adversary, "the inevitable question is what should Blacks do?" (1975:9). First, Wright suggests that Blacks must cast aside illusions that a psychopathic oppressor can provide strategies of liberation for those they oppress. Secondly, Blacks must recognize the oppressors as waging war against them and respond in equal measure. And finally, he (1975:11) states that they should seek the "answer to Blacks' problems in the works and lives of Black heroes" and heroines "whose minds have moved past the psychopath's imposed boundaries and have begun to blaze new paths towards Blacks' rendezvous with destiny."

8.3   ETHOS

The stress on the radical restructuring of the consciousness of Black people and persons by Black psychologists finds its logical parallel and support in the Kawaida contentions concerning the need for a proactive and positive ethos among African Americans (Karenga, 1980:Chapter VIII). Kawaida defines ethos "as the sum of characteristics and achievements of a people which define and distinguish it from others and gives it its collective self-consciousness and collective personality" (Karenga, 1980:90). Put another way, "the ethos of a people is often called its national or ethnic character which is not only defined by itself, but also assumed by others."

Now, ethos, or a people's self-consciousness and self-definition, is defined by their thought and practice in the other six fundamental areas of culture, i.e., history, religion, social organization, economic organization, political organization and creative production. This means essentially that we know ourselves and are known by what we have done and do. And from our knowledge of self and others' knowledge or perception of us, we acquire our self-concept. Thus, the contribution of the

Africans of Egypt to the establishment of the major disciplines
of human knowledge defines them in their own eyes as well as
the world's. Moreover, the Moorish African contribution to the
civilization of Europe, the African contribution to the Olmec
civilization and African Americans' contribution to the social and
cultural wealth of the U.S. and its political liberation and
development, all indicate sources of positive self-consciousness
and self-definition.

The achievement of a positive ethos lies then in historical
and current struggle and achievement. The struggle can be seen
as an ongoing struggle of humans, in this case Blacks, to realize
themselves. In Kawaida theory, self-realization has a double
meaning, i.e., to know and to produce oneself. To know oneself
is to grasp the essences of one's past, one's present and
especially one's future possibilities and thereby know who you
are by what you have done and thus what you are capable of
doing and becoming based on past achievement and current
conditions. To produce oneself is to create oneself through
struggle against natural and social oppositions and through
knowledge of what and who you can and ought to be. Thus, self-
knowledge and self-production are at the heart of ethos and are
clearly linked. For as a people struggles to overcome basic
oppositions, then, it creates and defines itself and informs the
world of its difference and distinctiveness, i.e., its ethos. Thus,
a people comes into being and knows itself by its achievements;
and through its efforts to become and know itself, it achieves.

Given this, it is a fundamental Kawaida contention that
a people whose achievements are minor, or whose knowledge of
its history and the possibilities it suggests is deficient, develops
a self-consciousness of similar characteristics. Moreover, in a
social context which defines and deforms a people's capacity to
realize itself, the problem of self-consciousness is not simply a
problem of thought, but also a problem of practice (Karenga,
1982). For the demand to end a deficient consciousness must be
joined to a demand to eliminate the conditions which caused it.
This is why Black psychologists advocate the social intervention

model of psychology advanced by Fanon (1967:11) who argued that mental health demanded a solution on both the subjective (mental) and objective (social) level.

In conclusion, then, the problem of self-consciousness is solved in the process of solving the social problems which cause it. This essentially means that through *study, work* and *struggle, building and becoming,* Blacks' real self, hidden under layers of false roles and identities imposed by the dominant society, will emerge. Through these self-conscious efforts and the resultant achievements in the various areas of human thought and practice as well as the model of work and liberational struggle Africans in America establish, they will, as I (Karenga, 1980:114) stated, transform themselves into a distinct self-realized and "self-conscious historical personality, proud of its past, challenged by the present and inspired by the possibilities of the future."

STUDY QUESTIONS

1. Define psychology stressing the reasons for its human focus.
2. Give a historical summary of the development of Black psychology.
3. What are the defining aspects of the traditional school of Black psychology?
4. What are some defining aspects of the reformist school of Black psychology?
5. What are some defining aspects of the radical school of Black psychology?
6. Discuss critically the contentions of the traditional psychologists presented.
7. Discuss critically the contentions of the reformist psychologists presented.
8. Discuss critically the contentions of the radical psychologists presented.

9.   Define and discuss the Kawaida conception of ethos.
10.   Discuss the link between self-consciousness, social achievement and social struggle.

REFERENCES

Akbar, Na'im (Luther X Weems). (1974) "Awareness: The Key to Black Mental Health," Journal of Black Psychology, 1, 1 (August) 30-37.

Akbar, Na'im. (1981) "Mental Disorder Among African Americans," *Black Books Bulletin*, 5, 2, 18-25.

Akbar, Na'im. (1976) "Rhythmic Pattern in African Personality," in *African Philosophy, Assumption & Paradigms for Research on Black Persons*, Lewis King, et al (eds.), Los Angeles: Fanon Center Publication, pp. 175-189.

Akbar, Na'im. (1991) *Visions for Black Men*, Nashville, TN: Winston-Derek Publishers, Inc.

Baldwin, Joseph (Kobi Kazembe Kalongi Kambon). (1992) *The African Personality in America: An African-Centered Framework*, Tallahassee, FL: Nubian Nation Publications.

Baldwin, Joseph (Kobi Kazembe Kalongi Kambon). (1976) "Black Psychology and Black Personality: Some Issues for Consideration," *Black Books Bulletin*, 4, 3:6-11.

Baldwin, Joseph (Kobi Kazembe Kalongi Kambon). (1980) "The Psychology of Oppression," *Contemporary Black Thought*, (eds.) Molefi K. Asante and Abdulai S. Vandi, Beverly Hills: Sage Publications, pp. 95-110.

Clark, Kenneth. (1965) *Dark Ghetto*, New York: Harper & Row.

Cress Welsing, Frances. (1980) "The Concept and the Color of God and Black Mental Health," *Black Books Bulletin*, 7, 1:27ff.

Cress Welsing, Frances. (1970) *The Cress Theory of Color Confrontation and Racism (White Supremacy)*, Washington, D.C.: C-R Publishers.

Cress Welsing, Frances. (1991) *The Isis Papers: The Keys to the Colors*, Chicago: Third World Press.

Cross, William E., Jr. (1980) "Models of Psychological Nigrescence: A Literature Review," *Black Psychology*, (ed.) Reginald L. Jones, New York: Harper & Row.

Cross, William E. Jr. (1991) *Shades of Black; Diversity in Africa-American Identity*, Philadelphia: Temple University Press.

Cross, William E. Jr., (1971) "The Negro-To-Black Conversation Experience," *Black World*, (July) 13-27.

Fanon, Frantz. (1967) *Black Skin, White Masks*, New York: Grove Press.

Fanon, Frantz. (1968) *The Wretched of the Earth*, New York: Grove Press.

Grier, William H. and Price M. Cobbs (1968) *Black Rage*, New York: Bantam Books.

Guthrie, Robert V. (1970) *Being Black*, San Francisco: Canfied Press.

Guthrie, Robert V. (1976) *Even The Rat Was White*, New York: Harper & Row.

Jackson, Gerald G. (1982) "Black Psychology: An Avenue to the Study of Afro-Americans," *Journal of Black Studies*, 12, 3 (March) 241-261.

Jackson, Gerald G. (1979) "The Origin and Development of Black Psychology Implications for Black Studies and Human Behavior," *Studia Africana*, 1, 3 (Fall) 270-293.

Jones, Reginald. (1980) *Black Psychology*, New York: Harper & Row.

Kagan, Jerome and Ernest Havemann. (1976) *Psychology*, New York: Harcourt Brace Jovanovich.

Karenga, Maulana. (1978) "Chinese Psycho-Social Therapy: A Strategic Model for Mental Health," *Psychotherapy: Theory, Research and Practice*, 15, 1 (Spring) 101-107.

Karenga, Maulana. (1980) *Kawaida Theory: An Introductory Outline*, Inglewood, CA: Kawaida Publications.

Karenga, Maulana. (1982) "Society, Culture and the Problem of Self-Consciousness: A Kawaida Analysis," in *Philosophy Born of Struggle*, Leonard Harris (ed.), Dubuque, IA: Kendall/Hunt.

King, Lewis M. et al (eds.) (1976) *African Philosophy*, Los Angeles: Fanon Center Publication.

Myers, Linda James. (1992) "Celebrating the Reality of Optimal Psychology: The African Healers are Here!" *Psych Discourse*, 23, 8 (November) 6-9.

Myers, Linda James. (1987) "The Deep Structure of Culture: The Relevance of Traditional African Culture in Contemporary Times," *Journal of Black Studies*, 4, 1-12.

Myers, Linda James. (1985) "Transpersonal Psychology: The Role of the Afrocentric Paradigm," *Journal of Black Psychology*, 12, 1, 31-42.

Myers, Linda James. (1988) *Understanding an Afrocentric World View: Introduction to an Optimal Psychology*, Dubuque, IA: Kendall/Hunt.

Nobles, Wade W. (1980) "African Philosophy: Foundations for Black Psychology," in *Black Psychology*, Reginald L. Jones, (ed.). New York: Harper & Row, pp. 23-26.

Nobles, Wade W. (1986) *African Psychology: Toward Its Reclamation, Reascension and Revitalization*, Oakland, CA: Black Family Institute Publications.

Nobles, Wade W. (1985) *Africanity and the Black Family: The Development of a Theoretical Model*, Oakland: Black Family Institute Publications.

Nobles, Wade W. (1976) "Black People in White Insanity: Issues for Black Community Mental Health," *Journal of Afro-American Issues*, 4, 1:21-27.

Poussaint, Alvin F. (1972) *Why Blacks Kill Blacks*, New York: Emerson Hall Publishers.

Thomas, Charles W. (1971) *Boys No More*, Beverly Hills: Glencoe Press.

Thomas, Charles W. (1978) "The Need for an Ethnically Specific Social Science," lecture, Tuskegee Institute, Tuskegee, Alabama, April 27.

Thomas, Charles W. (1974) "The Significance of the E(thnocentrism) Factor in Mental Health," *Journal of Non-White Concerns in Personal Guidance*, 2, 2.

Thomas, Charles W. (1979) "The Social Significance of Research," paper presented at Howard University Mental Health Research and Development Center, May 1-3.

White, Joseph L. and Thomas A. Parham. (1990) *The Psychology of Blacks: An African-American Perspective*, Englewood Cliffs, NJ: Prentice Hall.

White, Joseph. (1980) "Toward a Black Psychology," *in Black Psychology*, Reginald L. Jones, (ed.), New York: Harper & Row.

Williams, Robert. (1974) "A History of the Association of Black Psychologists: Early Formation and Development," *Journal of Black Psychology*, 1, 1 (August) 7-24.

Wilson, Amos N. (1991a) *Awakening the Natural Genius of Black Children*, NY; African World Infosystems.

Wilson, Amos N. (1978) *The Developmental Psychology of the Black Child*, New York: Africana Research Publications.

Wilson, Amos N. (1981) "The Psychological Development of the Black Child," *Black Books Bulletin*, 7, 2:8-14.

Wilson, Amos N. (1991b) *Understanding Black Adolescent Male Violence*, New York: Afrikan World Infosystems.

Wright, Bobby E. (1981) "Black Suicide: Lynching by Any Other Name is Still Lynching," *Black Books Bulletin*, 7, 2:15-17.

Wright, Bobby E. (1975) *The Psychopathic Racial Personality*, Chicago: Third World Press.

CHALLENGES AND POSSIBILITIES

9
CHALLENGES AND POSSIBILITIES

9.1   INTRODUCTION

Moving toward its third decade, the discipline of Black Studies faces challenges which, depending on the process and effectiveness of their solution, will determine and shape its future on campuses across the country (Turner, 1984; Karenga, 1988; Harris, Hine and McKay, 1990; Stewart, 1992). Assessing the state of the discipline, Robert Harris (1990:12) has observed that essentially "Africana Studies has achieved legitimacy and has become institutionalized within higher education." Moreover, he perceives an increased "theoretical refinement and more sophisticated analysis" along with the development of fundamental research tools which will, of necessity, continue to be updated and expanded. He concludes that "in general the field is in fairly good condition, but there are some problems or perhaps some opportunities to improve it."

It is these problems and opportunities which I designate as challenges to indicate their dual character of problem and possibility. For although these challenges suggest severe tests, the successful meeting of these challenges can only enhance the possibilities of further expansion and development of the discipline. By challenge, I mean to indicate and define, then, a demanding task or problem which calls for special effort, dedication and struggle. Surely, the problems and tasks confronting Black Studies demand special commitment and effort to solve and complete. Thus, the category challenge is used because it not only contains emphasis on tasks and problems, but also special dedication, effort and struggle to complete and solve them. A listing of these basic challenges to Black Studies, which are both internal and external, will aid in demonstrating the value of such an approach. In this context, two broad categories of challenges stand out: 1) the political challenge, and 2) the intellectual challenge. However, before discussing these challenges, it is important to put these challenges in historical perspective by providing a background of conditions which led to the current state of things.

9.2   BACKGROUND

Many of the current challenges to Black Studies appear, upon analysis, to be rooted in the very process of its birth and development as a discipline. Three fundamental factors among others contributed directly and most definitively to the development of these challenges. They are: 1) the dual mission of the discipline; 2) problematic administrators in the discipline; and 3) administrative opposition on campus.

The Academic-Social Mission of Black Studies

The first of these was the fact that initially Black Studies was not simply an academic enterprise, but also a political/social one (Anderson, 1990: Section One). As outlined in Chapter 1, Black Studies was part of the overall demand of the Black community for meaningful and effective participation in every decision and process that affected their destiny and daily lives. In fact, the struggle for Black Studies was viewed and posed as part of the overall struggle to rescue and reconstruct Black history and humanity and free Black minds and labor for Black people's use and benefit. As Nathan Hare (1972:33) observed, "early advocates of Black Studies sought both the collective elevation of a people with education of, from and for the masses, and the training of a mass minded Black conscious middle class."

Also, another expression of the political character and shaping of the Black Studies enterprise is that Black Studies rose, not from internal administrative enlightenment and decision to expand university offerings, but out of a struggle by Black students deeply immersed in the thought and movement of Black liberation. As I argued above, the demand for Black Studies is unavoidably linked to the rise of the militant Black Student Movement in the 60's. "In fact, it is no exaggeration to say that the establishment of hundreds of Black Studies curricula in colleges and universities across the land was a major achievement of the Black Student Movement..." (Allen, 1974:2).

This dual interrelated thrust to create Black Studies from the Black Liberation Movement in general and the Black Student Movement in particular was a political thrust as well as an academic one. This provoked cries of politicization of education and facile arguments against Black Studies by hostile administrators already eager to oppose what was considered an intrusion in the traditional academic arena. Also, this political thrust often led to the subordination of academic demands to political interpretations of relevance and to periodic halts in academic work and intellectual production. This, among other things, certainly interrupted necessary instruction and contributed to diminished production of literature in the field.

Problematic Administrators in Black Studies

A second factor contributive to the current challenges to Black studies is the fact that those who posed the issue, struggled for and won a space for Black Studies on campus were and are not the same as those who were brought in and chosen for the administration of the programs or departments (Brisbane, 1974:223-237). The students who spearheaded and led the struggle were obviously incapable of administration of the programs they fought for and won. Likewise, their community-organization allies could only obtain temporary teaching positions, never administrative ones. Thus, their theoretical orientation, their principles and motivations never became a fundamental part of the spirit, thought or practice in the discipline of Black Studies. In the place of these principles and motivations were inserted the ideas, interests and orientations of four basic types of administrators who shaped Black Studies in their own images and threatened to bring it to the brink of impotence and irrelevance on several campuses.

The four types of administrators, i.e., chairs, coordinators and directors, which assumed leadership of Black Studies were: 1) the pragmatists; 2) the Continental and Caribbean Africans; 3) the integrationists; and 4) the opportunists. The pragmatists were essentially resistant to ideological emphases and necessities. Instead, they reduced Black Studies to what was essentially an administrative and public relations program. Their guiding principles were legitimacy, harmony and action-by-the-book. Brisbane (1974:239) described the product of the pragmatists when he spoke of the courses offered at leading Black institutions like Howard, Morgan, Atlanta, Fisk and Lincoln. The courses these pragmatists put together to defuse the demands for Black Studies "consisted principally of the regular curriculum plus a few additional courses in Black history, politics, art, religion and the like." In fact, "none of them appeared to reflect a genuine long-term commitment to the teaching of the Black Experience." After all, the point for the pragmatists was not to be ideological or inventive, but rather to be successful in defusing the force of radical demands and reduce everything to efficient administration and effective public relations.

Many Continental and Caribbean African administrators proved problematic also for Black Studies for various reasons. First, they often came with less stake and orientation in the struggle for Black Studies and/or African American liberation and thus, with less commitment to build Black Studies in the image of the politically oriented groups who demanded and fought for its existence on campus. They were usually more acceptable to white administrators because of their non-problematic nationality, i.e., non-American, which often meant less or no stake in the struggle and therefore, less tendency to challenge or try to link what was considered to be essentially an academic enterprise to the embarrassing and disruptive demands of the Black community. Moreover, they were the prototype Africans (Continentals) or at least considered not as "mixed" (Caribbeans) as "so-called negroes" and thus, were often exempt from the intense criticism African American academic brokers in similar roles were subjected to by African American radicals and moderates alike. In a word, they easily met the racial criteria and often escaped the political criticism in the name of Pan-African unity and thru the naive assumption that Blackness was a function of geographical origin rather than cultural consciousness and political struggle.

It is this uncritical acceptance, the tendency toward accommodationist academics by many Continentals and Caribbeans, their lack of strong, viable links with the African American community and struggle and white administrator's apparent preference for them over African Americans which began to prove problematic for Black Studies. Moreover, another problem was the tendency of many of the Continentals and Caribbeans to focus on Continental or Pan-African Studies rather than African American Studies. This tended to create a problematic quandary of emphasis in a discipline which by origin and need should logically be and has been African American centered. None of this is to suggest that all Continental and Caribbean administrators fitted into this framework. Many were committed to both the academic and social missions of Black Studies. But it does suggest that there were enough uncommitted to have posed a problem for Black Studies in its early striving to establish itself, even as there were many African American administrators who posed similar problems for the discipline.

A third type of administrator is the integrationist who was embarrassed by what he/she considered the raucous political demands often placed on Black Studies to maintain its Afrocentric focus. The integrationists were split between the economic benefit of their position and the perceived liability of being a part of anything that resembles what they call separatism. Moreover, they were less prone toward community links which obviously would impose on them an identity and duty they would rather deny, downplay or dismiss. Also integrationists were usually those who advocated what can be called weak conceptions of Black Studies, i.e., non-discipline conceptions such as "an adjunct to Eurocentric metatheories;" "a subcomponent of individual discipliners," -- history, literature, etc.; or "a component of non-discipline aggregates -- African Studies, ethnic studies, etc." (Stewart, 1992:40-41). In a word, they did not see Black Studies as a self-justifying discipline but as an uneasy additive or component of some larger more legitimate enterprise.

Finally, the administrators include a group best defined as academic opportunists. They entered Black Studies not because they believed in its principles or supported its academic or political objectives, but simply because of its personal benefit to them. Some were there because they could not be in the traditional departments due to institutional racism or their own incompetence. Since in the confusion of knowing with being, all Blacks are supposed to be competent in Black Studies, and since Black Studies was considered in some quarters less than an academic enterprise, these Blacks often were appointed not so much on the basis of academic credentials as on the basis of racial identity and psycho-political orientation (Brisbane, 1974:241). Thus, they were appointed and promoted on levels and with a facility no other department would have allowed. In addition, they received increases in rank and step, not for theoretical production or professional achievement, but for non-problematic management of what was considered a pseudo-academic nuisance unscheduled for long endurance. It was this approach to Black Studies that led some to conclude that Black Studies was the first academic discipline "for which burial was in order before the labor pangs subsided" (Brisbane, 1974:239).

Administrative Opposition on Campus

The third factor which has clearly contributed to the development of these challenges is opposition and ambiguous acceptance of Black Studies by many campus administrations and traditional departments. Brisbane (1974), Walton (1974) and Hare (1972) all make this point and demonstrate how this opposition and ambiguous acceptance continue to plague Black Studies and pose for it a clear challenge. Actually, few administrations ever fully accepted Black Studies as a viable and valid academic enterprise. Generally, they conceded to its establishment only under various kinds of pressure and usually refused to grant it department status, conceding instead programs or just courses. Moreover, traditional white studies departments and administrators challenged its academic validity and viability and also felt threatened by the students it would take, the courses it would teach, the budget it would use and the challenges it would pose to traditional disciplines and to the paradigms and data on which they were based. As Hine (1990:17) states, "Many undoubtedly wished that Black Studies would go away; others tried to thwart growth and development. (And) Most of those who opposed the creation of Black Studies units claimed that these units would lower academic standards because they believed such endeavors lacked intellectual substance." Continuing this posture and recognizing that Black Studies does not have the level of active community and assertive student organizational support it had in the 60's, many campuses are now moving to dismantle, reduce or merge Black Studies departments and programs. Thus, these forces which never fully accepted Black Studies and opposed its establishment are continuing to pose one of its most critical challenges today.

Hine (1990:16) observes that she has witnessed an "attitudinal transformation" from the "initial vehement objections to the creation of Black Studies units." Moreover, Nellie McKay (1990:26) states that she sees "a renewed commitment among predominantly white institutions to strengthen Black Studies and to increase the number of them on their campuses." However, this optimism is not shared by the majority of Black Studies faculty and administrators who face challenges of cutbacks, budget restraints, hiring freezes and mergers as reported at annual meetings of the National Council for Black Studies. Furthermore, McKay (1990: 27) concedes that although much has been achieved through intellectual production and political struggle, "Black Studies, however, still has not achieved full acceptance in the scholarly community -- despite the fact that it has been one of the prime movers in revolutionizing the nature of accepted knowledge in the 80's." The answer to this dual perception is that there are and have always been individual administrators more favorable than others, but on the whole, the general climate is more often less receptive than ideal collegiality would require or less even, as she notes, than the climate for women's studies. It is thus in this context of ambiguous receptivity and resistance that the political and intellectual challenges are posed.

9.3   THE POLITICAL CHALLENGE

Continuing Opposition

The political challenge to Black Studies, then, begins with the continuing opposition and lack of support from campus administrations. As discussed above, this takes many forms, including dismantlings, subsuming Black Studies under Ethnic Studies, budget cuts, refusals to grant or support department status and other acts negative to the maintenance and development of Black Studies. As early as 1972, Nathan Hare (1972:34) one of the leading theorists and activists in the struggle for Black Studies, had noted that Black Studies was being systematically dismantled and diluted in the areas of its identity, purpose and direction. He observed that not only were the college and university administrators opposing the liberational thrust of an incipient Black ideology, but they were also in large part successful in destroying or diminishing the community links component of Black Studies and "in restricting Black Studies to culture and the humanities to the mere study of Blackness."

By 1974 Allen (1974:2) would report that Black Studies was "in deep trouble" and fighting a rearguard battle even though it "began with such enthusiasm and optimism in the late 60's." This, he continued, was due to the fact that "wholesale cutbacks in operating budgets and student financial aid, coupled with intellectual ambushes by academic critics, have crippled or destroyed dozens of Black Studies departments and programs around the country." In fact, he concluded, "In 1971 some 500 schools provided full-scale Black Studies programs; today that figure has dropped to 200." Although a rough estimate of existing programs still hovers around the figure 200, it is clear that many are on tenuous ground. The need, then, becomes one of building political support on and off campus for them.

In addition to cutbacks and dismantling, Black Studies has historically faced the challenge of establishing itself as a department in spite of a chilly climate. As Brisbane (1974:240) noted, one of the major problems at the beginning of Black Studies was the issue of "...whether the program should be administered by an autonomous department or by an interdisciplinary, coordinating committee." This problem has still not been solved. It was argued then and remains true that without departmental autonomy, a viable and effective Black Studies enterprise is difficult if not impossible. However, the vast majority of institutions resisted such autonomy and reduced Black Studies to programs managed by interdisciplinary coordinating committees.

Walton (1974:23) observed that it was this administrative crippling thru the refusal to build departments and give economic security thru tenure-oriented assignments that contributed greatly to the decline in the academic quality and stability of the Black Studies program. As he stated:

...unwillingness of the white controlled educational institutions to make any sort of long-term commitment to Black Studies created a situation wherein the academic quality of Black Studies programs was rapidly eroded by the fact of the unstable and temporary nature of the persons responsible for the implementation of the programs.

Moreover, instead of developing strong Black Studies Departments, colleges and universities have come up with three alternative structures: (1) courses only; (2) programs; and (3) institutes which lack the legitimacy, structure and personnel to achieve goals usually associated with departments (Smith and Yates, 1980:279).

The response to such continuing opposition, lack of support and attempts to dismantle, merge or divide through joint appointment must be multidimensional and philosophically grounded. Black Studies faculty, administrators and students must stand firm on the principle that there is, of course, no substitute for departmental status. As Hine (1990:16) notes, it is only departments which are "separate autonomous units possessing an exclusive right and privilege to hire and grant tenure to their faculty, certify students, confer degrees and administer a budget." Programs are tenuous, and joint appointments for their faculty only divide their loyalties and divert their intellectual energies from Black Studies as a discipline. Moreover, there is no serious discipline without departmental status. Thus, departmental status is not only basic evidence of a discipline, but it is also an indication of the level of campus support for the discipline.

In spite of claims of support by campus administrators, then, they can best show such support by conceding and facilitating departmental status, providing adequate budget to hire and sustain needed faculty and supporting a viable program to recruit and retain Black Studies students. Furthermore, degree programs beyond the B.A. degree must be established and maintained. The Temple University African American Studies Ph.D. Program offers an excellent model of the direction in which other departments should move, for the discipline both requires and demands Ph.D. programs in any and all institutions which grant Ph.D.'s. Otherwise, they are both thwarted in their ultimate task and diminished in status (Asante, 1992:115ff). As long as the Temple project remains the only Ph.D. program in the field, campus administrations cannot claim the dubious position of being favorable to Black Studies. Finally, Black Studies scholars and students must be active on campus, participating in academic and student government, and making appropriate alliances with other ethnic studies departments, women studies, and other progressive forces willing to support a truly multicultural education and campus. Likewise, they must build support in the community and compel the university to respect the aspirations and interests of the communities it claims to serve.

Professional Organizations

A second political challenge is the need to continuously expand support for and critical participation in effective national professional organizations for Black Studies. The National Council for Black Studies has assumed a vanguard role in this respect and should be supported and further developed. Also, the African Heritage Studies Association and the Association for the Study of Black Life and History have made tremendous contributions to the discipline and should likewise be supported. It is in the context of strong and viable organizations that collective strategies, a standard curriculum, rationales, resources, defense of interests and scholarly exchanges will evolve. Moreover, coordination and regular exchange must be achieved by these structures. For without such organized efforts and collective thrusts, each of these structures will tend to be reduced to struggle for attention, duplication of effort as well as counterproductive competition and division of effort where coordination is required.

Community Rootedness

A third dimension of the political challenge to Black Studies is to maintain and deepen its relations with the community. From its inception Black Studies saw itself in relationship and in service to the Black community. It defined itself as an emancipatory project dedicated to expanding the realm of freedom--intellectually and socially. Thus, the concept of mission was key to its self-conception. As outlined in Chapter 1, this mission was a dual mission--an academic and social one. Nathan Hare (1978:14) summarized this dual mission when he stated that "We must transform the community and make it relevant to the educational endeavor at the same time as we make education relevant to the community." This he also conceptualized as "bringing the community to the campus and the campus to the community."

Such a position also emerges out of an historical communitarian understanding of education evidenced in the writings of African American educators like W.E.B. DuBois and Mary McLeod Bethune who taught a concept of mission within their philosophy of education. For Bethune (1939: 9) education was essentially a process of searching for truth, critically interpreting it and sharing it with the masses. The central challenge of education, she asserted, is "to discover the dawn and bring this material within the understanding of the child and the masses." Moreover, the challenge of education includes, she states, "seeing that the fruits of science and invention are within the reaches of the masses who need it most." DuBois also posed mission as an inherent part of the educational process, advocating an education that would produce a Talented Tenth, the best and brightest of the community, who would guide and serve the community (DuBois, 1975; Paschal, 1971:31ff). These would be men and women of intelligence and character with vision beyond vulgar careerism and class bias (Stewart, 1984: 306ff). The vision here is one of an ethically focused education rooted in a conception of "knowledge for human sake" as distinct from "knowledge for knowledge sake" and of a dialectical link between intellectual emancipation and political emancipation, as well as between campus and community.

But such a conception which reached its most definitive stage in the emancipatory struggles of the 60's is not the sole or even major motivation in many Black Studies departments. The stress is often placed on the academic at the expense of the social and great effort is made to both disown and disengage from historical links with and roots in the community and its struggles for a just and good society. The need, then, is to reaffirm this link and rootedness, to reaffirm and reinforce Black Studies' link of critique and corrective, social knowledge and social practice. Rooted in such a mutually beneficial relationship, the power of Black Studies units and the Black community to define, defend and develop themselves is enhanced and consolidated. For the stronger the organization(s) and the alliances built and effectively utilized, the greater the power. Thus, the organization and alliance of Black Studies and the community can only enhance each other's power and unite them in an effective mutually beneficial project of the collective rescue and reconstruction of Black history and humanity.

Progressive Alliances

Finally, an important aspect of the political challenge is to build and sustain positive and productive relations, especially with other Third World ethnic programs or departments as well as with women studies and other progressive forces on campus. Too often relations with others are characterized by antagonistic competition for resources, positions and administrative favor (Allen, 1974). In some cases, there are no relations at all which lead to the cultivation of negative myths on all sides, gratuitous distance and dismissal of the importance of mutually beneficial exchanges. Such distance and/or hostility make ethnic departments and programs more vulnerable to administrative manipulation and eventual cancellation or forced combining. On the other hand, operational unity around clear principles of cooperation and common objectives would add to the meager strength most of these departments and programs have individually. In the current efforts to build and sustain a truly multicultural curriculum, campus alliances of progressive forces on campus are indispensable (President's Task Force, 1991).

However, the forging of an effective operational unity among ethnic studies departments and programs, and the development of positive and effective relations of these departments and programs with the community, students and other progressive forces, as well as the building and support of national professional organizations for Black Studies depend, in the final analysis, on the resolution of the intellectual challenge which would provide the necessary coherent set of views and values to initiate, sustain and develop such practices (Karenga, 1988).

9.4   THE INTELLECTUAL CHALLENGE

The Problematic of Philosophy

Like the political challenge, the intellectual challenge is multidimensional and, as mentioned above, clearly affects Black Studies' capacity to meet the political challenge. This intellectual challenge as other Black Studies scholars and I have noted, begins with the problem of paradigm and philosophy which defines the field and sets up its basic parameters of focus in intellectual production and allied practice (Weber, 1984; Le-Melle, 1984; Turner, 1984; Karenga, 1988; Stewart, 1992). As Turner (1984:xviii) notes, "Black Studies is a conceptual paradigm that principally tells us, like other academic discourse, what counts as facts and what problems of explanations exist." And this paradigm must be undergirded and informed by "a philosophy of Black Studies that offer(s) an analytic, empirical and ethical framework for studying, understanding and explicating African American life in its current and historical unfolding" (Karenga, 1988:401).

The imperative of theoretical construction which contributes to the development of a philosophy of Black Studies is well-recognized in the discipline. Shirley Weber (1984:411) has asserted that "the first challenge of (the discipline) is to develop a sound philosophy of operation." However, she recognizes the profound historical resistance expressed within the discipline to a definitive philosophy which would set basic guidelines and parameters of research and relevance. Thus, she goes on to say that while a philosophy "does restrict, it also gives direction and purpose to the program." The key to this problematic is an open-textured philosophy which both allows and encourages different ways of approaching the discipline but nevertheless sets basic guidelines and parameters of research and relevance which focus on intellectual *rigor* rather than ideological conformity.

LeMelle (1984:60) is correct in his assertion that "success or failure of Black Studies programs and departments will depend to a large degree on the resolution of ideological struggles within Black Studies." What is called for here, then, is not the triumph of an ideology, but the philosophical agreement and grounding in paradigms of research and relevance which characterize all disciplines. For "a discipline by definition is a self-conscious, organized system of research and communication in a defined area of inquiry and knowledge, not simply a literature, series of courses in schools and universities or research focus in a given area" (Karenga, 1988:399).

The project above all requires a self-consciousness, organization and demarcation of the intellectual enterprise, which only a philosophy of Black Studies can provide. Such a philosophy must be, as suggested above, an open-textured one, allowing for and encouraging diversity of perspective, but insisting on the integrity, essentiality and intellectual rigor and relevance of and in the discipline. It is within the context of such a philosophy that what Stewart (1984) calls "exemplars" of excellence in research and intellectual production can be both produced and evaluated on mutually agreed upon grounds.

Self-Definition of the Discipline

Within the context of a philosophy of Black Studies is the intellectual challenge for Black Studies to delineate and reaffirm its original self-definition, i.e., establish and reaffirm in clear terms in a body of critical literature its academic and social missions. The problem of self-definition is undoubtedly the core of the intellectual challenge, for its resolution and has implications for all its other aspects. In fact, it appears that unless effective self-definition is achieved and reaffirmed, the defense and development of Black Studies will remain not only a problem of theory, but also a problem of practice as well (Stewart, 1979).

At its inception, Black Studies was relatively clear about its broad objectives even if it were less so about specifics. As a product of the Black Liberation and Black Student Movements, Black Studies assigned itself two broad set of goals which overlapped and reinforced each other. These, again, were the academic and social missions posed in Chapter 1. As Hare (1972: 33) expressed it, "Black Studies was (essentially) a mass movement and a mass struggle based on the notion that education belongs to the people and the idea is to give it back to them." Given this, Hare argues that "Most crucial to Black Studies, Black education, aside from its ideology of liberation, would be the community component of its methodology." This essentially involved a process of gaining and utilizing skills to teach and assist the community in its defense and development and, in turn, seeking assistance from the community in the thrust to become and remain a viable and relevant academic unit on campus.

However, these goals once so clear have become on many campuses obfuscated by changes in the community and on campus which eroded clarity and called into question not only Black Studies' relationship with the community, but also its status as a discipline and in some cases its very raison d'être. Among these changes are: 1) decline of Black students' unions and their deterioration into social clubs or at best pale images of their once defiantly Black selves; 2) the lull in the Black Movement which inspired, informed and supported campus struggles; 3) the police and intelligence agency suppression of Black leaders and organizations who led the community and campus struggles; 4) the resurgence of racism in the face of weakened campus and community structures; and 5) the return to academic business-as-usual, given the inability of Blacks to intervene effectively in the process to introduce and impose their interests.

The Problematic of Primary Focus

Central to the philosophical problem of self-definition is the issue of focus and thrust which pose several dualities not easily reconciled. First, there is the issue of whether Black Studies should be African American centered or Pan-African (Turner, 1984:viff; Hine, 1990:15). Usually, a Pan-African emphasis means a Continent-centered program, but it may include Caribbean Studies, the study of South American and Islander Blacks or any other Blacks as well. As Nick Ford (1973:3) pointed out in the first decade of Black Studies development:

> ...The phrase "Black Studies" has become an acceptable designation for all studies primarily concerned with the experience of people of African origin residing in any part of the world. (Thus)...it includes the experiences of Africans, Afro-Americans, Afro-Asians, Afro-Europeans, and African descendants of the Caribbean and other island territories.

Although this definition is correct in its inclusion, it still leaves fundamental questions unanswered. For example, which of these areas or peoples should get the most attention, and if it is to be equally divided, why? If Black Studies is still to link the campus to the community, how does it now define the community given its expanded focus? Moreover, just as a point of departure and sound procedure, does not logic demand a thrust which is not over-ambitious, but begins where it is, in the U.S., among African Americans, and then as it grows stronger, expands outward? In other words, is not the study of African Americans the core of Black Studies in the U.S., the study of an African people neglected more than any other, certainly more than the study of Continentals or Caribbeans?

As I (Karenga, 1988:405-406) have argued, the priority focus on the African American experience is both necessary and correct for several reasons. "First such a priority focus is a due recognition and respect for the history of the discipline as an intellectual enterprise conceived and established by African Americans, first and foremost for their own intellectual and political emancipation." This, of course, does not exclude study of and linkage with other parts of the world African community. On the contrary, as Turner (1984:viii) states, Black Studies stresses linkage and knowledge of the global Black experience but "with understandably, primary concentration on African America." Secondly, "the priority focus on African Americans makes the praxis dimension of Africana or Black Studies, readily recognizable and easier to implement" (Karenga, 1988:406). As I have stated, "The original call by Nathan Hare to 'bring the campus to the community and the community to the campus' finds its practical expression in the African American community." Again, none of this is to deny the global branches of Black Studies, it is only to reaffirm its African American roots. Such a position allows for a concrete social theory on the African American social reality (Turner and Perkins, 1976:10) and facilitates developmental links with the community which will allow "the transmission of the gains and experiences of the struggle from one generation to another (which) is a vital task of education" (Chinweizu, 1977:24).

The Issue of Value Orientation

A third problem of paradigm and philosophy revolves around values. By values is meant here categories of commitment, categories of priorities and categories of possibilities. Stress is especially placed on possibilities, for what a person or people is committed to and set as priorities dictate their human possibilities. Thus, the value orientation of Black Studies is key to understanding the possibilities it offers its advocates and students. Among the value foci debated in the midst of the philosophical problematic are: 1) critique and correctives vs. acceptance and perpetuation of the established order in study and research; 2) stress on Black resistance and construction vs. the virulent character of our oppression and the assumed pathologies it engendered; 3) education of change agents vs. the vulgar careerists which DuBois (1961:42-54) and Frazier (1970: 71-76) criticized and challenged; 4) a multidimensional education vs. a one-dimensional education, and finally 5) program or department stress on development vs. stress on simple survival.

It would seem safe to say that the way to handle the value dimension of the philosophical problematic is to stress both aspects of the dualities, to stress alternatives and acceptance, resistance and oppression, change and careerism. However, such a position is not only dishonest, but negative to the clarity and strength necessary for Black Studies to successfully meet its challenges. As an African proverb says *"mpanda farasi wawili, hupasuka msamba"* (a rider of two horses is split in two), and we can add, in this case, both theoretically and structurally. Moreover, a challenge demands a clear and solid decision and that decision must, of necessity, be proactive rather than simply defensive or survival-oriented.

It is clear that the value orientation for Black Studies must be proactive rather than reactive, toward social change rather than simple protest or servile careerism, toward critique and correctives rather than sterile statements on social pathologies and the oppression which assumedly engendered them. As

Hare (1972:33) contended, "...Black education must be education for liberation, or at least for change. In this respect, it was to prepare Black students to become the catalysts for a Black cultural revolution." But to be an education for liberation and change, Black Studies must develop a new body of literature which reflects audaciousness and initiative in research and critical and corrective intellectual production. It must challenge established disciplines, develop its own social science methodology, and give a new meaning to social science, i.e., the science of social change and reconstruction. As William H. McClendon (1974:17) stated, "Black Studies, in remaining compatible with the assorted needs of Black people to obtain useful and purposeful formal education, is compelled to teach contrary to much of what has become customary and routine in a variety of disciplines."

The Standardization of Rationale

Another problematic of paradigm and philosophy is the development of a rationale for Black Studies, that is to say a standard justification or statement of relevance in terms of the functions it serves. This, although closely related to mission, is not the same and is essentially an answer to the question of how the discipline understands its fundamental contributions as a discipline.

The problem of rationale was engendered, as mentioned above, by the over-ambitious expansion of focus, the value crisis and the assumption of power by administrators who shared none or few of the motivations and objectives of those who launched and won the struggle for Black Studies. In addition to these problems was the problem created by the success of administrators in blocking the "incorporation of an ideology of liberation (particularly in scientific and technical courses) to replace that of acquiescing to the status quo,...rejecting the community component,... (and) restricting Black Studies to culture and humanities,..." (Hare, 1972:34). Such restriction of Black Studies to courses to appease emotionally but not develop intellectually, of necessity called into question the validity and value of Black Studies even among its supporters. For indeed, few people, if any, could claim academic and political relevance and at the same time support self-indulgence as a substitute for critical knowledge of society and the world. Nor could advocates of Black Studies support its reduction to the music, drama, dance and or even history courses which were taught as isolated, unconnected and self-contained subjects and passed off as the essence of the Black experience.

An equally fundamental problem of rationale was the theoretical and administrative thrust toward integration. The first thrust was a natural outgrowth of the introduction and the motivations of professors and administrators who, as mentioned above, saw assimilation as the highest goal and were intellectually and/or emotionally uncomfortable with focus on the Black experience as an experience equal in worth and instructiveness to any other. Nor were they supportive of the struggles on campus and in the community to define, defend and develop Black interests. Moreover, the administrative thrust was a practical and often racist effort to deny autonomy or reality to Black Studies and subsume it under already existing disciplines and departments. Thus, they found ideological allies in the integrationists who argued that Blacks were more definitively Americans or humans, not simply Blacks and that therefore, the need was for a good American or human education, not a Black one (Kilson, 1973).

The problem with this position, especially for the Black academicians, is that it puts them on shaky grounds, ideologically and practically. On one hand, they argue their essential American and human identities and on the other hand they seek, of necessity, to justify their positions, or more specifically, their jobs in a discipline which by their own admission not only does not really exist, but also does not need to exist. After all, how can one argue she/he is most definitively human or American and then justify a department for the study and teaching of a less important or irrelevant sub-identity?

However, as argued in Chapter 1, Black Studies has proved its relevance in seven basic areas and this should serve as a fundamental way of explaining its value and function in the academy and society. The question of rationale, then, is more a problem of standardization than creation. That is to say, Black Studies has established its relevance. The need is for Black Studies literature and faculty to reflect this achievement in a standard rationale. Obviously, I think that whatever its final form is should reflect the seven basic contentions of relevance I advanced in the first chapter, i.e., that it is a contribution: 1) to humanity's self-understanding; 2) to the university's realizing its claim of universality, comprehensiveness and objectivity; 3) to U.S. society's understanding itself; 4) to the rescue and reconstruction of Black history and humanity; 5) to the creation of a new social science; 6) to the creation of a body of conscious, capable and committed Black intellectuals who self-consciously choose to use their knowledge and skills in the service of the Black community and by consequence and extension, in the interest of a new and better society and world; and 7) to the critique, resistance and reversal of the progressive Europeanization of human consciousness and culture which is one of the major problems of our times.

It is this sixth contribution that in fact is key to all the rest, for the development of such a Black intelligentsia insures the realization and expansion of the other contributions which are at the same time tasks. Thus, the central responsibility for the successful meeting of all challenges to Black Studies as well as those which confront Black people, rest as DuBois (1969) argues, with the best minds of the people. Both Harold Cruse (1967) and E. Franklin Frazier (1973) were critical and doubtful of the consciousness, capacity and commitment of the Black intellectual. Frazier's criticism remains in great part valid. He contends that "they have failed to study the problems of (Black) life in America in a manner which would place the fate of (Blacks) in the broad framework of man's experience in this world." Moreover, he charges that "they have engaged in petty defenses of the (African American's) social failure. Even worse, "more often, they have been so imbued with the prospect of integration and eventual assimilation that they have thought that they could prove themselves true Americans by not (even) studying (Blacks)."

Cruse (1967:455) is more optimistic concerning the Black intellectual, assigning them the vital task of intellectual production which leads to a critical explanation of the economic and institutional causes of Black oppression and the development of solutions to it. These contentions are obviously supportive of the academic and social mission of Black Studies. For they pose education as a narrow and invalid process and experience, if it is not placed in service of Black people and is not a contribution to the intellectual conception and practical building of a better society and world. And they also place hope and educational focus on the creation of a conscious, capable and committed body of Black intellectuals who will self-consciously intervene in social reality and history and shape them in the image and interest of Black people (Karenga, 1990).

The Question of Curriculum

Another aspect of the intellectual challenge is the development of an effective and expansive standard curriculum (Hine, 1990:18-20; Stewart, 1992). Every discipline is in great part defined and introduced in a practical sense by its curriculum. Often Black Studies courses seemed to be offered based on the teaching interest or area of the department's or programs' current faculty (Smith, 1971:265-270; Harris, 1990:13). Although there should always be room for innovative and experimental development of courses, no serious discipline can establish itself or its academic legitimacy if all or the bulk of its courses are experimental and if it lacks a standard or core curriculum. Thus, Hine's (1990:20) concern for flexibility in course development does not and should not conflict with the need for a standard core curriculum, i.e., a base from which to expand and on which to build.

The problem of a standard curriculum can be traced back to the origins of Black Studies which, as noted above, was born in a time of confrontation and political urgency. Things were not always thought out nor was the emphasis always on the academic. However, credit must be given to pioneers who were treading on new grounds and in times not conducive to long critical academic exchange. As noted above, in the academic year of 1967-1968, a Black Studies program was adopted at San Francisco State which included eleven courses in Anthropology, Dramatic Arts, Education, English, Psychology and Sociology. These courses were tentative and ad hoc, and were supplanted by a more extensive curriculum designed and developed by Dr. Nathan Hare (Brisbane, 1974:226-227). Hare also built in a community component which included a Black Community Press, Black Information Center and specific methods of faculty, student and community interaction. Although important groundwork was lain by Hare and the Black students at San Francisco State, it seems that it was the struggle for the program rather than its construction and development which became the model. Therefore, in most cases the wheel was reinvented in almost each Black Studies program and a critical study of curriculum and structure proposals was never made on a widespread level.

Added to the inability of subsequent Black Studies programs to learn from the first historical model is the recurring problem of self-definition and definitive focus it requires. For until Black Studies is able to establish a *priority focus,* it is logically and practically impossible for it to design and develop a standard curriculum. With advocates torn between an African American centered focus and a general Pan-African thrust, a unified approach to curriculum is obviously problematic. Moreover, without basic agreement on value focus, the same limitation on standardization is imposed on curriculum development. Thus, Walton (1974: 27) is correct when he argues that:

> The offering of an uncoordinated patchwork of
> ethically oriented courses on an 'a la carte' basis
> will serve only to perpetuate the long term fru-
> strations and problems that many institutions of
> learning experienced because they readily adopt-
> ed uncoordinated courses and portions of Black
> students' program suggestions *prior* to the devel-
> opment of an *internally consistent* structure to
> support the implementation of such courses and
> programs.

The solution of this problem is obviously a major intellectual challenge and calls for serious and sustained critical thinking and exchange.

In terms of a standard curriculum, the seven core subject areas serve as a framework for that determination. A survey of Black Studies curricula shows that numerous variations are possible within such a curricular framework (Smith, 1971; Harris, Hine and McKay, 1990)). Moreover, since most Black Studies programs already have courses within this framework, the standardization process would be less difficult to initiate. Also, as argued in Chapter 1 these seven core subject areas are most definitive of the various aspects of Black life and culture and therefore, serve as core foci for inquiry and analysis. Finally, it is important in the standardization process to start with the establishment of core courses which mirror the core subject areas rather than the possible variations in them. For example, an introductory or advanced course in Black Economics per se should precede courses on specialized areas, i.e., Black Coopera-tives, Black Capitalism, etc. Likewise, a course in Black Politics or its equivalent should precede and take precedence over a course in Urban Welfare Politics or the Political Ideology of Racism. This is curricular base-building as opposed to academic hang gliding, i.e., catching whatever wind faculty members can ride. It is important to note here that NCBS has put extensive effort into developing a standard curriculum and should present it for discussion and action shortly. In addition to development of a standard curriculum, ongoing curriculum development is imperative. Stewart (1992) has suggested an "expanded range of subject areas" in Black Studies, including education, helping/ specialized professions, policy analysis, physical/ natural sciences and engineering. His stress here is on applied solutions to problems confronting the African American community and the larger society.

Finally, the Black Studies curriculum must reaffirm its commitment to and constantly expand in the areas stressed in Chapter 1: women studies, classical African studies, multicultural studies as well as international studies. For these areas are essential both to the definition and development of the discipline and the realization of its academic and social mission.

A Definitive Body of Literature

Finally, the intellectual challenge includes the task of continuing to develop a substantial and definitive body of literature for the discipline of Black Studies. It is obvious that teaching in and development of the discipline can only suffer if such a body of literature is not produced. Such a body of literature not only introduces the subject areas of the discipline but also establishes its focus and rationale, develops and presents its special language and introduces its paradigms, models, techniques, methods, theories, research strategies and research designs (Gordon, 1979; Turner, 1984; Anderson, 1990). Without a substantial definitive body of literature in Black Studies, the worth and future of the discipline will always be in doubt.

Hine (1990:25) notes that "in the early years Black Studies units justified their intellectual existence on the grounds that they shattered the confining and restricting boundaries of traditional disciplines." However, she tends to see this as no longer possible or desirable. She states that it was "naive and unrealistic" to expect young scholars to master and use Afrocentric methodology in the publication of manuscripts in the pursuit of tenure. But in fact at the heart of the Black Studies enterprise is the Afrocentric thrust to study, conceive and approach the world beyond the Eurocentric paradigm, to cross boundaries, challenge semi-sacred assumptions and speak our own special cultural truth to the world. To continue to be what McKay (1990:27) calls "one of the prime movers in revolutionizing the nature of accepted knowledge," Black Studies must be more than a colored duplicate of traditional white studies. It must do something different, creative and challenging. Otherwise, it writes its own intellectual obituary and brings about its own academic death. It is Fanon (1968:255) who challenged us saying, "If we want humanity to advance a step further, if we want to bring it up to a different level than that which Europe has shown it, then we must invent...make discoveries...turn over a new leaf (and) work out new concepts."

By way of paradigm construction, the Afrocentric thrust of Black Studies toward the development of a body of literature which brings into being a new social science and a new humanities and at the same time contribute to the rescue and reconstruction of Black history and humanity must have at least four characteristics. It must be holistic, critical, corrective and committed (Karenga, 1977:50-54). Such an audacious and urgent task:

> ...must take place within a definite *analytical* and *value* framework. It must, in both inquiry and presentation, adhere unashamedly and unreservedly to a core of basic values that express our priorities, aid us in choosing the most important problems, assist us in selection of data most relevant to solving those problems and provide categories and concepts which inspire and inform our inquiry and assumptions (Karenga, 1977:52).

A holistic approach is a comprehensive inquiry into the core process and practices of Black life as well as an investigation into related internal and external factors which confront and affect us as a people. Such an approach recognizes and respects the fact that society or social life is an interconnected, interactive and independent whole and that failure to view it in its totality as far as possible limits perception and intellectual production. A holistic approach places Blacks in interaction with society and the world, not in isolation. A holistic approach considers race, class, and gender factors and their interrelatedness. And it does not treat race, gender and class as topics but rather as fundamental constitutive elements of human reality and thus indispensable ways of understanding social and human reality. Also, it does not and must not sacrifice one for the other or fail to perceive that a faddist clamor for exclusive analysis in no way can deny or diminish the fundamental role each in interaction has played in the shaping of the human society and has played and will play in the struggle to reshape this country in a more human image.

A critical approach is a concrete, rational and incisive approach. It seeks to avoid sterile "protest and pomposity--the temptation to indulge in the maudlin, moralistic enterprise of cataloging injustices and tragedies to elicit sympathy..." (Karenga, 1977:53). Critical intellectual projection moves beyond the insubstantiality of free flows of consciousness and standard calls for survival, digs beneath the surface and raises that which is absent in traditional literature, i.e., the rich variousness and potential of Black life and the subversive content of our history. Its search is for possibilities as well as achievements, for contradictions as well as tendencies that will lead us beyond the established state of things.

A corrective approach strives to go beyond criticism to reconstruction. Thus, a corrective body of Black Studies literature must begin with a redefinition of the world in our own image according to our own needs. In fact, an essential, inevitable act of a people coming into consciousness of itself is to redefine the world and society in order to assure its rightful and true role in them. This is at the heart of the Afrocentric project (Asante, 1990; Karenga, 1988). Moreover, a people in the process of liberation must and does construct an alternative to the established order on the theoretical and practical level. For it understands that *the most severe and effective criticism of a society is self-conscious practice which transforms it.* This is, of course, at the same time a central challenge to its intellectuals (Karenga, 1990).

Finally, the intellectual production that contributes to a new social science and to the rescue and reconstruction of Black history must be committed. It must be unashamedly committed to a set of values contributive to its task--which in the final analysis--is both theoretical and practical. Committed intellectual work reflects the acceptance of one's role as an *unashamed partisan of one's people and their quest for the just and good society, human freedom and human flourishing.* Moreover, it recognizes the fact that there is no pure research isolated and divorced from the urgencies of the day. In fact, "all cultural work takes place in a definite social context, thus, either reinforcing or challenging that context" (Karenga, 1977:52). Or as Chinweizu (1977:234) maintains, "There is no neutral, value-free research, especially in the unnatural, or so-called 'social' sciences. Even in the natural sciences, what gets researched, when, and with what priority and thoroughness, are all matters determined by political and economic considerations." Given this then, "Afro-American researchers and educators should organize in ways to permit them to research what is of value to Afro-America, rather than what is against the interest of Afro-America."

Having accepted such a responsibility on the intellectual level, one cannot but recognize and respond creatively to the fact that a real and effective effort to rescue and reconstruct Black history and humanity in the academy must be at the same time a step toward doing the same thing in society. It is in recognition of this that Black Studies has defined for itself both an academic and social mission and is, thus, both an investigative and applied body of knowledge and practice.

9.5   CONCLUSION

At the beginning of this chapter, I advanced the proposition that challenges successfully met enhance possibilities. It is the history of humankind that overcoming social and natural oppositions strengthened them and pushed them further along the road to ever higher levels of thought and practice. The struggle to defend and develop Black Studies offers similar possibilities of development in the academic world. *Black Studies' need to defend itself is at the same time a demand to develop itself*. Moreover, whatever unsure steps or stumbling there was in the past offers a wealth of lessons for the future which will aid a quicker-paced development. For as an African proverb says, "To stumble is not to fall but to go forward faster." The need, then, is for bold and critical thought and planning, greater intellectual production, more vital research, effective organization, systematic exchange and development. In a word, the need is for self-conscious action which not only answers critics, but more importantly answers the critical questions the discipline continuously raises for itself in the constant refining and expanding of its capacity to carry out its academic and social mission.

In conclusion, Black Studies has shown a remarkable capacity for development and expansion and must continue to do so. Few, if any, of the traditional disciplines has shown such an adaptive vitality in meeting new internal and external challenges to change and expand. Part of this receptivity to and capacity for change and expansion is undoubtedly due to its relative newness, the absence of long-termed entrenched contentions grown hoary and semi-sacred with age.

Moreover, Black Studies is an open-textured and open-ended project, interdisciplinary and receptive to diversity as expressed in its ability to include various subject areas and various intellectual perspectives. But more important, it reflects also the history and character of the discipline itself which came into being as an emancipatory project which seeks to be both an ongoing and profound critique and corrective, intellectually and socially. Thus, if it holds true to its academic and social mission, it is compelled to practice internally what it demands externally, i.e., self-criticism and self-correction. The key to Black Studies continued growth and expansion and its continued vanguard role in the multicultural challenge to the established order paradigm, then, is its maintaining its open-textured, open-ended character which allows for and encourages the creative challenge of diversity and an intellectual rigor and relevance which both disarms its severest critics and honors its original academic and social mission. And the mission remains one, as Bethune (1939:9) said, of discovering the dawn and sharing it with the masses, of bringing the fruits of knowledge to those who need it most and thus laying the basis for maximum human freedom and human flourishing.

STUDY QUESTIONS

1. Define challenge and crisis in relationship to Black Studies.
2. What are three fundamental historical factors which contributed to the development of the current challenges to Black Studies?
3. What are the basic political challenges facing Black Studies?
4. What are the fundamental intellectual challenges facing Black Studies?
5. What were the basic types of administrators which posed problems for the development of Black Studies as an established discipline?
6. What changes in the community and on campus contributed to a blurring of the original goals of Black Studies?
7. What are the four structural forms of Black Studies in the academy? What are their strengths and weaknesses?

8.   What characteristics must Black Studies literature have if it is to fulfill its academic mission?
9.   Discuss suggested correctives to meet the challenges to Black Studies.
10. How will the intellectual and political challenges to Black Studies serve to enhance its possibilities?
11. Discuss Black Studies' need to be an open-textured and open-ended project.

REFERENCES

Allen, Robert L. (1974) "Politics of the Attack on Black Studies," *The Black Scholar*, 6, 1 (September) 2-7.

Anderson, Talmadge. (1990) *Black Studies, Theory, Method and Cultural Perspectives*, Pullman, WA: Washington State University Press.

Asante, Molefi. (1992) "The Afrocentric Metatheory and Disciplinary Implications," *The Afrocentric Scholar*, 1, 1 (May) 108-117.

Asante, Molefi. (1990) *Kemet, Afrocentricity and Knowledge*, Trenton, NJ: African World Press Inc.

Bethune, Mary M. (1939) "The Adaptation of the History of the Negro to the Capacity of the Child," *Journal of Negro History*, 24, 9-13.

Brisbane, Robert. (1974) *Black Activism*, Valley Forge, NY: Judson Press.

Chinweizu. (1977) "Education for Power," *The First World*, 1, 3 (May/June) 20-24.

Cruse, Harold. (1967) *Crisis of the Negro Intellectual*, New York: William Morrow & Co.

DuBois, W.E.B. (1975) *The Education of Black Folks: Ten Critiques, 1906-1960*, New York: Monthly Review Press.

DuBois, W.E.B. (1961) *The Souls of Black Folk*, New York: Fawcett Publications.

DuBois, W.E.B. (1969) "The Talented Tenth," in *The Negro Problem*, (ed.) Ulysses Lee, New York: Arno Press and the New York Times.

Ford, Nick. (1973) *Black Studies*, New York: National University Publications.

Frazier, E. Franklin. (1970) *Black Bourgeoisie*, New York: Macmillan.

Frazier, E. Franklin. (1973) "The Failure of the Negro Intellectual," in *The Death of White Sociology*, (ed.) Joyce A. Ladner, New York: Vintage Books, pp. 52-66.

Gordon, Vivian. (1979) *Lectures: Black Scholars on Black Issues*, Washington, D.C.: University Press of America.

Hare, Nathan. (1972) "The Battle for Black Studies," *The Black Scholar*, 3, 9 (May) 32-47.

Hare, Nathan. (1978) "War on Black Colleges," *The Black Scholar*, 9, 8 (May/ June) 12-19.

Harris, Robert. (1990) "The Intellectual and Institutional Development of Africana Studies," in Robert Harris, Darlene Clark Hine and Nellie McKay, (eds.), *Three Essays: Black Studies in the United States*, New York: The Ford Foundation.

Harris, Robert, Darlene Clark Hine and Nellic McKay, (eds.). (1990) *Three Essays: Black Studies in the United States*, New York: The Ford Foundation.

Hine, Darlene Clark. (1990) "Black Studies: An Overview," in Robert Harris, Darlene Clark Hine and Nellie McKay. (1990) *Three Essays: Black Studies in the United States*, New York: The Ford Foundation.

Karenga, Maulana. (1990) "The African Intellectual and the Problem of Class Suicide: Ideological and Political Dimensions," in Molefi Asante and Kariamu Welsh Asante, *African Culture: The Rhythm of Unity*, Trenton, NJ: African World Press Inc., pp. 91-106.

Karenga, Maulana. (1988). "Black Studies and the Problematic of Paradigm: The Philosophical Dimension," *Journal of Black Studies*, 18, 4, 395-414.

Karenga, Maulana. (1977) "Corrective History: Reconstructing the Black Past," *The First World*, 1, 3 (May/June) 50-54.

Karenga, Maulana. (1978) *Essays on Struggle: Position and Analysis*, San Diego: Kawaida Publications.

Kilson, Martin. (1973) "Reflections on Structure and Content in Black Studies," *Journal of Black Studies*, 1, 3 (March) 297-314.

LeMelle, Tilden. (1984) "The Status of Black Studies in the Second Decade: The Ideological Imperative," in James Turner (ed.) *The Next Decade: Theoretical and Research Issues in Africana Studies*, Ithaca, NY: Africana Studies and Research Center, Cornell University Press, pp. 47-61.

McClendon, William H. (1974) "Black Studies: Education for Liberation," *The Black Scholar*, 6, 1 (September) 15-20.

McKay, Nellie. (1990) "Black Studies in the Midwest," in Robert Harris, Darlene Clark Hine and Nellie McKay, (eds.), *Three Essays: Black Studies in the United States*, New York: The Ford Foundation.

Paschal, Andrew (ed.) (1971) *A W.E.B. DuBois Reader*, New York: MacMillan Publishing Co.

President's Task Force Report on Multicultural Education and Campus Diversity. (1991 *The Challenge of Diversity and Multicultural Education*, Long Beach, CA: California State University, Long Beach.

Smith, William D. (1971) "Black Studies: A Survey of Models and Curricula," *Journal of Black Studies*, 10, 3 (March) 269-277.

Smith, William D. and Albert C. Yates. (1980) "Editorial in Black Studies," *Journal of Black Studies*, 10, 3 (March) 269-277.

Stewart, James B. (1979) "Introducing Black Studies: A Critical Examination of Some Textual Materials," *Umoja*, 3, 1 (Spring) 5-17.

Stewart, James B. (1984) "The Legacy of W.E.B. DuBois for Contemporary Black Studies," *Phylon* 53, 296-311.

Stewart, James B. (1992) "Reaching for Higher Ground: Toward an Understanding of Black/Africana Studies," *The Afrocentric Scholar*, 1, 1 (May) 1-63.

Turner, James (ed.). (1984) *The Next Decade: Theoretical and Research Issues in Africana Studies*, Ithaca, NY: Africana Studies and Research Center, Cornell University.

Turner, James and Eric W. Perkins. (1976) "Towards A Critique of Social Science," *The Black Scholar*, 7, 7 (April) 2-11.

Walton, Sidney F. (1974) "Black Studies and Affirmative Action," *The Black Scholar*, 6, 1 (September) 21-31.

Weber, Shirley. (1984) "Intellectual Imperatives and Necessity for Black Education," in James Turner (ed.) *The Next Decade: Theoretical and Research Issues in Africana Studies*, Ithaca, NY: Africana Studies and Research Center, Cornell University, pp. 63-75.